The Adventure of CIRCUS in America

LaVahn G. Hoh & William H. Rough

BETTERWAY PUBLICATIONS, INC.
WHITE HALL, VIRGINIA

Published by Betterway Publications, Inc.
P.O. Box 219
Crozet, VA 22932
(804) 823-5661

Cover design by Susan Riley
Cover photograph of "Whizzer" (Don Bridwell)
by D. M. Chambers ("Elmo Gibb")
Typography by Typecasting

Library of Congress Cataloging-in-Publication Data

Hoh, LaVahn G.
    Step right up!: the adventure of circus in
America / LaVahn G. Hoh and William H. Rough
       p.   cm.
    Includes bibliographical references.
    ISBN 1-55870-140-0: $29.95 —
    ISBN 1-55870-139-7 (pbk.): $19.95
    1. Circus — United States — History. I. Rough,
William H. II. Title.
GV1803.H64   1990
791.3'0973 — dc20   89–29910
                                CIP

Printed in the United States of America
0 9 8 7 6 5 4 3 2 1

*To the artists who bring us
the contemporary circus,
who by their example teach us
to dream . . .
to reach beyond our limitations.*

Acknowledgments

So many people have helped in the preparation of this book, it's hard to know how to begin to thank them all. We'll start with our good life-partners, Joan Z. Rough and Mary Frances Hoh. They have offered their photographic artistry and their reading skills, as well as their encouragement and their suggestions; and they have patiently endured many months of being ignored. We also wish to thank all the other members of our families for their support, and in particular, LaVahn's mother, Mrs. Leland Hoh, for taking him to his first circus, and his daughter, Jennifer, for enduring eighteen years of being taken to the circus.

We particularly want to thank circus historians Joe McKennon, Fred D. Pfening, III, and Stuart Thayer, who have devoted many hours sharing their love of the circus with us, and assuring that our facts are rendered as accurately as possible.

We are grateful to all the good people who are directly or indirectly a part of circus in America—the performers, the owners, the roustabouts, the secretaries, the spectators, the fans, and the historians—old and new friends who have shared their stories, their suggestions, their knowledge, their experiences, their skills, and their observations with us. They have eased our access to information, and added life to our picture of the circus in America. Among them are Jan Rok Achard, David "Spider" Alton, Joe Anderson, Branden Baily, David Balding, Elvin Bale, Trevor Bale, Frank Ball, Bill Ballantine, Lou Bird, Betty Black, Allen J. Bloom, Lyman H. Bond, the Boumi Temple, Bill Brickle, Gordon Brown, Vince Bruce, Chuck Burnes, Guy Caron, Jim Carpenter, D. M. "Elmo Gibb" Chambers, Jimmy Cole, Robin Crivello, Nancy Cutlip, Fred Dahlinger, Wayne Daniel, Michèle Desmarais, Eileen Dillmann, Doris Earl, Jeff Earl, Kenneth Feld, Franklin O. Felt, Judy Finelli, June Forsythe, Jim Foster, Boris Frank, Pat Frank, Wayne Franzen, John Frick, Tim Frisco, John Fugate, John Fulghum, Hank Godlewski, Harry Hammond, Tommy Hanneford, Linda Heath, Kathleen R. Herb, John Herriott, Allan C. Hill, Barbara Hoffman, Yaro Hoffman, Doug Holwadel, Robert Houston, Susan S. Hurst, Conrad Hyers, Alan Inkles, Dolly Jacobs, Lou Jacobs, Lynn Metzger Jacobs, Terrell "Cap" Jacobs, III, Jimmy James, Dominique Jando, Mary Ann Jensen, Sheila Jewell, Patty Britt Johnson, Edward D. (Ted) Jones, Jr., Jim Judkins, Paul V. Kaye, John Kelly, Jim Kieffer, Dave Knoderer, Michael Kohlreiser, David Kovacs, Theresa Lamb, Brian LaPalme, Joshua Leeds, Betty Llewellyn, Fred Logan, Don Marcks, Bill McCarthy, John McGinn, Marian McKennon, Denise McLean, Rob Mermin, Alan Meredith, D. R. Miller, Florence Oliver, Donny Osman, Glen Parkins, Bob Parkinson, Greg Parkinson, Sacha Pavlata, Bob Pelton, Bruce Pfeffer, Manuel W. Phelps, Barbara Pike, Larry Pisoni, James M. Pitts, Carol Pizzo, David Poist, Jerry Polacek, Bruce Pratt, Brigitte Pugh, Johnny Pugh, Karen Pugh, Paul Pugh, Chris Rawls, David Rawls, Harry Rawls, Fred R. Reed, Nancy Renner, Michael "Buster" Rosman, Rod Ruby, Elka Schumann, Jerry Showalter, J. J. Silva, Alan B. Slifka, Dick Smith, Steve "T. J. Tatters" Smith, Peggy Snider, Ward Stauth, Renee L. Storey, Wilson Storey, John Stubblefield & Stubblefield Custom Color, Elissa "Freckles" Tatton, David Tetrault, John Towsen, The University of Virginia, David Van Derveer, Cliff Vargas, Bonnie Vickers, Rodney Wainwright, Darryl Wallace, Fred Weil, Mary "Sigmund Frog" Wengrzyn, Chuck Werner, Ben Williams, Rheva Williams, Thomas E. "Topper" Williams, Joan Zieger, and John Zweifel.

[5]

Foreword

In 1792, the renowned British equestrian John Bill Ricketts arrived in Philadelphia. On April 3 of the following year, he presented the first circus ever seen in America in a wooden amphitheater erected on the corner of Twelfth and Market Streets. On that site today at the foot of an office building, a 42-foot circular piazza (the diameter of a circus ring) and a plaque commemorate the event.

At the time, circus was mainly an equestrian show, with tumblers, rope-dancers, jugglers, and clowns offering comic relief between acts. This mixing of visual acts had originally been designed by another British equestrian, Philip Astley, who presented the first performance of that type in London over twenty years earlier. This new form of entertainment soon became the craze in Europe. But it was Astley's first competitor, Charles Hughes, who gave it a name—*circus*—and exported it to Russia. Ricketts, who had once served as an apprentice to Hughes in London, brought it across the ocean to America.

The circus soon became extremely popular on this continent. It was easy to appreciate, at a time when horsemanship and physical endurance were part of everyday living. It didn't have the upper-class coloration of the theatre, nor its distinctive British tone—a positive selling point to a newly independent people. Presidents Washington and Adams both patronized Ricketts' circus.

Just as actors managed their own theatre companies, so too did circus performers operate their own shows in those early days. But this new enterprise was becoming so successful that soon businessmen took over. It began with farmers turned menagerie owners, in the region of Somers, New York, who quickly realized that they could increase profits by combining the two most popular traveling attractions of the day, the circus and the menagerie. Fortunes were quickly amassed.

In the late 1870's, the true popularity and financial potential of the American circus was realized by P. T. Barnum, the legendary impresario. Barnum, who was then in semi-retirement, together with his associates, William C. Coup and James A. Bailey, turned the circus into America's favorite entertainment—the richest, the biggest, and the greatest show on earth...and so it remained for the next five decades.

As so often happens in these situations, commercial success slowly disfigured the art form. From a rather intimate show-in-the-round, where audiences could appreciate the individual skill and artistry of each performer, American circus evolved into a garish spectacle, presented on three (and up to seven) rings or stages at a time. The introduction of multiple rings arose from a commercial need to increase tent capacity while simultaneously allowing the most remote spectator to catch a glimpse of the performance. By feeding on the American audiences' developing taste for high pageantry and extravaganza, the original perception of circus as a performing *art* was soon lost.

LaVahn Hoh and William Rough, who have studied the history of the theatre as well as that of the circus, well understand how much the two are interrelated. Jerome Robbins once stated that Circus is the original theatre. Many circus historians have related the history of the circus from a business perspective, or stunningly described the impressive logistics involved in moving the huge cities of tents in the heyday of the American circus. The merit of this book is that it offers a closer look into the evolution of the *art form*, from its introduction in this country, to its subsequent decline and, as it now seems, to its revival. For any serious theatre, circus, or performing arts scholar, this is an important book — as it also should be for anyone interested in the history of this country. The circus, as we will see, played an important role in the development of America. Finally, this work offers a wonderful adventure, as does circus itself, and that alone is enough to make it endearing.

Dominique Jando
Associate Artistic Director
The Big Apple Circus

Contents

1.
LADIES AND GENTLEMEN, STEP RIGHT UP!

"Cotton candy! Popcorn! Snow cones! Soda pop! Hot dogs!" "Right this way, Ladies and Gentlemen, Right this way! Don't be afraid to step right up!" "Get your Souvenir Programs here! Buy 'em while they last!" "Souvenirs! Balloons!" "Peanuts! — Hot roasted peanuts! Get 'em right here!" "Ladies and Gentlemen, and Children of all Ages, the circus is about to begin!"

It's irresistible, isn't it? All that noise, all those smells, and all that color. Magnificent, and beautiful — and a little bit frightening. There are all those strange people and animals, and all those painted faces. The unpredictability of the clowns, the enormity of the elephants, the roar of the big cats, the dizzying height of the big-top peak from which the trapeze hangs: it's all more than a little overwhelming. We go in anyway, full of joy and anticipation, but perhaps clutching the hand of a parent or a child just a little more firmly. If this is to be our first exposure to the circus, we have no idea what to expect. We are just "First of May," the circus term for a greenhorn at this whole experience. However, most Americans do have some experience with the circus, at least as spectators, and all but a few of us have toyed with the concept of "running away with the circus." "First of May" or not, we have come because we need it. It's been a change of pace — something to lift us out of the ordinariness of our lives.

Many of us for one reason or another haven't been to the circus in a long time — perhaps since our parents took us as children. We may think we've forgotten what it was like, but the sounds and images and smells of the circus are a part of our heritage and our collective memory. Sensual memories are far more direct a path to who we really are than remembered thoughts, ideas, or words. It's not the clever words, the funny lines,

or the meaningful dialogue from a good movie or play that seem to stick with most of us; it's the images, and the sounds. Words we must struggle to *understand*, but smells, noises, and pictures we can simply *experience*. The senses become the substance of our dreams.

If we seem to have forgotten the smell of the circus, it takes only a few instances to make it all come tumbling back: ripe horse sweat; sweet hay mixed with pungent elephant dung; fresh sawdust; and the oily mustiness of waterproofed canvas. That sour aroma of canvas alone can still call up a multitude of reminiscences associated with our last trip to the tented circus — even up to 1988, when the last American real canvas major big top was finally folded up for good.

Most of us can probably still taste the same stale popcorn drowning in fake butter that first passed our mouths years ago while the circus band blared, or the mustardy hot dogs which went to war with our stomachs. Could we really ever forget the smell, or the taste, or the gritty, sticky texture of the circus' most popular treat, for instance? Cotton candy was originally called "Fairy Floss," when it was first invented in 1900 by Thomas Patton. But none of that matters to the amazed child inside each of us, as the pink or blue spun-sugar magically disintegrates and disappears on the tongue in less time than it takes for that acrobat to complete a quadruple somersault high over our heads.

There are thousands of such memories. Once we have experienced them, we will never forget the trumpet of the elephant, the changing color of the chameleon, the agony of a burst balloon, or the heart-stopping fall into the net of the perfect man-on-the-flying-trapeze. We'll remember the time when that clown hit Dad over the head with

The Midway. Photo by Joan Z. Rough

Photo by W. H. Rough

Photo by Joan Z. Rough

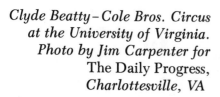

Clyde Beatty–Cole Bros. Circus at the University of Virginia. Photo by Jim Carpenter for The Daily Progress, Charlottesville, VA

his inflated baseball bat; or the time when little sister spilled her purple snow cone down her brother's neck and no one yelled at her for it; or when Mom missed the whole act with the lions in the cage because she didn't dare open her eyes. And we'll remember the sticky hot summer day when we were allowed to visit the back yard; we saw the wire-walker in his tights, torn and stained at the knee in the light of day, and the unshaven boss elephant man without his shirt, all paunchy, and grouchy, and smoking a cigarette.

The circus has always been one of the most popular forms of public entertainment in the world. It's hard to conceive of just how popular it was in its American heyday. America grew up with the circus. Whole towns shut down on circus day — schools, shops, and offices — an occasion when everything but fantasy and excitement stood still. The day the circus came to town was every bit as memorable to us as Christmas, the Fourth of July, and our own birthdays.

The circus is not, however, all memories and past tense. The convenient and regular appeal of television and the extravagance of the movies may have lessened its impact on society as a whole for the time being, but the circus is still very much with us. The largest entertainment empire in the world today remains the Ringling Brothers and Barnum & Bailey Circus; they are once again in the process of expanding their circus activities and widening their concepts, and their business is

thriving. The Ringling show is but one of the well over fifty circuses that continue to travel throughout America every year, many of which still play under a tent. In 1989, reports abounded that the box offices of these shows had seen ever-increasing ticket sales, and that despite appearances, more people are going to the circus than ever before. New circuses were being born, and new concepts and ideas for the circus were being successfully tried.

In periods throughout its history, the circus has been through many cycles of lean years. Weather, wars, economic hardships, cut-throat competitions, and tragic accidents have always plagued its existence. Often the circus has not been deemed fashionable or wholesome entertainment, although even so it may be the only art form in the world which has never been subject to censorship. As a result of all of this, many circuses have gone broke, and many circus entertainers have gone hungry. But never in known human history have circus-like entertainments been entirely driven out of business.

Thirty years ago, at the bottom of the current cycle, economic conditions in America were once again threatening to finish off the circus industry, and doom-sayers were reporting the imminent end of the circus as a form of entertainment. But the circus, as always, has hung on by its proverbial bootstraps. While many people apparently remain unaware that the circus is thriving, it is, and

Photo by Joan Z. Rough

it will continue to do so. There are signs that people reared on the impassivity of television are thirsting for a return to the live entertainment arts. People seem to be growing tired of the shallow world of make-believe. They want to see real people, performing real and genuinely challenging feats. Today, despite the high cost of fuel, which has always plagued the circus, and despite the now soaring insurance rates and bureaucratic red tape associated with various permits, we may in fact be on the edge of a new circus renaissance. At the very least, the circus remains deeply entrenched in the culture of America.

Few of us are aware of just how thoroughly the circus has permeated every facet of our civilization. Over the years, it has become a part of our technology, our language, and our art. Circus is ingrained in our imagination, in our collective memories and dreams, and even in our most basic fears.

INNOVATIONS

The circus is certainly a part of the technological history of our country. In 1879, "The Great London Circus! Sanger's Royal British Menagerie, with Cooper, Bailey & Co.'s Famous International Allied Shows" advertised the first major popular demonstration of the dazzling electric light. For the September 26 performance of the show in Rockford, Illinois, the circus bill talked of "Creating a spectacle of most entrancing loveliness, ravish beauty, and supernatural splendor; transforming the very earth into a Paradise of Bliss, and carrying the imagination to the Realms of Eternal Heaven. It brings to the soul of every human witness a sense of imperishable ecstasy and enduring charm, and it gilds every object within a radius of two miles, animate and inanimate, with a subdued enchantment that realizes in every intelligent person the silvered dreams of beauteous fairyland." Bailey called the electric light "Heaven's own gift to earth of lightning." It illuminated far more than his 420,000 square feet of canvas; it

illuminated the imaginations of the American people and created a thirst for electricity in the home. In 1897 there were three movie theaters in the entire United States: One in New York, one in Chicago, and one in the Ringling Brothers Circus, a black tent which showed the Corbett–Fitzsimmons fight. The year before, and twenty years before the horseless carriage was commonly seen on the streets of America, the Barnum & Bailey Circus paraded a Duryea automobile. But of all the technological wizardry invented and popularized by the circus, it was the logistical system of rail travel that had perhaps the most far-reaching implications. When the Barnum & Bailey show toured Europe at the turn of the century, the German army were eager students of the circus' methods of loading and unloading flat cars rapidly and with maximum efficiency. The American army quickly followed suit, and soon the two most powerful military forces in the world were both modelling their entire transportation systems on the highly organized methods they had learned from the circus.

*The Great Britain bandwagon.
Photo by L. G. Hoh*

LANGUAGE

The circus has also been made an intrinsic part of our very language, providing us with words which we may no longer even associate with the circus. A *jumbo*-sized object, used to describe anything larger than expected, is perhaps one of the best examples of circus linguistic influence. The word *"jumbo"* comes from the nickname of the oversized African elephant displayed from 1882 to 1885 in the Barnum & Bailey Circus. That lovable "ponderous pachyderm" sent Americans into a tailspin of Jumbo-phoria that would put 1989's Batman craze to shame. *"White-Elephant* Sales," used to describe items reduced in price because no one wants them, are so-named because of the 19th century "White Elephant War" between Barnum & Bailey and a rival circus, from which the public came away with the belief that all white elephants were hoaxes.

"Rain or shine" is now a common expression in our language, but we can trace its origin to advertising in the era when circuses first played under canvas big tops. Some of us can remember our father impatiently clapping his hands to get us to hurry into the car at the beginning of a family outing: "Let's go! *Let's get this show on the road!"* he used to plead. Or conversely, when his children got a little too rambunctious in the car near the end of the trip, and he wanted us to calm down, he would warn, *"Hold your horses,* now! We'll get there." The first expression clearly comes from the

anxious call of the circus manager at the end of a long day of performances and packing, eager to get his wagons rolling towards the next stand in the next town. But "Hold your horses"? Why, we wondered, was Dad worried about our *horses?* We didn't have any *horses!* Once again, the expression derives from an old circus call: "Gentlemen! Hold your horses! The elephants are coming!" It was intended to protect onlookers or passersby on horseback, when the elephants were about to bring up the end of a circus parade. Horses tended to panic at the sight and smell of an elephant in the early days of the circus; so when elephants were nearby and the warning call was heard, wise horse owners held on tight to the reins, soothing their mounts' excess anxiety.

When a politician announces his candidacy for office by *"throwing his hat in the ring,"* he is following in the shoes of Woodrow Wilson, who did so literally in 1916: Wilson began his bid for re-election when the Barnum & Bailey Circus came to Washington, by throwing his hat into the center ring. One final example here also has its source in a political candidacy. When Dan Rice was parading his circus through the streets, while seated atop the leading bandwagon, he shouted down to his friend Zachary Taylor, "Come on up here where the people can see who's going to be their next president! *Get on the bandwagon!"* In the course of the next chapters, we'll find many other examples of how the circus has insinuated its way into our daily language.

THE ARTS

The circus has become the preoccupation of many of the world's finest businessmen, artists, and craftsmen. Some claim that it is merely a commercial enterprise, designed only to take as much money as possible from the wallets of its spectators. Most circus folks would say that is patent nonsense. Certainly the circus is far more than a commercial entertainment business. While some contemporary American circuses are strictly commercial self-supporting organizations, others are not-for-profit corporations, designed primarily to serve as non-commercial "artistic" enterprises.

However it is organized or described, the circus exists primarily for the display of the performer and the amazement of the audience. Its function as a money-maker ranks only after those essential ingredients. Performers, owners, technicians, and workers do what they do, not because they want to get rich, but because they choose to amaze — despite the difficult lifestyle imposed on them by that choice, and often despite incredibly low financial returns. No one whose primary motive in life is to make money stays long with the circus.

In its own way, then, the circus lays claim to being an art form which demands to be treated with the same attention, love, and respect as our literature, fine art, music, and theatre. It certainly does not deserve the haughty dismissal of a public which thinks of art as only something to hang in a gallery or ponder from the comfort of a velvet-upholstered arm chair. Some of the best creative minds in the world have failed to come up with any consistent definition for what or why art is, and no such lofty attempts will be made here. At any rate, for most circus folk, such questions are irrelevant. If the circus is art, it is food for the soul of the common man, as Peter Schumann of the Bread & Puppet Theater suggests: "It is like good bread, and green trees." If it is art, it is cheap, and primitive, and soothing. And if it is art, it is unlike theatre art, which is a representation rather than a presentation. Theatre by nature pretends to be something it is not — "truth in the pleasant disguise of illusion," as Tennessee Williams contends in the opening to his masterpiece, *The Glass Menagerie.* The circus, on the other hand, is a direct presentation of the truly unusual, the best of genuine human and animal behavior — truth without artifice or pretense.

Artists and craftsmen have always been a part of the circus, and in return the circus has provided the subject matter for many a fine artist and artisan whose imaginations have grown preoccupied and fascinated with its scope and colorful appearance. Fine model craftsmen have spent entire lifetimes capturing the essence of the circus in their work. An entire organization, Circus Model Builders International, exists to serve the 1,500 members for whom building model circuses is a profession or a major hobby, and they publish a bimonthly magazine called *Little Circus Wagon.* Among the many superb models on public display in the United States is one which took sixty years of labor by William Brinley to create and which includes more than 3,000 hand-carved objects. It's now on display at the newly reopened Barnum Museum in Bridgeport, Connecticut. The largest such display is the impressive three-quarter-inch scale layout of Howard Tibbals, now on exhibit at Circus World Museum in Baraboo, Wisconsin. One-eighth-inch scale circus models have been known to take over the garages and basements of hundreds of hobbyists around the country.

From its earliest beginnings, the circus has been a subject for treatment by prominent artists fascinated by the human truths it could reveal. Calder's elaborate wire and metal sculpture *Circus* resides at the Whitney Museum in New York. Many paintings by Toulouse-Lautrec, Matisse's *Sword Swallower,* Auguste Renoir's *The Clown,* and Seurat's *La Parade* and *Le Cirque* underscore the fascination of artists for the surreal qualities of the circus. The painter Fernand Léger wrote that "The ring is freedom. It has neither beginning nor end." Picasso was perhaps the most famous artist of the circus; he was frequently to be found in the audience at Paris' Cirque Medrano, and several of his paintings, especially during his early Rose Period, center around circus themes: *Girl on a Ball,* and *Les Saltimbanques.*

The circus has often been treated in the literature of the world by writers who have become fascinated with its process. Ernest Hemingway once claimed, "The Circus is the only ageless delight that you can buy for money. Every thing else

William R. Brinley's miniature circus. Quick-Silver Productions, courtesy of The Barnum Museum, Bridgeport, CT

Howard Circus midway, Howard Tibbals circus model at Circus World Museum. Photo by W. H. Rough

Author's model. Photo by L. G. Hoh

Alexander Calder. Le Dompteur et Ses Fauves. *1932. Ink on paper. 21³/₄ × 20³/₄ inches. Collection of Whitney Museum of American Art. Gift of Howard and Jean Lipman. 80.50.2. Photo by Geoffrey Clements*

is supposed to be bad for you. It is the only spectacle I know, that while you watch it, gives the quality of a truly happy dream." On the other side of the globe, the great Russian writer Maxim Gorky wrote of his feelings after experiencing his first circus: "I don't know exactly what the circus gave me. Except that I saw people risking their lives while being beautiful, for the enjoyment of their neighbors. But I think that's enough." In fact, circus imagery is a major part of the works of some of the world's greatest writers and philosophers, including Franz Kafka, Thomas Mann, Friedrich Nietzsche, John Steinbeck, Booth Tarkington, and Mark Twain. And circus themes surface in short stories by such well-known American writers as Stephen Vincent Benet, Paul Gallico, O. Henry, Evan Hunter, MacKinlay Kantor, Alice Lide, Jack London, Katherine Anne Porter, William Saroyan, Mark Van Doren, and Thomas Wolfe. "The smell of the sawdust, the crack of the ringmaster's whip, and the ancient jokes of the

clown, and the wonderful linguistic performances of the lemonade man," wrote O. Henry, "are temptations that most of us strive to resist in vain."

Much less ambitious popular entertainment media arts have also used the circus as a subject matter extensively in their work. Those of us who as small boys and girls used to listen to the radio will remember the adventures of Tom Mix, Clyde Beatty, or Sky King. Sky King? Yes: Kirby Grant, one of many cowboy heroes who used to travel with the circus, worked as Sky King for the Tom Packs, James Bros., Gatti, and Carson & Barnes circuses. In the early days of television, does anyone remember *Circus Boy*, which starred future "Monkee," Mickey Dolenz? Or Don Ameche's *International Showtime*, or *Big Top*, or the long line of circus performers who amazed and delighted Ed Sullivan's audiences?

Finally, the circus has not been ignored in popular film arts. Some of the many landmark movies which have treated circus themes and stories include Charlie Chaplin's *The Circus* (1928); Tod Browning's cult film, *Freaks* (1932), the Marx Brothers' *At the Circus* (1939), Walt Disney's *Dumbo* (1941) and *Toby Tyler* (1960), Cecil B. DeMille's *The Greatest Show on Earth* (1952), Ingmar Bergman's *Sawdust and Tinsel* (1953), *Trapeze* (1956) with Burt Lancaster and Tony Curtis, Rodgers & Hart's musical *Jumbo* (1962), *Circus World* (1964) with John Wayne, Federico Fellini's *The Clowns* (1971), and most recently Wim Wenders' *Wings of Desire* (1987).

Fears

Another facet of the circus concerns each of us in the audience, and may in large part account for this kind of show's overall undying popularity: As individual human beings, we may have a private, deep-seated psychological need for what we can get out of a circus performance that goes far beyond its mere entertainment value. American master poet e.e. cummings once wrote, "Were Congress to pass a bill compelling every adult inhabitant of the United States of America to visit the circus at least twice a year...I believe that throughout the country, four out of five hospitals, jails, and asylums would close down, and millions of psychoanalysts would be thrown out of employment." The remark may not be so far-fetched and whimsical as it sounds. The circus, like an athletic competition and a religious mass, fulfills part of our human need for order, ritual, and spectacle on a grand scale. And perhaps even more important, it forces us to confront our own most basic fears: fears of who we are and who we might be if the normal fetters of society were removed from us; fears of falling, of being laughed at, and of death in the jaws of some primitive beast.

Circus performers face head-on the fears that paralyze the rest of us. They are the ideal illustration that fear can be managed. In watching them, we see that fear is something to be controlled, something we can learn to live with, if not to overcome. No good aerialists, for instance, ever stop being afraid. The lack of fear, they tell us, makes for careless and much more dangerous work. The kick comes from facing the continuing fear, and going ahead anyway. Burt Lancaster, who performed on the flying trapeze at the beginning of his long career, summarized the exhila-

ration of the circus: "Like getting up in front of a camera or on a stage for the first time, when it's your turn under the big top, you just got to go out and do it all by yourself. The excitement is nothing compared to that fabulous feeling of accomplishment after turning a double somersault, breaking out, and finding yourself safe in the strong secure hands of your catcher, saying, 'I did it. I really did it!'"[1]

Circus folk are not really fearless, any more than the rest of us who keep our feet safely on the ground. They simply substitute their own peculiar set of fears for our more conventional ones. They would never dare to eat peanuts in the dressing room, or to put a costume on backwards, or to enter the ring on a left foot. Any such rash actions could jeopardize the safety of a performer or a whole show. Jinxes and superstitions are taken very seriously. Just as an actor would never dare whistle or utter the name "Macbeth" within the confines of a theatre, circus folk would never dare move a wardrobe trunk once it has been spotted; it would mean only that, like it or not, the performer was leaving the show. On the other hand, to see three white horses in succession, and no red-headed women, is good luck.

CARNIVALS AND KIDS

Before we leave this brief introduction into the nature of the circus and its impact on us, let us be clear about two things that a circus is definitely *not*. First, a circus is not a carnival. Carnivals are commercial interests; they exist without artistic goals, primarily to make money. Also unlike a circus, they are not a show, and they are not meant to be a display of excellence. Except for special event audiences and side-show crowds eager to see the rare or the forbidden, there are no spectators. Carnivals are mostly a series of activities in which ordinary people are meant to be engaged as participants. On one side of a booth or ticket stand are the Ferris-wheel riders, the balloon-poppers, bell-ringers, ball-throwers, and thrill-seekers—all of us eager to engage in any activity which might distract us from the mundaneness of our daily lives. We all spend a large portion of our waking hours securing our own and our families' safety and security. But since we

child's face, wide-eyed and open-mouthed, gathering into his consciousness a new awareness: "So this is what I am. So this is what I can do." There is complete acceptance in his face of what he sees. No immediate questions or doubts ensue. But years later, the images he takes in as a child will haunt his memory.

Without life experience, we can't fully appreciate the circus as children. The adult can be much more responsive, because he or she has already decided: "I'm not, and I can't." Those kinds of self-limiting convictions and preconceptions are what allow circus acts to make such a stunning impact on us. When we see performed in front of our very eyes what we had thought to be an impossibility, our convictions become questions: "If she can, could I?" and "Can I be...?" And sometimes, just as in the aftermath of a religious miracle, our questions generate new convictions. The flight of an acrobat, the personality of an elephant, or the antic of a clown is the stuff of dreams, and it is our dreams that define who we are. The circus is one of the few places on earth where we normal human beings can complete the line, "I wish it were possible to..." or "I wish I could..." The circus offers the undeniable proof that "It is possible," and that "I can."

The business of defining ourselves and what we are capable of has preoccupied the hearts and minds of mankind since we first walked on two feet and concluded that we were somehow different from other animals. We will see that that search for definition is the business of the circus as well. And we will come to recognize that that business is vital and necessary for the health of our society. All this is certainly far removed from the seedy status the circus is often mistakenly accorded as a distant, impoverished relative of the entertainment industry. In fact, during the coming chapters, we may well be brought to the realization that in the circus lies the ultimate metaphor for the human condition. As American poet Vachel Lindsay wrote in 1928:

can't "play it safe" all the time, we tell ourselves that we need and want the illusion, the pretense of risk that a carnival can offer. It's a very different kind of entertainment from the circus, which presents us not with illusion but many times with the real risk of the performer. Meanwhile, on the other side of the carnival booth and ticket stand are a lot of people eager to take our money from us. Crooked or clean, carnivals provide most of the amusements on the midway at American state and county fairs. They are popularly viewed as at least as good a way as any state-sponsored lottery for Americans to risk and lose our hard-earned money, and a lot more fun. The biggest of American carnival troupes, the giant Strate show, still travels on rail, the only self-contained amusement company outside the Ringling Brothers and Barnum & Bailey Circus to do so. Indeed, carnivals are a huge industry, but they are not circuses.

Second, there is a popular misconception that the circus is just for the kids. In the coming pages, it will become clear that circus is not "children's entertainment." It is entertainment for "children of all ages," for the child in each of us. Nothing can so warm the cockles of an adult's heart as a

> For every Soul is a circus.
> And every mind is a tent,
> And every heart is a sawdust ring
> Where the circling race is spent.[2]

2.

TRACES

Tracing the evolution of the circus to what we see in the rings today is not an especially straightforward task. Towns and countries are eager to lay claim to history with "Home of..." or "Biggest...!" The field of circus history is flush with experts who accord honors to this or that person who was the first to perform this or that stunt. Grown men and women spend hours or lifetimes deciphering who did the first back flip off of a horse's back, or which was the first elephant in America, or in what country was the art of rope-dancing invented. It's almost as hard as trying to decipher what "the biggest" means. Among elephants, for instance, who was bigger: Jumbo, or Tusko, or King Tusk, or now the Circus Vargas' Colonel Joe? And does "bigger" mean higher, or heavier, or with longer tusks? Does the "biggest" show under canvas mean the biggest tent, or the biggest elephant herd, or the largest truck fleet, or the most number of people traveling with a circus? Of course, it all only means what the P.R. man wants it to mean. Usually, such phrasing has more to do with how many tickets can get sold than with any accuracy or historical relevance.

Of course, claims of superiority are just the kind of thing we want to hear. Americans have been brought up to place high value on the best, the strongest, the biggest, and the first. We wouldn't have it any other way. We wouldn't go across the street to see a circus or anything else that didn't claim to being the first, or the best, or the biggest at something. And who remembers second or third place at the horse races? We'll have to play the "biggest" game in this book too, at least a little bit. It's impossible not to play at all, and it wouldn't be any fun anyway. P.T. Barnum may not have been an especially able circus man, but we still associate the old shyster with the "Greatest Show on Earth," the Ringling Brothers and Barnum & Bailey Circus. He used to say that the public liked to be fooled, and he was only giving them what they wanted. How right he was. This moral, kind, temperate man may have been full of himself, but he never lied without a twinkle in his eye which entered him into an unspoken partnership with his listener. And he never did give the public anything but what we still want, just for the sheer fun of it.

In the Barnum tradition, many people who ought to know better will insist that the circus is strictly a part of our American heritage. It isn't, of course. Americans didn't invent the circus, or even any of the traditional acts we have come to expect in a circus performance. In the 500 years since Columbus "discovered" America in 1492, the circus as we know it today has evolved in England more substantially than in any other place, although even England has no exclusive claim to be the birthplace of the circus. Die-hard circus fans may insist, "At least the three-ring tradition came from America, didn't it?" Well, no, not really. Even something so basically "American" as a three-ring circus was tried in England by George Sanger long before W. C. Coup and Barnum claimed to have staged the first three-ring circus in the new world. And what Barnum first meant by his claim of three rings was really only two rings, with an oval hippodrome track, the "third ring," surrounding the two conventional rings. Furthermore, Roman arena managers must have staged three or more events at the same time on frequent occasions, in the vast spaces of the Colosseum and the Circus Maximus. Thorough research would undoubtedly turn up still other times and other countries where three or more simultaneous presentations were common practice, so there is no justification for any American claim for originating the three-ring circus. The point is that in the circus, there are no genuine exclusives. In the larger picture, "firsts" and "biggests" and "mosts" tend to lose their dramatic impact. And of course, dramatic impact is why such claims are used in the first place.

As we begin this brief history of the American Circus, then, two cautionary notes are in order. First, it is advisable to cast a skeptical eye on all such claims. Firsts, mosts, and biggests can usually be contradicted with a little bit of digging, just because of the nature of the human animal. More than a few "Firsts" have turned out to be "Seconds" and "Thirds." After all, we've been walking on ropes and jumping off and on horses for many thousands of years. Records have been accurately kept only relatively recently; and because of the typically itinerant circus lifestyle, many of those records have been lost.

The truth is that there are huge gaps in what we know about circus history. Some American circus historians, like George Chindahl, Richard Conover, Fred Dahlinger, Chappy Fox, Earl Chapin May, Joe McKennon, the Parkinsons, the Pfenings, Stuart Thayer, and a host of others, have worked very hard to provide accurate information and sort it all out. Still more have relied purely on intuition, hearsay, a little memory, a lot of imagination, and a gift for blarney and bull. Or worse: They believe the literature and claims of the circus P. R. people, who are after all paid to lie and exaggerate. While almost all circus literature is fascinating and magnificently entertaining, a great deal of it is also full of distortions and made-up facts, with just enough truth to make telling the difference difficult. The unavoidable result of all this is that most histories struggle with truth and fall prey to inaccuracy. In our turn, we have tried in this book to be as accurate as possible, and not a few myths of circus history will fall by the wayside. However, we are not historians, and

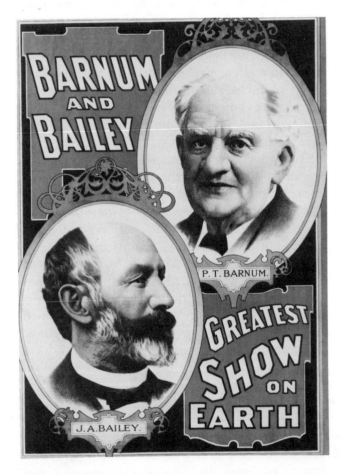

Barnum and Bailey poster, 1897. QuickSilver Photographers, courtesy of The Barnum Museum, Bridgeport, CT

Interior of 3-ring circus tent. Photo by Joan Z. Rough

inconsistencies, gaps, and conflicting "facts" are inevitable. We've done what we can to sort them all out, and we share the rest in the spirit of Barnum.

Second, while this is a book about circus in America, we have found it impossible to deal fairly with the historical aspects of the subject without tracing its evolution during the thousands of years before the American nations acquired their own political identities. We have chosen to spend the rest of this chapter doing just that. After all, not only did Americans not invent the circus: there are those who even charge that we killed it. In truth, we've done some fertilizing and pruning of branches which have led us in a unique direction. American circus may look and feel very different from the varieties of circus to be seen in other countries, but it is all part of the same tree. And it's pretty hard to kill a good tree with a deep and healthy root system.

Ancient Roots

When, where, and how did the circus come about? The answer is much less specific than history books would indicate. The roots of the circus can be found in virtually all civilizations. We are often asked to accept the notion that the tradition of circus began in Rome, which is patently absurd, as we shall see. Some say that circus comes from ancient Greece, because it is Greek art and literature that provides us with some of our first records of circus-type acts. In the 15th century, the European Renaissance, despite plenty of competing evidence, began to attribute the origin of all things civilized, whether art, politics, or recreation, to the classical Greeks. Scientists, artists, and men of letters traced the evolution of civilization down through the Roman Empire to their own time, ignoring that unfortunate period of barbarianism known to us as the "Dark Ages." Despite clear evidence of other cultures with alternate traditions, arts, and scientific knowledge of their own, Europeans preferred to think of themselves as "the unique inheritors of the only genuine and truly special civilization known to man". . . and all that. Our own inherited western tradition of circus has fallen victim to the same prejudice, and it merits another look.

Our modern circus is a genuinely international art form, and any attempt to assign its origins to a single cultural tradition is misleading. If there is anything the circus teaches us, it's that people are pretty much the same the whole world over. Eventually, more balanced and internationally oriented archeological and historical studies may convince us that circus-type arts developed independently in most civilizations and were rapidly shared between them. In the meantime, we need no history books or time capsules to develop some healthy skepticism of single-origin theories.

There are three logical considerations that lead us toward a more inter-cultural explanation of circus origin. First, circus-type stunts are a universal expression of an individual's freedom to challenge the physical, social and political restrictions of his or her culture, wherever they existed. Second, demonstrations of super-human skills are usually perceived by the more "normal" elements of a given society as extra-human, capable of being performed only by God-like men and women, or with the intercession of the gods. Thus certain types of performances that we now associate with the circus developed as a part of the religious ritual of various tribal cultures all over the world. Finally, those individuals who were skilled and independent enough to perform these stunts did not always have the sanction of their family or tribe. They generally became nomadic, whether they went by choice, or they were driven out. They would have carried their skills and traditions freely across all political and cultural borders. This movement between disparate civilizations alone makes it extremely difficult to assign the origin of any single circus tradition to a particular locale. So before we begin to identify geographical origins, let us take a brief look at each of these more universal explanations for early circus performance.

The urge to triumph over commonly accepted limitations, far from being exclusive to any one civilization, lies within the nature of the human animal. Paradoxically, we are driven both by the desire to remain safely within our limits, and by the urge to challenge our limits. When the cave boy was told by his mother not to go outside of the cave entrance because the lion would attack him and carry him off, he undoubtedly listened at first.

Gunther Gebel–Williams in command. Photo courtesy of Ringling Bros. and Barnum & Bailey Combined Shows, Inc.

Dolly Jacobs, 1987 Big Apple. Photo by Martha Swope, courtesy of Big Apple Circus.

A magical heel hang. Photo courtesy of Elvin Bale

Xochitl, 1989 Clyde Beatty–Cole Bros. Photo by Joan Z. Rough

Josip Marcan, 1988 Clyde Beatty–Cole Bros. Photo by Jim Carpenter for The Daily Progress, *Charlottesville, VA*

But this prehistoric Gunther Gebel–Williams also set about devising schemes first to exert his mastery over the lion, and then to show all his friends and other members of the tribe that it could be done. And when the cave girl was told she couldn't climb trees because she would fall, she undoubtedly hesitated only briefly before she climbed the tallest tree she could find and swung on a vine to its neighbor, astounding her audiences then every bit as much as Dolly Jacobs astounds circus audiences today.

We all find that we must ordinarily live from day to day within the limits imposed on us by parents, teachers, employers, and leaders of all kinds. It's easier, after all, to stay indoors and on the ground, to keep house, to bring home the bacon, and to do as we are told. Such conformity earns us rewards from the authorities, because when we play out our given roles in the social pecking order, and perform duties within our expected limitations, it's generally safer for everyone...up to a point!

At the same time, however, we all delight in those who can find ways of demonstrating to us that expectations and limitations are not so final, not so inviolable after all. Just in the last century, mankind has climbed Mount Everest, dived to the depths of the ocean, flown to the moon, circumnavigated our little world in a mere fraction of Jules Verne's "impossible" eighty days, and defeated dozens of medical plagues. Yet everyone said it couldn't be done! Well, none of it would have been done if someone hadn't been driven to challenge his or her apparent limitations and risk performing outside the norm of expected human behavior. On the most basic level of human physical capability, everyone also knows you can't hang by your hair, or walk on a rope, or stand on a finger, or juggle seven hunting clubs in the air at the same time, or bend over backwards and look forward between your own legs, or balance your dinner plate on a stick, or put your head in the lion's mouth and live to tell the tale. "None of it can be done!"

Oh, how we chuckle and wink when we have the opportunity to see it all being done after all. And as we sit comfortably on the sidelines, how we love to laugh in the face of the most trying circumstances: circumstances which by rights ought to make us either afraid or depressed. Watching a performer who can break out of expectations and limitations is our revenge on all of those who have ever told us, "You can't...!" And so it has always been.

Ritual Origins

There is an alternate response to the chuckle and the wink, however, when we see someone do something we believe to be impossible. We can react with fear and amazement, convinced that some supernatural force is at work. It leads to the second multi-cultural source for circus performances. God-like stunts, which challenge our perceptions of what humans are capable of, put the performer in the powerful position of claiming god-like powers. These powers may be useful to the culture in curing sickness, in defeating death, or in exorcising evil spirits. In this manner a shaman or witch doctor can make himself absolutely indispensable to the welfare of his society.

Anthropological evidence suggests that "circus"-like stunts have been a part of social and religious ritual, in hundreds of widely separated cultures, since the dawn of man. In a routine paralleling the origins of modern sword-swallowing, an Alaskan Eskimo shaman could swallow eighteen inches of a smooth stick. Native American shamans commonly engaged in clowning, violent acrobatics, sleight-of-hand magic, and Houdini-like escape acts to convince their audiences that they had unique psychic powers on which the future survival of their civilization might rest. In the South Pacific, an ancient "fly-away," not unlike Jaqueline Williams' stunning climax to the Andrews trapeze performance in the 1988 Cirque du Soleil, or the hair-raising conclusion of Sacha Pavlata's cloud swing act with the Circus Flora, is commonly practiced by young men entering manhood. These tribesmen for centuries have been proving their worthiness by leaping from a high tower in trance-like states which assure them of the protection of the gods. Their fall is broken inches from the ground by vines secured to their ankles, a primitive but effective bungie cord. In India, the ancient mystical traditions of sitting on swings of sharp stakes, contorting the body into unbelievable shapes while in a trance, and charming dangerous snakes all suggest protection by supernatural forces, and they remain a part of the national heritage. The domestication of elephants, with the blessing of the gods, to perform useful "tricks" has been going on throughout Southeastern Asia for thousands of years. In Cambodia, we know that something resembling a circus existed at least eight hundred years ago. Temple carvings in the city of Angkor illustrate one such performance before a large crowd. There are jugglers, a trained monkey act on a perch pole, equilibrists, musicians, and even a high wire act with flaming torches. [1]

The manipulation of fire is one of the most commonly used demonstrations of god-like powers, with separate traditions in many different cultures. Fire-walking appears in ancient India, and it is an ancient tradition which today remains a major annual tourist event in northern Greece. In America, it is currently undergoing renewed popularity among radical spiritualists. Fire-eating, such as is practiced by ringmaster Brian LaPalme with the Roberts Brothers Circus, Red Johnson with Culpepper–Merriweather, John Strong III, and others, is an ancient art, a powerful demonstrtion of man's domination over his environental and human limitations. Any man or woman who can perform these kinds of activities paradoxically inspires in us both awe and fear. Thus it is that the performer who defies human limitations gains a considerable power over mere mortals, because the rest of us define ourselves by our very limitations. Once we see those limitations transcended, our definition of human potential grows. A simple circus-type stunt becomes associated with the universal quest for identity: Who are we, and where do we fit into the universe? Mystical superhuman power is an essential element of man's common search for selfhood, for an understanding of whatever limits there are that define us as human beings.

The third and final argument for a multicultural explanation for the origin of circus lies in the fact that circus people have always been nomadic. After all, if they can cross the barriers of human physical capability, why shouldn't they also cross political and cultural boundaries? "Home" would have represented all the restrictions, limitations, and expectations which he or she was dedicated to challenging. Over the ages,

thousands of people really have "run away to join the circus"! As any of them will tell you, the challenger is usually given plenty of incentive to leave home. A limited number of shamans and medicine men can be accommodated within any one group of people, and these priests would not have been particularly tolerant of rivals exhibiting the same "magical" super-human skills. What's more, that young cave boy demonstrating his control over ten lions in front of the family cave may have been impressive, but he was after all ignoring more productive duties like bringing home the meat. He was challenging authoritative traditions cherished by the warriors and shamans, and he must have been a tremendous emotional and mental strain on his parents and friends. Part of their fascination with him, after all, was the fear that at any minute he could lose control, and the result would be a shared wholesale slaughter. It was a fear which could not be sustained indefinitely. As for the young woman who spent her days swinging through the trees instead of playing it safe and performing her more conventional obligations, she too must have become a constant source of aggravation and frustration for her community. Neither of these prehistoric performers played their expected roles, and neither was long welcome in the cave. As impressive as their demonstrations of skill may have been, tribal leaders, both secular and spiritual, would have encouraged them to leave: "If you must behave like that, not in my cave, please."

One of the most intriguing paradoxes of the circus, to which we will return over and over in this book, is that while we flock to see circus performers, we then want them gone. We need to be amazed and impressed by them, and to identify with them, but then we need to reject them. Circus people will tell you that they don't feel welcome or at home among "towners." Both they and we prefer them to be outsiders. We may want them to come into our towns and show us what is humanly possible, but we don't think we would quite want them to stay. They would only confront us with the extent to which we are content to live within our own more traditional limitations. "Their presence is too painful a reminder of the compromises we have made, thank you very much." Challenge, after all, has its place, but

"Towners" on circus lot. Photo by Nancy Renner

challengers are both frightening and dangerous to a way of life that has been carefully designed within the safe boundaries of the known world.

Animal trainers, jugglers, acrobats, clowns, dancers, contortionists, and rope-walkers from many different civilizations and cultures all over the world, all rejected by their own people, thus found themselves wandering freely and widely in search of new audiences who would be impressed with their skills. They brought with them performance traditions that had been developed independently in dozens of different civilizations in which they had outworn their welcome. They could perform their deeds only until amazement inevitably gave way to fear, and familiarity bred the usual contempt. Then they had to move on once again. Thus, they were no more likely to be members of the civilizations for which they performed than they are today. Instead, we know in many instances that they were exotic strangers, "barbarians" from some foreign land. In the great Roman circuses, for instance, the legendary animal trainers were not Roman but Egyptian.

Wherever groups of such performers banded together to perform their stunts for the amazement and amusement of a rich man, an emperor, a pharoah, or a king who was eager to impress his court or his subjects, or for an audience of ordinary people gathered on a village green, there was circus. It may not have been called "circus," but surely it has existed all over the world for thousands of years.

EARLY RECORDS

In the Nile Valley of Egypt, acrobats and balance artists are depicted on wall paintings that date to 2500 B.C. As long ago as the Sixth Dynasty, around 2270 B.C., we have evidence of an early clown: We know from a tomb inscription that the nine-year-old Pharoah Pepi II wanted to be entertained by a Sudanese dwarf "that dances like a divine spirit" more than he wanted all the gold and silver of Sinai and Punt. One of the largest "circus parades" known to man took place in Egypt in the Third Century B.C., when Ptolemy II mounted a day-long procession involving hundreds of wagons and chariots, drawn by thousands of animals of every variety.

Large wild animal parks, similar to our modern day zoos, were apparently common both in Egypt and in the Far East. They contained fabulous collections of exotic wild animals, which seemed to be completely domesticated and trained to obey the commands of their owners, according to travelers whose recorded observations have survived to our own day. Marco Polo himself observed Kubla Khan's great zoo at "Xanadu" in the 13th century.

In fact, China has a long and venerable tradition of circus-type performers, who traveled throughout the vast provinces and earned respect in the Emperor's courts. We know there were court jesters as early as the Chou dynasty, which began around 1027 B.C. The tradition of Chinese acrobatics that is making such an international impact in the contemporary circus goes back at least to the Han dynasty, two thousand years ago, when the "Hundred Entertainments" included rope dancing, juggling, balancing on balls, and pole climbing. On a tile excavated from a Han tomb is a drawing of an acrobat balancing a stack of bowls on his head while standing on one hand. And in another tomb is a large mural illustrating three girls cavorting on a rope suspended over four sharp sword points.

Over a thousand years ago, a special school was established by the T'ang dynasty for the purpose of training and organizing acrobatic dancers and musicians. The "Pear Garden," which was established in A.D. 714, must have been one of the first theatrical schools in the world. Many traditional acrobatic tricks, such as the art of spinning plates on bamboo poles, were developed and taught at this time. From the Sung dynasty which followed come stories of performers who juggled everything from clocks to children with their feet. Eventually, the Chinese classical theatre of the 14th and 15th centuries would develop from the groundwork of the Pear Garden. The white-faced clown was to become one of the four basic types of roles in classical Chinese Drama. "Lotus Drama" had developed by the Ming dynasty in the 15th century, and it included such circus elements as jumping through hoops lined with swords and turning somersaults on a ladder. Eventually, acrobatic skills were to become an integral part of Chinese drama and opera.

Nanjing Acrobatic Troupe, 1989 Big Apple. Photo by W. H. Rough

Mediterranean Origins

Perhaps the earliest evidence of circus activity combining acrobatic prowess with wild animal training comes from the Mediterranean. On the island of Crete, there is a famous mural in the Palace of Minos at Knossos. This fresco depicts three figures engaged in a genuine "circus" stunt. A young man is in the process of a backward somersault, apparently having flipped himself over the bull's horns. He will land on the bull's back and then flip back off into the arms of his catcher, a woman. The third figure, also a woman, is grasping the bull by the horns and evidently preparing to follow the man's somersault. The Minoan palace was built in 1700 B.C. to replace a 300 year old palace destroyed by earthquake, so the fresco is at least that old. But no one knows how old the tradition of bull-leaping itself might be. We have no idea whether it was an entertainment, an athletic competition, or some sort of religious ritual, but we can guess that bull-leaping must have been a popular activity, and that it was open to equal participation by men and women. The same scene is repeated on a variety of other Minoan artifacts. Interestingly enough, in later periods of Mediterranean cultural development, where athletics and the theatre rapidly became the province of men only, acrobats and clowns continued to feature women in their ranks. Argument over the image at Knossos rages, and

some modern rodeo men have vowed that the routine could never have been done by anyone.

By the time the great city states of Greece emerged from their own dark ages, in the eighth century B.C., the circus arts were a well-established part of Greek culture. The great strongman Herakles, or Hercules as the Romans would come to call him, was the hero of the age, and his exploits in overcoming the Nemean lion should probably earn him the title of world's first lion trainer. Completing the picture of his circus heritage, a clown version of Herakles was also the butt of much of the humor in later Greek theatrical comedies. Homer includes pictures of festive dancers and acrobats in his description of Achilles' great shield in Book 18 of the *Iliad*.[2] In the *Odyssey,* the sorceress Circe, daughter of the Sun, certainly lends her spirit if not her name to the origins of the circus. She is surrounded by men whom she has turned into lions and pigs. Or, like the 20th century American lion trainer, Mabel Stark, has she perhaps instead cast her spell on the animals and endowed them with human-like behavior? Earlier in the poem, there is a revealing description of acrobats, jongleurs, and dancers who are entertaining Odysseus:

Halios and Laodamos. . .took in hand a fine purple ball, one of the clever works of Polybos. One of them would bend his body backwards and throw up the ball into the

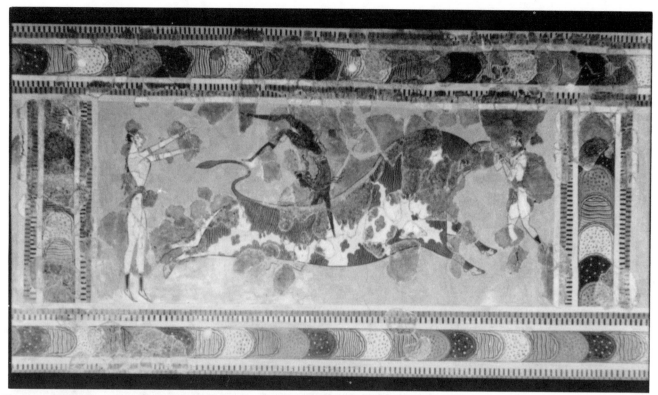

Fresco, Knossos: Bull Leapers, *Heraklion Museum. Scala/Art Resource*

clouds; the other would jump lightly and catch it in the air before his feet touched the ground again. After throwing it straight up in this way, they danced on the level ground, throwing the ball one to the other, again and again: the lads beat time standing around the ring, with clapping hands. [3]

The acts were clearly most appreciated, and Odysseus honors the "ringmaster"-minstrel: "In every nation of mankind upon the earth minstrels have honor and respect, since the Muse has taught them their songs and she loves them, one and all." The Muses included in their jurisdiction not simply music but all of the fine arts. Earliest evidence suggests that minstrels were not only singers and reciters of poetry, but were also well-established as accomplished dancers, acrobats, jugglers, and all-around entertainers. In short, there is ample evidence to suggest that circus arts flourished in the mythological age of prehistory in ancient Greece.

Also emerging from the Greek dark ages was an already ancient, well-established tradition of comic mime to which many of the antics and traditions of the modern circus clown may be linked. We know very little about this early comedy, but depictions on vases suggest it had its roots in Megara, and spread with the Dorian influence throughout Greece, Sicily, and southern Italy. We can see sources here for the spotted, striped, and flowered costumes of the modern clown, along with painted and blackened faces or masks, bald heads, and exaggerated noses and feet. Their comedy was evidently improvised, and dealt satirically with mythological, political, domestic, and sexual themes. Many of the routines of modern circus clowns might well be recognized by time travelers from ancient Megara.

Furthermore, at various times and cities throughout Greece, competitive athletic games provided five consecutive festive days of events and noise, and vendors of food, drink, and souvenirs, in an atmosphere which must certainly have resembled that of the modern circus. Poets

*Mabel Stark. Photo courtesy of
Circus World Museum,
Baraboo, WI*

"The Big Juggle." 1989 Pickle Family Circus, Stony Brook, NY. Photo by W. H. Rough

came to recite their verses, and dancers and singers abounded. Chariot and horse races, requiring the design and construction of the first hippodromes, or "places for horses to run," were to become an integral part of Greek athletic competitions. In the later games at Olympus, the *kalpe* was a race for mares in which the rider jumped down from his horse and ran part of the race holding on to the horse's mane.[4] It was an event in which many of today's circus equestrian acrobats might have excelled. The athletic Pythian Games at Delphi also included a variety of "musical" events and related acrobatic dancing, adding to a circus-like atmosphere.

At the height of the Greek classical period, Xenophon describes a dinner party given by Callias in 421 B.C. As he presumably watched a Syracusan dancer and juggler keep twelve hoops in the air at the same time, the philosopher Socrates, who was one of the guests, concluded: "This girl's feat, Gentlemen, is only one of many proofs that woman's nature is really not a whit inferior to man's, except in its lack of judgment and physical strength."[5]

During Greece's Hellenistic period, subsequent to the reign of Alexander the Great, there was a rapid expansion of Greek influence among the many cultures of the Eastern Mediterranean, Africa, and India, accompanied by an internationalization of Greek culture itself. New trade routes and a spreading common language ensured a co-mingling of many different cultural traditions, and bands of itinerant entertainers, including actors, acrobats, comedians, rope-walkers, and animal trainers freely roamed around the known world, amazing their new spectators with exotic acts derived from a variety of strange traditions. As Rome gradually overwhelmed the successors of Alexander in the last two centuries B.C., circus arts probably became the most widely-accepted form of popular entertainment. The early Roman playwright Terence bemoans the lack of public appreciation for his play *The Mother-in-Law*. In the Prologue for a later revival of the play, he recounts what happened during its first production for the Ludi Megalenses in 165 B.C.: "It was interrupted by a strange and stormy scene, so that it could not be seen or heard. In fact, the people's thoughts were blindly preoccupied with a rope-dancer [fu-

nambulo]."[6] Terence evidently liked his play better than the public, which had similar reactions to two later revivals. They firmly expressed a preference for popular circus arts over the "high culture" of Terence's theatre.

ROMAN TRADITIONS

Many histories trace the roots of the modern circus to the circuses of ancient Rome, and the result is misleading. It is true that Rome first gave us the word circus, but Roman circuses were certainly something very different from what we know as circus today, and in fact they had little if anything to do with the derivation of modern circuses. They began as chariot races, a tradition the Romans had acquired from Etruscans, Greeks, and Egyptians. One of the early Roman "circuses" was the Circus Flaminius, which was not even a

Chuck Burnes. Photo courtesy of Periwinkle Productions

The Colosseum in Rome.
Photo by W. H. Rough

built structure at all and had no permanent seating. Evidently it was only a relatively small and confined rectangular space, which was eventually surrounded by many temples, and traditionally used for horse and chariot racing. On the other hand, the Circus Maximus, the largest structure in ancient Rome, was an elongated horseshoe-shaped amphitheatre, over a third of a mile in length. The Latin word *circus* means round, or around, and the word was evidently used for such disparate and odd-shaped places and events because horses and chariots raced "around" the turning posts.

As Rome aged, going to the circus became the single most popular form of entertainment. In the second century A.D., Juvenal wrote in his *Satires*, "The people that once bestowed commands, consulships, legions, and all else, now concerns itself no more, and longs eagerly for just two things — bread and circuses." The Latin word *circenses* here would be more properly translated as "races." Nonetheless, the "circus" rapidly evolved into much more elaborate games than mere chariot races, eventually ballyhooing the wholesale slaughter of animals and human beings among their featured events. The Emperor Augustus, for example, claimed to have staged 10,000 gladiatorial combats in his career. And when the Colosseum was built in Rome in A.D. 80, one hundred days of games were dedicated to its opening, during which over 4,000 tame animals and 5,000 wild animals were slaughtered. The new amphitheatre was even designed to permit flooding so that full sea battles could be fought to the death, for the enjoyment of the public. Such events were hardly anything like what we go to the circus for today.

On the other hand, the Colosseum did exhibit some concepts that would later be incorporated into the modern circus. Its oval shape allowed 50,000 spectators to surround the spectacle from seats close to the action. On hot sunny days, a huge canvas, stitched together with colorful patches, was stretched from poles over the entire arena, to create shade for the public and add to the festive mood. This *velarium*, as it was called, is our first record of a "big top."

Nonetheless, for all the major festivals, spectacle on its grandest scale was staged at the Circus Maximus, which seated 150,000 spectators, one-sixth of the entire population of Rome. By comparison, the New Orleans Superdome can accommodate only 95,000 people, and the record attendance in a Barnum & Bailey tent was a mere 16,728, set in 1924 in Concordia, Kansas.[7] Twelve Colosseum arenas would have fit inside the 1900 by 259 foot arena floor alone of the Circus Maximus, and after it had been remodelled by Augustus, Dionysius of Halicarnassus called it one of the most beautiful and admirable buildings in Rome. It is little wonder that we are mistakenly drawn into attributing the origin of the modern circus to this spectacular building.

Jean–Leon Gérôme, Chariot Race, *oil on canvas, n.d., 86.3 × 156 cm, George F. Harding Collection, 1983.380.* © *1989 The Art Institute of Chicago, all rights reserved.*

Festivals and holidays took up half the Roman calendar, and for each holiday a circus was held. So circus fans could indulge in their favorite habit to their heart's content. The biggest circus event was the Ludi Romani, games held annually over a ten to sixteen day period in the middle of September to honor the god Jupiter. Elaborate and spectacular circus parades were held to promote the festivities and lead the populace to the Circus, and Dionysius has left us a detailed description of one he witnessed: legions of young men on horseback and on foot; charioteers; athletes; dancers in scarlet tunics and bronze belts, with swords, helmets, and spears; flute and lyre players; satyrs, mimicking the warrior dancers; incense burners; floats carrying images of gods, and thousands of sacrificial animals. The great circus parades of the last century in America would have been dwarfed by such a procession.

The chariot races immortalized on screen in William Wyler's *Ben Hur* were held in the Circus Maximus. It's possible that Lew Wallace, who wrote the original book in 1880, was inspired by imitations of the ancient Roman chariot races that he had seen featured by the huge early American circuses. In the original, each race was seven laps around the course, for a total of about five miles, and lasted approximately fifteen minutes. Little or no rules restrained the chariot drivers from seeking to win at all costs. Drivers were culture heroes, the Roman equivalent of our sports heroes and movie stars, and the best were worshipped by tens of thousands of fans.

We know that these races were interspersed with other entertainments as well. In addition to the criminals and Christians who were condemned to die by some spectacularly gruesome means, there were acrobats, runners, gladiators, boxers, wrestlers, elephant and camel races, trained animal exhibitions and animal fights, and lots of equestrian events. A Roman post-riding event exhibited standing riders astride two horses, a skill often exhibited by equestrians in modern circuses. In still another form of racing, riders reined two horses together, and leapt from one to the other, perhaps at the end of each lap. [8] And in the "Troy Game," another equestrian event, two squadrons of noble Roman youths paraded before the audience and performed a complicated drill and a sham battle. [9]

Many of these events do seem to have a remote connection to the circus as we know it. However, it can't be denied that the grim blood-letting of the Roman circus spectacle was even more fascinating to the public, and it was not to be a passing fancy. The slaughter that typified the Roman circuses continued for over four centuries. All around the Mediterranean, wherever Roman influence was felt, ancient Greek theatres were converted to permit more elaborate staging of spectacles, and new amphitheatres and circuses were built. Evidence suggests that up to seven new circuses were built in the fourth century alone. [10] Elaborate chariot races were held not only in Rome, but in Spain and the northwest and eastern provinces. [11] Only with the full Christianization of the Roman Empire in the fifth century did the circuses begin to disappear. Not only were they suppressed as being morally depraved, but the leisure class which had supported such activities could no longer afford them. Finally, when the Roman Empire collapsed altogether under attack by Attila the Hun and the Visigoths in A.D. 455, the institution, the place, and the word circus disappeared from public use altogether. For the next thousand years, the Circus Maximus and the Colosseum, and other structures like them all over Europe, the Middle East, and North Africa, served only as stone quarries for newer and less ambitious building projects.

The Roman parades, the chariot races, and the less bloodthirsty events of the old Roman circuses have often been recreated, albeit in scaled-down versions, in the opening spectacles and stunts of modern circuses from the Franconis in France to the Ringlings in America. In 1890, Imre Kiralfy staged a gigantic "Nero Spec" for the Barnum & Bailey show, featuring sea battles, chariot races, triumphant marches, casts of thousands, and of course a conflagration scene. P. T. Barnum and his partners built the first Madison Square Garden in New York to house just such a performance. Only since the staging of such events, beginning at the end of the 19th century, has it become fashionable to attribute the source of the modern circus to Ancient Rome.

ROMAN MIMES

On the other hand, in the heyday of Rome there were additional forms of public entertainment, alongside of the circus. One of them proved to be just as popular, far more enduring, and much more deserving of the title of ancestor to the modern circus. While Pompey was promoting his bloody circuses, he was also building the first permanent theatre structure in Rome in 55 B.C. Others soon followed, most notably the Theatre Marcellus, in 11 B.C. It was the home of comedies, Atellan farces, tragedies, and the mime shows. While the latter were originally used as encore pieces to more formal theatrical presentations, gradually they became so popular as to drive out their theatrical competition. Roman mimes very probably had inherited their comic traditions from the Dorian colonies in Sicily. They bore no resemblance to the silent pantomimists we have come to associate with the contemporary word mime. In fact they seem to have much more in common with the modern artists of the circus. Small companies of men and women called histriones performed as acrobats, dancers, clowns, and actors for audiences gathered at the theatre, on the streets, and at private dinner parties. In the *Satyricon*, Petronius describes one such dinner party in approximately A.D. 80:

> Finally the acrobats arrived. One was a silly idiot who stood there holding a ladder and made his boy climb up the rungs, give us a song and dance at the top, then jump through blazing hoops, and hold up a large wine-jar with his teeth.
>
> Only Trimalchio was impressed by all this: art wasn't appreciated, he considered, but if there were two things in the world he really liked to watch, they were acrobats and horn-players. All the others were not worth a damn. [12]

The young slave-acrobat slipped and fell onto the couch of his host, Trimalchio, instead of throwing him to the lions for his clumsiness, freed him.

Poster for Imre Kiralfy's "Nero." Photo courtesy of Ringling Bros. and Barnum & Bailey Combined Shows, Inc.

Mime performances were largely improvised little playlets, usually farcical, combined with all kinds of acrobatic stunts. Some of the mime companies were not so small, and approached the size of a full modern circus troupe. One troupe in the third century, for example, had sixty members, including rope-walkers, trapezists, jugglers, contortionists, sword swallowers, fire eaters, stilt walkers, animal trainers, flute players, and of course, the clowns.

Their little playlets were usually much bawdier than modern clown acts, although some of the more risqué contemporary acts have probably come close to their old models. The clowns operated then much as today's Auguste and tramp clown work together in the circus, as straight man and *stupidus,* as the Romans called the poor fool who served as victim. The *stupidus,* or *sannio,* was usually a talented leader in the mime troupe. One such was Genesius, who was martyred in the Colosseum in A.D. 303. Although he became the patron saint of the theatre, he was more of a circus man than an actor. Typically he would have worn a patchwork cloak and a long pointed dunce cap which were the uniform of the mimic fool, and which in all likelihood are the direct ancestors of the pointed cap and polka dotted suit that were still being worn by early 20th century circus clowns.

In later mime performances, trained animal acts were also featured. According to Plutarch, for example, an unusually talented dog appeared in the leading role of a farce which required it to be poisoned, play dead, recover, and greet the audience. Lou Jacobs used to do a similar routine with "Knucklehead" with the Ringling Brothers and Barnum & Bailey Circus, "shooting" instead of poisoning the dog, who was disguised as a rabbit. Bears also acted in Roman farces, and there are even reports of elephant rope-walking during the period of Nero's successor. [13]

The continuing tradition of women being involved as full participants in mime activities, including at the managerial level, is particularly noteworthy. Unlike their counterparts in the formal theatre, mimes, clowns, jugglers, rope walkers, and acrobats had never been limited to male participation, even in Greece. Theodora herself, who was to become Empress of the Eastern Empire in the sixth century, was a mime in her youth. [14] It's very hard to account for this continuing lack of chauvinism in the mime tradition, especially when we consider that the more formal theatrical profession would remain an all-male bastion from the Greeks through the English Elizabethan age. Some have suggested that the status of both women and mimes was so low that it didn't matter. If women chose to perform as mimes, it was not considered surprising that they should choose a low life comparable to prostitution; the phenomenon was so insignificant that it merited no social restrictions. Another less demeaning explanation lies in the fact that itinerant players, then as now, came from many varied and worldly cultural traditions. Some of the best mimes in Rome were not Roman; they came from Greece

Lou Jacobs and "Knucklehead." Photo courtesy of Ringling Bros. and Barnum & Bailey Combined Shows, Inc.

and Syria. This allowed them to cast a skeptical eye on regional religious and social laws and limitations, to which the more formal established theatre had to adhere. The mimes, the genuine "circus" people in the modern sense of the word, were, after all, in the business of violating limitations and expectations, just as we have suggested their ancestors had been doing since the dawn of social interaction. Perhaps because they were not associated with the norm of Roman society, mimes were not expected to conform to the social customs restricting the role of women.

Historical traditions notwithstanding, we suggest that when Rome fell, the mimes did not! The reasons are similar to those which permitted women to participate in the art: mimes were outsiders by nature. Unlike the charioteers and gladiators, they were not associated with any particular arena; they were not cultural icons, nor were they saddled with particularly Roman values. With no "establishment" role to play, they adapted, first to Christianity, and then to the Visigoths, because they were and are most of all survivors. Besides, the new "barbarians" could hardly have been all that much more barbaric than the

Romans had shown themselves to be in their circuses. As they moved into the medieval ages, then, mimes and other popular performers simply had to readjust to more self-employment than they had been accustomed to in the golden years of Rome. That practice of adaptation, of adjustment to the times, still continues among circus people today.

THE DARK AGES

The medieval age was clearly anything but "dark" for Western popular entertainers. Walls tumbled, new trade routes with the East were established, and armies marched, helping to provide a further mix of cultural traditions. Arabs and Vikings invaded Europe, and the Crusaders invaded the Holy Land. And wherever trade routes developed, so did the roads on which circus people traveled. In fact, bankers and mountebanks were the two parasites who accompanied every big medieval trading fair. The two words both derive from the French word *banc* (bench), upon which the money changers and entertainment promoters stood to deliver their pitches. It was a period rich in opportunities for adding exotic new material to the repertoires of the small bands of mountebanks, minstrels, troubadours, and jongleurs. They traveled widely throughout Europe, just as their counterparts were traveling about Asia Minor, North Africa, and China. There were new influences, such as the arrival in Europe of Chinese plate spinning, but the minstrels were essentially the same kinds of people who had performed the Roman mimes, doing variations of the same kinds of things, if under a new name. They were often accomplished poets who sang songs of courtly love, but they also served as ringmasters. They either presented, or themselves performed as sword-swallowers and balancers, magicians, acrobats, jugglers, curers, contortionists, actors, jesters, puppeteers, and trainers of horses, goats, pigs, and various less likely animals. The itinerant troupes played for the public on town squares, gathering their audiences like the Pied Piper. Sometimes they were paid by the mayor for their efforts, and at other times they had to pass the hat. Or they played in banquet halls for rich lords and kings who were eager to keep their subjects happy.

Persecution of the players on moral grounds was not unknown; but so long as they represented no political threat, and their humor did not grow too blasphemous, they were tolerated and even employed by both church and state. There was at least one ecclesiastic fraternity of fools founded by the church, for instance, to combat the fear of death during the Black Plague; the Company of the Fool of Arrau, under the patronage of St. Sebastian and the Virgin Mary, presented masquerades and parades designed to lift the spirits of the people. The annual Feast of Fools, sometimes even featuring a parody of the mass, celebrated by a "Boy Bishop" or the "Lord of Misrule," was held in many parts of Europe up to the 16th century. During those January festivities, no custom or high officer in church or kingdom was immune to mockery. At a time when very little was written down, when the average man did not live past forty and life was difficult in the extreme, the fools, troubadors, and minstrels managed to amaze people and make them laugh and feel good; and the people loved them for it, even when they got fleeced.

In our examination of the roots of the modern circus, a second medieval practice merits just as much attention as the traveling minstrels. With the age of chivalry also came increased emphasis on horsemanship, to which the period owes its name. Horses eventually were to provide the core around which the circus would be reinvented. Knights in shining armor rode highly trained steeds into battle and against dragons, whether real or imagined. In times of peace, they competed on horseback in the lists, in jousting tournaments that were almost as full of pageantry as the old Roman circuses. Educated horses that could do tricks were frequently on display by the minstrel troupes, and eventually at the country fairs that grew to be so popular particularly in England and France. Perhaps the most famous of such animals was a horse named Morocco, owned by an Englishman named Banks. Morocco could dance, count, distinguish colors and people, return gloves to their rightful owner whose name had been whispered in his ear, and even climb the steps to the steeple at St. Paul's Cathedral. Wayne Franzen's horse Tonto is among those still performing some of the same tricks today. By 1600, the tradition had already been established that a highly trained horse spoke for the prestige of its owner. The smarter the horse, the more people would pay to be entertained by the animal, and the more impressed they would be with the talents and skills of its owner. The enterprise was not without risk: Ben Jonson reported that both Morocco and Banks were burned at the stake for practicing witchcraft by the pope in Rome.

Commedia dell'Arte

By the end of the 16th century, with the Renaissance well under way in Italy, and Elizabethan England at the peak of new artistic expression, two phenomena had developed which particularly deserve our attention: in England, the development of the bear-baiting rings and theatres, which for the first time in centuries gave their potential audiences permanent locations existing solely to provide a regular schedule of entertainments; and in Italy, the emergence of the Commedia dell'Arte.

Scholars continue to debate the possible origins of the Commedia dell'Arte, but the similarities to the ancient itinerant traveling performers of the Eastern Mediterranean, the Roman mimes,

Sandy Kozik. Photo by D. M. Chambers "Elmo Gibb"

and the medieval minstrels would seem to make their descendency all too clear. No one labelled these new troupes "commedia dell'arte" until the 18th century, but their art was firmly established by the 1550's. Small traveling companies of Italian professional players performed short plays, primarily for the common people of Italy, first on the streets, and later in the new state theatres. Most, but not all, of their scenarios were farcical, and they involved the same character-types in varying comical situations. The eight hundred or so commedia scenarios which have survived to the present have proven to be excellent source material for modern clowns and comedians. Scenarios were only loose outlines of a given situation. They might have included a few set speeches which had to be memorized. There were also a series of *lazzi*, slapstick-like and highly energetic sight gags, pratfalls, and tricks tying the plot elements together, and which the audience expected to see in every performance. But everything else was improvised by the actors.

The popularity of the commedia dell'arte troupes was enormous, and their long-range effect on the world of popular entertainment is without parallel. Their influence is expressed by Shakespeare and Molière, in vaudeville and burlesque routines, in TV situational and late night improvisational comedies. Literally every type of clown and comedian can be traced to some variation of a stock commedia character. And in turn, many commedia characters are at least indirect descendents of earlier performers.

All but the *inamoratti*, the young lovers, wore very distinctive masks and costumes. Among the "straight-man" professional characters, the doctor, or Il Dottore, for instance, was a pretentious windbag who had already been established as a common stock clown in ancient Dorian mimes. The mustachioed Spanish captain, El Capitano, all braggart but pure coward, wore the wide ruffled Spanish collar which we associate now with early 19th and 20th century circus clowns. Finally, the old miser and lecher, Pantaleone, from whom we derive our modern word pantaloons for the costume he wore, had a familiar balding head, hooked nose, and potbelly. It was but a new name for a stock character already often seen on ancient Greek vase paintings.

It is in the foolish servants of the above characters that we find the most similarities to modern clowns. They were called *zanni*, from which we derive our word "zany," meaning silly, or clownishly crazy. The similarity to the sannio of the Roman mimes can't fail to be noticed. There were many zanni, but we are particularly concerned with four. The character of Pulcinella, with hunchback and hooked nose, and roots in ancient

Greek puppetry, eventually produced the English puppet character of Punch. His friend Pedrolino in France eventually became Pierrot; with his ruffled collar and white suit with big buttons, he was the model for the clean-cut white-faced clown. The cunning and cynical Brighella, who lacked all scruples and seemed dangerously tinged with evil, like Batman's "The Joker," is perhaps a source for many of the more aggressive Ringling clowns, as well as the ruthless Benny Le Grand, who now travels with the Cirque du Soleil. And finally, there was the most popular of all the zanni, Harlequin himself, who is often portrayed as the joker in a deck of cards. He wore a black mask and a diamond patterned costume, and frequently carried a slapstick. The ultimate trickster, Harlequin was highly acrobatic, both cunning and stupid, and always at the center of any intrigue.

In addition to the zanni, there were also the faithful confidantes and servant-maids, like Columbina. They and the female inammorata, descendants of the Roman mimae, were still played by professional actresses, unaffected by more sex-restrictive policies such as those practiced by the established theatre in England.

Bear-Baiting

England was indeed slow to change in this regard. As late as 1754, well after actresses were appearing regularly on the English stage, a troupe of Italian players, including at least one female rope-dancer, were violently attacked for the "unchaste, shameless, and unnatural tumbling" of their women. Nonetheless, to England fell the specific role of combining all the various elements and reinventing the circus itself. This process began to gain momentum as early as 1560, when we know that there were at least two circular buildings in Bankside, across the Thames from London, that were devoted to the sports of bear and bull baiting.

Like the Roman circuses of over a thousand years earlier, the Bear Garden and its twin are not a particularly wholesome source for the family circus. Nonetheless they played a key part in its development. The primary activity involved chaining a large bear, or perhaps a feisty young bull, to a stake in the center of a ring, where large mastiff dogs were encouraged to attack it. The

dogs were particularly courageous, and they would continue to attack over and over again until they were too weak from loss of blood to stand. Bets were taken on how many dogs would be killed before the bear or bull died. Interspersed with these main events were other acts, which by now are familiar to us as ancient arts. There were vaulters, and rope dancers, and fencing exhibitions, and even a company of apes performing on horseback.

The relevance of the bear rings lies in the fact that they assembled in one place a wide variety of animal and human performers, including every imaginable variation of human physique from giants to midgets. It was one big variety show that was probably not all that different in spirit from 19th-century side shows and carnivals in America, where cock fights took the place of the larger animals. Significantly, itinerant performers were no longer limited to street corners and country festivals; there were permanent places dedicated for their performances. Second, bear-baiting formalized the tradition of an audience seated all around a central ring, close to the action. The Bear Garden itself was a round building, with three tiers of seating, surrounding a ring approximately fifty-five feet in diameter. Finally, the bear-baiting rings, together with the one private and six public playhouses that had been established by 1605, also reawakened the long lost tradition of regular attendance at a fixed place of entertainment.

Although they represented a habit abhorred by the Lord Mayor of London and his Puritan friends, such places were extremely popular with Londoners struggling through the filth of daily existence. The two sporting rings were not enough, and more space was needed. Phillip Henslowe, manager of the Bear Garden, speculator, entrepreneur, and diarist, built the Rose Theatre nearby in Bankside in 1587, and it was joined by the Globe in 1599, rebuilt from the lumber of James Burbage's Theatre. The latter was England's first permanent playhouse, which had originally been raised in 1576 in London. When the mayor threatened to close it, Burbage's men, including William Shakespeare, allegedly tore it down in the middle of the night, moved it across the Thames to Bankside, and rebuilt it as the Globe, possibly now in the same circular shape of its established neighbor, the Bear Garden. When the regular theatre season was closed, both the Rose and the Globe were inevitably also used for popular juggling and acrobatic entertainments. When the Globe burned down in 1913, Henslowe converted the Bear Garden into the Hope Theatre, which was used both for plays, on a portable stage, and for the popular sporting entertainments, with the stage removed.

English clowning also blossomed during the Elizabethan and Jacobean age. The "Clown," as he appeared in a variety of Shakespearean plays, developed a simpler, less sophisticated country bumpkin personality than his counterpart on the continent. On the other hand, much about the character of this fool suggested that he might be wiser than everyone around him. A great lover of food and drink of all varieties, and usually the victim of a shrewish wife, he was played on stage by the likes of Will Kempe, Richard Tarleton, and Robert Armin, an actor in Shakespeare's company. The typical English clown was known by many names, including Merry Andrew, Simple Simon, Jack Pudding, and Pickle Herring. Shakespeare's representations of Falstaff, Lear's Fool, Hamlet's grave digger, Macbeth's porter at the gate, and Olivia's jester, Feste, are all variations on the character of the English clown. In describing Feste in *Twelfth Night*, Viola summarizes the universal paradox of the English clown: "This fellow is wise enough to play the fool, And to do that well craves a kind of wit." [15]

The Puritans were outraged by the popularity of all of the theatres and bear-baiting rings in Bankside on the grounds that such places generated open displays of immorality. Nineteenth century historian Thomas Macaulay quipped that the Puritans hated bear-baiting so much not because of the pain it gave to the animals, but because of the pleasure it gave to the people. They were further piqued by the support that both Queen Elizabeth and King James I had extended to the players. And the disposition of the Lord Mayor could not have been soothed by the knowledge that all those theatres clustered in Bankside were outside of his taxing jurisdiction. Eventually, in 1642, the Puritans succeeded in killing the king, establishing the

Commonwealth, and banning all performances of any kind, in bear and bull rings, in theatres, or on the streets, for the next eighteen years. In so doing, one of the plans they succeeded in thwarting was that of an elephant showman named John Williams. He had twice proposed to build in London a huge "amphitheatre," for the exhibition of exotic animals and all kinds of human skills. It seems that the circus just missed being born in the 17th century.

During the Commonwealth, some popular performers were imprisoned, but most of them simply moved out of London and into the countryside to wait out the Puritan mood of the government. When the English court was restored in 1660, Charles II returned from his exile in France with a whole new variety of entertainments. English clowns and their friends emerged from hiding to join the multi-talented performers from the continent, who brought with them two especially strong traditions: the Commedia dell'Arte, now in full blossom, and a mature respect for fine horsemanship.

In both England and France during the next century, laws were in effect which indirectly were of considerable significance in the development of circus arts. Legitimate theatres were licensed by their governments and tightly protected from competition by outside performers. By the end of the century, for example, the Italian Commedia dell'Arte troupes were banned from France, allegedly because of their immorality. Faced with every conceivable kind of bureaucratic ban on theatrical material, popular performers in both countries were forced to be inventive. Both the renewed popularity of the puppet show and the French tradition of silent mime developed specifically because unlicensed performers were forbidden to speak dialogue from a stage. Performers thrived at country fairs, with their carnival-like atmosphere and a location outside the restrictive regulations of the big cities. New forms of entertainment, such as the English pantomime, with its songs and silent clowning, were born as alternatives to the highly regulated theatres. And by the end of the 18th century, the circus would finally come into its own.

THE FATHER OF THE MODERN CIRCUS

Among all the activities that we would call circus-related today, it was horsemanship that most caught the public fancy in the 18th century, and in several generations, the English were to develop it into a fine art. Legendary high schools of horsemanship were being formed all over Europe, including Vienna's Spanish Riding School in 1735. A number of prominent English riding schools had been established by 1760, which gave popular exhibitions of trick riding. Among several early equestrian stars of the era was a young Sergeant-Major just discharged from Colonel Elliott's Light Dragoons. Philip Astley had a reputation for superb horsemanship and bravery against the French in the Seven Years War. In 1768, he and his wife advertised a demonstration of horsemanship in a little field called Halfpenny Hatch. It was located on the south bank of the Thames, where people had congregated for restriction-free popular entertainments for centuries.

The Astleys conducted neither the only nor the first of such exhibitions, but the young veteran displayed showmanship and panache, as he galloped around the ring. His dramatic stance, with one foot in the saddle and the other on the horse's head, swinging his sword around his head, earned him instant fame. Even more importantly, Astley was an entrepreneur with an extraordinarily fine business sense. In order to bring his audiences back on a regular basis, he quickly added variety to his performances, including our old friends the clowns, the tumblers, the rope walkers, the daredevils, and the illusionists. He created an educated horse demonstration, reminiscent of Morocco. He was responsible for developing the "Tailor's Ride to Brentford," an act combining clowning and horsemanship which survives in many variations to this day. Astley played Billy Button, an inept little tailor who is determined to ride to the village of Brentford as quickly as possible in order to cast his vote for a popular underdog of a politician named Wilkes. The problem is that he can't even get onto his horse. When he finally does succeed in mounting, the horse won't move, but then it gallops off so fast he is thrown off again. The act concludes with the horse chasing the clown around the ring.

With his talents for riding, clowning, and business, Astley successfully developed his little equestrian variety show into an entertainment empire. He first built a covered grandstand for his riding ring, and then in 1779 he built the first indoor ring, Astley's Amphitheatre Riding House. Now he could have night performances, as well as full protection from the elements. Rapidly expanding his enterprise, he began an ambitious touring program, and built several new amphitheatres around the country. Astley also performed in the first known circus tent in Liverpool, in 1788, but curiously he rejected the idea of canvas after only one season.[16] It is not clear why it would be left for the Americans to establish the tradition of circus tents a half a century later. It is likely, however, that at least some of the hastily built amphitheatre-circuses that were built in the next twenty to thirty years were wooden structures with canvas roofs, an inexpensive way to span a large center ring. Many were considered temporary, or even portable circus buildings, that could be moved to other locations and reconstructed.

Since performances at the new theatres and other such interior structures now had to be lit with candles or oil lamps, they were prone to frequent fires, and Astley's enterprises were no exception. Back in London, many of his amphitheatres were destroyed by fire. He stubbornly rebuilt each one, bigger and more elaborate than the last, for the staging of bigger and more elaborate entertainments and displays of exotic animals. His Royal Amphitheatre, originally built in 1804, combined a forty-four foot diameter circus ring with a separate raised proscenium stage. Such amphitheatres signaled the invention of the dubious art of hippodrama, combining horsemanship with legitimate theatre. Shakespeare's *Richard III* was staged at Astley's, for instance, in 1856, undoubtedly adding a completely new dimension to Richard's famous battlefield cry, "A horse! a horse! my kingdom for a horse!"[17]

The forty-four foot ring diameter, with a subsequent minor reduction to forty-two feet, or thirteen meters, has become the industry standard dimension for the circus ring. It was probably determined by Astley to be the smallest practical size for circling horses. It must have also been influenced by the economics of engineering a roof over such a span, since his ring was at least twenty-five percent smaller than it had been in his outdoor riding school.

Philip Astley built nineteen amphitheatres in his lifetime, including many on the European continent. The circus has never recognized national boundaries, but it is a significant tribute to Astley's diplomatic skills that in a time of almost perpetual war between France and England, he was a favorite of both the French royal family and the revolutionary citizens. Defying a bureaucratic law which prohibited the staging of any two spectacles at the same time on any permanent stage, Astley stubbornly resorted to mounting a portable stage on horseback and parading his circus through the Parisian boulevards full of cheering throngs. His eventual Paris amphitheatre was never closed, even during the "Reign of Terror"; he was asked to leave France only when she officially went to war with England. He returned in 1802, and Napoleon soon threw him in jail when he declared yet another English war. With the help of French circus friends, Astley escaped to England, but he later returned once more to rebuild his Paris properties.

When Philip Astley died in Paris in 1814, the family business continued with his son. John, named by Marie Antoinette "the English Rose," had begun to ride in his father's entertainments when he was five. He survived until 1821, when the Paris Astley's was taken over and later renamed the Cirque Olympique by Antonio Franconi. Franconi had operated the amphitheatre in Astley's absence during the wars. His descendants became one of the premiere circus family dynasties of Europe. In 1845, it was Victor Franconi who would build Europe's first new outdoor hippodrome, which restaged huge Roman-type spectacles and races, and after whose idea the Franconi Hippodrome in New York was built.

Back in London, Astley's amphitheatre was taken over in 1823 by Andrew Ducrow, the "Colossus of Equestrians," and the brother of the clown John Ducrow, who had created Mr. Merryman at Astley's. A later member of their family, William Ducrow, would become the first equestrian director of the Barnum & Bailey Circus in 1890. Astley's remained in operation under various owners until it was closed in 1893.[18] During his life,

Philip Astley had invented no new circus skills. But he did combine all the elements that we have come to call the circus into a single entertainment. More important, he created an industry that spread throughout England and Europe like wildfire. For that he is traditionally credited with the title of "Father of the Circus." However, "circus" was a name he himself was never to use. Audiences simply went to the "Amphitheatre," or to "Astley's."

Dibdin and Hughes

The first modern use of the term "circus" came in 1782 from Charles Dibdin (the Elder), a cantankerous musical composer. In seeking out a new business opportunity, Dibdin had formed a partnership with the gifted rider Charles Hughes. Hughes had just as fine a talent and reputation as Astley, and in fact he had worked for Astley for a brief period back in 1771. At that time, Hughes was already an accomplished horseman, and he claimed to have performed in America and Africa in 1770. The relationship between Astley and Hughes developed into a monumental clash of egos, and in 1772 Hughes entered into a long and nasty rivalry with his former employer by opening his own neighboring riding school. The two fought bitterly; they lost few opportunities to publicly insult and accuse each other of underhandedness, and they blatantly plagiarized each other's material. Hughes perhaps got off the best salvo when he held a benefit performance for Astley's poor old father, to whom Astley was not speaking.

Dibdin and Hughes called their new 1782 enterprise the "Royal Circus." Rather than basing his name on the old Roman circus, as is commonly supposed, it is more likely that Dibdin chose the name because "circus" was a term in common usage for describing a place for riding horses around a circular path. London's Piccadilly and Oxford Circuses share the same derivation.[19] At any rate, the Royal Circus was a twin to Astley's amphitheatre in both design and purpose, but more ambitious in scope. The roof could be opened, for instance, to allow the escape of smoke from fireworks exhibitions, as well as from the large number of candles needed to light the stage and the ring. Most notably, though, it is the new name which was significant. The word caught the public fancy, and soon "circuses" were being built everywhere, far outnumbering even the proliferating amphitheatres.

Dibdin himself didn't last long in the circus business, but his name was to have further impact on the world of the circus in the next generation. It was his son, Charles Dibdin (the Younger), the manager of the Sadler's Wells Theatre, who first spotted young Joseph Grimaldi's talent, and thus nurtured the most famous clown in the world. Although he was never to appear in a circus, Grimaldi became the model of all circus clowns to come, as we shall see in Chapter 7.

Meanwhile, Charles Hughes had gone on to become instrumental in the spread of the circus throughout the world. His trip to Russia in 1790, where both he and his horses were favorites of Catherine the Great, formed the basis for the Russian circus. He was more horseman than businessman, however, and when he returned to England in 1793, he found that his competition from Astley and others was now insurmountable. In a quarrel with the magistrates, he lost his license, and in 1797, Charles Hughes died a broken man. Eight years later, the Royal Circus burned to the ground. Its immediate reincarnation was bigger and grander than before, but ultimately the enterprise failed. In 1810, the ring was filled in with benches, and it became the Surrey Theatre.

Charles Hughes also figured prominently in the spread of the circus to America, to which we will turn our attention in the next chapter. He was himself apparently among several expert showmen who performed trick riding exhibitions in the colonies in the 1770's and could well have been the first English equestrian to do so. Others who had contributed to making the art of horsemanship all the rage in America included John Sharp in Boston, and M. F. Foulks, Thomas Pool, and Jacob Bates, in Philadelphia and New York. Pool was probably English, but later claimed to be American-born, taking fashionable advantage of the new American patriotism. Bates introduced Astley's "Tailor's Ride to Brentford" to America in 1772. In that same year back in England, a young Scotsman named John Bill Ricketts was serving his apprenticeship with Charles Hughes' riding school.

3.
NEW WORLD ROOTS

A look at the annual Great Circus Parade, conducted every July in Milwaukee, Wisconsin, suggests an American circus history rife with colorful people and events. Nowhere else can a spectator experience so much of the spirit of the circus which grew up alongside of America. Every year, the Circus World Museum loads up its collection of restored antique circus wagons, and transports them on an old-fashioned circus train south from Baraboo, Wisconsin, down into the northern suburbs of Chicago, back north again along the shores of Lake Michigan, and into Milwaukee. In small towns all along the way, the tracks are lined with enthusiastic circus fans and children of all ages, eager to capture a sense of what the circus was and is. After four noisy and colorful days of exhibition on the Milwaukee Lake Front, the wagons are paraded through downtown streets lined with sunburns, laughter, balloons, and peanuts. Of course, the parade is not just wagons, as if those beautiful hand-carved masterpieces of fantastical circus art would not be enough to delight us all. There are also around 750 magnificent Percheron, Belgian, and Clydesdale horses; the marching, mounted, and riding bands; the dignitaries and stars; the clowns; the novelties; the elephants; and the inevitable pooper-scoopers. They all make up what is undoubtedly one of the most colorful events in the world. Indeed, the Great Circus Parade has been telecast around the world, and its audiences number in the millions.

Few of us can experience the Great Circus Parade without a sense of wonder at all that contributed to the history of this spectacle. How hard it is to believe that parades of this sort used to be a regular feature of America's past, when small towns would be awakened by gigantic processions featuring three or four separate bands, great herds of elephants, cages of wild animals, sequined performers, and beckoning clowns, all trailed by the thundering calliope. In fact, the first and maybe the greatest Barnum & Bailey daytime parade, held in New York City on March 18, 1893, had no less than three thundering calliopes, together with fifty wagons, assorted floats, tableaux and vehicles, 300 animals, not counting the horses, and 500 people, all strung out in ten long sections. So captivating was the circus parade that towns would literally have to shut down all operations later in the day, because everyone would be at the circus. There was a time when such parades were demonstrations of how the circus actually used to travel, before the days of trucks and trains, across the frontiers of America. There was a time when the tall telescoping tableau wagons did not have to telescope, because there were no electric wires across the streets that hindered their passage. There was a time when a forty-horse hitch was thought necessary to pull a ten ton wagon onto muddy lots.

Except for the Milwaukee parade, the circus parade has been a thing of the past since 1939. The King Brothers–Christiani Circus staged one in 1952, and occasionally a Zerbini or Vargas Shrine unit might still mount a special parade. But economics does not permit any regular continuation of the practice.

There is so much to see and hear and smell and feel at the Milwaukee Circus Parade that it's easy to get lost in it all. There are clowns and animals galore, and food of every variety. During circus week every year, one of America's contemporary traveling tented circuses is invited by Circus World Museum to be the official parade circus, holding regular performances throughout the week. But the main feature is the museum's magnificent collection of wagons. They've been gathered from empty fields and abandoned warehouses all over

Circus World Museum wagons loading in Baraboo, WI, 1989. Photo by Mary Frances Hoh

Fans watching the wagons. Photo by W. H. Rough

Photo by L. G. Hoh

Photo by L. G. Hoh

Ready for the 1989 Great Circus Parade.
Photo by W. H. Rough

Wherever there are elephants,
wheelbarrows are close behind.
Photo by Joan Z. Rough

The Forty-Hitch. Photo by L. G. Hoh

Nellie Hanneford aboard the Wedding Cake telescoping tableau wagon, 1989. Photo by L. G. Hoh

the country, and lovingly restored to mint condition. The magnificent Buffalo Bill ticket wagon was being used as a chicken coop. Some of the wagons are on special loan to the museum by the Ringling Brothers & Barnum & Bailey Circus. Seventy-five of them graced the 1989 parade, featuring the world's largest: John Zweifel's Twin Hemispheres Bandwagon, ten tons of Americana created for the Barnum & Bailey Circus in 1903, pulled by the forty horse hitch driven by Paul Sparrow, and carrying twenty-eight musicians. From the topmost seat to the elaborately decorated wheels, all the wagons feature wildly imaginative carvings and colorful paint schemes, representing some of the finest folk art in America. Very few museum collections could match the splendor of the Pawnee Bill Wagon, the Twin Lions Telescoping Tableau, and the Golden Age of Chivalry Tableau, depicting a spectacular two-headed dragon. No one could deny the charm of the Cinderella, the Mother Goose, and the Old Woman in the Shoe children's floats, the only three surviving out of seven gilded pony carts originally built for the century old Barnum & London Circus. The Cinderella wagon was found just in time

to save it, rotting and embedded in grass in a midwestern field. And no one can fail to be impressed by the seniority of the big-wheeled Bostock & Wombwell wagon, at 150 years the oldest circus wagon in existence.

The circus wagons all carry titles that conjure up two hundred years of a mysterious past. Every name carries with it dozens of questions. Who was Adam Forepaugh, anyway? When was the John Robinson show on the road, and what kind of circus was Hagenbeck and Wallace? Did my father or my grandfather ever crawl under the sidewall of a big top to see the Gollmar Brothers' Circus, or was that the Gentry Brothers, or the Christy Brothers, or the Downie Brothers? And seriously, were they really all brothers? Did Sparks, or W. W. Cole, or Sells–Floto, or Howe's ever come to my town? When did Barnum get together with Bailey, and how did the Ringling brothers get involved?

Sorting all this out is not an easy process, and we may not ever get around to understanding all the facts of circus history in America. Some of it we'll never know, and some of it really ought to remain a mystery. After all, what we see in the circus is both real and unbelievable, both

*"Sidewalling." Photo courtesy of
Circus World Museum,
Baraboo, WI*

impossible and true. We used to discover a circus in town in the morning, and go to it later in the day. By the following morning it would be gone again, leaving only an empty lot and a lot of people wondering if it had all really happened. Maybe part of it must always remain an ethereal part of our unconscious. To understand it all might rob us of its magic. As for the rest, those wagons suggest a time when a frontier spirit of adventure, a joy of life, and a determination to succeed against all odds were at the core of the American soul. We had best start at the beginning.

THE AMERICAN FATHERS

Twenty years after his apprenticeship with Charles Hughes, a Scotsman named John Bill Ricketts arrived in America, an experienced, accomplished performer and horseman. He set up in Philadelphia "at very considerable expense" an outdoor riding ring he called a "circus" at the corner of Twelfth and Market streets, which he opened on April 3, 1793. We now call this enterprise the first complete circus in America, because it incorporated the elements of clowning, music, acrobatics, and horsemanship. In his program, Ricketts promised that he would dance a hornpipe on horseback, throw a somersault backward, and leap from the horse to the ground and with the same spring remount with his face towards the horse's tail. His May 15 notice gives us a hint of the full flavor and extent of the circus:

This day, at the Circus in Market, the corner of Twelfth Streets. The doors will be opened at 4, and the Performance begin at half past Five o'clock, precisely

Will be Performed — A Great variety of
EQUESTRIAN EXERCISES,
By Mr. & Master Ricketts, Master Strobach and Mr. McDonald, who is just arrived from Europe.

In the Course of the Entertainment, Mr. Ricketts will introduce several New Feats, particularly he will ride with his Knees on the Saddle, the Horse in full speed; and from this position Leap over a Ribbon extended 12 feet high.

Mr. Ricketts, on a single Horse, will throw up 4 Oranges, playing with them in the Air, the Horse in full speed.

John Zweifel's giant Twin Hemispheres Bandwagon. Photo by W. H. Rough

Detail of old wagon. Photo by Joan Z. Rough

The Pawnee Bill Wagon. Photo by Joan Z. Rough

"Old Woman in the Shoe" and "Mother Goose" wagons on flatcar. Photo by W. H. Rough

The Bostock & Wombwell wagon. Photo by L. G. Hoh

Detail from the Asia wagon. Photo by Joan Z. Rough

Ricketts' Circus, 1794. Photo courtesy of Circus World Museum, Baraboo, WI

Mr. McDonald will perform several
COMIC FEATS
(Being his First Appearance in America).

Seignior Spiracota will exhibit many Sur-prizing Feats on the Tight Rope.

The whole to conclude with Mr. Ricketts and his Pupil in the Attitudes of two Flying Mercuries; the Boy pois'd on one Foot on Mr. Ricketts' Shoulder, whilst Mr. Ricketts stands in the same Manner with one Foot on the Saddle, the Horse being in full speed.

Those Ladies and Gentlemen who wish to embrace the present Opportunity of seeing the Exercises of the Circus, are respectfully informed, that Mr. Ricketts intends closing it for the Season within three Weeks from the present Time, as he is about to take a Tour to some other Parts of the Continent.

Tickets sold at Mr. Bradford's Book Store, Front street, and at the Circus. BOX 7/6— PIT 3/9.

As Philadelphia was the nation's capital, President George Washington is traditionally thought to have been in attendance at one of the first performances, hours after he had signed a declaration of neutrality at the onset of new hostilities between the French and the English. He and Ricketts later went on recreational rides together and soon became good friends, sharing among other things their uncommon love of horses. In fact, Washington ultimately sold his favorite white charger, Old Jack, to Ricketts for $150, for display at his circus.[1] Gilbert Stuart, famous for his portrait of the "Father of Our Country," also painted John Bill Ricketts, the "Father of the American Circus," as he has come to be called, and his portrait now hangs in the National Gallery in Washington, D.C.[2] Like Astley in England, Ricketts' "Circus Father" title comes not from having invented anything new, but from popularizing circus skills and arts and establishing the business of circus entertainment in America.

Ricketts' circus expanded rapidly, although "circus" was still a term reserved for describing the place, and not the event. He and his younger brother, Francis, and their small company were soon joined by other acts. They included Master Long, the popular clown Mr. Sully, John Durang, the first American-born clown, and other riders, acrobats, and rope walkers. In 1795, he built his most famous "New Amphitheatre," containing both a riding ring and a stage, on Chestnut Street in Philadelphia, just behind Independence Hall. Drawings suggest that it was a round white wooden structure that may have had a canvas roof. It was probably typical of the same kind of buildings apparently being hastily constructed in England, which saved expense and provided at least some degree of mobility.

Many Americans, emerging from the Revolution and a temporary law banning all theatrical and ring exhibitions, were eager for escapist entertainment. However, many others were not so enlightened as President Washington, and they were convinced that the theatre and the circus could be lumped together into a common den of iniquity and sin. In fact, to escape various prohibitions of one kind or another, theatres frequently played circus acts, and circuses frequently included brief skits and melodramas. In 1796, for example, only months after she had arrived in the country, America's first elephant made a "grand triumphal entry" in Nathaniel Lee's *The Rival Queens* on stage at The New Theatre, which was just across the street from the Ricketts' circus. Conversely, both Ricketts brothers were frequently forced to present and sometimes appear in theatrical productions as a matter of necessity.

Many Philadelphians, who only totalled about 60,000 people, would have never attended such "immoral" demonstrations. Clearly, potential audiences were too limited to support a full-time circus, and to make matters worse, the city was frequently a victim of outbreaks of yellow fever. As a result, in search of new audiences, Ricketts instituted an ambitious touring program as soon as he arrived. He traveled up and down the east coast, from Quebec to Charleston. On at least one occasion he even framed two units of his show to tour separately, although that plan was not especially successful. In his eight year career, he built at least twenty circuses, located in every major eastern American city, including several amphitheatres in Philadelphia and New York.

Ricketts was almost immediately imitated by competitors from both England and France, who opened similar shows, and sometimes employed his performers. One such was a Swede named Philip Lailson, who built a permanent domed amphitheatre only several blocks from Ricketts' Chestnut Street circus. However, Lailson's fancy ninety-foot-high dome collapsed for no good reason in 1798; some undoubtedly said it was God's justice. None of the competitors was as energetic and stubborn as America's first circus owner, but even he could not sustain for long his enthusiasm

for circus in the New World.

Ricketts' luck changed dramatically in 1799, when both the Greenwich Street amphitheatre in New York and his remodeled Philadelphia amphitheatre burned down. Financially ruined, he nonetheless struggled through several more touring attempts, and even tried to play in Lailson's collapsed amphitheatre. Finally, as his friend John Durang described him, "out of heart at doing business in this bodge way," Ricketts and most of his company set sail to try their luck in the West Indies.[3] Luck proved to be no better there, for en route he was kidnapped by French privateers. Rescued, the circus played for several months throughout the islands; several of the company died, probably from the same yellow fever that would kill one hundred thousand British troops in the region by 1802.[4] When his brother Francis went to jail for deserting his new native wife, John Bill Ricketts had had enough. "The Father of the American Circus" sold his horses and set sail for England. He and all hands were lost at sea, a final twist to the pattern of ill luck that had plagued his last years. Francis was eventually released and returned to America to tell the little-known story of his brother's Carribean adventures, and as late as 1810, he was a clown with the Boston Circus.

In the meantime, while the French were killing each other off by the thousands, and the British were rattling their sabers, Americans were basking in their neutrality and independence. It was a time for expansion, of both frontiers and ideas. In that regard, it wasn't only circuses and theatres who were competing for the two-bits Americans might be willing to pay for entertainment. For some time there had also been an established tradition of importing strange-looking animals that could be exhibited in cities and towns for a fee. By the middle of the 18th century, for example, lions, camels, and polar bears had all been exhibited singly in Boston. On April 13, 1796, Captain Jacob Crowninshield brought into New York harbor America's first elephant, an unnamed two-year-old Asian female. The enterprising ship's captain sold her to a Mr. Owen at the Bull's Head Tavern for what at the time was the stupendous sum of $10,000. Owen must have felt he could make a lot of money by displaying her; if the morality of the stage was questionable, and the ring was guilty by association, certainly no one could object to paying for simply viewing one of God's largest creatures, could they? Documents show this elephant on the stage in Philadelphia later that year, and for at least the next ten years she was led up and down the coast, on exhibit from Boston to Charleston.

Hachaliah Bailey

A second elephant was evidently on the scene by 1804, and at least by 1809 she was being displayed by one Hachaliah Bailey, born in Somers, New York, and a cattle dealer and owner of the stagecoach line there. Bailey named her Betty, or "Bet" for short, perhaps after his ex-wife, Elizabeth. Records of early American elephants are scant and contradictory, and historians have had a field day trying to figure them out. There is some circumstantial evidence to suggest that because his cousin and partner's name was John Owen, and because it was a Mr. Owen who bought that first elephant from Captain Crowninshield, Bailey may have been involved with exhibiting it. In fact, as a twenty-one-year-old New York cattle dealer, Bailey would probably himself have been a frequenter of the Bull's Head Tavern in 1796. Some historians have even speculated that the first elephant was Bet. However, Stuart Thayer, one of America's more thorough circus researchers, has done an impressive job of sorting it all out for us, showing among other things that Bet was a four-year-old African female when she was brought into Boston Harbor, and that there were at least two elephants touring the country by 1806. [5]

At any rate, so successful were Hachaliah and his partners in exhibiting Bet, that they decided to add tigers and other animals. The early elephants were generally displayed as separate attractions, but other animals were quickly imported and shown in traveling menageries after 1813. Intrigued neighbors rapidly turned Somers into a mecca for entrepreneurs and wild animals. When they weren't on the road, the animals were hidden away in local farmers' barns, some of which are still standing.

Bet was murdered by an irate farmer in Alfred, Maine, in 1816. He evidently felt it was sinful to spend money to see such a wicked beast, so Bet was a victim of religious fervor after all. A memorial plaque erected by the contrite people of Alfred marks the spot where she fell. By then, Bailey and his friends knew they had tapped into a lucrative business, and they lost no time in importing another Betty, named after the first, as well as a male named Columbus. "Little Bet" was also murdered, pointlessly shot down on May 25, 1826, by six adolescent boys on the bridge over the Chepachet River in Chepachet, Rhode Island. So remorseful were the citizens of Chepachet that the site became known as Elephant Bridge. And one hundred and fifty years later, in 1976, they too attended a ceremony at the bridge, at which a modern elephant unveiled a bronze plaque commemorating the death of her prominent ancestor. [6]

When possible, Hachaliah preferred to leave the actual road tours to others. One of his early business associates was Nathan A. Howes. "Uncle Nate," whose name would later become legendary in circus history, once toured Old Bet on an early trip into Maine. [7] By 1820, Bailey had retired from the road to build his Elephant Hotel in Somers. The inn was built on the profits from travels with his first elephant. In the foreground of the building, he later erected a twenty-five foot granite shaft topped with a wooden statue of "Old Bet," as she was now called, carved from glued together blocks of white ash. A major stage stop, the hotel became the favorite watering hole for the likes of Aaron Burr, Washington Irving, and Horace Greeley. Hachaliah spent a brief period with his menagerie in Virginia, where he established Bailey's Crossroads, ironically only a short distance from where the Ringling Brothers and Barnum & Bailey Circus has established its modern corporate headquarters. However, he soon returned to Somers, where he was killed by the kick of a horse in 1845 at the age of seventy. After the last of the Somers Baileys died in 1957, Hachaliah's hotel became the Town Hall and Historical Society, and a replica of "Old Bet" still stands proudly out front.

Other Early Showmen

On January 14, 1835, a group of 135 young, hard-nosed, blue-blooded, business-minded farmers and menagerie showmen and corporations, almost all from the vicinity of Somers, gathered in the ballroom of the Elephant Hotel. For

The Elephant Hotel, Somers, NY.
Photo by W. H. Rough

some time, these men had been involved in an increasing number of circuses and menageries, and they were eager to solidify their positions as America's premier showmen. By the end of the day, they had formed a powerful "trust" called the Zoölogical Institute, capitalizing a traveling menagerie show by that name. They then controlled at least thirteen menageries and three circuses — literally every show on the road except for six resistant circuses. Shows under their control could then travel on lucrative routes designed for efficient operations and avoiding all competition. Although the Institute itself did not survive the financial panic of 1837, three of its survivors, John J. June, Lewis B. Titus, and Caleb S. Angevine, from nearby North Salem, were owners of a joint stock company which continued to thrive. They and their associates, Jesse Smith and Gerard and Thaddeus Crane, formed the core of another group of powerful showmen calling themselves the "Syndicate," according to Earl Chapin May.[8] With their relatives and friends, they would maintain a firm monopoly on both the menagerie and circus businesses lasting until 1877. They were able to combine their capital, to launch major expeditions abroad to capture exotic new animals, and to buy out competing shows. They soon earned the somewhat derogatory nickname "The Flatfoots," allegedly because they thwarted all competition, threatening to "put their foot down flat" on anyone who tried to enter the menagerie business without their permission.

Circuses and menageries originally developed in competition with each other. They sought the same audiences, and they often coordinated their productions so that circuses played in the afternoon and menageries were displayed at night in the same location. In 1832, J. Purdy Brown, a cousin of Hachaliah Bailey, toured his circus with a menagerie for the first time. Circuses and menageries prior to that had been known to be mistrustful and jealous, and even stole each other's livestock on more than one occasion. In the 1840's, differences between the two kinds of traveling shows grew less distinct. In 1851, Aron Turner, a North Salem shoemaker and an old friend of Hachaliah Bailey, grew tired of putting up with monopolistic control of wild animals by the Syndicate. At the urging of his manager and son-in-law, George Fox Bailey, he leased his animals from them outright for use in his own circus. He thus became another early circus owner to completely combine the menagerie and the ring acts into a unified performance. This Bailey was another one of Hachaliah's nephews from North Salem, who would go on to become one of the top circus showmen in the country when he later inherited Aron's circus. He died in 1903, calling himself the last of the Flatfoots. Syndicate shows quickly followed the leads of Brown, Turner, and Bailey, and by the late 1850's menageries were completely absorbed into circuses.

New York had been a circus town since the days of Ricketts. The French Canadian circus

The Hippodrome at Madison Square, 1853. Photo courtesy of Circus World Museum, Baraboo, WI

master, Victor Pepin, built his Olympic Circus on Broadway in 1810. The Institute moved into New York City in 1835, occupying quarters at 37 Bowery. Within three years, the Flatfoots were operating the Bowery Amphitheatre, featuring a full circus ring. In 1853, the Franconi Hippodrome was built in New York in only twenty-five days. Located at Madison Square, at 23rd and Broadway, it was a two-acre building seating about 6,000 spectators, with 20-foot high brick side walls, a canvas roof, and a wide 1000-foot hippodrome track. Franconi and his troupe staged recreations of the great Egyptian, Greek, and Roman games, gladiatorial combats, and chariot races. Twelve years later, Lewis B. Lent, by then one of the most widely traveled and experienced of the Flatfoots, first rented and then bought another big circus building on Fourteenth Street called the Hippotheatron, one of New York's favorite amusement spots, and opened it as Lent's New York Circus. It was much more permanent than either Franconi's Hippodrome or Nixon's Alhambra, which it had been built to replace in 1864. The Hippotheatron sported a roof of corrugated tin instead of canvas. It had a 43½ foot ring, larger than Astley's in London, and held about 2300 people. Lent operated it successfully for four years, until P.T. Barnum bought it for his menagerie. Despite its reputation as the iron building, it subsequently burned down, as circuses were still prone to do. P.T. Barnum's canvas-roofed Great Roman Hippodrome was later built on Madison Avenue at 27th Street in 1874, on the site of an abandoned N.Y. and Harlem passenger railroad station, and after it was remodeled in 1881, it

became the first Madison Square Garden. These buildings, and others like them, represent some of the earlier American efforts to create permanent circus buildings in the European tradition.

However, Ricketts, Bailey, Lent, and their imitators were quick to discover that a different approach to performance would have to be taken by circuses in the new world from what was becoming the norm in the old world. In England and Europe, Astley, Hughes, and the Franconi Family assured themselves of big audiences by building relatively permanent circus buildings in the heavily populated major cities. Despite the experiments with semi-permanent circuses in New York, American cities did not have the population base to support the new industry by themselves, and early American circuses grew almost immediately into road shows. Enterprising individuals designed and built their circuses to travel. They played in the open air or in whatever theatres and meeting houses they could find in the small towns they visited, and when necessary they built makeshift amphitheatres. However, they soon discovered that it simply wasn't practical to spend the money and time required for permanent buildings, no matter how cheaply they might be built. The full canvas tent was the logical outgrowth of such limitations. According to Stuart Thayer, Joshua Purdy Brown toured the first American tented circus in 1825. [9] Brown was the same benevolent and gentle circus man who would eventually join his operation with the Wright Brothers menagerie in 1832. In 1826, Hachaliah's old associate, Nathan Howes, and friend Aron Turner, tried a tent for the first season of their new circus.

Finally, in 1830, Turner took on the road a complete ninety-foot round tent, which is generally considered the true forerunner of the American big top.

Tents proved to be the ultimate solution for problems faced by the circus in frontier America, and one of the great mysteries of circus history is why they didn't catch on sooner and faster. Not only did they guarantee audiences protection from the weather, but they provided the performers with a consistent set-up for their acts, protected the circus from those who would watch without paying, allowed rapid set-ups and take-downs, and increased the mobility necessary for seeking new audiences. After 1840, playing under canvas became the norm in America. It soon grew popular in Europe as well, after the American Richard Sands, a former clown in Aron Turner's circus, took his tented pavilion circus to England in 1842, fifty-four years after Philip Astley had performed in his Liverpool tent.

Turner and Nate Howes split up in 1828, and both continued to operate small circuses independently. Seth B. Howes, who had been working for his older brother as a performer and gaining managing experience on other shows, would become a proprietor of the Howes and Mabie Circus in 1843. Seth was to become the most famous and powerful of all circus men, accumulating a fortune of $20 million by the time he retired in 1870. Dozens of circuses eventually bore his name, one of the most often used titles in the history of circus, including Howes' Great London Circus, a big American show so named because it was a smash hit on its London tour. Marian Murray suggests that Seth B. Howes has also been called "the Father of the American Circus," because of his outstanding success and the number of contributions he made in the development of the circus.[10]

P.T. Barnum

A young Phineas T. Barnum, from nearby Bethel, Connecticut, once worked for Hachaliah Bailey, or so Barnum would have us believe. Barnum later became a ticket seller, secretary, treasurer, and occasional clown for Aron Turner's circus in 1836. Allegedly, it was a practical joke by Turner that taught Barnum the value of notoriety.

Victor C. Anderson's "The Old Circus Horse." Photo courtesy of Circus World Museum, Baraboo, WI

Turner told an Annapolis, Maryland crowd that Barnum was wanted for murder, and as a result he was barely able to rescue him in time from a lynching. The following year, Barnum briefly took out his own "circus," called Barnum's Grand Scientific and Musical Theatre. But he was not really cut out to be a circus man, and the show was caught in the 1837 financial panic. It failed in Nashville, Tennessee, after only two months on the road.

Years later, in 1871, Barnum had retired to Bridgeport, Connecticut politics, on the remaining profits of his famous American Museum in New York, and his astounding promotion of such financial successes as Joice Heth, "George Washington's 161 year old nurse"; Jenny Lind, the Swedish Nightingale; Tom Thumb; the Feejee Mermaid; and an assortment of bearded ladies and side-show attractions. In the intervening years, he had been involved in at least one behind-the-scenes partnership with his old friend Seth Howes. Barnum and Howes financed the acquisition and showing of the first genuine herd of elephants in America back in 1851.[11] However, that tour had no ring acts; it wasn't officially even called a "circus," and Barnum didn't travel with the show. Still, by 1871, his name was one of the best known in America, and his success at drawing crowds had earned him the title the "Shakespeare of Advertising." He had made and lost several fortunes; his museum had burned down twice; and Barnum, now past sixty years old, was fully prepared to enjoy his retirement years in leisure. However, two successful Wisconsin circus owners, William C. Coup and Dan Castello, succeeded in luring him back into the circus business in a big way. They convinced Barnum to join them in framing a new enterprise with the profitable but unwieldy title, the "P. T. Barnum Museum, Menagerie and Circus, International Zoölogical Garden, Polytechnic Institute and Hippodrome."

Barnum's new enterprise was then the largest modern circus ever to be mounted. Barnum himself was not an enthusiastic participant, although he never hesitated to take credit for the show's successes. During the next five seasons, under W. Coup's persuasive leadership, the show expanded rapidly. It played under the largest big tops ever seen; it became the first circus to travel completely by rail on its own cars; and it established the pattern of staging huge street parades for promoting the show.

By 1873, the title had grown to perhaps the longest in history: "P. T. Barnum's Great Traveling World's Fair, Consisting of Museum, Menagerie, Caravan, Hippodrome, Gallery of Statuary and Fine Arts, Polytechnic Institute, Zoölogical Garden, and 100,000 Curiosities, Combined with Dan Castello's, Sig Sebastian's, and Mr. D'Atelie's Grand Triple Equestrian and Hippodromatic Exposition." Notably, the title contained neither Coup's name nor the word circus. Barnum's large ego, combined with an inherent fear that he would lose what was left of his fortune, did not make life easy for his partners. Veteran circus performer Dan Castello was the first to leave. Coup quit in 1875, finally giving up when Barnum insisted on splitting the show into two units, one managed by John "Pogey" O'Brien, one of the most notorious "grifters," or gyp artists, of the day. Left without an effective manager for either unit, Barnum turned to his old friends the Flatfoots for help. Barnum's became the last major circus to be operated under the Flatfoot aegis. They auctioned off what was left of Coup's unit, saving the best to consolidate into one successful new show.

By 1880, Barnum and the Flatfoots were getting a lot of competition from circuses that had developed outside of their monopolistic influence. One of them was Cooper & Bailey's Circus, a huge show that had toured successfully as far as California, Australia, Java, and South America. Having recently bought up Seth Howes' Great London Circus from James E. Kelly, Cooper & Bailey was one of the largest railroad shows in the country. It was headed by a young man calling himself James Anthony Bailey. Seeing a mutual advantage, the two shows combined and evolved into Barnum & Bailey's "Greatest Show on Earth," as it came to be called for the first time in 1888, although the title had been briefly used in 1872, by the Coup and Barnum show.

James Bailey is often labeled the best manager in the history of the circus for his efficiency and generosity. He kept at least 200 disabled or retired employees on his payroll, and he used his vast wealth for charitable purposes.[12] Bailey was initially a retiring behind-the-scenes manager, who

The Barnum Museum, Bridgeport, CT.
Photo by W. H. Rough

contented himself with chewing quietly on his rubber bands and letting Barnum take all the bows. But significantly, no one ever dared to confront Mr. Bailey when he was indulging in his nervous chewing habit; only when he spit the rubber band out was it considered safe to talk to him.

When Barnum first met him, Bailey was only thirty-two years old. He had been an orphan, born in the old circus town of Detroit as James Anthony McGinniss. In his youth, he had been befriended by Frederick H. Bailey, an advance man and bill-poster for the Robinson & Lake Circus who was staying in the hotel where he worked. Bailey adopted young James, gave him his name, and raised him in the circus. Significantly, Frederick H. Bailey was still another distant cousin of old Hachaliah himself.

Thus it was that Hachaliah Bailey and his elephant were responsible for a considerable sphere of influence, inspiring a second birth of the circus quite apart from John Bill Ricketts; and thus it was that the area around Somers, New York, about forty miles north of Manhattan, came to be called the "Cradle of the American Circus." Almost every major show in the country had at least some connection to this area and to Hachaliah's relatives, imitators, and followers. It was P.T. Barnum himself who labeled Hachaliah Bailey "the Father of the American Circus," a title he deserved fully as much as any of the others to have been so called.

As for P.T. Barnum, although he is still generally thought of as a circus man, his actual involvement was only peripheral. The real credit for conceiving and operating his circuses goes to his visionary and talented partners, particularly William Coup and James Bailey. Barnum added his considerable talents in promotion and the enormous drawing power of his name. Before he died, thanks in no small part to Coup and Bailey, Barnum had regained his stature as one of America's richest and most popular men. In a spirit of lovable chicanery, he fooled us all: Few of his audiences ever claimed they had not gotten their money's worth. Few grumbled about spending a few pennies to see an exotic "Egress" only to find an exit door, or discovering that a "Man-eating Chicken" was really an ordinary man seated at a table chewing on a drumstick. If he really had said, "There's a sucker born every minute," which has been wrongfully attributed to him, it would have been in a spirit of shared fellowship. Barnum's home in Bridgeport, Connecticut, where he had served as benefactor and mayor, was for a half a century the home of the "Greatest Show on Earth." An exciting new $8.5 million remodeled Barnum Museum opened its doors in Bridgeport in 1989, to commemorate the man who had attracted 82 million people to his museums, circuses and traveling shows around the world. Barnum would be happy to know that attendance is setting all-time high records.

THE MOVE WEST

In the first half-century following 1793, when Ricketts had arrived in Philadelphia to open a circus, Americans moved rapidly westward. Within thirty years, there were several small but significant circuses touring the new world with two or three wagons, some horses, and a clown. New circus troupes, eager to search out new audiences away from the crowded competition in the East, were never far behind the settlers. Early circus troupers had to be a rugged bunch of pioneers: roads west were little more than widened trails when the first circus wagons challenged them. Much easier for traveling were the great waterways, the Ohio and the Mississippi. In 1825, when the Erie Canal was opened connecting the Hudson River at Albany to the Great Lakes, entrepreneurs and ordinary settlers began to flock westward in even greater numbers. By mid-century, there were dozens of circuses, small and large, criss-crossing the country and playing wherever new populations justified a performance. Within the context of this brief historical perspective, we can only touch on a few of their names, in order to suggest the relationships between them and to show just how fast the American circus developed. By 1849, for instance, Joseph A. Rowe's Olympic Circus had already gotten all the way around Cape Horn to San Francisco, where it played to gold rush audiences at gold rush prices: Admission to box seats was set at $5.00, compared to 50¢ back East.

Edmund and Jeremiah Mabie, from Flatfoot country in Putnam County, New York, had started their first circus in 1841, with the help of Nathan and Seth Howes. After six years of touring from New York, they paused for a rest one day in Delavan, Wisconsin. So struck were the brothers by its beauty, as well as the practical consideration of establishing a midwestern base for new territories, that they bought a 400 acre farm there, and the circus stayed. The word spread, and by the next spring, other entertainers were moving in. Their loose living habits rapidly earned Delavan the title of the "wickedest town in Wisconsin," an ironic description for a place just founded in 1836 as a temperance colony and named for an internationally famous prohibitionist.

Somers, New York may have been the "cradle," but Delavan's reputation as the "home" of the American circus was earned by the twenty-three circuses who called the town their home. In fact, the two towns would engage in a modern battle of words in 1966 over which one was entitled to issue first day cancellation for the American Circus commemorative stamp. That brouhaha was eventually settled when Somers, the earlier "birthplace," won the privilege of re-cancelling covers flown in from Delavan, the official site. Among the residents of Delavan in 1870 was Dan Castello's Circus, managed by W. C. Coup. Castello, who was a talented equestrian and one of the most popular song-and-dance men in America, had started with the Mabie Brothers, and he had extensive experience in traveling shows around the country. His partner was on the train on May 10, 1869, the day that the Golden Spike was driven joining the Union and Central Pacific Railroads in Promontory, Utah. Castello's became the first circus to cross the continent by train. New towns had been founded all along the new railroad tracks as they stretched across the country. In 1872, it was W. C. Coup and Dan Castello, recognizing the value of the new territories and the potential for traveling farther and faster, who persuaded P.T. Barnum that their circus should be placed on brand new specially made circus railroad cars. Other circuses had been traveling on the rails for several years, but the Coup–Barnum enterprise was the first to move its entire circus, including all the annexes and a parade, to daily rail transportation, on April 18, 1872. They used Pennsylvania R.R. cars at first, but later in the same year they ordered their own specially-built flat cars.

William Cameron Coup had had earlier experience with Barnum, the Mabies, and Yankee Robinson, of whom we shall hear more. By 1870, Coup was perhaps the most forward-thinking man in the industry. In addition to his historic train initiative, it was Coup in the first place who proposed the union with Barnum's name that would evolve into "the Greatest Show on Earth"; Coup who insisted on expanding to two rings; and Coup who proposed Barnum's New York Hippodrome, the precursor of Madison Square Garden. Yet outside the world of the circus, his name is virtually unknown. After he split from Barnum, he failed at several subsequent enterprises, more from bad luck and high principles than lack of talent, and he died in Florida in 1895, a pauper. His body was brought home to Delavan.

Delavan today is just as proud of its circus heritage as Bridgeport, Connecticut and Somers, New York. Not to be outdone, it too has an elephant memorial in the center of town. This one is a colorful, fiberglass, standing representation of the Mabie Brothers' notorious elephant, Romeo, who was reputed to have killed twenty-five horses and five trainers. Delavan is also the home of the International Clown Hall of Fame.

Mud Shows

Fayette "Yankee" Robinson was both a preacher and a Shakespearean actor before he decided to become a flamboyant lion trainer. By the mid-1850's, he had established a successful circus career in the midwest and northeastern parts of the country, and he went on to become one of the biggest circus names in the country after the Civil War. His operation was typical of the rapidly multiplying wagon shows of the era, the true "mud shows," in which life was neither easy nor romantic. These circuses played one-night stands in tiny communities, and moved only an average of ten miles between towns, under cover of darkness, no matter what the weather or the condition of the roads. In the blackness of night, an advance man would tear apart a farmer's fence and place a fence rail across any road the circus caravan was not to take. "Railing the road" was standard operating procedure to prevent misdirections and circus wagons lost in the dark. At dawn, they would pause at a stream or pond near the next stand to wash and decorate the wagons. The bandwagon was moved to the head of the line, and everyone dressed up for their parade entry into town. Their task on arrival was to "make the nut," meaning to make ends meet, or earn enough income from doing the show to pay all salaries and costs. The expression derives from the town officials' habit of confiscating an all-important nut from the hub of one of the big wagon wheels, in order to keep a show from skipping town. It would be returned after the performance only when the circus had paid all its bills and "licensing" fees in full.

Some of the mud shows were not small by any

stretch of the imagination. By the middle of the century, some vast circus wagon trains carried 100 wagons, 400 horses, 6000 seats, one or two 40-foot poles, and rhinos and hippopotamuses. Some smaller shows could not afford a supply of stock, and horses were rented from local farmers. Neither could they afford the weight of carrying their own tent poles, which had to be cut in each town. Large or small, these early circuses were called mud shows not because they played on muddy lots, which they certainly did, but because they often had to travel on roads made all but impassable by mud. In 1869, for example, twenty-two out of twenty-eight traveling circuses were driven out of business by the endless rains that year. [13] Nonetheless, circus wagons were a long-lasting tradition in America. The M. L. Clark & Sons Circus was still using horse- and mule-drawn wagons to move show equipment as late as 1930. The wagons on display in the annual Milwaukee Circus Parade and some in Peru, Indiana are among the few that remain of the thousands that were built for hundreds of traveling circuses.

Delavan's "Romeo." Photo by W. H. Rough

They are the ones that survived abandonment, fires, and intentional destruction for the prevention of competition.

During the Civil War, "Yankee" Robinson's famous nickname did not endear him to southerners, and on more than one occasion his circus was shot at by the local townspeople. He narrowly avoided a lynching in Harpers Ferry in 1859, and circus historian Joe McKennon tells the story of how Yankee's circus was attacked and burned to the ground in Richmond by a gang of rebel hoodlums. The rebs just missed the chance to tar and feather the whole troupe, but the troupers had been tipped off in advance. Such treatment of early circus troupes was not all that uncommon in frontier America.

River Shows

In 1843, an Albany pharmacist named "Doc" Gilbert R. Spalding got hooked on the circus business by a bad debt. He soon earned a considerable name for himself up and down the Ohio and Mississippi Rivers with various partners and circuses for over twenty years. He was an important, inventive risk-taker, generally credited with a lot of firsts in the circus business, many of which may be reliable records. He is said to have invented the quarter pole, to keep the canvas off the heads of his audiences. He is also credited with developing the efficient jack-and-stringer type of seating arrangement which survives in small circuses to this day. His was the first circus to use a mechanical precursor to the calliope, and the first to convert from candles and oil lamps to gaslight. In 1853, he was among the first to experiment with railroad travel: his "Railroad Circus and Crystal Palace" exhibited in Detroit, although probably only with a few stock cars. Three years later he ordered nine specially-built railroad cars for his new Spalding & Rogers Railroad Circus, which carried no menageries or parade equipment. The cars had adjustable axles and may or may not have been designed to actually drive off the tracks to a circus lot, but this isn't really clear. In any case, they were used for only one season, before Spalding evidently decided that railroad circuses were not yet practical.

Spalding's most famous enterprise was the Floating Palace, which he undertook in partnership with the English equestrian Charles Rogers. From 1852 until the Civil War made them stop, this luxurious barge visited ports all along the Mississippi and Ohio, and usually wintered in New Orleans. The barge had only a four foot draft, but it contained a full 42-foot circus ring, and could seat perhaps as many as 2,400 spectators. The menagerie was carried on the tow boat, one of two magnificent show boats owned by Spalding, the Banjo and the James Raymond, on which other performances were also presented. They ranged from minstrel shows to dramatic performances, from Shakespeare to the temperance comedy, *Ten Nights in a Bar Room*.

On a later circus, "Doc" Spalding would give a headstart to the talented young clown, Dan Castello. But with his very first circus, he had acquired a feisty young singer, fighter, and strong man named Dan Rice. He and Rice began a stormy partnership, and later a lifelong rivalry marked by bitter "billing wars" when the two men attacked each other with dirty tricks and slanderous advertising. One year, after a legal foreclosure by Doc Spalding had reduced his menagerie to a single horse, Rice was determined to continue performances of his own show. As he led Aroostook into the ring, a distinguished-looking man suddenly rose from the audience to call out, "Ladies and Gentlemen: Introducing Dan Rice and his one-horse show!" Without missing a beat, Rice bowed to him and replied: "After all, Dr. Spalding, the taking of Troy was strictly a one-horse show." To the roaring approval of the audience and the ironic embarassment of Spalding, Rice planted a kiss on Aroostook's nose and proclaimed that "quality is never measured by numerical standards." Thereafter, the "one-horse show" became a national catch-phrase used as a mark of distinction for any small operation priding itself on quality. [14]

At one time or another, Rice owned several circuses, one of which was probably used as the model for the traveling troupe described in Mark Twain's *The Adventures of Huckleberry Finn*:

> It was a real bully circus. It was the splendidest sight that ever was when they all come riding in, two and two, a gentleman and lady, side by side, the men just in their

drawers and undershirts, and no shoes nor stirrups, and resting their hands on their thighs easy and comfortable—there must a been twenty of them—and every lady with a lovely complexion, and perfectly beautiful, and looking just like a gang of real sure-enough queens, and dressed in clothes that cost millions of dollars, and just littered with diamonds. It was a powerful fine sight; I never see anything so lovely. [15]

Rice wowed audiences with his political songs and conversations with his "educated" pig, Lord Byron. His brand of political humor didn't always endear him to his audiences, although he was a favorite of Zachary Taylor, Jefferson Davis, Robert E. Lee, and Abraham Lincoln. He even considered running for president himself in 1868. Rice sported a goatee and frequently wore a top hat and a striped red, white, and blue outfit. His appearance has led several historians to suggest that political cartoonist Thomas Nast used him as the original model for the renowned character of Uncle Sam, although plenty of contrary evidence exists to establish that he merely dressed the part of an already well-established political caricature. In any case, Dan Rice became America's most popular clown, the Will Rogers of his day. At one time he was also America's highest paid clown, earning about $1,000 a week. However, spoiled by success and the bottle, he would die broke and forgotten in 1900.

It was probably Rice's Great Paris Pavilion that was unloading on the banks of the Mississippi in McGregor, Iowa, one morning in 1870, inspiring the biggest circus story in American history. Five brothers sat on a nearby grassy knoll and watched every move of the process. Their German harness-maker father, August Rungeling, was doing some repair work for the strong man, and he earned free passes for them all to go to the circus that night. And so it was that the Ringlings caught the circus fever. The oldest brother Al soon left home to earn a living with a carriage company, but was lured into joining Doc Morrison's circus in Delavan as an acrobat and juggler. Morrison was a smooth talker and a self-taught "dentist," and under his tutelage and the influence of the wickedest city in Wisconsin, Al learned all the

Dan Rice as "Uncle Sam." Photo courtesy of Circus World Museum, Baraboo, WI

circus tricks he'd ever need, including how to get out of a Green Bay hotel room without paying the bill. [16] Meanwhile, back in their home town of Baraboo, Wisconsin, Otto was becoming an expert at geography; Alf T. and Charles were studying music, and young John was doing a lot of acting and minstrelsy. Reunited by 1882, when Al was thirty and John was sixteen, the five brothers mounted their first show together: The Ringling Brothers Classic and Comic Opera Company. The show was apparently a financial and artistic disaster, but the boys were too stubborn to care, and they kept at it. In the following year on tour, they stumbled on down-and-out old "Yankee" Robinson himself, and talked him into letting them use his name and old equipment to put out their first real circus. The handbill that Otto posted in Sauk City, advertising the second performance of the new show, read as follows:

Behold the Old Hero of the Arena, coming Tuesday, May 20, 1884. Old Yankee Robinson and Ringling Bros.' Double Show!! The largest and most elegantly conducted and perfectly equipped Arenic Exposition

*The Ringling Bros. first parade?
Photo courtesy of Circus World
Museum, Baraboo, WI*

*The Big Top at Circus World Museum,
Baraboo, WI, original home of the
Ringling Bros. Circus. Photo by
W. H. Rough*

ever witnessed. The Great 25 Cent Show! (Not 50 cents as was reported.) Two performances daily, Rain or Shine. Doors open at 1 and 7 p.m. See our Street Parade! At 11:30 a.m. on day of show.

Yankee agreed to serve as manager and advisor for the boys during that first season. Dean Jensen, in his excellent chronicle of Wisconsin circuses, *The Biggest, the Smallest, the Longest, the Shortest,* describes Robinson's ringside speech for the opening performance:

Ladies and Gentlemen, I am an old man. For forty years I have rested my head on a stranger's pillow. I have traveled every state in the Union and have been associated with every showman of prominence in America. I will soon pass on to the arena of a life that knows no ending, and when I do, I want to die in harness and connected with these boys. If I could have my dying wish gratified, it would be that my name should remain associated with that of the Ringling Brothers. For I can tell you, the Ringling Brothers are the future showmen of America. [17]

In September of the same year, Yankee died on the road.

THE GOLDEN AGE

The Ringling Brothers Circus grew rapidly, along with other American circuses. They were entering the age known as the "heyday," or the "golden age" of the American circus, something short of a half-century of progress which ended abruptly with the 1929 stock market crash. Ringling's winter quarters in Baraboo is now the site of the Circus World Museum. We have seen in both Somers and Delavan that circuses tend to attract more circuses by seducing neighbors and relatives into the business, and now Baraboo was also to become a circus capital. In 1890, when the Ringlings were finally ready to put their show on rail, their five cousins bought all their old wagons and established a second Baraboo circus, which eventually became The Gollmar Brothers' "Greatest of American Shows."

At the end of the century, The Ringling Brothers' "World's Greatest Shows" went head to head in a bitter competition with its chief rival, the Barnum and Bailey Circus, which was solely managed by James A. Bailey after Barnum's death in 1891. The boys from Baraboo had by now been joined by their two remaining brothers, and their management expertise together was legendary. They may have argued loudly in private, but there was never a public disagreement between them. Traditionally they wrote down very little about their day-to-day decisions, and most Ringling deals were made with verbal agreements. Any decision affecting the circus was made by consensus, and once it was made, the brothers worked hard to bring the plan decided on into effect. In this case the plan was to overtake and acquire the legendary Barnum & Bailey Circus. Taking advantage of Bailey's five-year European tour, they were able to achieve the status of the biggest and most popular circus in America.

Finally, in 1907, a year after the death of the popular "Mr. Bailey," the Ringlings gained control over the Barnum and Bailey Circus and its other interests at bargain prices. For a while, they continued to operate their several shows separately under their own names. John Ringling insisted their show would never leave Baraboo: "The members of our company have invested a quarter of a million dollars in homes that cannot be dupli-

cated in the state of Wisconsin."[18] Nevertheless, The Ringling Brothers Circus remained in Baraboo only until 1918, when the three remaining brothers elected to combine the two biggest shows, creating The Ringling Bros. and Barnum & Bailey Combined Shows, Inc., the title it retains today. From 1918 until it moved to Sarasota, Florida in 1927, the "Big One" was winter-quartered in Barnum's Connecticut barns. Bridgeport was thought to be a better location from which the brothers could keep tabs on what had become nothing less than a circus empire. Thus did Bridgeport and Sarasota join the select community of American circus cities. Sarasota in particular later became a major capital, when other circuses seeking warm climates for their winter quarters settled in the vicinity. Nearby Gibsonton, or "Gib'town" as it is affectionately called by circus people, became a retirement home for hundreds of ex-circus performers. However, relations between the big Ringling show and its host city were from time to time strained, and in 1960 winter quarters were moved fourteen miles south to Venice, Florida, where they remain today.

BLACK CIRCUSES

Before we turn our attention too far away from Wisconsin, however, a word must be said about a phenomenon much overlooked by most American circus histories: the role of the black man.

There were early isolated examples of black performers in the circus, like James Sandford and Robert White, who had both appeared with Aron Turner's Circus and then with Barnum in 1836. Minstrelsy became popular in the late 1840's, but early groups such as the Virginia Minstrels, the Kentucky Minstrels, and the Original Christy Minstrels were white men performing in blackface. These touring shows were played in big city theatres, in tents, and on show boats like Spalding's. With song-and-dance, lectures, and short playlets, they purported to show "life on the plantation," that is, the "amusements" of Negro slaves. But with few exceptions, prior to the creation of the Original Georgia Minstrels in 1865 by Charles B. Hicks, there had been no blacks in the mainstream of the American entertainment industry.[19] It wasn't until after the Civil War that black managers like Hicks, Lew Johnson, and Henry Hart established popular and successful minstrel shows with well-trained black actors and bands. By the 1880's, the old format of minstrelsy was already growing tiresome; the playlets grew longer, and the specialty acts opened up opportunities in the shows for acrobats, wire-walkers, and jugglers. This new direction bridged the gaps between minstrelsy, burlesque, vaudeville, and the circus, and paved the way for Ephraim Williams.

Ephraim Williams

Ephraim Williams was the owner of several of the over 100 circuses which were eventually spawned in Wisconsin. Born around the middle of the century, he spent his youth as a shoeshine boy and hotel porter in Milwaukee, dreaming of growing into this country's black Barnum. He became an accomplished horse trainer and magician, as well as a pleasant but stubborn gentleman, dressing dapperly in tailor-made evening wear with a bright red vest. He took his first circus, the Ferguson & Williams Monster Show, out of Appleton, Wisconsin in 1885. This was more than a decade before another black man, the brilliant comedian Bert Williams, would make his celebrated vaudeville debut and become the country's first black star. Ephraim Williams was later joined at various times by the German trapeze artist and sword-swallower Frank Skerbeck and his family. By 1893, Prof. Williams' Consolidated American and German Railroad Shows were based in Medford, Wisconsin, with a fifteen car railroad circus. The Medford newspaper wrote "...it is beyond question that with the company selected for this year, Prof. Williams need not turn out of the road for any show going.... His skin is dark, but he will come out on top yet, or know the reason why." In 1898, Eph was the only black circus owner in America. He owned 100 Arabian horses and employed twenty-six people.

Ephraim Williams was operating a show with as much extravagance and talent as the best little circuses of the day when he was only in his thirties. However, he soon had to face a not particularly rare run of circus man's hard luck: bad weather and bad creditors. His fall from prominence was probably aggravated by white resistance to the initial success of this upstart black proprietor, who

was performing with white employees, and for white audiences. He endured several financially "down" years working for Skerbeck, framing one additional show of his own, and working menial jobs. In the summer of 1907, Williams and his "ponies" appeared in Philadelphia with Cole and Johnson's popular Negro dramatic company, in a play called *Shoo-Fly Regiment*. Bobby Cole, by the way, was one of the greatest of black comedians, particularly known for his appearance in a clown's white-face, in an era when even blacks were blackening their faces for the stereotypical amusement of all. By 1910, Eph had once more returned to the circus: He had become the founder, sole owner, and manager of Prof. Eph Williams' Famous Troubadours, touring an all-black tent show called "Silas Green from New Orleans." This circus–revue played one-night stands throughout the South, and became one of the longest-lasting tent shows in American show-business history.[20] Williams managed the show, and continued to perform his horse tricks alongside such performance greats as Bessie Smith, the legendary blues singer. It was enormously popular among both black and white audiences, many of whom can still remember the Silas Green show, still touring in the 1950's, and old Eph Williams. However, when he died in Florida, sometime in the 1930's, apparently no one considered his death important enough to announce in an obituary or to mark his grave.[21] A much-overlooked figure in the history of American circus, Williams was a victim of the same racial discrimination that has blocked the paths to success and happiness of many Americans throughout our history.

Black Performers

For over a hundred years, the circus industry, which on one level seems so accepting of every variety of human being, paradoxically has been no exception to that discrimination. Black circus performers after the mid-19th century, when racial lines were firmly drawn, have traditionally been limited to minstrelsy, freaks, colored side show bands, and tribal warriors. The most menial jobs of the circus labor force were usually reserved for the black roustabouts, and train crews were traditionally filled with blacks. On white circuses, blacks were fed in their own dining tents, and they were generally segregated from the rest of the circus community at every level. Such a tradition makes black circus stars, and especially entrepreneurs like Ephraim Williams, all the more exceptional. Yet among the circus histories, only Dean Jensen's has treated his story in any depth.

It is still difficult to find reliable information about black participation in circus history, although it certainly existed. "Shufflin' Sam from Alabam'" was a copy of the Silas Green show, and Pat Chappelle's Rabbit's Foot Company was one of the most successful tent shows of the day, featuring among others a performance by Allie Brown on the slack wire. The Famous Mahara Minstrels, for which W. C. Handy was band director, included an act by Prof. Charles Carr and his ten performing Shetland ponies and thirty dogs, as well as a trick bicycle act by Snapper Garrison. These were among the dozens of black entertainment companies that developed out of the minstrel tradition around the turn of the century. This was the era of the great elaborately-costumed minstrel or mummers parades that rivalled the white circus parades for sheer spectacle. The Doc Bartok Medicine Show, before it was taken over by Hoxie Tucker, also carried a complete black minstrel show. Billy Kersand's, the Georgia Minstrel, and Al G. Field's shows were all popular and successful black companies. The great Al G. Field, born in Virginia as a Hatfield, had traveled with Ben Wallace's first circus out of Peru, Indiana in 1884, working as equestrian director and head clown on the show, and touring his own minstrel show in the winters.[22]

During the year after the Civil War, Harriet Beecher Stowe's 1852 novel *Uncle Tom's Cabin* became a dramatic production toured by several circus men during the winter months as an additional source of revenue, and many of their casts included black actors. As might be expected, such shows were not made especially welcome in the old South. Other blacks performed in circuses, dramatic companies, minstrel shows, burlesque, and vaudeville theatres. Littlejohn's and the Russell Brothers employed hundreds of black artists over the years. Many of them also practiced their circus arts within the context of the minstrel shows. They performed trick unicycling and bicycling (Maxwell, Adams, Montrose Douglass,

and Snapper Garrison). They were acrobats: Pauline Freeman and George Bradshaw, in Hogan and McClain's Smart Set Co.; Pearl Woods in Tom McIntosh's "Hot Old Time in Dixie Company"; George Woods with Geo. W. Hall & Sons; as well as Evans Fuller, Wells and Wells, Charles Gaines, Walter Jones, and "Master Duffee." They were wire artists, like "The Great Layton." Particularly popular were the slack wire artists like La She, a wire man with Richards and Pringle's Georgia Minstrels, and A. L. Prince, Manzie Richardson, Alfred Drew, Gray and Gray, and George Baker with Silas Green. There were outstanding black jugglers like Ben Toledo and Rowland, the "Brainstorm Juggler." There were some superb black magicians, like Black Carl, and W. A. Barclay. The first American magician was a black man named Richard Potter, who was born in 1783 and traveled with several circuses during his career.

Blacks were no strangers to the Wild West, either. Bill Pickett, the great steer wrestler with the Miller Brothers 101 Ranch Wild West Show, virtually invented the art of bull-dogging; the great black American cowboy and horse trainer Tom Bass trained Buffalo Bill's famous horse Columbia, and sold a horse to Teddy Roosevelt. The list of fine black circus artists is a long one, but their names and stories are comparatively unknown in circus histories. Documentation of both

The "Uncle Tom's Cabin" cart awaits display at Circus World Museum. Photo by L. G. Hoh

black circus managers and performers in America is sparse, and major research has yet to be undertaken.

THE WILD WEST

The "wild west" show was a uniquely American part of circus history that developed early in the "golden age." In May of 1883, Buffalo Bill Cody opened the "Wild West, Rocky Mount and Prairie Exhibition" in Omaha, Nebraska. His show was a huge success and would eventually make three tours to Europe. The last one ended in 1906, when Annie Oakley shot the cigar out of Kaiser Wilhelm's mouth; she later commented, "I wish I'd missed that day."[23] But Annie, the "Little Sure Shot" who hated guns, rarely missed, and she was one of Buffalo Bill's prime drawing cards. Her most popular trick was to shoot holes through the pips of playing cards thrown into the air. A circus ticket with a special hole punched in it denoted free admission, and to this day, a free pass

Annie Oakley. Photo courtesy of Circus World Museum, Baraboo, WI

is called an "Annie Oakley."

"Buffalo Bill's Wild West" always called itself just that. The word "show" was never attached to the end of it, because the "West," a noun, is what he was presenting. The Wild West included huge demonstrations, usually in the open air, of horsemanship, the Pony Express, cowboys and Indians (including old Sitting Bull), shooting skills, the attack on the Deadwood stagecoach, and of course, the spectacular presentation of the veteran Pony Express rider, army scout, and Medal of Honor winner himself. Later the Wild West staged a more international riding exhibition entitled the Congress of the Rough Riders of the World, featuring three hundred riders in various uniforms, charging around the arena, hell-bent for leather. It may not have been pure circus, but audiences loved it, at least in the beginning. Buffalo Bill's Wild West was soon imitated by Pawnee Bill's Wild West, featuring Gordon Lillie, an Indian interpreter, by the new Wild West unit of the Adam Forepaugh circus dynasty, and by the 101 Ranch Real Wild West. Gradually, circuses and wild wests became inextricably intertwined: Pawnee Bill's show included an incongruous herd of elephants, and Buffalo Bill's included a circus side-show in the 1890's. And for a period in the 1920's, it was common for many circuses to have a "Wild West" feature in the "concert," an after-show which always followed the "blow-off" at the end of a circus performance. Contemporary circuses such as Flora and Big Apple continue to commemorate the tradition of the "Wild West" with old west themes and western acts like the impressive lariat work of the "cockney cowboy," Vince Bruce.

It was Miller's 101 Ranch Wild West that gave a down-and-out Buffalo Bill Cody his last job before he died in 1917. There is a postscript to the old scout's story. Just a month after he died, Congress stripped him of the Medal of Honor he had earned in 1872 as a civilian army scout, in a retroactive decision to restrict eligibility to enlisted men and officers. But in July of 1989, after seventy-two years of argument, his grandson was finally successful in persuading the army that the famous scout was worthy of our nation's highest award, and his name has been restored to the honor roll.

Vince Bruce, 1989 Circus Flora.
Photo by W. H. Rough

THE CRASH

When the Ringlings acquired the Barnum and Bailey enterprise in 1907, they also acquired full control over the Forepaugh–Sells Bros. Circus, which Mr. Bailey had combined in 1896.[24] By 1910, the Ringlings controlled three of the top five circuses, all but Hagenbeck–Wallace and Sells–Floto. At this time, about the midway point in the golden age of the circus, there were at least ten large railroad shows and more than thirty smaller wagon shows on tour.[25] Many of the smaller shows were regional operations, such as Mollie Bailey's circus in Texas, but there were other huge circus operations as well.

John Robinson's Ten Big Shows claimed to have been founded in 1824, although 1842 is a more likely beginning, and it was operated under four successive John Robinsons. Old John frequently had to point out that his circus had no relation whatsoever to "Yankee" Robinson's show, or to the circus operated by his adopted son, James Robinson, a champion equestrian of the day

known simply as "The Man Who Rides."[26] Before it was retired in 1930, the John Robinson name was thought to be the oldest title in the circus business, with somewhere around a century of continuous use. During the Civil War it was called the "Hog Show," and it freely crossed back and forth across the Mason–Dixon line. Although Old John was loved in the South, he nearly got himself killed on several occasions when he talked a little too openly about freeing the slaves.

The Robinson show and others like it are closely associated with the whole frontier spirit of a rapidly expanding America. Life in the circus was always an adventure and a challenge, and it could be downright dangerous. One day in 1875, in Jacksonville, Texas, Robinson circusmen were challenged to a pitched battle by townspeople out to destroy the circus. Perhaps they were seeking revenge for losing all that money at "games of chance" with the last circus that was in town; on a grift show, games of "chance" didn't necessarily have anything to do with chance. The traditional circus call-to-arms "Hey, Rube!" produced guns, stakes, knives, and clubs, and the "Battle of Jacksonville" left six or seven dead and dozens injured.[27]

As everyone knows, shootings were commonplace in frontier America, and circus men were frequent victims. The famous clown-manager William Lake was murdered in the ring by a gunman, leaving his circus in the very capable hands of his widow. Along with Mollie Bailey in Texas, Agnes Lake was one of the two most successful female circus managers in the country; some years before, it was she who had made James Bailey the general agent for the old Robinson & Lake show, thus launching his career. She was eventually remarried, to the famous gunman Wild Bill Hickok, who would also be shot to death. As often as not, for self defense, circus men were armed. Even band members occasionally carried pistols tucked into their belts underneath their shabby blue serge uniforms. Circus band man Earle M. Moss once described a not untypical frontier circus audience he witnessed as late as the 1920's:

> During the show, some of our male customers would become carried away during the performance, partly because they happened to like the performance and partly on

account of too many visits with the bottle. On such occasions they might whip out a .38 and pointing up their pleasure with a "rebel yell," perforate the top of the tent with a couple bullet holes. Generally, some of their compatriots would follow suit. Some times, it would sound like a rehearsal for the Battle of the Marne. At such times, Uncle Ernie would barge in under the sidewall with hat in hand, admonish the crowd, saying 'Shoot, pshaw, now folks. I want you to have a good time, but shoot, pshaw, you're making a lot of holes in my little old tent; if it rains, we'll all get wet, I'm afraid, so if you don't mind, I'd appreciate it it if you'd put away those shooting irons until you get outside my poor old tent. Thank you kindly, gentlemen.' "[28]

The John Robinson show was among several to become part of another major circus dynasty that would soon challenge Ringling supremacy. The American Circus Corporation had its roots back in 1884, in Peru, Indiana, usually pronounced by circus people as *Pee*-roo, although the natives use the more conventional Puh-*roo*. "Uncle Ben" or "Colonel" Wallace, the owner of the largest livery stable in Indiana, had acquired the remains of W. C. Coup's Circus, sold at auction in Detroit, and the menagerie of a circus which couldn't pay its feed bill. The animals included a lion, a black bear, a wolf, one deer, two goats, two hyenas, and a camel, and the *Miami Herald* duly reported in true circus fashion that the new "Wallace & Co.'s Great World Menagerie, Grand International Mardi Gras, Highway Holiday Hidalgo, and Alliance of Novelties" was a show which was "second in size only to that of P.T. Barnum." Al G. Field, the talented black Virginian who would become one of the country's top minstrels when he wasn't traveling with the circus, was Wallace's head clown and equestrian director. The Wallace, or Great Wallace, or Cook & Whitby show frequently had to use different titles because it was so well-known for its grift operations. When Ben bought the great German wild animal trainer Karl Hägenbach's show in 1907, it became the Hagenbeck–Wallace Circus. Three years later it was traveling on about forty-five railroad cars, compared to the Ringling

Brothers and Barnum & Bailey units at eighty-five cars each, one indication of their relative size. Also by 1910, the John Robinson show was traveling on forty-two railroad cars. The Sells–Floto Circus had about thirty-one cars; the Gollmar Brothers had twenty-four, and Al G. Barnes had ten. The total number of circus railroad cars across the country was then approaching 700.

Rivalries

There were rare occasions when cooperative efforts among circuses were made, but for the most part, circuses were prepared to go to war with each other in order to win their audiences. And wars were won by buying out the competition. Outside the Ringling conglomerate, a young man by the name of Jerry Mugivan, carrying the same kind of twinkle in his eye as had P.T. Barnum, emerged from nowhere as the leading competitor. His fast and furious rise to fame began in 1893, when he and his lifelong partner Bert Bowers were ticket sellers for the Sanger & Lentz show. In 1900, he went to work for Ben Wallace. After the devastating 1913 flood, Wallace had sold the show to a syndicate soon to be headed by Peru real estate magnate Ed Ballard. By 1920, after a lot of buying, selling, wheeling, and dealing, Mugivan, Bowers, and Ballard owned the Hagenbeck–Wallace Circus, sold to them for a bargain $36,000 after the disastrous train wreck in 1918 had all but ruined it. By then they also owned the John Robinson and Sells–Floto circuses, and claimed the titles to the Great Van Amburgh, Yankee Robinson, Gollmar Brothers, Dode Fisk, Sanger's Greater European, and Howe's Great London circuses, as well as Buffalo Bill's Wild West. Recognizing the worth of a name, they had resurrected the Van Amburgh, Sanger, and Howes titles, changing the location of the apostrophe from Howes', even though they had no connection to the original shows. The circus has survived for so long because of just this sort of daredevil tactics — fast deals carried out in the baths of the Majestic Hotel in Hot Springs, Arkansas, or in the smoke-filled rooms of the Sherman Hotel in Chicago. The following year, Mugivan and his partners organized the American Circus Corporation, based in Ben Wallace's refurbished old Peru winter quarters.

American Circus Corp. winter quarters.
Photo by W. H. Rough

Peru, Indiana, was the "circus capital of the world" in the 1920's, eventually the home base for five big American circuses. Since 1960, it has been the home of the celebrated amateur Festival Circus, an annual circus involving some 200 youngsters from Miami County. The show is staged in one of the few permanent circus buildings in the country, which also houses a small circus museum. In 1989, the International Circus Hall of Fame, Inc., also now based in Peru, launched a fundraising campaign to establish a major circus museum in Peru. It will use as its nucleus the twenty-three circus wagons and more than 1,000 artifacts it acquired in 1985 from the now defunct Circus Hall of Fame in Florida. Several of the old white barns of the American Circus Corporation are still there outside Peru too, carefully preserved by the present private owners, as is the old Terrell Jacobs farm. Peru, like the other American circus towns, has a heritage to be treasured.

The American Circus Corporation continued to acquire circuses, including Sparks and Al G. Barnes, so that by 1929, virtually every major circus in America was owned by one of the two giant syndicates. By far the larger of the two was now being vigorously led by the last of the original Ringling brothers, "Mr. John." The Ringling Brothers and Barnum & Bailey Circus had become the largest and most successful circus in the world, and John Ringling was counted among the world's richest multi-millionaires. He had accumulated

one of the finest private art collections in the country; what's more, his Sarasota mansion had solid gold fixtures in the bathrooms, and during Prohibition a Titian nude painting hanging in the basement concealed an icebox full of fine Bremen beer. Nevertheless, the five traveling Corporation shows (Hagenbeck–Wallace, John Robinson, Sells–Floto, Sparks, and Al G. Barnes) were a continual thorn in his side. Mr. John's pride was further challenged by Mugivan's public boast that he would one day own the Ringling show.[29] The last straw came with unfortunate timing for Ringling. Mugivan and his partners had managed to secure the opening date for Madison Square Garden for the spring of 1930, for their Sells–Floto Circus. It was a traditional opening date for the Ringling show, in a building with which it had been associated since Coup and Barnum had built the prototype in 1874. Ringling was even a vice president of the Garden corporation. In an ill-considered fit of pique, and primarily to preserve his own opening dates, Ringling renewed an old offer to buy out the American Circus Corporation, lock, stock, and barrel. Mugivan's partners recognized that the time was right for them to get out of the business, and he reluctantly went along with them. Just a little over a month before Black Friday, October 29, 1929, they sold all their shows, titles, and equipment for about $2 million to John Ringling, now the undisputed king of American circus.

American Circus Corp. barns. Photo by W. H. Rough

The stock market crash caught Ringling badly unprepared and financially overextended, but he was unwilling to sell any of his circus and real estate properties or any part of his impressive art collection to finance the hefty debt he had just acquired. The economic pressures brought on by the onset of the Depression cut deeply into box office receipts, and it was expensive to keep all those railroad shows on tour. So Mr. John was forced to begin a process which over the next eight years would shelve five of the six active circuses he now owned, whose names had been around for generations. In his effort to protect "The Big One" from competition and shore up its economic underpinnings, he began by closing down John Robinson, Sells–Floto, and Sparks. But it was a losing battle, and he was in way over his head. In 1932, he lost control of the Ringling syndicate and was ordered out of Madison Square Garden by Samuel Gumpertz.

Gumpertz was an interesting man, often overlooked in circus histories. When he took over as manager of the Ringling–Barnum shows with the support of the widows of both Charles and Richard Ringling, he was sixty-four years old. He had been a rider with Buffalo Bill's Wild West, where he met Flo Ziegfeld, the man who outshot Annie Oakley. Later, when he moved into the executive end of the business, he would give Ziegfeld the start in the entertainment industry he needed to launch his famous *Ziegfeld Follies*. Gumpertz had

supervised the construction of Brighton Beach, Long Beach, and Coney Island's Dreamland amusement parks, and he managed Dreamland until it burned down. He also even owned the Half Moon Hotel, where Ringling was staying when he signed the agreement giving up his authority.

John Ringling died a broken man only four years after his ouster. He left an estate of over $23 million in property, most of which ended up going to the state of Florida. Yet at the end he was unable to buy a hot dog on his own circus lot on credit, or have use of his own personal Pullman railroad car, the largest and one of the most luxurious ever built. The car was named for John and Mable Ringling, "Jomar," and it still languishes in a Sarasota rail yard, although there are plans to restore it.

John Ringling's will was a lesson in "How NOT to Create an Estate" that would be studied in law schools for years to come. Surviving relatives entered into a protracted bitter battle over control of the circus, and even over the frozen remains of John and Mable. Their bodies are involved in a bizarre debate to decide whether they can be buried as requested near their magnificent home, Ca'd'Zan, in Sarasota's Ringling Museum complex. As of November 1989, they were being held in Port Charlotte, Florida, where they had been moved from an unidentifed location in Fairview, New Jersey.

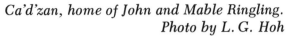

Ca'd'zan, home of John and Mable Ringling.
Photo by L. G. Hoh

The North Era

The Hagenbeck–Wallace and the Al G. Barnes shows succumbed to the recession of 1938. In the same year, control over the Ringling Brothers and Barnum & Bailey Circus was won, if only temporarily, by John Ringling North and his brother Henry. Ironically, the Norths were the sons of Ida Ringling, the original brothers' only sister, who had never wanted anything to do with the circus. It was mainly John Ringling North who brought The Big One back from near ruin. He could be a ruthless businessman, as is evidenced by his decision to burn 126 beautiful old circus wagons on the grounds of his American Circus Corporation property on November 21, 1941, in an effort to keep rival shows from buying them up. Occurring as it did only a few days before Pearl Harbor, this event is viewed by many circus people as their own "day of infamy." North also made many enemies by firing great numbers of old-timers and hiring new "Hollywood" types who ran roughshod over tradition in the name of glitz. Nevertheless, he endured years of near financial ruin, labor troubles, family squabbles, and the biggest disaster the cir-

cus world has ever seen, the 1944 Hartford, Connecticut fire.

Fortunately for him if not for the circus, Johnny North was not in control on July 6, 1944. He had been temporarily ousted by Ringling relatives the year before, and the big show was under the control of Charles Ringling's son, Robert. There are many reasons why the big top was not flame-proofed that season, headed by the obvious wartime scarcity of effective materials. Some say that the early flame-proofing chemicals were destructive to canvas, and many circus men were reluctant to use them because their tents didn't last as long. About 7,000 people were watching the matinee performance in Hartford, when a small line of flame was spotted at the south end of the tent at 2:40 p.m. Panic ensued, and spectators, forgetting they had only to duck under the loose side walls, stampeded for the nine visible exits, two of which were blocked with animal chutes. A gust of wind spread the fire to the big top and guy ropes, and six minutes later it was over. There were 412 hospitalizations, and 169 people were burned, smothered, or crushed to death in the

After the fire: Ringling Bros. and Barnum & Bailey, July 6, 1944. Photo courtesy of Circus World Museum, Baraboo, WI

disaster, including one blonde six-year-old girl who has come to be known as "Little Miss 1565," after the number on her morgue tag. To this day, no one ever claimed her body, and despite years of investigation by police and private detectives, no one has ever determined who she was, who she might have been with, or why she was there on that terrible day.

The Ringling show returned to Florida for rebuilding, and within a month it was back on the road, at the insistence of Mrs. Ringling, and playing under open skies and in arenas. The bitter aftermath of the fire included more family feuding and board squabbling, which ultimately returned Johnny North to the seat of power in 1947. It took ten years of all the profits they could make, but the Ringling show paid every penny of the over 600 uncontested damage claims, a total of over $4.5 million. The most important result of the fire is that federal and state regulations now ensure that every circus tent anywhere in the country is thoroughly flame-proofed. Five circus officials symbolically held responsible for the fire, including the vice president, the general manager, and the boss canvasman, were sentenced to prison terms for involuntary manslaughter. The real cause remains in doubt. At first it was thought to be carelessness with a cigarette. But in 1950, a Robert Dale Segee was arrested in Columbus, Ohio, and signed a confession saying he had set the fire. Segee was a bitter, self-confessed murderer and pyromaniac, who had worked for the Ringling show briefly during the period of the fire. He was indicted, but charges were later dropped,

and no further investigations have been pursued.

Despite the controversies and disasters, and the brief period in which they were not in control, the Norths operated the big show more or less effectively for almost three decades. Johnny North was a high spender, and at the end the show was falling into a precarious financial position. Finally, in 1967, they sold it to Irvin and Israel Feld, Washington, D.C.-based promoters of the circus and rock-and-roll concerts with whom they had been associated. Today, the Ringling Brothers and Barnum & Bailey Circus is a thriving part of a highly successful multi-million dollar corporate enterprise run by Irvin's son, Kenneth Feld.

Two years after John Ringling's death in 1936, economics and the Ringling syndicate had reduced the number of railroad circuses on the road from twenty-two in 1901, to two: Cole Brothers and Ringling. The Ringling syndicate had successfully stifled competition, claiming to own all the other old major titles. Careful readers of the 1989, 119th Edition Souvenir Program for the Greatest Show on Earth may notice that the Hagenbeck–Wallace name owns the costumes and props, and Sells–Floto publishes the program. Since these Corporation titles are still legally in use, they can't be used by any rival circus. The prominence of "The Big One" was preserved, albeit at a high cost. New circuses like the Clyde Beatty and the Kelly–Miller shows slowly began to be born as the nation emerged from the Depression, and they continue to be born today, as we shall discover in the next chapter. However, the industry recovered only gradually from the setback that the syndicate monopolies and the market crash had dealt it.

John Ringling North was a major controversial figure in recent circus history. Certainly one of his more difficult decisions, and one which can still generate hot debate among circus fans and historians today, was to take the circus out from under the canvas and away from the rails. It is difficult to know whether the decision was made on the basis of indifference, bad judgment, or good economics. Carrying all those tents and labor crews on the railroad was growing inordinately expensive. The same economic factors had driven other circuses off the rails and into far more cost-effective trucks. North's practical-minded manager, Art Concello, had tried for some time to persuade him to abandon the canvas big top; but it was Irvin Feld who finally convinced him to make the change, on the basis that he would promote the new indoor shows, and that they would be far more lucrative. The result was that on July 15, 1956, North dropped a press bombshell: "The tented circus is a thing of the past!" The next day, in Pittsburgh, Pennsylvania, the Ringling Brothers and Barnum & Bailey Circus folded its tents for the last time and went home to Florida on the "funeral train." It has since been limited to presentation in indoor arenas, civic centers, and coliseums, except for recent tours of their new third unit in Japan in a bright gold vinyl tent. By the end of the same year, the Clyde Beatty Circus had converted from rail to a truck show, although it elected to remain under canvas. It was the last of the big tented railroad circuses.

There were of course dire predictions in the press that the circus had died and could never recover. But of course, it didn't die, and tented circuses have not yet become "a thing of the past." Despite all the packaged entertainment that Hollywood and the television industry have pitched to us, people have never stopped craving live performances, which stretch the limitations of human capability before our very eyes. A *New York Times* reporter wrote in 1938, paraphrasing the old Roman maxim, that we still needed our circuses as much as we need our bread. The proof is in the numbers: In 1840 there were at least twenty traveling circuses; in 1873, there were at least twenty-two; in 1901, at the peak of the golden age of the American circus, there were eighty-nine; and in 1931, at the peak of the Depression years, there were still at least twenty-three big and little circuses on the road, six of them on rail. According to Earl Chapin May, circus attendance in 1931 was double that of 1870, and he estimated that 15 million Americans were buying circus tickets annually. [30] And in 1990, when many Americans even claim to be unaware that there are any circuses outside of the Ringling organization, tens of thousands of circus performances are still being staged in a variety of settings around the country, many of them under canvas.

And so we find that that part of the human spirit which makes circuses has only once more adapted itself to the economic and social demands of its age. The animal trainers, acrobats, trapezists, clowns, and all the other circus artists whom we have been following for three or four thousand years in the last two chapters, simply did what they have always done: Some died, but others were born with identical instincts; some moved to other circuses, carnivals, to television, or into the movies; some retired; some shifted the nature of their acts; some carried forward their long-standing family traditions; and some framed their own new shows, better adapted to the fast-paced mechanized world that America was becoming. In the next chapter, we'll take a look at who some of the new circus proprietors are, where they've come from, and what their guiding principles are. And we'll examine some of the big and little shows that are crisscrossing the America of the 1990's.

4.

RED WAGONS

The managerial hub of every circus is still called the red wagon. It may be in a modern white air-conditioned tractor-trailer rig, in a Pullman coach, or resting on four spoked, steel-banded, wooden wheels, but it's still the red wagon. That's where the tickets are sold, the men are paid, and the telephones are connected. It's where the owners and managers hang out when they're on the road; and behind its high caged windows, policy is established and major decisions are formulated.

Despite the continuing renaissance of American circus, many city folks remain unaware that the circus still exists outside the annual arrival of the Ringling Brothers and Barnum & Bailey Circus in their civic arena. Many folks in the country and small towns across America completely escape the attention of the tent show booking agents that are still crisscrossing the country. "I thought the circus was dead—I mean, except for the Ringlings," is a common response to our inquiries into what Americans know of the modern circus.

Nonetheless, rumors of the circus' death, like that of Mark Twain, are greatly exaggerated. There are dozens of tented shows, ranging from one to five rings, visiting small towns annually across America. Some of the larger shows are developing the capacity to play in civic arenas in competition with "The Greatest Show on Earth." Both traditional and "new-wave" tented shows are making inroads into larger city markets; and indoor Shrine circuses help to comprise a coast-to-coast, year-round circus season.

There have probably been over 2,000 circuses entertaining Americans since troupes first began to perform in the New World. Over the years they have come and gone in response to economic and social pressures governing both taste and pocket money. In 1890, perhaps a hundred shows toured the country, but numbers were drastically re-duced by the 1893 depression. We have already seen the effects of the great 1929 stock market crash on the circus business in America. However, economic crises and depressions somehow seem to result in increased social needs for the escapism and wonder of the circus arts, and the cycle renews itself. The circus goes on. Pointedly, Judy Finelli, current Artistic Director of the Pickle Family Circus, recently suggested that the current resurgence of interest in the circus is at least in part symptomatic of a modern world which is sick enough to need the circus more fervently than ever.

The circus by its very nature is a transient business. Owners, performers, and titles come and go, passing into and out of public awareness with alarming frequency. The Big Apple Circus' Associate Director Dominique Jando points out that it is one of the most expensive forms of entertainment in the world, and that makes it inevitably a high risk business. The Beatty–Cole show, for example, has a daily overhead of about $21,000. Rain or shine, show or no show, the people, the animals, and the machinery need feeding, and merchants need to be paid, and it all must come from gate receipts. With no such incoming receipts in the off-season, a circus still must maintain equipment and personnel, and owner salaries may have to be cut to keep expenses down.

Circuses continue to die every year, overwhelmed by low attendance, retirements, changing priorities, sloppy artistry, rising insurance rates, sickness, or by any of a number of large and small disasters that can cut the tenuous life lines of a risky and expensive business. Recent years have seen the passing of Circus USA, the Toby Tyler, the John Herriott, the Mighty McDaniel, and the Lewis Brothers circuses, for example. But new circuses continue to be born every year, sometimes from scratch, and sometimes out of the ashes

Payday at Clyde Beatty–Cole Bros. "Red" Wagon. Photo by L. G. Hoh

1989 Circus Flora in St. Louis. Photo by W. H. Rough

of a dying circus. Some of the newest are the much-respected Circus Flora, the little Culpepper–Merriweather Circus, the Jordan International Circus, the Reynolds Circus, and Bill & Martha Phillips' Phills Bros. Circus, new in 1989. The new Double M Ranch Historic American Circus, a tent show quartering in Hastings, New York, hits the road in 1990, and will be routed throughout the Northeast. There are even plans to make it a rail show in the future.

What seems clear from the many names of circuses dying, being reborn, being launched, combining, and spinning off, is that circus itself is a permanent institution. Some of the newer circuses will not be around in a few years, and probably even some of the older ones will join them in oblivion. But others will spring up to take their places. And somewhere in the back yards of every circus in America, there are unknown individuals, truck drivers, talkers, candy butchers, or performers, who long to take out their own show. From their ranks will spring the next generation of circus impresarios: future Ringlings and Forepaughs and Robinsons and Baileys.

It takes a special breed of human being to run a circus. In 1973, the program of the Circus Vargas, then still called the Miller–Johnson Circus, called its manager an "entrepreneur, impresario, businessman, progressive showman, unrealistic traditionalist, foolhardy administrative genius, dreamer, perfectionist, and impossible nonconformist." That list of attributes, unlikely and contradictory combination though it may be, might well be applied to any circus owner of the last 200 years. It is no wonder that the number of long-term circus owners who have owned or managed their shows for, say, twenty or more years, is deceptively small. The business takes its toll.

ALL FOR FUN

Circus owners are a varied lot indeed. Some were born into circus families. Some ran away with the circus as youngsters and worked their way up through the ranks of ticket takers and candy butchers. Others are entrepreneurs and businessmen. And still more see themselves as creative artists, sometimes even serving as headline performers. There are owners who never miss seeing a performance of their own shows, and others who never leave winter quarters.

Why would anybody want to own a circus? Everyone knows that it's a very tough business. The short historical list of people who were successful at running or owning their own shows suggests that a lot of pain went with the job. The daily task of "making the nut" takes its toll. Plenty of owners, including P.T. Barnum, made fortunes only to lose them again. Many, like Dan Rice, died as forgotten alchoholics. Yankee Robinson, the boom-or-bust pioneer owner who gave the Ringlings a boost at the beginning of their career, died broke. At least for these and many other men, there was always a chance for economic success. That had to be enough, and in many cases success was irrelevant. Consequences and the possibility of failure were not part of the equation when the enterprising Gilbert Spalding began his circus career. He took over the management of the Nichols Circus because they had defaulted on a personal loan and were behind in their payments for paint he had sold to them. He was a bored pharmacist with little to lose. The great Philadelphia meat and horse dealer, Adam Forepaugh, like P.T. Barnum, needed a little humbug in his own life; and he recognized that his circus audiences needed it too. Using his own first name to justify the inclusion of biblical references in his advertising, he allowed himself to challenge the anti-circus prejudices of the church with a smile. Despite his deceptive claims, his circus was neither religious in its thematic approach, nor was he reputedly very "Christian" or honest in his relationships with his employees and audiences. A ruthless businessman, he nonetheless created one of the largest and most successful circuses in the world.

For all these men, the norm, the mundane, the ordinary, were simply not acceptable. The fun of owning a circus was in the process, in the game itself, and not in the final score. D. R. Miller would rather have a patron tell him how much he enjoyed the show than hand him a thousand dollar bill. No false sense of permanence, stability, or security lures circus owners into the business. They continue to feel that circus enterprises last as long as they last, and then they're over; that's

all. Only a handful of today's shows have been around or expect to be around for more than twenty years.

The allure does not always come from potential fame, either. As we saw in the last chapter, Coup and Bailey deliberately chose to remain modestly out of the limelight, despite the fact that both were the great driving forces behind Barnum's circus enterprises. In his day it was Bailey's circus; every major decision and order was his to make, yet few outsiders ever saw him. Many modern owners too are rarely seen by the public, content to remain quietly in the background.

For both the loved and the hated, the winners and the losers, money was never the issue either. It's true that in the last chapter, we saw enormous fortunes being made by the likes of Seth Howes, Jerry Mugivan, John Ringling, and many others. But these people were aggressively enterprising individuals, and there were undoubtedly easier, cheaper, and less stressful methods for them to earn their fortunes had they so chosen. More to the point is that circus owners and managers were men and women on the fringe, on the edge of the socially and culturally acceptable, and they thrived on a sense of adventure, risk, and the unusual. What was most important to them was having a good time, living their dreams.

The great Sells–Floto Circus is a good example of a show which was created for the sheer fun of it all. It was started by two publishers with the *Denver Post*, who whimsically named the show after their sports writer, Otto Floto. In 1906 they hired Willie Sells, adopted son of one of the original Sells brothers of circus fame, to be their general manager. Sells took the show on tour for only one season and then left, but his name remained as a perpetual part of the show's extended and more impressive title.

All these men were possessed of a positive spirit in the face of adversity that they were determined to share with the public at large. They wanted people around them to have fun, so that they too could have fun. Such is the ambition of contemporary owners as well. To a person, when asked why they were prepared to accept all the risks of putting a modern circus on the road, they replied, "It's fun."

Obviously there's an element of nostalgia to it

all, a joy in recreating a time from America's past when values were clearer and simpler. But it's more than that. Contemporary circuses exist in a contemporary world, and they have value to us only when they can speak to us in our world. Owners and designers of the modern circus experience recognize that. They want above all to teach us that the imagined boundaries of our lives, the ones that prevent us from having fun, are only illusions. They want to demonstrate to us that despite all the pressures, dangers, and demands we face from society and the modern world, life is still full of wonder, and joy, and fun. It is just the kind of spirit that the circus has been and will always be so well equipped to convey. Fourteen-year-old Matthew Colbert, traveling with the 1989 edition of Vermont's little Circus Smirkus, sums up the driving philosophy of most circus owners simply and honestly: "I like to see people laugh. That's hard enough."

The Circus Smirkus kids. Matthew Colbert is in the middle on the right. Photo by W. H. Rough

TRADITIONAL BIG TOPS

At least three of the big tented shows of today have the scope and polish to make their audiences feel what some of the giants of the golden age of the circus must have been like: The Clyde Beatty–Cole Brothers Circus, the Carson & Barnes Circus, and the Circus Vargas. They may serve as examples of the kind of large tented circus which emerged directly from our historical traditions, and which is still successfully operating in contemporary America. The backgrounds and approaches of their owners and managers are typical of those found throughout the business since it first began.

The Clyde Beatty–Cole Brothers Circus carries one of the oldest names in the circus business. Winter-quartering in Deland, Florida, it has earned the nickname the "I-95 Show," because it travels primarily up and down the east coast along Interstate 95. It's an old-fashioned, three-ring circus, presented as their 1989 program states as "a continuance; a salute to the oldest purely American form of entertainment . . . in the time-honored tradition of an era gone by, under a rope and canvas arena larger than a football field." In its eight months on the road, the Beatty–Cole show claims to present 486 performances, seven days a week, traveling across 10,000 miles in seventeen states, with 170 performers and staff in seventy-eight vehicles.[1]

Since the stroke of midnight that ushered in 1982, the show has been owned by John W. Pugh, joined several months later by E. Douglas Holwadel. When bought from Florida State University, Beatty–Cole was in shabby condition, both artistically and financially. In what Holwadel calls a real "sweetheart" deal, they acquired the circus and $600,000 in bad debts for $2 million, payable over twenty years at 3% interest.[2] Just the year before it had been appraised at $2.5 million and donated to Florida State by Jerry Collins, a multi-millionaire dog track owner and the last survivor of a triumvirate that had owned the show since the mid-1950's.

Soft-spoken, articulate, and always nattily dressed, Johnny Pugh glows with a look of professional competence. He provides the vital practical experience and the expertise in the logistical and performing operations needed on the Beatty–Cole show. He is the son of "Digger" Pugh, a British show business entrepreneur who produced theatrical and variety shows throughout England and the Continent. Johnny got his first stage contract when he was less than a year old, and in August of 1988, he passed his fiftieth anniversary in show business. He first came to America as a boy in 1942, and he appeared with the Cole show before returning to England with his family during the war. When he came back to the Cole show in 1948, all of ten years old, he appeared in a center-ring trampoline act with the great clown, Otto Griebling, and remembers being terrified as a boy by Zack Terrell and his unpredictable cane. Following a three year stint with the Mills Bros. Circus, he returned to England and worked in the television and film industries. He appeared at the Palladium with Benny Hill. During the filming of Burton's and Taylor's *Cleopatra*, he was Richard Burton's double, and the man in charge of the elephants; only later did he discover that he and every last one of his elephants had been left on the cutting room floor. Once again back in the U.S. in 1961, he went to work for the Beatty–Cole show, and has been there ever since. He likes to say that's longer than anyone still active in the circus has worked on any one show. In 1964 he broke his leg while working on the trampoline, and began to shift his focus from performance to the front office; within two years, he was the manager, and by the time he became a co-owner eighteen years later, he was thoroughly experienced in every aspect of circus operation.

His new partner, on the other hand, was brand new to the field. Doug Holwadel was a Vice-President of Marketing with the Santee Cement Company in South Carolina, and he traded on the New York Stock Exchange. He led a stressful life, and three operations for cancer led him to seek a change. Since he had loved the circus all his life, when Johnny offered him the opportunity, he jumped at the chance to buy in, helping to raise the $200,000 in working capital needed to put the show back on the road so it could start earning income. Three years later, he joined the show on the road as the booking agent, and brought with him his marketing techniques and business expertise. He introduced computers and streamlined the whole operation, helping to cut costs and identify prime audiences. He likes to say that he left New York's Wall Street in a Brooks Brothers suit, and he is still wearing it. He approaches prospective lot leasers — mall owners who might perhaps be expecting a circus owner to be someone in cowboy boots and a gold chain — as though he were closing a real estate deal, in his Brooks Brothers suit and a button-down oxford shirt and tie. He takes his time and seeks no immediate answers. "If they give you an answer off the top of their heads, they haven't thought it through clearly," he says.

Photo by Joan Z. Rough

Clyde Beatty–Cole Bros. big top. Photo by W. H. Rough

Photo by Joan Z. Rough

Clyde Beatty-Cole Bros. tent interior. Photo by L. G. Hoh

The enterprise and the partnership have been successful in returning the Beatty–Cole show to a state of fiscal and artistic good health. Johnny Pugh is fiercely proud of the turn-around he and Doug have managed to pull off in only a few short years, and he plans to extend his records by remaining actively involved on the lot for many years to come. Despite the new stresses inevitable in running a circus, even Holwadel's cancer has been in remission. He says he has never felt better in his life, although he still finds it impossible to sit still during a full circus performance. The two owners often take turns traveling with the show, although Johnny finds it hard to stay away. They remain good friends, and their different styles, areas of expertise, and backgrounds complement each other to serve well the famous names and long tradition their circus carries.

The Cole title goes back to William Washington "Chilly Billy" Cole, who was born in 1847, the son of an English clown and contortionist. In 1871, the same year that W. C. Coup was persuading Barnum to get into the circus business, the Cole & Orton Circus was founded, and was later among the first to play in small western towns. By 1884 the W. W. Cole show was traveling on thirty-one railroad cars out of St. Louis, Missouri. From that show the modern Beatty–Cole circus measures its lineage, celebrating its centennial year in 1984. One of the most widely respected names in the circus business, Cole sold his popular and successful show in 1886 and became a partner for a while with Barnum & Bailey. Ten years later he rescued a financially insolvent James Bailey on his European tour. One of the circus' most successful entrepreneurs, "Chilly Billy" left an estate of $5 million when he died in 1915.

W. W. Cole's great-great-nephew, James M. Cole, represents a separate line of the Cole name in circus history. Born in 1906, he saw John Robinson's circus when he was a boy, and dreamed of owning his own. He began by working for American Circus Corporation shows until they were sold to the Ringling empire. In 1938, he started his own indoor circus, a "school" show operating in high school gymnasiums along the backroads of New York and Pennsylvania. "Mr. Cole," as he is affectionately called by friends and strangers alike, operated the little Cole All Star Circus for short winter tours every year for fifty years, "taking the circus to the kids in the gym," as he says. It is still operating successfully, now under the aegis of his former ringmaster, Billy Martin. In the summers he operated the James M. Cole Circus under tent, and managed a variety of others over the years. Why? Because he "enjoys being around people, loves seeing them have fun, a good way to be if you own a circus," he says. [3] When he retired to Sarasota, Florida in 1987, he had become one of our oldest and most widely loved premier circus showmen. Like so many circus men, Mr. Cole can look back and smile on a long and fruitful career, living out a boyhood dream and adding to our rich circus heritage.

Meanwhile, the "Cole Brothers" title itself was created in 1906 by Martin Downs. The title was subsequently used by a variety of people before the big Depression. In 1935, Jess Adkins and Zack Terrell revived it, and with equipment from the Christy and Robbins shows they built it back to prominence. It featured for their first three years a young wild animal trainer named Clyde Beatty. Beatty had already appeared in every major circus of the day, and had almost been killed by his powerful lion, Nero, in 1932. In 1939 the Cole Brothers show became the last circus to abandon the tradition of the horse-drawn circus parade. The circus was acquired in 1957 by the Acme Circus Corporation—Frank McClosky, Walter Kernan, and Jerry Collins—who merged it with the Clyde Beatty title they had rescued from bankruptcy just the year before. McClosky and Kernan had only just been fired from the Ringling show in 1955, and they were eager to provide their former employer with some competition.

In the meantime, Beatty had been performing in circuses bearing his own name and others throughout the '40's and early '50's. It was Beatty's show under the new management that became the last to leave the rails in 1956. Following the merger, Beatty remained a featured performer in the combined show until his death from cancer in 1965. The following year, Art Concello came on as manager, and almost succeeded in duplicating his old Ringling solution and sending Beatty–Cole into Madison Square Garden, which would have doomed it as a tent show. However, Jerry Collins and Frank McClosky, among the last of the old

Carson & Barnes circus tent. Photo by L. G. Hoh

The Carson & Barnes menagerie. Photo by W. H. Rough

Carson & Barnes. Photo by W. H. Rough

D. R. Miller with author LaVahn
Hoh and Mary Frances Hoh. Photo
by W. H. Rough

Carson & Barnes tent-folding.
Photo by W. H. Rough

The 1989 Carson & Barnes elephant
herd. Photo by L. G. Hoh

school of circus showmen, prevailed. The show survived under canvas, albeit meagerly, until 1979, when McClosky passed away. In 1981, on Johnny Pugh's advice, Collins gave his circus to Florida State as a tax write-off and thus set the stage for its recovery to one of the largest and healthiest tented shows in modern America.

Another huge tented show leaves Hugo, Oklahoma every March. The gigantic Carson & Barnes Circus plays only one-day stands in small towns across America, mounting two performances and raising and tearing down its five-ring big top every day for 240 days. In 1988, moving on eighty vehicles, the 200 men and women on the tour traveled 18,000 miles, through twenty-eight states, border to border and coast to coast. They carried with them a large collection of animals: thirty-seven horses, a rhinoceros, a giraffe, a hippopotamus, a liger, lions, tigers, llamas, camels, a moose named McDermott, and most crucial, twenty-three elephants.

In fact, the show's owner, Dory R. Miller, is one of the biggest elephant lovers in the country. His favorite bull is Barbara, who was named after his daughter and who has been with the show for almost forty years. As a young "punk," Barbara was a frequent escapee. Spooked by a falling pole in Prairie du Chien back in 1977, she decided to take a long stroll through the Wisconsin countryside, pursued for miles through backyards, corn fields, and a nursing home by her handler and a large crowd of troubled officials and onlookers. Unruffled, Miller grumbled, "If so many people hadn't chased her, she wouldn't a' run so far!" He excused the feisty Barbara's second escape with "Youngsters have to have a little fun while they're growing up, don't they?"

Dory Miller is a living circus legend, who with his wife Isla celebrated fifty years of circus ownership in 1986. No other owner alive today can make such a claim. D. R., as he likes to be called, has been involved in more than 24,000 performances; that's over 12,000 set-ups and tear-downs in over 12,000 towns.[4] He is responsible for training and launching the careers of many younger circus managers and performers, and for importing from Mexico some of the finest aerial acts ever to appear in American circuses. D. R. can still be found at performances, settled into his lawn chair by the back door at center ring, wearing his baseball cap, and with a bag of Red Man tobacco always at hand. His small lanky frame is alert to everything that happens in the big top, as he nods his approval of the performers, or occasionally registers his dissatisfaction with a sidelong spit of tobacco juice. "We sometimes don't got the best," he says, "but we got the biggest." He obviously loves every part of the circus world he helped create, and his crews and performers love him too. They are all his family. Carson & Barnes is a true family show: D. R.'s daughter and son-in-law, Barbara and Geary Byrd, are co-owners of the show, as is Isla; and his grandchildren Kristin and Traci are performers.

In his 1985 route book, General Manager James K. Judkins wrote of the effect of D. R.'s absence from the tour due to a hospitalization:

The entire season was clouded with the fact that they were not here. If you think about it, D. R. and Isla really didn't have to do anything. Others easily took over the miriad of chores that D. R. and Isla attended to. It's not what they did, it's who they are. It is their presence. Isla can make you feel good just by laughing. D. R. can see more sitting in the tent with his eyes closed than most can with binoculars. Just knowing he is in the tent causes everyone to do their best. He can straighten out a problem by just addressing it. Having the Old Man show that he was interested in the situation was enough to clear it up. One of his scowls could sober up even the drunkest soul, or at least make him head for his sleeper. He would say good morning to a Big Topper that everyone else forgot. Compliment the cookhouse people, when others might complain. Check on a new baby. Smile when he parked you in the morning. Tell a joke, that wasn't funny but would cheer you up. Straighten out the camels. The Old Man could make your day. Years ago D. R. wasn't the Old Man. Obert was. It took D. R. nearly 50 years to become the Old Man. Nobody is in any hurry to assume that title, and for now it belongs to D. R.[5]

D. R. first entered his father Obert's circus business in 1924, when he was eight years old. When he wasn't working the side show platforms, he was a trick pony rider or the calliope driver, and eventually he was known for his wire act. In 1939, he and his brother Kelly and their father started a small dog-and-pony show called the Miller Brothers Circus, which grew into the Al G. Kelly–Miller Bros. Circus. Kelly–Miller was where the great American truck circus was developed: The spool truck, the seat wagons, and an impressively efficient logistical system for "high grass" operations were all originated there. In 1942, at the invitation of a local circus fan and businessman, the circus moved to Hugo, in the Red River Valley of Oklahoma, where it has been quartered ever since. Hugo then joined the ranks of Somers, Delavan, Baraboo, Peru, and Sarasota, taking on the role of still another Circus City, USA. Since that time, it has been the home of at least one and sometimes as many as five circuses.

Even during the war the Kelly–Miller show prospered, thanks to the efforts of Isla and Kelly's wife Dale, who moved the show while the boys were away. The ladies drove the trucks and rigorously followed the 40 mph rule, reputedly holding to that speed in the city, in the country, and on the lot—saved on gas, clutches, and shifting, and everyone else learned to stay clear!

Kelly died in 1960, and Obert in 1961, leaving behind them a morass of estate taxes and a greedy Uncle Sam. In 1962, the ship carrying the circus to Canada caught fire and sank off the coast of Nova Scotia. No lives were lost, but it was the final blow to a show by then plagued with financial and legal worries. Still, D. R. would not cry "Uncle!" He gathered the remnants of the old show and others and invented a new name he and his family picked out of thin air, uninfluenced by anyone ever named Mr. Carson or Mr. Barnes. He mounted the current Carson & Barnes Circus, and turned it into what is today one of America's greatest circuses.

D. R. is justifiably proud of his career, his accomplishments, his elephants, and his circus. He was once introduced to Kenneth Feld, the impresario of the Ringling show: "Oh, Mr. Miller," said Mr. Feld, "you're the fellow with all those elephants." "That's right, Mr. Feld," said Mr. Miller,

biting off a characteristic plug of Red Man, "and I've got a circus to go along with them, too."[6]

Both the Carson & Barnes Circus and the Beatty–Cole show lay claim to being the biggest circus under the big top. Still a third major American circus enterprise calling itself the "largest" and "greatest" tented show touring America today was owned and operated by Clifford E. Vargas before he succumbed to cancer on September 5, 1989. Actually, Vargas was fully equipped to play indoors as well as in a tent, although he preferred to use his new Canobbio 150 by 300 foot big top. The three-ring circus traveled mostly in the West, spending over half its touring season in California, where it was based. It moved on twenty-three trucks, two of which were reserved just for the elaborate wardrobe, and carried twelve elephants. Its members were proud of the quality of their show, and they claim to have been fiercely loyal to their dedicated and energetic manager. Vargas was involved at every level of his show, which seems to be a common factor in most of the successful circuses on the road today. "I don't sit behind a desk. I'm right out in the circus all the time. And I don't ask anybody to do anything I can't do myself," he told the *Oakland Tribune* in 1976. Vargas was completely devoted to re-establishing the positive values of our circus heritage, "a return to the rich tradition of the circus as it once was in America," as he said, although it's difficult to say whether it's a return or an evolution. His emphasis on quality rather than quantity, and his high level of energy and zeal made him one of the more important forces in the industry. The Circus Vargas headlined talented performers and brimmed with patriotism and energy. The "Let Freedom Ring" spec which closed the 1989 edition, with performers glittering from the center ring in red, white, blue, and gold is an example of the lush excitement marking the Circus Vargas' production values.

Cliff Vargas was another in that rare circus breed of men who managed a show for over twenty years. Born and raised in California, he got into the circus business originally as a young man, by stumbling into the back door of the Chicago Shrine show. Seduced by what he saw, he did

"America's Big Top Giant." Photo courtesy of Circus Vargas

"The Dancing Vargettes." Photo courtesy of Circus Vargas

The late Clifford Vargas with "Colonel Joe." Photo courtesy of Circus Vargas

promotional work for them for a while before he returned to California and began his own promotion company. In 1972 he bought the Miller–Johnson Circus with which he had been associated, together with the contracts that went with it, for $250,000. It was a small outdoor tentless show, with some trucks, props, ring curbs, and seating. California weather made a tent the first priority, and since that time the show has grown steadily in size and quality. With the elaborately sequined 1989 edition, the Circus Vargas celebrated the twentieth anniversary of Vargas' association with it. As of this writing, it is unclear whether the Circus Vargas will survive the death of its dynamic owner–manager, or whether in another decade it will have become one of the thousands of circuses that have faded from memory.

LITTLE TOPS

There are probably two dozen relatively small old-fashioned tented shows currently traveling throughout the United States and Canada, and hundreds more in Mexico and Central and South America. They play in the outlying fields, the parks, and the recreation grounds of very small towns, and sometimes in the bedroom communities surrounding our cities, but rarely in the cities themselves. The circuses may be as small as the modest companies of performers with one-man bands, who, like the two Liebel Family Circuses, play on the midways at county fairs and town festivals. The Liebels' origins, incidentally, go back to 16th century Europe, and their red unit plays in a stunning 100-foot round tent, with four center poles topped by an unusual ornamental steel arch arrangement. Small top circuses may range up to the three-ring affairs which are big enough to create their own events, like the Olde Tyme Circus, taken out by veteran animal trainers Alfred and Joyce Vidbel for the first time in 1984. The Vidbels are quartered in the Catskill Mountains of New York, and their enterprise is popularly known among audiences along its central East Coast route as "America's Finest Family Entertainment." Some little tops are more impressive than other little tops: they may have more daring acrobats, more stunning jugglers, funnier clowns, cleaner set-ups, friendlier staff, or more elephants. But

all of them are exhibitions of real skills, not illusions; and all contain the elements of humor and challenge to human limitations that give their audiences such a fun and honest perspective into what we are and what we can be. It is always a wonderful surprise to discover the friendliest clowns or the most impressive balancing acts ever seen in a little family circus, where they are sometimes least expected; and yet we get surprised all the time. To describe each of those circuses thoroughly would take up several books. Here we can take a brief look at only four shows, who must represent for us small circus in America. At the same time, we mean to suggest that there may be twenty others, equally deserving of our attention, and we expect that American audiences will continue to seek them out.

In 1974, Wayne Franzen was a twenty-seven-year-old Wisconsin high school teacher who loved the circus. His lifelong dream of owning a show finally won him over on June 6, when he took out the Franzen Brothers Circus for the first time. "Brothers" is an invented part of the title of so many circuses because many owners evidently feel it has a traditional family appeal. But in this case there really was another Franzen brother originally involved. Neil left the show after only three months of its first tour, having discovered that more money could be made with less work in almost any other line of employment. Wayne has been the driving force behind every aspect of the show. He began with a little 40 by 60 foot tent, a herd of goats at liberty, a horse named Tonto, a spool truck made from a converted potato truck, and a corn crib for a lion cage.

From those small beginnings, the Franzen Brothers Circus has developed in fifteen years into one of America's favorite little shows. Its new bale-ring two center pole Scola vinyl tent is small, focusing attention on its single ring. It would accommodate well over 1,000 spectators, but Wayne frequently chooses to set up only one side for seating. Now quartered in Florida, with an office in Wapakoneta, Ohio, the circus travels throughout the Midwest and East on thirteen trucks. Wayne Franzen is an excellent example of the kind of single-minded determination and devotion to the

1989 Franzen Bros. Circus. Photo by L. G. Hoh

business that still marks the character of the small tent show manager in America today. Despite a reported 1100% increase in liability insurance costs in 1986 alone, he stubbornly continues to move his show from town to town, and audiences continue to support his efforts. To control costs, everyone in the small company doubles up on jobs, and Wayne remains involved at every level of show management, from truck driving to performing. In fact he is the most prominent performer, opening the show with his full cage act, and later reappearing with his elephant and Tonto, the educated horse who has been with him from the beginning. He also appears on the aerial ladder, but it is the animal acts with which he is most closely associated. It is highly unusual for such a small show to have a full cage act, with six tigers and two lions, but that was Wayne's dream from the beginning. Raised on a Wisconsin dairy farm, he has a natural feel for working with animals. He prefers to work with each cat, goat, dog, horse, elephant, camel, and llama singly in the training process, feeling that they all thrive on the personal attention. It is clear that Wayne thrives on it, and his love for the animals pervades the atmosphere of the whole show.

The other three little tops that are to serve as our representatives for small circuses in America are three-ring affairs. Two of them, the Roberts Brothers and the Great American shows, are quartered near Sarasota, Florida, still the most popular circus haven in the country, as it has been since the Ringling Brothers and Barnum & Bailey Circus moved there in 1927. The third one, the Kelly–Miller show, is based in Hugo, Oklahoma.

The Roberts Brothers Circus is a genuine family affair. It is run by the charming Doris Earl and her two sons Jeff and Robert T. Jeff is the vice president and secretary, who manages the show, and Robert is the president, remaining in Florida to run the main office. Doris is the treasurer, and frequently travels with the show as a candy butcher. The Earl boys were raised in the circus; Doris and her late husband took the Robert G. Earl show out as early as 1964, when Doris was a featured aerialist. Now, the Earls are on the road from March to October, playing up to 200 stands with two shows per day. They travel from Florida to Maine and back, and for three of the seven months of their tour they are in Pennsylvania. They know they'll never get rich in this business, but they love it; and they're proud that after years of hard work, they've paid off debts and are beginning to show some profits.

Roberts Bros. moves on about twenty vehicles. It carries no wild animal or cage acts, but there are a variety of ponies, llamas, and small animals, and one elephant, Lisa, whom they have leased from D. R. Miller since the show began. Their tent is about 70 feet by 210 feet long, small enough to fit on the ball fields of back road America.

Once again the whole tone of the show is determined by the active presence of congenial owners. It's clear that everyone on the lot likes everybody, and that carries through to ringmaster Brian LaPalme's personable appeal to his audiences. Not only is LaPalme the ringmaster, the magician, and one of the country's most impressive fire eaters; he also runs a popular cook house, although his cohorts often accuse him of preparing meals by blowing on the food with his "volcanic breath." It's a small troupe, and everyone pitches in to help with the big jobs. The tear-down takes little more than an hour, and when they've gone the lot is so clean it's difficult to tell that the circus has ever been in town. Of course, they've had some help from the armies of happy local youngsters who hang around to pick up trash. In return they get all the hot dogs and popcorn they can eat from the concession stand, the last truck to pack up and leave.

The Great American Circus is also quartered in Sarasota, and it plays exclusively in the eastern half of the United States, covering 246 dates and an estimated 15,000 miles in 1989. It's a small show, traveling on about ten trucks of its own with seventy-five people. The new incarnation of the Great American has developed into a tidy little three-ring show, featuring several elephants including four baby Africans, a lot of dogs, and some very nice acts. No longer is Tiny Tim featured "Tiptoeing through the Tulips," and the new red-topped blue and white vinyl tent, which can seat over 2,200 spectators, gives a unique, warm, reddish glow to all the performances. Circus people always look as though they have long and fascinating stories to tell, but the wonderful group of characters assembled for this show could

Roberts Bros. circus marquee. Photo by Joan Z. Rough

1989 Roberts Bros. tent. Photo by W. H. Rough

Photo by W. H. Rough

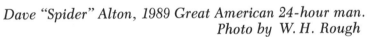

Dave "Spider" Alton, 1989 Great American 24-hour man.
Photo by W. H. Rough

1989 Great American Circus,
Charlottesville, VA. Photo by
L. G. Hoh

undoubtedly keep us enthralled for hours. They range from the 24-hour man, feisty David "Spider" Alton, a former Ringling employee and ex-prizefighter weighing in at ninety-one pounds, through the variety of multi-faceted performers like Yaro and Barbara Hoffman to the quiet and personable business manager, Rod Ruby, an ex-Methodist minister.

The Great American and the title to the now defunct Circus USA are owned by Allan C. Hill. He runs his entire operation from phone banks in Sarasota and doesn't often travel with the show. Allan has been close to the circus all his life. He is the son of Bill Hill, once boss canvas man and general manager for Hoxie Tucker's circus; his mother was a third-generation aerialist and equestrienne. Allan has never been a performer, but he was raised as a candy butcher, and quit school after the eighth grade to stay with the circus. He joined the Hoxie Brothers Circus as a promoter in 1972, after a stint in Vietnam had earned him a Bronze Star. In three years he quadrupled the market for Hoxie by instituting a new, up-to-date telemarketing system he still uses today, and in 1983, Allan was able to buy the show. Hoxie's second unit became the Great American Circus. In the winter of 1989, his Children's Theatrical Group toured "Santa's Magical Circus."

The Kelly–Miller Circus is quartered in Oklahoma, under the shadow of its giant sister, the Carson & Barnes show. In fact, the two shows spring from the same roots, and D. R. and Isla Miller are also part owners of this one, along with Lorraine Jessen and David and Carol Rawls. When the Big John Strong tent show went out of business in 1983, it was acquired by the Millers. Because the Al G. Kelly–Miller Bros. title had been retired since the old show became Carson & Barnes, it was decided to resurrect it for a new show using the Strong equipment as its nucleus. David Rawls became its manager, and the title was later reduced to Kelly–Miller. It travels primarily throughout the South and the Midwest.

The Rawls family is a good example of just how thoroughly one circus family can provide talent for many different circuses. David manages Kelly–Miller, and his wife Carol is the Artistic Director. In 1989, their sixteen-year-old daughter, Sasha, is an office assistant, and six-year-old Kelly is an occasional performer. David is the oldest son of Harry E. Rawls, a respected circus veteran who has worked with the likes of Jimmy Cole and D. R. Miller. Harry helped to launch the new show and serves as its contractor in Hugo. Bobby, his second son, used to be the manager of the Beatty–Cole show, but he has given up life on the road and now owns the AAA Sign Shop in Mead, Oklahoma, making a career as a talented circus and sign painter. His creative work appears on the Beatty–Cole, Carson & Barnes, and Kelly–Miller circus lots. A third brother, Chris (Harry C.), took over his management job, and Chris' delightful wife Maria is now the Beatty–Cole office manager. The fourth brother, Michael, is Concessions Manager, and the youngest, William, is the newest announcer for Kelly–Miller. Three sisters have opted out of circus careers.

With three generations of the Rawls family involved, Kelly–Miller is proud to call itself a family circus. David is a knowledgeable circus businessman, trained by D. R. Miller, and he is eager to promote his show as friendly, responsible, clean family fun. It travels on thirteen show-owned vehicles, and another thirty or so private trailers and campers. There are from sixty-five to seventy people on the tour, including what seems like an army of small happy children. One of them, ten year old Dora, is an amazingly accomplished contortionist and equilibrist, and a reminder of the true paradox of "children of all ages." One summer day before a show in Frederick, Maryland, she borrowed a friend's bike to play with. As she wobbled precariously past a circus fan, as tremulously as any other uninhibited little girl with no balancing skills whatsoever, she was overheard to say, "Oh, oh! I don't know whether I remember how to ride a bike!" Yet a half hour later she was perfectly balanced on a tiny platform in the center ring, gracefully bending over backwards and through her legs to drink a cup of pink lemonade placed on the floor in front of her.

Kelly–Miller carries a full menagerie tent, open as a side show attraction for separate admission, and stocked with three elephants, three camels, three goats, one llama, the requisite snake, and one tiger. The declawed tiger was acquired

1989 Kelly–Miller Circus, Frederick, MD. Photo by W. H. Rough

Bobby Rawls' work for the 1989 Clyde Beatty–Cole Bros. Circus. Photo by Joan Z. Rough

Kelly–Miller. Photo by W. H. Rough

for humane reasons, and is a non-performing pet, kept in an oversized cage and lavished with love. David no longer believes in carrying wild-animal acts because of safety concerns for both the animals and the public, not to mention skyrocketing insurance rates. The blue and gold, three-ring, four-pole main tent is a new Italian Scola Teloni design, housing a talented and dedicated family of performers. David Rawls and the company were to have a unique opportunity to combine the best of both the tented and indoor circus worlds by setting up their entire big top and back yard inside the Lansing, Michigan Civic Center for the 1989 Labor Day weekend Riverfest celebration. However, when the Center discovered how many holes they were going to drill in the floor, it was decided to place the tent conventionally outdoors.

Each of the four representative circuses discussed in this section has a unique contribution to make to the American circus scene, but they have much in common. They must all sink or swim on the income from the red wagon alone, and they are at the mercy of the wind and the mud. Nonetheless, box office receipts are up in all four shows, a sign of renewed interest in the circus experience which is encouraging to their owners and managers. Increasingly more common for them all are old-fashioned "Straw Houses," the traditional name for sold-out shows, when straw was spread out in front of the seating for overflow audiences. None of them would choose another line of work,

despite all the headaches of salary-juggling, booking, transportation, insurance hikes, and local regulations that make modern circus management so difficult. Although Franzen's single-ring one-sided presentation breaks with some preconceptions of what circus is, all four shows are expressions of a genuinely American folk art form, steeped in the traditions and lore of the American frontier spirit. At the same time, they have modernized their operations with trucks, computers, and telephone communications which allow them to improve their connection with the people of contemporary rural America.

Other Small Circuses

These four shows and their managers are certainly not alone. There is the spiffy little Culpepper–Merriweather Circus, quartered outside of Phoenix, Arizona, which features among several fine acts the bullwhip routine of "Cap" Terrell Jacobs, III, grandson of the famous wild animal trainer and the aerial artistry of Cap's wife, Lynn, one of the circus' original founders. There are only twenty-two people on owner Red Johnson's payroll, and they can fit only 700 spectators in their tent, but everyone is happy. John and Betty Reid's Reid Bros. Circus in Oregon is still plugging away in the far West, as are the Cirque du Plaisir and Cirque Universal in Canada. There is the Plunkett Circus in Texas; the Flores Family; and the Allen and Bentley and Frazier

Photo courtesy of Culpepper–
Merriweather Circus

Lynn Metzger Jacobs and Terrell "Cap" Jacobs, III in the "Gorilla Act." Photo courtesy of Culpeper–Merriweather Circus

and Farnum and Friendly Brothers Circuses: The list goes on and on. Small tented circuses are quartered all over the continent. The people who run them, as well as the people who attend them, are having fun. They always have, and there is no reason to expect that they will ever stop having fun.

COLISEUMS

"The Ringling Brothers and Barnum & Bailey Combined Shows, Inc." remains too long a title for most of us to wrap our tongues around. It's interesting to note that even today, over seventy years after the combined show was created, it gets informally abbreviated to "The Ringling Show" in the midwest, where the brothers had a strong reputation, and the "Barnum," or "Barnum & Bailey Show" in the East. Whatever it's to be called, there is little question that it has been the king of the indoor circuses since its last canvas tear-down in 1956. Its history was outlined in the last chapter, and few circus-goers need any introduction to "The Greatest Show on Earth."

Since 1969 there have been two units of the Ringling circus, the Red and the Blue, traveling at any one time in North America, and then in 1988 the special international "Gold" third unit

was created to play under tent in Japan. The two arena units travel for eleven months of the year, and return to quarters now located in Venice, Florida every other year. In less than one month they mount a completely new show, with a new theme and new acts, and they're off again. Every year brings a new edition out on the road for a two-year tour; in the middle of the tour, everyone gets one two-and-a-half week vacation. So the year 1990, 120 years after Messrs. Coup and Barnum went into business together, embraces both the second year of "Gunther Gebel–Williams' Farewell Tour" for the Red Unit's 119th edition, and the Blue Unit's new 120th edition of the Big One. The new Blue Unit show features the best of a fine Italian circus, the Circo Americano, that Kenneth Feld purchased in its entirety in 1989. His father had carried out a similar coup once before, when he bought the entire German Circus Williams in order to get Gunther Gebel–Williams as his headliner. This time, Flavio Togni and his family, the fourth generation of another of Europe's oldest circus families and twice the winners of Monte Carlo's Golden Clown Award, make their American debut. Flavio presents liberty and high school horse acts, a mixed horse and elephant act, an elephant menage, and a rhinoceros–panther–leopard act.

The Ringling units are the headliners in an entertainment empire which also includes five Disney ice shows, the Siegfried and Roy Magic Show, and a variety of live entertainment special extravaganzas. The statistics are impressive indeed. By their own estimates, Kenneth Feld productions are seen by some 40 million people every year. In an average year, each unit of the Ringling Brothers and Barnum & Bailey Circus travels over 14,000 miles, to thirty-nine cities, over a forty-nine-week period, giving an average 535 performances a year. Each unit carries around 250 performers and 100 animals, depending on the particular year. Each unit travels with almost 100 animals, including 21 elephants and 32 horses. Each week, each unit consumes 12 tons of hay and 5½ tons of meat, and hauls away 210 cubic yards of trash. Every year, one of the two circus units travels within 100 miles of 85% of the American population, and business is booming.

Its sheer size and Las Vegas show-quality have led some old time circus fans to think of the Ringling enterprise as fostering size and quantity over quality, form over substance, profit over art, and glitz over talent. There have always been critics who rightly or wrongly level such charges against the circus, and especially against the new directions instituted by Johnny and Henry North. Johnny died in 1985, while the affable Henry Ringling "Buddy" North still serves as a vice president of the Corporation. It's true that when Kenneth Feld's father and uncle took a big chance and finally bought the show from the Norths in 1967, they thought they could make money. Profit was quite naturally the primary goal among these seasoned show businessmen, and they were outrageously successful: Irvin and Israel Feld assumed a $1.7 million debt and bought the circus for a bargain $8 million. They revitalized its presentation and doubled its size. Four years later they sold it to Mattel Toys, Inc. for $50 million. But they weren't through with profit yet. Mattel had no idea what to do with a show earning them major losses, and sold it back to the Felds in 1982 for only $22.8 million. "The good Lord never meant for a circus to be owned by a large corporation," said Irvin. [7]

Ironically, the Feld enterprise is today the largest entertainment corporation in the world,

and it is still raking in enormous profits. Son Kenneth took his own firm hold on the reins when Irvin died in 1984, and he vehemently denies any allegations by his critics that he may not be sufficiently interested in the true art of the circus. He insists that his lifelong dream remains "to create the best...present the finest...to enliven...to enlighten...to entertain!" Feld is a passionate, devoted and tireless businessman. He is a generous supporter of any enterprise seeking to expand awareness of circus arts, and supports the efforts of both the Circus World Museum in Baraboo, Wisconsin, and the Circus Hall of Fame in Peru, Indiana. He oversaw the creation of the "Ringling Readers," an innovative new series of publications designed to encourage children to read. Most important, he strives to produce every new edition of the circus to top the last one, seeking a unique combination of displays that will both preserve circus traditions and experiment with new ideas. The Ringling show can afford to pay its acts top dollar, and they can afford to seek out the best acts from all over the world. The great tramp clown,

"Ride that tiger!" Photo by Joan Z. Rough

Introducing...
EUROPE'S INCOMPARABLE

GUNTHER GEBEL-WILLIAMS

Name an animal, any animal and, chances are, it has been successfully trained by Germany's unique Gunther Gebel-Williams.

Americans abroad have for years brought back tales of the amazing Gebel-Williams and his unbelievable animal performances as star of the celebrated Circus Williams. This season, as the result of the considerable persuasiveness of Irvin Feld, president of *The Greatest Show on Earth*, Gunther Gebel-Williams and his troupe have finally consented to make their long-awaited American debut.

Throughout the 99th edition of RINGLING BROS. AND BARNUM & BAILEY CIRCUS you will thrill to Gebel-Williams and his amazing animals.

Gunther Gebel–Williams' 1969 American début. Photo courtesy of Ringling Bros. and Barnum & Bailey Combined Shows, Inc.

Kenneth Feld. Photo courtesy of Ringling Bros. and Barnum & Bailey Combined Shows, Inc.

Emmett Kelly. Photo courtesy of Circus World Museum, Baraboo, WI

Ringling Bros. Circus in its heyday: Red Wing, MN; Aug. 31, 1915. Photo courtesy of Circus World Museum, Baraboo, WI

Emmett Kelly, when he and the show were still on good terms with each other back in 1954, wrote: "You can troupe all over the world, and you can listen to applause in far-away places and you can read flattering publicity from hell to breakfast, but when you open with Ringling Brothers and Barnum & Bailey Circus in Madison Square Garden, New York City, you have 'arrived.'"[8] Among performers and audience alike, there is no question that the same incomparable prestige still prevails for "The Big One."

However, "The Big One" is far from the only major circus currently playing indoor dates in the United States. The Shriners have established an annual tradition of sponsoring circuses ever since the Mystic Shriners' Yankee Circus in Egypt was produced in Detroit in 1910. Almost everyone has heard of the Shrine Circus, but Shriners don't actually operate circuses, except for some concessions and amateur clowning. Circus committees of local Shrine Temples simply lease the services of professional circus promoters, who put together a show for them from available circus artists; or they may hire a complete circus to perform under the Shrine name. Some circus producers like Paul V. Kaye, George Carden, George Hubler, Tarzan Zerbini, and Tommy Hanneford play the majority of their dates under Shrine sponsorship. Shrine-produced circuses are no small enterprise. Taken all together, they employ more people, attract more audiences, and play more performance dates than any single circus possibly could.

The Zerbini and Hanneford enterprises may be used as examples of the extreme flexibility with which indoor arena circus producers operate. They are perhaps the biggest and the best known, and they both can keep several units on the road at the same time. They can provide employment for performers in a virtually year-round operation, putting off-season unemployed acts together into entire circus performances on demand. They will play in arenas and coliseums, in the open in stadiums and race tracks, or under canvas. They will play under the Shrine name or under their own: The Tarzan Zerbini International 3-ring Circus, and the Royal Hanneford Circus.

Photo courtesy of Tarzan Zerbini Circus

1989 Royal Hanneford Shrine Circus, Timmonium, MD. Photo by L. G. Hoh

The Hanneford name must be one of the oldest in circus history. In 1621, young Irishman Michael Hanneford toured rural England with an early menagerie, and in the next century an Edwin Hanneford participated in a juggling contest before King Edward III. The current Royal Hanneford Circus was just created by Tommy Hanneford and his wife "Struppi" in 1975, but Tommy figures that his sister's daughter Nellie is at least a seventh generation circus artist. "Royal" came into the title originally as "Royal Canadian," when the old Irish show was touring in England, and Edwin's family posed as Canadians in order to avoid British antagonism. The modern Hanneford show is based in Osprey, Florida, just south of Sarasota. It can be split into two units as necessary, and about 80% of their dates are played under the Shrine name. Beginning in 1990, at least one of the Royal Hanneford units is expected to play in one of the new European-designed cupola'd tents.

The Royal Hanneford Circus is reknowned for its clowning and horse acts, which developed out of a long family tradition. A nephew of the famous "Poodles" Hanneford, Tommy grew up along with his brother George and sister Kay Frances on the Downie Bros. Circus. As soon as he was old enough to walk, he worked on his father George Sr.'s bareback riding act. In the mid '70's, he was himself "the Riding Fool" of the Hanneford Riding Act, and he still serves as equestrian director for its newest incarnation. His wife Struppi, who was famous not only as a rider, but in a trained tiger act and as the trapeze artist "Tajana, Goddess of Flight," now works in every phase of circus production with Tommy.

John "Tarzan" Zerbini's popular nickname stems from the sensational entrance to his own wild animal act that he developed in 1960, when he debuted as "Tarzan Zerbini, Lord of the Jungle." Standing on the back of an elephant, he thundered into the arena dressed only in a loincloth, grabbed a rope "vine," and swung over the bars of the steel cage, to be confronted with a variety of "dangerous" cats. His more contemporary shows may include variations such as the substition of a tuxedo for the loincloth, and a pink Cadillac convertible for the elephant.

Zerbini was born into a French circus family, and came to this country in the 1950's to appear with the Mills Brothers Circus. He subsequently went on to work for the old Dobritch show, one

Tommy Hanneford. Photo by L. G. Hoh

1989 Royal Hanneford Circus, Milwaukee, WI. Photo by W. H. Rough

of the top Shrine shows in the country. In the late 1970's he was finally able to mount his own show by purchasing the assets of Hubert Castle's International 3-Ring Circus. He now operates two circus units and occasionally a third, based in Webb City, Missouri, which tour throughout the North American continent each year. The two indoor shows, a western and an eastern unit, are 3-ring affairs, and the third is a European-style single-ring circus that plays under canvas. The Canobio round tent seats around 3,000 people, and Tarzan likes to use it whenever he can. The tent unit travels with a fleet of fifteen new company-owned Freightliner tractors. Tarzan's performances are growing rarer, as he and his wife Elizabeth frequently wing back and forth between units supervising operations. Elizabeth's father, Joseph Bauer, who was once a world-class perch-pole artist and is now a major circus producer himself, also works with the show, and his son Joseph Dominic Bauer does both ringmaster and "Giant Space Wheel" duties. Tarzan and Elizabeth's lovely and graceful daughter Sylvia, the ninth generation of the Zerbini circus family, is a frequently featured aerialist on the single trapeze and Spanish web. The Zerbini Circus style betrays its owners' European backgrounds, emphasizing fast-paced, strong acts in a no-frills format, and de-emphasizing the big production numbers that tend to predominate in big American shows.

There are of course dozens more small circuses who make it their regular practice to play indoor dates around the country. They operate all year round but more often in the winter time, thus avoiding the summer tent season and assuring a better pick from available talented performers who are committed to the summer tours. George Hamid, Jr., another old and respected name in the circus business, operates his not-so-small popular Hamid–Morton Shrine Circus for a spring tour in the East and Midwest, opening regularly at the Roanoke, Virginia Civic Center. At this writing, "Big John" Strong, who may never manage to retire completely, still operates at least six touring indoor shows. David & Trudy Harris' Circus Kingdom is a Christian show which performs at prisons, orphanages, and homes for the mentally

disturbed, among other audiences. From the big Circus Gatti and the internationally famous Circus Zoppe Europa to the little shows like Jimmy Cole's All Star and the Century All-Star Circuses, indoor circuses are big business. If we were to include all indoor Shrine circuses and the many small "school" shows that play short tours in high school gymnnasiums for less than one season before they reorganize under a new name, our list would undoubtedly amount to over a hundred contemporary circuses.

SCHOOL TOPS

Any look at the whole spectrum of circus in contemporary America must include the school tops that may be helping to create tomorrow's circus artists. We are not referring here to those dozens of tiny circuses mentioned above that play around the country in school gymnasiums. Our concern is for a new circus phenomenon that is growing in both numbers and quality. Circus schools offer training grounds to future artists, as well as periodic exciting and energetic performances, which American audiences would be well advised to seek out.

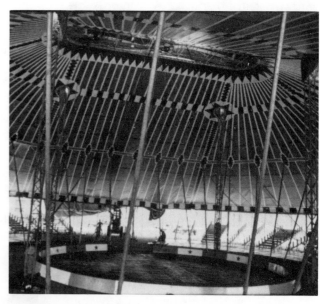

Zerbini Big Top interior. Photo courtesy of the Tarzan Zerbini Circus

Until recently in most of the world, and still in the United States, the most reliable supplier of each new generation of circus professionals has always been family on-the-job training. Some circus people are out to change all that. In order to understand where Americans are on the scale of circus education, let's take a brief look at the rest of the world. The most famous circus school in the world is in Moscow, which since 1930 has offered a demanding four-year curriculum in circus arts. The 300 or so students range from fifteen to twenty years old when they are admitted; only seventy-five of them survive each year's final examinations. The school's sense of the aesthetics of circus art, combining harmony of gesture, beauty of performance, and strength of feeling, as well as the quality of its graduates, has had a major influence on virtually every circus in the world. There are now two other such national circus schools in Russia. Nearly all the socialist countries of Eastern Europe, as well as North Korea and Cuba have schools based on variations of the Moscow model. In China, each of the 130-odd state-run acrobatic troupes serves as the equivalent of a circus school. In France there are three big circus schools. In Spain, Los Muchachos is the International Boys Circus, a whole self-governing village of 2,000 boys ranging in age from four to the late teens. It was founded like "Boys Town" in this country, as a refuge for runaway and homeless boys, but its Circus Training School attracts applicants from all over the world to its five-year course. And in much of the rest of Europe and Latin America, where the circus is a revered tradition, circuses provide plenty of on-the-job training opportunities. Wherever circus people are valued for their artistry and not dismissed as social parasites, there is encouragement for young people to learn the skills.

The current trend in American circus schools stems in part from the scarcity of talented American circus artists. To the casual observer, the number of Americans who are genuine stars as aerialists or animal trainers is surprisingly small. It is true that circus is an international field; American circus artists are in higher demand in Europe and the Asian countries than they are here, while American audiences have more interest in seeing exotic acts from Russia, the Balkan states, Mexico, and especially China. But the fact remains that we see very few American acts. There may be a somewhat nationalistic reversal of that trend in the offing, instigated by Chinese reluctance to tolerate the kind of defections that followed the massacre at Tiananmen Square in the summer of 1989. Travel limitations imposed by restrictive governments seem to make it a good time for American producers to tap into an American talent supply.

But where exactly is that American talent supply? As long as there are so many state-supported acrobatic schools in China, where circus is the most popular mass art form, there will be superior Chinese acrobats. As long as Russia teaches, funds, and reveres its circus arts, there will be superior Russian performers. And as long as truly talented Mexicans have the incentive of a far superior pay scale for performing in the United States, there will be superior Mexican aerialists. But in this country, we offer neither the training nor the financial incentives to prospective circus artists. Only a few major circuses can generate a pay scale that encourages American performers. Certainly few Olympic athletes would consider the daily drudgery of circus life when they can get much higher pay by sponsoring sneakers on TV. Circus is still a dirty word when it comes to legitimate career concerns, and few non-circus families would ever think of encouraging their children to become circus performers. With no formal American circus training available, the result, quite naturally, is that there are very few first rank American circus performers.

The best of the North American circus training schools is located in a renovated train station in Old Montreal, Canada. Under the general direction of Jan Rok Achard, the National Circus School was established in 1980 by Guy Caron, who would also later direct the big school of circus arts at Châlons-sur-Marne in France. He is the former artistic director of Canada's Cirque du Soleil, and is for the most part responsible for the abundance of genuinely talented young artists that become Soleil performers. In the brief decade of its existence, the school and its students have won major international recognition. Over 200 students, both beginners and professionals, may enroll in a four-term variety of courses including mime, dance, commedia, trick cycling, trapeze, juggling, acrobatics, circus history, French language, and philosophy. The school is recognized by the Quebec Ministry of Education as a "private school of public interest," able for the first time in the world to grant a degree in circus arts. Also available are individual courses and workshops, and special programs for children. But its chief goal is a thorough professional training for future circus artists, and it has the firm support of city, provincial, and federal governments.

Several American circuses now also provide specific training opportunities for interested youngsters to learn circus skills. The Big Apple Circus operates the New York School for Circus Arts, whereby disadvantaged youngsters at Harbor Junior High School in East Harlem are taught a variety of circus skills and academic subjects. The Pickle Family Circus School in San Francisco offers periodic classes for children and adults. In St. Louis, the Circus Arts School serves about 150 youngsters in gym classes in several schools and YMCA's, out of which has developed a crack performance team called the "Arches." Their instructors, Alexandre Sacha Pavlata and Jessica Hentoff, are aerialists with the Circus Flora, with which the school is closely associated. The idea is that teaching circus skills also involves teaching fear control, stick-to-it-iveness, trust, self-confidence, and self-discipline. When emotionally troubled and economically strapped kids get good positive strokes and a lot of personal focused attention for three hours a week, they start to feel better about themselves. Circus skills are intended to combat the feelings of hopelessness and low self-esteem that lead to all sorts of abuses. "A kid who walks a wire can see what he can do with his life, dream to be something more," says Ivor David Balding, founder of the Circus Flora.

Several American communities have begun to share the feeling that circus training makes an excellent education for children who are not

Lizzie Uthoff on Russian Barre with Sacha Pavlata, 1989 Circus Flora. Photo by W. H. Rough

One of the Arches at 1989 Circus Flora. Photo by W. H. Rough

necessarily bound for circus careers. Fine Arts departments like the one at South Mountain High School in Phoenix, Arizona, and physical education departments like that of Eastmont High School in Wenatchee, Washington, are developing basic circus skills courses. At least two communities, one in Florida and one in Indiana, have developed outstanding independent circus programs that operate in tandem with their public school systems.

The Sailor Circus in Florida is open to all students from Sarasota County schools who maintain a C average or better. Director Bill Lee identifies "the pursuit of excellence" as the school's governing philosophy, and he and his professional staff seek to engender in each student feelings of accomplishment and mutual respect. In October, the youngsters begin practicing a variety of performance skills in their own permanent circus building. By the end of March some sixty-odd students are ready to present their annual Sarasota Sailor Circus. Because many of the kids are from circus families clustered in the Sarasota area, it's not surprising that the show generates both a considerable talent among its performers and a con-

siderable enthusiasm among its audiences. With a special dispensation from the Ringling show, ordinarily fiercely protective of its famous copyrighted title, the Sailor Circus calls itself "The Greatest Little Show on Earth." In 1989, it celebrated its fortieth year.

In the same year, the Peru, Indiana Amateur Circus celebrated its thirtieth anniversary. It is the feature event of an Annual Circus City Festival held to preserve the heritage of the American Circus Corporation's residency in Peru. It also exists to serve youth, and it is an enormous community effort involving volunteers and professionals. Circuit Court Judge Bruce Embrey, who serves as one of three volunteer ringmasters, suggests that the circus teaches a sense of community and responsibility that is hard for kids to come by these days. "I've never had a circus kid come before me in court," he grins. In a week of frenetic activity capped by a two-hour circus parade, over 200 young people from Miami County, ranging in age from six to twenty, put on ten performances. A spot is found for anyone who wants to work hard enough. A smaller group of fifty or so youngsters also perform as a road tour company throughout

The web, 1989 Circus Festival, Peru, IN. Photo by W. H. Rough

1989 Circus Festival, Peru, IN. Photo by W. H. Rough

the region during the summer months. The Festival performances are held in the Peru Circus Building, which also contains a well-stocked small circus museum; it was adapted from an old lumber warehouse, and has a high, tent-like roof specially designed for the circus. The performances are the culmination of a year of preparation by the kids, under the guidance of head trainer Bill Anderson and his staff. Adults are involved only as trainers, staff and teachers, clowns, and in a magnificent sixty-piece circus band led by high school band director Tom Gustin. The kids do all the rest.

Other circus schools are privately-run operations, such as San Francisco's "Make a Circus," which teaches children in the audience circus skills as part of the show, or Camp Winnarainbow, a kind of counter-culture summer circus camp for California children. Much more comprehensive and thorough professional training is provided by Paul Pugh's venerable Wenatchee Youth Circus in north central Washington State. It has operated since 1952, with forty to eighty performers, high school-aged and younger. They sometimes tour up to 10,000 miles in the summers to pay their yearly expenses. Their extensive equipment is loaded into eight custom-built "circus wagons" and carried on a flat-bed truck. They carry no tent, performing in the open air, and their shows display every aspect of the traditional circus with the exception of animal acts. It is an ambitious and popular program, demonstrating professional quality in its youngsters and enjoying the firm support of its community.

Still another approach is taken by the Circus of the Kids, formed by Bruce Pfeffer in 1982. He was then was joined by Tammy Lutter, a fire-eater, clown, trick bicyclist, and elementary school teacher. Tammy had been spending her summers teaching circus skills at the French Woods Festival, a summer performing arts camp for children in upper New York State. Together, Bruce and Tammy developed a plan whereby they approach a school system and offer one and two-week circus training workshops to one or more groups of

*Guppo and Chula, a.k.a. head clown
Chet Andrizzi and director Paul K. Pugh.
Photo courtesy of Wenatchee Youth Circus*

Photo courtesy of Circus of the Kids

students in grades one through twelve. They bring in all the safety equipment and costumes, and can offer complete workshop programs in acrobatics, juggling, trapeze artistry, and clowning. The program also extends to workshops for parents and teachers. Part of the goal is to promote academics and responsibility, and Bruce has developed with associates at the University of Louisville an extensive syllabus, "Circus across the Curriculum," to go with the circus skills workshops. There are separate curricula with circus motifs in reading, creative writing, math, science, history, and geography. Each one is broken into sections appropriate for students in kindergarten through high school. The workshop period is capped by a final "all-star" demonstration–performance for the public. In the summers, a longer and more extensive training program now serves as a part of the performance offerings at French Woods. The Circus of the Kids has reached over 50,000 enthusiastic youngsters since Bruce began it. The program has garnered some rave reviews from administrators, teachers, and parents, who talk about their students' dramatic improvements in attitude, in capacity to trust, and in self-esteem.

The charming little Circus Smirkus, begun in 1987 by Rob Mermin as a summer camp program in northern Vermont, taps into the energy and idealism of its young performers. In July, twenty young people aged ten to seventeen show up at Mermin's farm for two weeks of intensive training in circus skills; then they embark on an ambitious tour around the state, performing twenty-eight shows in nineteen days in eleven towns. Their teachers are caring professionals, like Irina Gold, former coach of the USSR Olympic gymnastics team and consultant with the Big Apple Circus. A non-profit enterprise, the Circus Smirkus was at first funded in part by the Catamount Arts Foundation, but it is now self-sustaining from contributions, tuition, and box office receipts, along with some corporate support. Mermin, who "ran away" for at least several blocks to the circus when he was a young boy, and then again more seriously when he was in college, wants to provide the opportunity for his performers to run away to the circus for at least six weeks in their young lives. He describes it as "a metaphor for stepping outside self-made boundaries, taking risks, accepting un-

foreseen challenges, and tasting the potential of our human spirit. First dreaming, then going for it!" [9] Donny Osman, the circus' ringmaster and associate director, who is also the director of the Governor's Institute on the Arts, describes the primary value of the circus as "empowerment." Smirkus is a process of planting the suggestion that their students, and by extension their audiences, have a sense of power over their own lives, that they are free to dare and define their own limits, and that they may both offer and seek cooperation with others involved in the same quest. One look at the faces of these performers suggests that the Circus Smirkus is working. They are ordinary children, but they are also talented, intense, dedicated, supportive of each other, proud, determined, and full of joy. The true spirit of the show was amply demonstrated midway through the summer of 1989, when a tragic automobile accident resulted in the death of a much-loved counselor and the hospitalization of the severely injured Mermin for the rest of the tour. Hours after the accident, the kids gathered together to mourn. They hugged, and they cried; and then as a group they made a decision, and they took action to raise the level of their own, each other's, and their audience's lives. The next day, they performed, and they smiled. Few spectators knew how they suffered and how they grew, but they did both; and nowhere has the paradox of the true spirit of circus been more evident.

All of these school enterprises have in common that they are in one way or another geared towards at least one public performance by the students. Spectators fortunate enough to be in the audience have a unique opportunity to participate in a circus spirit that is greatly enhanced by the naïve, wide-eyed enthusiasm and commitment of the young performers. None of them take their own new accomplishments for granted; emotions run high, and the excitement is catching. If the execution of an acrobatic trick doesn't always match the level of those who have spent their lives in performance, the energy, the determination, and the genuine expressions of joy often far surpass the professionals.

At the college level, there are a few courses in circus skills offered at Florida State University, New York University, and other campuses around

Circus Smirkus marquee. Photo by W. H. Rough

The Smirkus elephant awaits his act. Photo by W. H. Rough

Jade Kinder-Martin, Smirkus wirewalker. Photo by W. H. Rough

the country, usually taught as part of the theatre department offerings. The Gamma Phi Circus at Illinois State is the oldest ongoing college circus program in the country. Celebrating its 54th edition in 1990, it was actually founded in 1929 by Clifford "Pops" Horton as an honorary gymnastics fraternity, but shut down for five years during World War II. Now with over 1,000 alumni, Gamma Phi performs annually with about sixty members, all full-time students and faculty at Illinois State. The Flying High Circus, begun in 1947 by Jack Haskin at Florida State, is a one-semester, one-credit course in stage and aerial skills that results in completely self-supporting full three-ring performances under their own tent. In 1989, sixty-eight students performed in the Flying High, "just for the fun of it." Since 1960 the Flying High has also conducted a summer residency at Callaway Gardens in Pine Mountain, Georgia, and an ambitious road touring program which includes Europe. There is only one course on the history of the circus, which has been taught for the past seven years in the Drama Department at the University of Virginia. The Ringling enterprise has operated its famous Clown College at winter quarters in Venice, Florida, since 1968, and now has over 1,000 alumni. It is actually not a college at all, but a purely professional training school, designed to add new faces to the diminishing pool of American circus clowns in the late sixties, with an incidental eye on its public relations value. Every American citizen might well benefit from completing its comprehensive psychiatric questionnaire–application, but the school is intended only for those seeking professional careers as clowns. Virtually every major American circus employs at least one graduate of Clown College. Its intensive program is only ten weeks long, and tuition is free. Out of the 2,000 to 3,000 yearly applicants, Clown College can accommodate at best only sixty men and women. They range from fresh high school graduates to older professionals seeking new careers, and approximately one third of them will be offered contracts with the Ringling show. Their final school performance is sometimes called the funniest final exam in the world.

Other clown schools springing up around the country, such as those in Houston, Atlanta, and the University of Wisconsin–LaCrosse, provide only brief introductory or professional refresher courses. All such schools, of course, focus only on clowning, and pretty hastily at that. There is little opportunity for a comprehensive, substantive circus education anywhere in the United States outside the circus itself.

There is a noteworthy difference between all the American offerings and the Canadian and European schools. With the exception of Clown College, the usually non-profit American circus school efforts are geared so far primarily as liberal arts education or as community service programs, rather than as professional training schools. Some of their public and private funding is undoubtedly predicated on the condition that they perform social service. Their goals are well illustrated by the New York School of Circus Arts' boast that its students "discover that balancing commitments is as difficult as balancing on a wire, and that juggling

David and Trudy Harris' Circus Kingdom, a traveling student circus offering college credit. Photo courtesy of Circus Kingdom

responsibilities is as tricky as juggling oranges." While circus aficionados admit that the goal of educating committed and responsible citizens with circus training is certainly a commendable one, they worry that American circus schools don't necessarily provide the grounds for exceptional circus talent. On the other hand, they may be re-assured that these schools do teach about the cir-cus; and what's more, that we in the audience can learn from their performances to value all that the circus can be. Furthermore, exceptional talent does indeed emerge from the American schools. Competent and sometimes inspired students do in fact go on to professional circus careers. The Back Street Flyers, a black break-dancing acrobatic company trained by the Circus Flora's Sacha Pav-lata when he was a master teacher with the Big Apple's New York School of Circus Arts, won a silver medal at the International Circus School competitions and went on to perform for three years with the Big Apple. Talented eleven-year-old Lizzie Uthoff wowed Flora audiences in 1989, after only a few months of working with Sacha, and she shows considerable promise as an acrobat. And two veteran trapezists from the Peru Amateur Circus, young Chris Robinson and Peggy Ma-theny, took a third place bronze medal in the 1989 International Youth Circus Competition in Verona, Italy. These and other signs of excellence from American circus schools are no small achievements.

Circus educators are eager to find new and better paths for American would-be circus artists to achieve excellence. Pavlata, for one, hopes that in addition to its goal of lifting students out of the lost world of the ordinary, the Circus Arts School will become a major circus professional training institution, that will funnel its students into the major circuses of the world as readily as Canada's National Circus School is starting to do. The "Pic-cola Flora," a mini-circus performed by the Flora troupe's dozen or so children, which was insti-tuted in the summer of 1988, is perhaps one step in that direction. But without a major shift in values that many Americans are unprepared to pay for, we will never have the training oppor-tunities equivalent to those that create the mag-nificent Chinese acrobats. Here, the circus is not the established social institution that makes such

excellence possible; and we do prefer after all to leave the responsibility for the pursuit of excel-lence up to the individual, and not to the state. So perhaps one or two outstanding professional circus schools on the North American continent are sufficient to accommodate the rare artist who will seek them out. But it's too soon to tell. Con-temporary American circus schools are all young, and the 1990's will determine how or if they are to meet the needs of the American circus.

NEW TOPS

This brings us to four major "new-wave" cir-cuses and one new "spectacular" one that many critics have already been calling the circuses of the future. That may be an ironic label for at least three of these shows, who profess to be more in-terested in rediscovering the circus of the past; and all five of them are in one way or another based on traditional European circus performance formats. In 1988, Clive Barnes, long time circus fan and theatre critic for the *New York Post*, wrote a series of articles primarily on three of the circuses. His words have been widely quoted as heralding the beginning of a new circus renaissance. Be that as it may, during the end of the '80's the Pickle Fam-ily Circus, the Big Apple Circus, the Circus Flora, the Cirque du Soleil, and the Circo Tihany are redefining what circus is.

What the five shows do and how they are structured is new to American audiences. They are distinctly different from all the traditional cir-cuses we discussed in the early pages of this chap-ter. For one thing, all five were created within ten years of each other from scratch, out of the sweat and hard work of contemporary dreamers. Second, all five have earned a considerable inter-national reputation for excellence. Third, they have taken a much more theatrical approach to the circus than their traditional colleagues, and have often been described as having "redefined the circus." Within that context, four of them are intimate one-ring circuses in which performers seem to be an integral part of a single theatrical performance, each act proceding logically from the one before in a loosely-structured story line. Fourth, because they are different and have re-jected traditional formats, they have sometimes

Photo courtesy of Ringling Bros. and Barnum & Bailey Combined Shows, Inc.

*Lizzie Uthoff with 1989 Circus Flora.
Photo by W. H. Rough*

been the objects of resentment or jealousy among some traditional fans. All five generate hot debate on what circus really is: Can there be a circus without animals, or without a death-defying sense of danger, or without spectacle, or with too much spectacle, or without circus music, or without even a ring? And finally, all but one of the circuses are non-profit operations that depend heavily on outside contributions from their own fans and grants from foundations, corporations, and all levels of government. In some cases less than 50% of production costs are borne by ticket sales. Although these shows tend to have higher ticket prices than traditional circuses, no one would suggest that raising admissions any higher is any answer to the precarious state of circus economics. The Big Apple's Dominique Jando reminds us that the spiralling cost of Broadway musical theatre tickets has virtually eliminated ordinary middle-income audiences. The arts are expensive, the circus is especially expensive, and they both need supplemental income. Like musical theatre and opera, circus is extravagant by its very nature. The arts, including circus arts, have always been state-supported in some fashion in Europe, and we may have to get used to that idea here too if we want them preserved at all.

But despite their similarities, the five shows are just as different from each other as they are alike. Only Soleil and Tihany boast of being a brand new circus art form, and they have little in common. Only two of the shows, Big Apple and

Flora, have animal acts. The five headquarters are geographically widely separated, reflecting philosophical goals aimed at very different audiences. And their approaches vary from intimate clowning, through death-defying high-tech, to Las Vegas spectacle.

The Pickle Family Circus, the oldest of the five in their present forms, was started in San Francisco in 1974. It travels mostly in the West, but it has made occasional side trips to Alaska and London, and most recently to New York, where in the summer of 1989 they were invited to appear at the International Theatre Festival at Stony Brook. Customarily, the Pickles play in parks and playgrounds under the open skies, with canvas side walls and no top, although they also enjoy the chance to escape California weather in indoor auditoriums.

The first thing spectators notice when watching Pickle is that the clowns are in control. It was founded by clowns, and it is designed and performed by clowns, and they are experts at the whole range of comedy, pathos, physical slapstick, and especially juggling. Audiences don't take long to get the idea that they are participating in an event which is an expression of love, respect, and support. It is being passed like juggling balls and clubs between company members and between the audience and the company. Entire silent conversations take place with juggling clubs. And

Photo courtesy of Pickle Family Circus

Photo courtesy of Pickle Family Circus

Photo courtesy of Pickle Family Circus

The clown-jazz musicians, "Round Midday."
Photo courtesy Pickle Family Circus

Diane Wasnak as "Baby." Photo
courtesy Pickle Family Circus

yes, one giant balloon, maybe eight feet in diameter and probably the biggest juggling ball in the world, is passed among audience members, bouncing over outreached arms and laughing faces until it bursts and showers confetti all over the place. The feeling is one of belonging to the proverbial one big happy family, and of course that is exactly what is intended and what the word "family" is doing in the title. The approximately thirty troupers are not a biological but a social family. Fourteen of them perform, but everybody, from Judy Finelli, the artistic director, to Ranna Bieschke, the much loved road manager/massage therapist, to the kids, contributes to the family spirit. The audience is invited to share in it too. Every show is like a party: strangers in the audience talk to each other, and cast members sit down to chat with audience stragglers when it's over.

There is more to Pickle than clowns and family, even though traditional fans may search this circus in vain for "death-defying" acts or even one four-legged animal. Accidents and falls can happen in any circus, but no one here courts disaster or uses life-threatening danger to titillate audience palates; safety wires or nets are in evidence when deemed advisable. As for the animals, it's not that the Pickles have any bone to pick with traditional circuses and their animals, it's just that they themselves would prefer not to put animals in a truck and haul them around the countryside. Their interest lies exclusively with the two-legged sort.

There are acrobats, wire-walkers, hand balancers, and trapeze artists, all demonstrating expertise and enjoyment. They perform with a dramatic flair which is inspired by a unifying theme, such as myth and folk tales. In fact, the second half of the shows is given over to a theatrical story, loosely told in the tradition of turn-of-the-century jugglers and set in a Parisian restaurant, the "Café des Artistes" in 1988, and the "Café Chaotique" in 1989. The real Pickle trademark, "the big juggle," comes at the end of the show: The entire company — everybody — juggles, and the air is filled with assorted crockery, glassware, and pies moving in every conceivable direction. The flying dishes are accompanied by the sounds of frenetic shouting and laughter, and a dynamic five-piece jazz band.

There is youth and idealism and energy at the Pickle which can almost be classified as zeal. It is the legacy of Larry Pisoni, also known by his clown identity as Lorenzo Pickle, from whom the show takes its name. Larry and Peggy Snider were both members of the San Francisco Mime Troupe, one of America's top guerilla theatres in the late 1960's, and their decision to found the Pickle Family Circus was perhaps as much a socio-political statement as an aesthetic one. It was an idealistic way to combat a decaying society with fun. There was to be no artificial division of labor and pay scale, no racism, no sexist use of scantily clad chorines, and no cynicism. There was to be an emphasis on community and social responsibility. The ideals remain valid today, as Pickle performers continue to devote themselves to sharing their art without undue concern for monetary rewards. Peggy continues as their executive director, after Larry left in 1988 to pursue a career as an independent clown performer. The Pickle Family Circus is now undoubtedly the only circus in the country featuring women as both executive and artistic directors, and for that matter even as boss clown. She wouldn't be called "boss" on the Pickle, but Queenie Moon can hold her own among the great clowns of all time.

There were (at least) two other future circus founders juggling with the lively San Francisco Mime Troupe in the early '70's: Paul Binder and Michael Christensen. The two became fast friends and developed a comedy juggling act which they toured through the streets of Europe and at the exciting Nouveau Cirque de Paris. Paul had never gone much to the circus as a child: "It seemed distant and smelly and seedy to me." [10] But the French circus was different. With business degrees from Dartmouth and Columbia, he was as much a businessman as a juggler, and he now dreamed of bringing "classical" circus to America. On July 20, 1977, with a lot of help from knowledgeable friends, he and Christensen opened the first Big Apple Circus season, which would play to 45,000 people in New York's Battery Park. He became its artistic director and ringmaster; Michael became the popular Mr. Stubs, clown extraordinaire and the show's clown coordinator. The talented Katja

The Binders: Katja Schumann, Max, Katherine, and Paul. Photo by Martha Swope Associates/Linda Alaniz, courtesy of Big Apple Circus

Schumann, a member of the famous equestrian Schumanns who have operated circuses in Germany and Denmark since 1870, added grace and class when she made her first appearance with the Big Apple in 1981. She soon became the wife and partner of Paul Binder and mother of a new circus dynasty, and she continues as the prize-winning architect and performer of one of the best varieties of equestrian acts in the country.

Within ten years of its founding, annual Big Apple audiences have grown to well over a quarter of a million people. Its colorful round tent holds about 1800 patrons. Thanks to the persistent efforts of Judith Friedlaender, then Executive Director and Producer of the circus, it was pitched at Damrosch Park at the Lincoln Center for the Performing Arts, where it has become a regular feature of New York's Christmas season. They have gained the corporate support of Exxon, Macy's, The New York Times Foundation, Viacom, Warner Communications, Columbia Pictures, several major banking enterprises, and many others. Big Apple's mission as a not-for-profit educational and performing arts institution and its charter with the host city for which it is named assure that the circus will be brought directly to the people in all five boroughs. It has also embarked on annual tours as far south as Washington, D.C., as far north as Shelburne, Vermont, and as far west as Cleveland. They travel the road with about 120

people, forty of whom are performers, two elephants, and Katja's horses.

The style, tempo, character, and sensibility of this circus are strongly American, but its format uses the classical European circus for its model. The Big Apple defines classical circus as taking place in a "single, intimate ring with the surrounding audience interacting with both performers and each other." It includes "performances by acrobats, gymnasts, aerialists, clowns, trainers and animals. Animals as performers are central to the classic mode, and the respect for animals is reflected in their treatment as a part of the circus and in the presentation of relationships between humans and animals."[11]

Big Apple is also following the European trend called "new circus," which emphasizes theatricality rather than spectacle. "It evokes a wide range of feelings with the use of strong lighting and music."[12] This results in an energy not unlike that of a Broadway show. The traditional ringmaster's intrusive announcements have become increasingly rare, as the high-quality international acts are left to speak for themselves. The performances are moved forward by a central thematic story around which they are loosely organized. The 1988–89 season featured an East–West détente theme called "The Big Apple Circus meets the Monkey King." It focused on the imagined adventures of a legendary comic folk hero from

The 1987 Big Apple at Lincoln Center, New York. Photo by Michael LeClair, courtesy of Big Apple Circus

China's Beijing opera tradition. The détente theme was made extremely poignant at the end of the tour, when real events in Beijing's Tiananmen Square resulted in a series of traumatic defections, including six by members of the celebrated Nanjing Acrobatic Troupe appearing with the show. For the 1990 season, the Big Apple brought back Barry Lubin, one of their original featured clown troupe, to headline a new story-theme called "Grandma Goes West." The show is a "loving tribute" to Buffalo Bill and his co-stars, Annie Oakley and Chief Sitting Bull. It has an "Old West" theme similar to one used by the Circus Flora several years earlier, and incorporates several unique western-oriented acts, such as a superb "Pony Express Ride" by Katja Schumann, the marvelous lariat work of Vince Bruce, and a trained buffalo.

The Cirque du Soleil, the "Circus of the Sun," is a strictly Canadian enterprise, and some may question what it is doing in a book focusing on circuses in the United States. The answer is clear to anyone who has seen it on any of its tours through Canada's neighbor to the south: Since it was founded in 1984, it has had as much impact on contemporary American circus as any show developed and operating exclusively within the United States. Its success has been nothing short of phenomenal: In five short years it went from entertaining 30,000 to a half-million spectators annually; from fifty performances a year to 312; from forty-five employees to 150, now including thirty-five performers; and from an annual budget of $1.3 million to $11 million. At the same time subsidies from the various levels of the Canadian government have fallen from 97% to under 10%. Proud Canadian corporate sponsors like Bombardier, Inc., Canadian Airlines International, Dominion Textile, and La Laurentienne have eagerly participated in picking up the slack, and the necessarily higher admission prices have not kept happy audiences away. In 1987, the Cirque du Soleil was a finalist with the likes of Molson Breweries and IBM Canada for a "Business of the Year" award. The business success of this ambitious enterprise has created some internal problems, as must inevitably arise when artistic and commercial interests vie for priorities.

But the Cirque du Soleil is no slouch in the artistic department either. Straw house performances in Chicago, Miami, New York, San Francisco, Washington, and other American cities have earned it rave reviews. The brilliant young Guy Caron was the artistic director for the first five years of Soleil's existence, and is largely responsible for the show's unique approach. Performances are given in a 130 foot, blue and yellow round tent made by the French sail-manufacturer Voilières du Sud-Ouest, which seats a relatively intimate 1750 spectators. They are marked by a polished, high-tech look and flow, complete with special effects, smoke and fog, dramatic lighting, colorful modish costuming, and a stunning mod-rock musical accompaniment. All of this is kept to an intimate level, however, and technology is never allowed to impress for its own sake. There is no pomp or pure spectacle, and there are no processions or armies of clowns and chorus girls. And to the dismay of traditionalists, there are no animals. "I'd rather feed three artists than one elephant," says founder and circus president Guy Laliberté. [13] In fact, the presence of animals in this show would even be distracting to its real purpose: an exploration of the psychological and physical nature of the human being.

Despite all the technical wizardry, the human element is the real focus of the Cirque du Soleil.

It is completely devoted to playing with the idea of what makes humans funny, and with exploring the outer limits of what humans can do. A heavily theatrical and intimate emotional approach has replaced the big production numbers of more conventional circuses. In the 1989 performances, the clowns' and acrobats' routines were framed by a dream-like transformation. In a swirl of magical smoke, a group of "ordinary" people wearing

The Nanjing Troupe acrobatic lions. 1989 Big Apple Circus, Shelburne, VT. Photo by W. H. Rough

1989 Cirque du Soleil. Charivari. Photo by Martin Lavoie, courtesy of Cirque du Soleil

1989 Cirque du Soleil Acrobatic Dance. Maia Taskova and Mariela Spasova (Bulgaria). Photo by Martin Lavoie, courtesy of Cirque du Soleil

Circus Flora. Photo by W. H. Rough

Ivor David Balding. Photo by
W. H. Rough

The 1989 "Baldini" Family. Photo by W. H. Rough

Cecil "Yo-Yo Baldini" McKinnon.
Photo by W. H. Rough

masks in a style suggested by the commedia dell'-arte were changed into magnificent circus artists. But they eventually had to turn back into the ordinary people, happy for the opportunity to have dreamed, but disappointed that their dreams can't last. At the end of the show they go off to resume their less than demanding lives.

The Cirque du Soleil performers are mostly under twenty-five years old, and some are no more than children. They are gifted with the zeal of youth that has thus far kept the show fresh and energetic. When they move on, whether because of other ambitions, artistic or salary disputes with management, or sheer exhaustion, their ranks are immediately filled from Chinese and other international sources, and from the rolls of the Canadian National Circus School, with new faces eager to participate in the dream. For the 1989–90 edition of Soleil, Guy Caron, the original artistic director, had been replaced by Gilles Ste-Croix, and 90% of the performers were new and fresh talent. In fact there is a constant struggle to find ways of preserving artistic freshness in the face of the demands of circus big business. Laliberté likes to book shows as little as ten days in advance, just to help keep everyone flexible and avoid a sense of the routine. And improvisational rehearsals keep everyone guessing what the clowns will do next.

It is impressive how funny a single clown in a circus ring can be, and it is often embarassing to see how much he reveals about our own human nature. The variety of ways in which the human body can be made to bend, balance, fly, dance, walk, and cope with flying objects is disarmingly bewildering when demonstrated by these young circus artists. Part of our surprise as spectators at their display of talent comes from a deceptive sense of their ordinariness. They do not appear to be perfect, super-human, muscle-bound, or unusually beautiful: it is an unimpressive, ordinary-looking human body lifting that weight, leaping from that dizzying height, or dancing so gracefully on that thin wire. These circus performers don't strut or flaunt capes, and there is no razzmatazz build-up into super-star status for any of them. The youth and beauty and strength that they exhibit is not for self-aggrandizement. It is to make all of us young and beautiful and strong.

The Cirque du Soleil was created in 1984 by young Guy Laliberté when he was himself only twenty-four years old. Like Paul Binder, the Big Apple founder, he was a street performer who had spent some time traveling among circuses in Europe, and he too had a keen sense for business. The two men also share a common reputation for mincing no words when sharing their opinions of traditional American shows: "I hate traditional Circus!"[14] he says, causing hundreds of traditionalists to gnash their teeth. Nonetheless, he stubbornly applied for and received a grant from the Canadian government to tour a new kind of circus in celebration of the 450th anniversary of the discovery of Quebec. Although plenty of American circuses and their imitators had toured throughout Canada in the past, the country had never had any strong national circus traditions of its own; Laliberté was free to make up his own definitions of the genre. He found a name for his show by looking in a dictionary of symbols. He saw " 'Soleil, sun.' It means youth, power, freshness. Everything was there."[15] Michel Clair, in 1984 the Minister responsible for Quebec's participation in International Youth Year, agrees. Looking at the new circus for the first time: "Observe them," he said. "Are they not of the sun?"[16]

The most recent of the four new-style circuses to come into existence is the Circus Flora. It is named after the baby elephant who is its star, and who was herself the namesake of Babar and Celeste's first daughter, Flora, in Jean de Brunhoff's charming "Babar" stories.

The Circus Flora is the brainchild of Ivor David Balding, the son of a British polo player who came to America to sell horses. Another circus runaway, Balding dropped out of his freshman year at Harvard University in the 1950's to train with the Cirque Medrano in Paris on the advice of actress Eva LaGallienne. But it was the theatre that would capture his early career interests; during the '60's he was the highly successful Broadway producer of such plays as *Steambath, The Man in the Glass Booth, Lenny,* and *The Ginger Man.* Nonetheless, he found himself increasingly drawn to the circus, feeling that the reality of circus had the capacity to transcend the illusion of theatre. He began to produce several television circus specials, and he became the celebrated Jimmy Chipperfield's general manager for a European tour of Circus World. In 1980, Paul Binder hired him as a consulting producer for the Big Apple Circus, and he became involved with several Shrine circuses productions as well.

All this time, David was formulating plans to take out his own circus, committed to "reviving the circus as an art form." He began with a loan from his sister and brother-in-law, Sheila and Sam Jewell, who have found themselves enmeshed in the world of the circus ever since. While he was on a photo safari in Africa in 1984, Balding bought Flora, a three-year-old African elephant orphaned by poachers. He had her flown to the U.S. and designed his circus around her. "You can't have a circus without an elephant, a horse, a clown and a pretty girl," he said, "and that's the order of importance."[17] The Circus Flora was invited to make its debut at Gian Carlo Menotti's prestigious Spoleto Festival in Charleston, South Carolina in 1986. A stunning surprise to the culturally elite audiences of the Festival, it was an immediate popular, artistic, and critical success. In fact it was such a hit that it was invited back for a second appearance at Spoleto in 1988, the first production of any kind to be so honored. The following year Menotti issued an unprecedented invitation for them to appear at the 1990 Spoleto Festivals in both South Carolina and Italy.

Except for the special lighting effects, Circus Flora performances are for the most part recreations of the circus arts as they existed in the 19th century. They tend to range between comedy and the classical dangerous presentations of skill on horseback and in the air, and they are presented in an intimate setting. Even the costumes are authentic nineteenth century designs with heavy overtones of the commedia troupes. Performances are not only theatrical but narrative, and in a format which allows them to exhibit the best of European circus traditions in an American historical context. They begin always with a "come-on" or "charivari," the arrival of all the performers together, with a special appearance by the charming Flora. For every performance, the clown Yo-Yo narrates the story of her fictional Italian family, the Baldinis, who have brought their circus and their elephant to tour America.

In 1986, the Circus Flora "recreated" the arrival of the Baldinis in Charleston in 1810, suggesting they were the first European circus to come for such a tour. In fact, although early European circuses did land in Charleston, the Baldinis never existed except as a Balding creation. Coincidentally, though, there was an early American Flora: She was in 1827 the seventh elephant to be imported into the United States, and the first to travel with a menagerie. The 1988 edition of Circus Flora was called *The Journey West* and included exciting troupes of Native American dancers among its features. Following the Baldinis as they moved westward into the new frontier from St. Louis in 1843, it provided opportunities for Flora to meet a friendly performing buffalo, and Yo-Yo to meet an Indian guide. Finding the mountains impassable, the Baldinis returned to St. Louis and took a river boat to New Orleans for the 1989 edition, *Back to the Bayou*, which had a Cajun theme. A pirate's theme takes over in 1990, as the Baldinis once more set sail for the West, and attempt to cross the isthmus at Panama.

Flora's single-ring performances are given in a red and white striped, light-tight round tent essentially similar to Big Apple's, Soleil's, and Zerbini's. This one is made by the Baches company in Bordeaux, France; it seats less than 1500 people in a 120-foot round, but is somewhat higher than the others, at the request of Sacha Pavlata, now a full-time partner, Technical and Performance Director, and aerialist with the show. Its all-white interior also adds to the illusion of height. Seating keeps audiences no further than forty feet from the ring.

Among the thirty-five or so talented performers are some of the oldest and most widely respected names in the business: Wallenda, Zoppe, and Pavlata, among others. In 1989, after a year of hunting for a permanent home, the company offices moved into St. Louis' Grand Avenue Performing Arts Center. St. Louis thus became the third contemporary American city, after San Francisco and New York, to have its own resident circus. Impressed by both their performances and the obvious value of Sacha's circus-in-the-schools program, the city has given them a five-year lease on some vacant land. The 1989 performance tour was considerably abbreviated, as the directors and their supporters devoted their time primarily to establishing the credibility of the school, reexamining their goals, and struggling to solidify their financial base. St. Louis audiences have been enthusiastic, and if Balding and Pavlata are able to muster sufficient funding from private, corporate, and public sources, there are plans for a permanent winter quarters, a school building, and an indoor performance arena. Balding claims the circus is now permanently in his blood, and he could never be drawn back into the New York theatre scene. Baby elephant Flora, on the other hand, who by the summer of 1989 was a gangly, strapping eight-year-old, began a series of ballet lessons from internationally acclaimed avant-garde choreographer Martha Clarke. She will make her New York acting and dancing debut in 1990, in a new theatre piece by Clarke at the Brooklyn Academy of Music's Next Wave Festival.

Before we leave our look at influential new circuses in the United States, with a slight overlap into Canada, we might do well to take a brief look at what is going on south of the Rio Grande. In Mexico, circus is big business, and people tend to take their circus arts much more seriously. There is a long-standing tradition of proud family circuses which are at least as fine as any in the United States. Many of the great Mexican flying families own their own circuses. Outstanding among traditional Mexican circuses are the Circo de Renato, the New York Circus, the Circo Sventes and finally, the Circo Atayde, an arena and tent show with a polished appearance and a variety of outstanding international acts. If outstanding Mexican acts in some Mexican circuses like the Atayde are rare, it is only because D. R. Miller and others have lured them north of the border with the promise of better wages.

Much of the talk in the Mexican circus world centers around a unique, giant new show that has been touring there for several years and is anything but traditional. It recently moved from South America into Mexico, where it has been a huge success. For sheer size and spectacle, the already legendary Circo Tihany promises to give the Ringling Brothers and Barnum & Bailey Circus a run for its money as it seeks to expand its routes with the "Circus Tihany Spectacular Celebrates America 'The Magic Is Here' 1990 Tour" into the United States. Tihany is the brainchild of a Hungarian, Franz Czeisler, and named after the town of his birth. Czeisler has been a circus man for forty years. He speaks eleven languages, performs sparkling magic tricks he personally learned from the likes of Houdini and Blackstone, and captivates his audiences with his infectious enthusiasm. The 180 people in his cast and crews travel on sixty-five trucks and trailers, and he uses two immaculate 200 by 240 foot Italian tents. It takes four full days to set them up, so the show hopscotches between tents from stand to stand. Stands are usually a minimum of ten days. Each tent holds almost 4,000 people in luxurious contoured seating; there are no bleachers. There is no ring. Everyone faces in one direction, towards a massive 80 by 100 foot proscenium stage made with the elevated flatbeds of Czeisler's trucks. Two long curved stairways on either side, lit by crystal chandeliers, form the show entrances. It's a spiffy, Las Vegas-style production, with even the stagehands working in tuxedos.

Many would consider Tihany a tented theatrical extravaganza, and not a real circus at all. Czeisler can perhaps best describe it himself:

> My show is an original blend of the Las Vegas type extravaganza—embellished by hydraulic stages that go up and down, colorful dancing waters, and music hall dancers—with the traditional circus. In it, I have introduced and developed a presentation that has never existed under the big top anywhere. Yet it is one which is still rooted in the European circus tradition of excellence, and commitment to treating people with love and respect.

Whatever it's called, Tihany is yet another example of the many directions from which American circuses might choose their future. Circuses must continue to evolve and change, just as they have for thousands of years, despite the protestations of traditionalists. Only the passage of time will reveal whether this or any of the four "new-wave" circuses is a passing fad, or the harbinger of a new epoch in circus performance that might compare favorably with Coup's and Barnum's 1872 circus enterprise.

Photo courtesy of Circo Tihany

Photo courtesy of Circo Tihany

5.
BACK YARDS AND GETTING THERE

For those of us who sit in the seats of an old-fashioned tented circus, the mere fact that the place exists is an absolute wonder. The spell is upon us even before the first act begins. What had been so far as we knew an eminently forgettable muddy vacant lot, or a dried out field of weeds, or a deserted corner of a mall parking lot only a few hours ago, has been transformed. When we drove by this spot yesterday, we never gave it a second look. In our wildest imaginations, we could never have dreamed up this multi-tiered city. It is teeming with activity and colored lights, costumes, and with noises and smells that completely violate the ordinariness of our daily lives. If we give ourselves over to the circus for only a few hours tonight, the reward will be absolute magic. We'll forget all the impossible problems and annoyances which demanded that we worry too much, and that we settle for stop-gap solutions which we know darned well won't work. Tonight, we'll gasp at performances that are unbelievably magical, mostly because we know they're not. We'll laugh out loud at jokes we've seen many times before, and make fools of ourselves with the kids' cotton candy and popcorn. But when we drive by the place again tomorrow, we will ask ourselves whether it was ever really here. Not a trace of any of this will remain, except in our own hearts and minds. The field or the parking lot will go on being deserted and ordinary once again.

What magician snapped his fingers and made all this appear? "How did they do that?" we will ask. If it wasn't really magic, somebody — a lot of people — worked very hard to make this performance happen for us right here and now. The logistics of getting the performance in front of the public are often as intriguing as the acts themselves. Perhaps they instigate even more curiosity, be-

cause, unlike the acts, this work is usually hidden from us. "Who made the arrangements? How did all these people get here, and how did they manage to get us to come here to watch them? When did they get here, and how did they put this thing together so fast? Where do they keep the elephants, and how much do they feed the lions? Why did they set it up like this, and have they always done it like that? What is holding that trapeze up there, anyway, and who will take care of cleaning up all this trash?" There are so many questions, ranging from the big top peaks to the dirt under the seats. One small boy was recently heard leaving a circus lot loudly and fervently demanding to know what happens to all the elephant poop. Now the program doesn't always tell us that, does it?

EARLY PREPARATIONS

Gone are the days when circuses arrived on the doorsteps of little American towns and announced a performance for that evening. Only a few years ago, an advance man could arrive in town, make all necessary arrangements and book a show for two weeks later. Today, most advance bookings are made five or six months, sometimes over a year ahead of when the circus will actually come to town.

Booking may be initiated either by the circus itself or by a town or sponsoring civic organization like the Shriners. Shrine sponsorship of circuses originally began as a fund-raising activity for the charities supported by temple. But more recently, circuses have become a major income-producer for the annual operation of the temple itself. In 1986, according to a September 28 story in the Orlando, Florida *Sentinel*, national Shrine leaders asked all 189 Shrine temples in North America to publish the following clarification in their circus programs: "Proceeds from this Shrine circus benefit Shrine operations only. They do not benefit Shriners hospitals for crippled children."

There are other equally effective but less ambitious forms of circus sponsorship as well. Local organizations such as auxiliary fire departments, police units, schools, service clubs, and charities may contact a circus and ask to sponsor them, either for profit or for benefit performances. Just as often it is the circus that seeks dates that conform to its route schedule. It then plays under its own name and splits the ticket revenue with a local sponsor on a prearranged basis. The Pickle Family Circus views their role as fundraisers for the non-profit sponsoring organization as a major aspect of their responsible interrelationship with the audience and the community. Contracts can vary widely, from set fees to percentages and guaranteed minimums. For their "take," the sponsor usually, but not always, agrees to do some degree of advance publicity and ticket sales for the circus, so that everyone ends up happy.

Occasionally, circuses will play "cold dates," with no local sponsor. Some, like the Ringling show, prefer to operate on their own, relying on their own professional staff to generate all relevant contracts and publicity. In other cases, either local regulations or insurance worries may have kept sponsors from being interested. When it establishes its routing, a circus may find it convenient to play in a location where no sponsor is available. A cold date may be desirable, for instance, in a town strategically located between two sponsored dates. Where there is high audience potential, and no restrictive local statutes, a cold date also generates more revenue for the circus, without the need for a sponsor split.

Some circuses preferring cold dates view their policy as a responsible step away from the "boiler-room" telephone tactics, which encouraged the sale of bogus tickets for allegedly charitable purposes. Sponsors sometimes turned a blind eye to professional high-pressure circus salesmen, who operated from banks of telephones outside the community. Very little of the money raised by such means went to the named charity. Instead it went quietly under the table either to the sponsor or to the circus. Boiler-room tactics are the logical extension of the old grift shows. As regulations have grown more effective, boiler rooms have grown more temperate and honest, but scruples continue to be questioned. As recently as 1988, according to *The Circus Report*, a Maryland judge ordered Dick Garden, owner of the Toby Tyler Circus, to pay $1.7 million in civil fines and $615,000 in restitution to the state's handicapped and mentally retarded children, who were supposed to have been beneficiaries from several of his shows. Although the case was settled for only $20,000 in fines, Garden will not be permitted to raise "charitable" funds again in Maryland.[1] Incidentally, for those who have always wondered, *Toby Tyler, or Ten Weeks with a Circus* was a fictional novel written by James Otis in 1880, and popularized by the Disney film. There was never a real Toby Tyler. This and other circuses have been named after the book.

Where to Put It?

Regardless of sponsorship, one of the biggest problems in planning a circus performance today is where to put it. The old pros insist that the greatest factor in the success of the circus is where it plays. Charles Sparks once said, "Any boob can run a circus, but it's the wise showman who knows where to put it." It's no longer an easy matter to put a tented show on an empty lot which is convenient for the public and large enough to hold the tents and all the necessary support equipment, and which has ample parking facilities. A major show like the Clyde Beatty–Cole Brothers Circus requires a space at least 300 by 500 feet, not counting public parking, for example. Even the smaller shows like the Franzen or Roberts Brothers Circuses need something approximating the size of a football field. The lot must have proper drainage, access for the trucks, and ample parking for circus and performers' vehicles. In the old days of the railroad circus, it also had to be adjacent to or near the rail yards.

Today, the fields down by the old railroad yards are covered with condominiums, and the tracks have been torn up for urban renewal. Land values near America's cities and towns are far too attractive to permit maintenance of an empty lot for the occasional circus which may come to town.

*1989 Clyde Beatty–Cole Bros.
Fishersville, VA. Photo by
L. G. Hoh*

At one time, Otto Ringling suggested that Ringling Brothers Circus purchase fourteen acres of centrally located choice real estate in every major American city. If they had done that, they could have certainly avoided the financial troubles that plagued them in later years. In the long run, of course, they couldn't have afforded to maintain the acreage as empty lots either, but at least it would have been a fruitful investment.

Contemporary circuses occasionally find communities that still have their old county fair grounds or ball fields on the edge of town, which makes life easy for everyone. If there is night lighting and stadium seating, and if sponsors are willing to risk bad weather, some outfits like the Royal Hanneford circus are rigged to play to large stadium audiences without a tent. Big sponsors, like the Shriners, may even be able to buy insurance to cover their expenditures if a show is cancelled because of rain. Tented circuses can also play on the asphalt parking lots of major shopping malls, if the management is receptive and recognizes a good drawing card when it sees one. The Beatty–Cole and Vargas shows are sometimes called the king and queen of the shopping malls. When those options are not available, shows are often reduced to playing on outcast land that has proved unsuitable for development because it's too rocky, or too marshy, or located too near the town dump.

For all of the foregoing reasons, many circuses no longer travel under canvas. Instead, the small shows contract for dates in high school auditoriums, and big shows like the Shrine productions go into civic centers. Of course the Ringling Brothers and Barnum & Bailey Circus now plays exclusively in large civic centers, except for the "Gold Unit"

in Japan. As we saw in the last chapter, some of the larger shows, including Tarzan Zerbini's, Cliff Vargas', and the Royal Hanneford are equipped to play either indoors or in tents. Several producers also take tented shows out in the summer and arena shows out in the winter, providing year-round employment for circus personnel.

It would seem that life ought to be easier, headaches fewer, and houses larger for indoor circuses. Weather and parking facilities are no longer a concern. Circus owners have no "blow-downs" to worry about, nor concerns for the high expenses needed to maintain the crews and truck fleets necessary for raising and lowering the canvas at every stop. There is usually plenty of seating, and there are often permanently established networks for publicity and concessions. However, indoor shows playing in small arenas and school gymnasiums find different conditions in every location, and they have their own share of headaches. If Monday's show is in a civic auditorium and Tuesday's is in a high school gym, the physical conditions for the acts can vary widely. Tents allow more consistent control over the space and layout. Indoor circuses frequently derive no income from in-house concessions, and are also forced to pay exorbitant fees to local musician's unions. In addition, small indoor circus managers may have to carry or contract for a false floor, pay excessively high rental and insurance fees, worry about whether the elephants will fit through the doors or fall through the floors, and make last minute adjustments when the school superintendent forgets to unlock the outside doors for the public. How many proprietors would agree that if economics permitted, they would rather be performing under the big top?

Advance clown Elmo Gibb. Photo by Jim Carpenter for The Daily Progress, *Charlottesville, VA*

Tenting really should be cheaper than the rising costs of renting super domes and civic arenas these days, and there are places that circuses might want to play which just don't have auditoriums of adequate size. Even the Ringling organization is considering a brand new tent for its international operations. If a move back towards tents and away from arenas can be detected as a trend for the 1990's, it is not only nostalgia that is at work; tenting can often reduce the high cost of renting, insurance, and local union fees and regulations. Besides, there is something about the combined smell of mud, sawdust, canvas, and elephant dung that circus folks just can't quite get out of their heads.

Most tented circus people vow to stay "under canvas" no matter what, threatening to take their shows off the road rather than go indoors. Carson & Barnes owner D. R. Miller is among the many who claim that a circus is not a circus in a building. And Cliff Vargas, who played in both, insisted that he much preferred the tent. On the other hand, America has never known the European tradition of the modern permanent circus building, with the possible exception of the school circus buildings in Peru and Sarasota. Dominique Jando of the Big Apple Circus claims that a permanent home is the ideal, and that no one in his right mind would prefer tented life to a building which allows precise and completely flexible control of lighting, rigging, entrances and exits, and provides permanent rehearsal and training space

for the ultimate development of circus arts. Such a site in New York remains the dream of the Big Apple Circus, and in St. Louis, of the Circus Flora. Nonetheless, circus in America is still closely associated with the nostalgic image of the old tents, and our primary interest in this chapter will be devoted to the contemporary American tented circus.

Logistics

There is a long process involved in bringing a circus to town, and each circus handles the logistics in its own way. Some kind of general agent, called by various names, and often an account executive or a vice-president of the circus, is in charge in front of the show. This "booking" or "tour," or "traffic," or "bushing" agent/director makes the initial contacts, sets up the routes and lots, and draws up contracts with the sponsors and advertisers. Circus routing is generally kept a secret until advertising begins, in order to prevent smaller or less conscientious shows from slipping into a town and taking advantage of the publicity of a big show. The booking agent must discreetly accomplish a great deal: Lot owners must be contacted to negotiate rental, and necessary permits must be secured from county or city officials. Some municipalities require fire, health, police, sanitary, zoning, building, and electrical permits, even for tented shows which carry their own generators.

The media and marketing directors arrange for the sale of advance tickets and promotional events. A number of complimentary tickets, "Annie Oakleys," are traded for favors to the circus. Special promotions may include discounted family days, coloring contests, elephant races, newspaper coupons, free giveaways in schools, drawings, and the involvement of morning disk jockeys and TV weather people. One of the more celebrated circus giveaway traditions is the opportunity for individuals and garden clubs to cart away wheelbarrow loads of free elephant poop, that magical guarantee of giant tomatoes in home gardens. That's one answer to the small boy's question cited at the beginning of this chapter. The Beatty–Cole show promises free fuel for life to the first person to invent an automobile which runs on elephant dung.

Many circuses employ an advance clown who arrives in town a few days before the circus to generate interest wherever he or she can, and to do personal appearances for schools, the media, and service organizations. The advance clown often performs demonstrations and distributes educational materials that may not be directly related to the promotion of his or her particular show; rather, they are designed to raise circus consciousness and knowledge about circus in general.

Hundreds of other not always insignificant details must be considered, including the procurement of food for the cookhouse and the various stands and "joints" on the midway, as well as the locating of such necessities of life as dry cleaners and laundromats. Supplies for a Ringling tour at one time included 1,144 tons of hay, 135,000 pounds of oats, 506 tons of sawdust, and 20,000 rolls of toilet paper. For today's Clyde Beatty–Cole Brothers Circus, advance arrangements must be made to deliver by 9:00 a.m. on the opening day of the circus: 30 bales of high quality hay, 450 pounds of grain, 5 to 10 bales of shavings or sawdust, two 20-yard dumpsters, provisions for 250 daily meals prepared in the cookhouse, and 1400 gallons of diesel fuel for every day the circus plays in that town. The agent must also arrange in advance for a water hook-up, asphalt repair for about 400 stake holes if they are to play on a mall parking lot, extra labor if needed, lot-cleaning, and the emptying of six portable chemical "donnikers," as toilets are traditionally called in the circus.

All jobs and deliveries are essential. If anything is overlooked, it can affect the performance in many unsuspected ways. For instance, one of the ten Beatty–Cole marketing directors, Dick Smith, recalls a day in Salisbury, Maryland, when the local contractor forgot to empty the donnikers at the appointed 9:00 a.m. hour. Since the donnikers always travel full from the previous stand so as to be less apt to tip, it was one miserable day at the circus.

As Marketing Director, Smith arrives in a town three weeks before the Beatty–Cole circus and up to five months after media teams and agents have made brief initial contacts. He doesn't leave until he is sure the lot has been thoroughly cleaned after

"Love those oats." Photo by W. H. Rough

Cat food. Photo by Joan Z. Rough

the circus has left town. It is his job to be the liaison between the circus and the community, and to solve all problems that might interfere with a successful experience for both. He arranges for gravel deliveries to fill in the low spots on a muddy lot. He also seeks to earn respect and trust for his show, providing a reliable face for local people to identify with the Beatty–Cole Circus, and convincing them that they can't do without circus in their lives.

Many smaller shows do more of their preliminary work from their headquarters. The Great American Circus, for instance, plans much of its advance work by telephone from Sarasota. Only a few advance men, often with the help of local circus fans, can then take care of any preparations which must necessarily be done locally. The Kelly–Miller Circus plans its tour from its winter quarters office in Hugo, Oklahoma. In addition to the advance agents who travel through each town to set up contacts, they do follow-ups from the home office and keep several WATS lines busy year-round, assuring sponsors of a permanent responsible contact. The Pickle Family Circus, on the other hand, relies on its sponsors to do all the advance work, providing suggestions by telephone and a thorough guide book of proven publicity techniques.

Every circus has its own system for making local arrangements and generating interest. They have in common a desire for the circus experience to be a happy one for all concerned. The Beatty–Cole show has even been known to spend over $3,000 just to returf a lot they had damaged. After all, good circus business depends on being invited back, and children of all ages count on the circus coming back to town again next year.

BILLING AND BALLYHOOING

If where a circus plays is vital to its success, so is the very complicated process of making us aware of the time and place of performances. So too is the often not-so-gentle art of persuasion that is designed to convince us that we, the public, can't live another day without the circus. Since 1893, that process has been called ballyhooing, a word which developed at the Chicago Columbian Exposition. It was an English mispronunciation

of an Arabic expression used for calling side show performers out in front of the tent to do a free show to attract a crowd. Ballyhooing involves a lot of flamboyant language and exaggeration that are the legacy primarily of two masters at it: Barnum and Charles Ringling. It has caught the public fancy, and we are rarely offended by exaggerated circus claims made in the same spirit as a challenging child: "I'll bet you a hundred million dollars that . . ." Said John Ringling: "There is no effort to deceive the public—but to express the hugeness of everything in figures that carry the idea. If we have fifty elephants, and say a hundred, it pleases rather than offends."[2]

Ballyhooing also meant that anything goes in advertising a circus. Hot-air balloon ascents were once an integral, spectacular opening for every circus performance, because balloons could be seen for miles by thousands of prospective spectators. Coup & Barnum's "Professor" Donaldson once took off in a balloon over Chicago in 1875; he's still missing. Today, the bulk of such advertising is handled by the media. The Ringling, Beatty–Cole, Carson & Barnes, and other big shows or sponsors rely on TV spots and newspaper ads; smaller shows put more emphasis on radio. Everyone is eager for the free and more meaningful coverage that can be generated by feature newspaper stories related to the circus. And a picture of the advance clown with a handicapped child outdraws thousands of dollars' worth of paid advertising.

Wherever possible, posters and handbills are still a vital circus tradition. Some shows use stock posters, and others develop unique looks, styles, shapes, and color combinations that identify a specific circus. Billing agents are responsible for "papering" towns, or putting up circus posters in store windows and on telephone poles where they will be seen by the greatest number of people. The success of P. T. Barnum's paper promotion of Joice Heth, George Washington's "nurse," as "the first person to put pants on the first president," established his genius at the art of ballyhooing. Madison Avenue virtually owes its beginnings to this "Shakespeare of Advertising," as he was sometimes known.

Modern billers have to contend with city ordinances against posting on utility poles, or

Circus paper. Photo courtesy of Ringling Bros. and Barnum & Bailey Combined Shows, Inc.

regulations requiring paper to be removed before the circus leaves town. They may be limited to the walls of vacant buildings, store window fronts which can be traded for Annie Oakleys, and fences around construction sites. Gone are the days when circus paper completely covered window fronts and the sides of buildings, and when large banners, hung across main street, announced the arrival of a show. But billing is still an important way to ballyhoo the circus coming to town. For an average stand on the Beatty–Cole tour, for example, Dick Smith has 400 pounds of posters ready for his billing crews.

Circus paper comes in sizes referred to as sheets. Their 28 by 42 inch dimension was originally determined by the size and weight of the lithograph stone that could be easily lifted by the printers. Every kind of bill was determined by combinations of sheets. Dates were printed separately on half-sheets, 21 by 28 inches, and twenty-four sheets made up a full 12 by 25 foot billboard. Panels for narrow window spaces were in half- and one-sheet sizes; one by 28 sheet "streamers," usually containing the show's title, were used for pasting over the tops of a long row of other signs. The biggest lithographs ever printed were for the W. W. Cole, the Forepaugh–Sells, and the Buffalo Bill shows, consisting of 100 sheets each, mounted on billboards 15 by 60 feet.[3] "Guttersnipe" referred to circus paper several feet wide by only a few inches high that was intended to go on rain gutters over store fronts; and "banners," for outdoor displays, were usually mounted on thin stiff cloth. The colorful old lithographs, offering a lot of printed and pictorial information, were designed for a more appreciative, slower-paced society than today's. Of the many major lithograph companies that handled circus printing, only one or two remain today. In the electronic age, the lithographs have been replaced by color TV. Today's circus paper is much simpler; in the tradition of video art, it is intended to provide the minimum necessary amount of information from only a casual glance.

Billing crews will now post or paper a town about a week before a circus is to open. In the old days of the giant railroad circuses, the major shows had from one to five advance "bill" cars, which would roll into town two to three weeks before the main show, attached to a regular passenger train. In 1923, John Robinson's bill car typically carried twelve billposters separated into two brigades, seven lithographers, a paste maker, a chef, and a car manager.[4] It contained sleeping facilities, storage for a month's supply of dated paper, ladders, brushes, tacks, and a complete shop for mixing glue and posting bills.

Circus paper was traditionally attached in one of two ways: It was either tacked up or pasted up. The tack-spitters were so called because of their dangerous-sounding cobbler's tradition of approaching their targets with a mouthful of tacks.

They were very good at spitting them onto their magnetic tack hammers and driving them into place with one smooth blow. The practice was probably begun by the North Salem (NY) shoemaker and circus founder, Aron Turner.[5] A good tack-spitter traditionally carried with him a loaf of bread; if he accidentally swallowed a tack, he would quickly follow it with a piece of bread, presumably to protect his stomach and bowels. A new and safer system for posting paper was clearly in order.

According to current scholarship, it was Van Amburgh who first used paste for bill-posting in Cold Water, Michigan, in 1855. May claimed that the system of pasting pictorial paper on locations open to the weather was ordered by Seth Howes.[6] Bill-posters had their own language: any stand of pasted circus paper was called a "daub," but they never "daubed" glue on anything.

The billing crews had to be a tough bunch. They had to work in rain, sleet, or hail, and sometimes they worked from high scaffolding and in high winds. On an average day, each man was supposed to post a "hod" of 300 to 600 sheets, covering up to 7,000 square feet of space. Added up, circus paper accounts for one of the major expenses of early shows. The 1911 Ringling show, for instance, allotted 914,000 sheets for the season, and the Hagenbeck–Wallace Circus of 1934 posted a total of 101,108 sheets in Chicago alone. Under average conditions, a show might be expected to use anywhere from 5,000 to 20,000 sheets per town, depending on the potential and the opposition.

Once the initial billing was complete, the job of the billing crews wasn't yet over. They were occasionally called on to engage in fist fights with rival billing brigades determined to cover everything with their own circus paper. Such tactics frequently launched full scale "billing wars." Circuses preferred to call them, more euphemistically, "opposition," but they could be ruthless indeed. Special opposition brigades were organized whose whole purpose was a campaign of dirty tricks that would put Watergate to shame. Supplies of new paper might be intentionally rerouted to the wrong city. "Rat" sheets were printed to cast doubt on the morality of a rival circus, or the truth of its advertising. They were most likely to

be libelous lies themselves, but they almost always got away with it because the printed slanders generated publicity for both shows. People would have to see them both to know who was telling the truth. Opposition crews might change the date and show title on rival circus paper. Some shows would bill a town with "Coming Soon" paper, even if they had no intentions of doing so, just to make trouble. "Wait Sheets" called for the public not to attend one circus but to wait for the "real" circus. At one time, the Ringling show was even called the "Wait Bros." because of its efforts to undercut any show preceding its arrival in a town. To the casual observer, the bright red bills insisted in big black letters, "Wait for the Big One!"

Gentlemen's agreements beginning as early as 1883 have always tried to reduce the billing wars to more subtle forms of persuasion, but there are still recent remnants of opposition to be found. In 1959, the Adams Bros. & Sells Bros. Circus used ten times its normal amount of paper crying "Why

Photo courtesy of Ringling Bros. and Barnum & Bailey Combined Shows, Inc.

Pay More?" as it struggled against the larger Cristiani Brothers Circus in Green Bay and Appleton, Wisconsin. Again in 1974, a public war of words in print broke out between the Felds' Ringling operation and the newly founded Circus America, both of which opened in Washington, D.C. on April 2 to packed houses. In 1983, almost four months ahead of their scheduled fall dates in Chicago, Ringling crews posted wait paper clearly aimed at a summer stand of the Vargas Circus: "Why Settle For: Paying more for less show and trudging across a dusty/muddy lot to swelter under a canvas tent in the hot and humid July/August heat while sitting on a hard bench?" Finally, as recently as 1988, in El Paso, Texas, a Disney ice show promoter was accused of posing as a Circus Vargas employee and stealing 100,000 Vargas free and discount admission coupons. According to the *El Paso Times*, he allegedly stole the coupons so people wouldn't know the circus was in town and instead would go to the Disney show.[7] Clearly, billing wars and opposition are not entirely a thing of the past.

With all the circuses, large and small, still crisscrossing our country, most of whom keep their routings a closely-guarded secret, it is inevitable that they will run into each other and compete for the same audiences. But good circuses generate business and enthusiasm for other good circuses, and responsible owners don't object if they have been preceded into their territory by a good clean rival. Mutually supportive relationships have begun to form, such as the one between the Pickle Family and the Cirque du Soleil, which resulted in a 1989 Soleil performance in San Francisco to benefit the Pickle. Pickle and the Australian Circus Oz have a mutually supportive arrangement as well, and Lorenzo Pickle found it possible to make a guest appearance with the Circus Flora in 1989. Such expressions of level-headed circus brotherhood were not unknown in the past, either, but they certainly didn't receive the exposure of the great billing wars. There is much more to be said about the fascinating world of circus advertising, but this is not the appropriate place. At any rate, the whole story has already been ably told in *Billers, Banners & Bombast*, by Charles Philip Fox and Tom Parkinson.

Arrowing

Leaving aside the job of ballyhooing the circus, there is one additional person, called the 24-hour man, who comes to town before the circus itself arrives. His jobs might include bringing the circus from one stand to the next by "arrowing the road." It is no easier, although probably far less offensive to local farmers, than the old practice of "railing the road." Small, easily seen arrows are temporarily taped to existing road signs and utility poles along the highway. Some roads are obviously easier to post than others, depending on traffic speed, available pull-offs, and the number of signs. As might be expected, the New Jersey turnpike has a reputation for being one of the more demanding of American highways to arrow. If two shows are following the same road, different colors, initials, or other characteristics may be used to distinguish one show from another. The

"Turn Here!" Photo by W. H. Rough

arrows are the "rails" which guide the circus vehicles to the lot of the next stand, and if the public
spots them and knows how to read them, they are
an easy way to find the circus in a new town.
Their language is simple. For instance, either a
"SLO" sign followed by an arrow pointing down-
ward, or two or three arrows pointing at the
ground mean "Slow down." Three arrows pointing at a 45 degree angle to the right mean "Take
the next exit."

The 24-hour man is usually responsible for
laying out the circus lot. He determines where the
center poles of the big top will be placed and where
the front and back doors will be. He marks each
key location with a ribboned wooden stake or
metal pin, if the lot is dirt, or a spot of color-coded
spray paint, if it's an asphalt lot. Working from a
single point, perhaps the front door, and using a
chain or other measuring device, he sets all subsequent measurements from that point, including
the placement of every stake line and center pole
and all the trailers and trucks. If physical obstruc-
tions interfere with his ideal stake lines, the general manager or owner may choose to find another
lot, modify the standard stake lines if it can be
done safely, or as a last resort blow the date.

Circuses haven't traveled in a tight convoy
since World War II, in order to avoid both highway traffic hazards and the congestion that would
result if everyone arrived on a lot at the same time.
The 24-hour-man meets the first trucks when
they arrive to show them where to park. But once

drivers are oriented to the location of the front
door, everything else is usually the same on every
lot. The peculiarities of a lot may demand flexibility for interior seating and back yard design,
but trailers almost always have the same neighbors, and the trucks are always parked in the same
relationship to each other. There are practical considerations governing parking procedures, as well
as the remnants of the old circus caste system.
Owners and managers are always on the front end
of the lot, near the ticket wagon. Performers'
trailers and motor homes are parked together, and
dormitory trucks are well out of sight in the back
yard, near the cookhouse. Animals are located
together on the same part of the lot, sometimes
tethered out on the grass, when practicable, and
downwind when possible.

GETTING THERE

With the exception of the Ringling Brothers
and Barnum & Bailey Circus, today's circuses all
travel in trucks. Before they can even leave their
winter quarters, the list of preliminary preparations is long. They must obtain and meet the rules
and regulations of all the various states governing
the transportation of animals across state lines.
Their trucks must be licensed in every state whose
borders they will cross, and display Department
of Transportation approval stickers guaranteeing
that all fees have been paid.

Any manager knows that a reliable means of

Circus red tape. Photo by Joan Z. Rough

reaching the site of a promised performance is absolutely essential. Because circus people can't afford the inevitable loss of income and reputation resulting from a blown date, they must either own and maintain or lease a fleet of reliable trucks.

The size and nature of the fleet varies from circus to circus. At minimum, every show under canvas carries at least one self-contained generator truck, which provides all the electric power the circus will use. The constant noise from the generator trucks and the rapid-fire talk of the candy butchers and side-show grinders have always been associated with the atmosphere of the circus. Another truck included in all circus fleets is the ticket office, still called the "red wagon." In addition, there are usually concession trucks, canvas trucks, pole and seating trucks, dormitory trucks, animal trucks, and the cookhouse. The three largest tented shows in the country, Beatty–Cole, Vargas, and Carson & Barnes, travel with a total of twenty-six, twenty-three, and forty-two show-owned vehicles respectively. Smaller circus outfits like Wayne Franzen's and the Great American travel with only thirteen and ten. These figures do not include the many privately-owned motor homes and trailers where individual performers prefer to live, or the trucks that belong to complete acts that are leased by the circus. For example, flying acts and animal acts usually own their own vehicles and equipment. Privately owned trucks and motor homes can double or triple the number of vehicles that must be accommodated on a circus lot.

Increasingly, circuses seek to own similar model trucks to simplify repairs with uniform replacement parts. Clearly, among the most sought after and well-paid employees of the circus are reliable, safe, and loyal truck drivers, able to maneuver onto some pretty inhospitable sites, and willing to carry strange cargoes and share the demanding hours of circus life.

Traveling by truck is a complicated process, and the Ringling show still finds it profitable to do their moving by rail, the only one to do so since the end of the railroad era in 1956. Starting in 1957, they too scraped by without their own train, moving like a regular truck show, except that the animal acts were shipped ahead via three railroad-owned stock cars. But in 1960, the Ringling show went back on the rail in fifteen of their own tunnel and stock cars, redesigned from old coach cars by manager and former flyer Art Concello. Since 1969, there have been two Ringling Circus trains crisscrossing the country, one each for the Red and the Blue Units. In 1989, the Red Unit used forty-four cars and the Blue Unit forty-five, and the flat cars have grown to almost 90 feet in length; all their cars together are as long as any circus train ever, except for the big Ringling tented show trains in the heyday of the railroad circus. Of course, both contemporary units are strictly arena-based, so they don't have to undergo the old logistical nightmare of carrying canvas, poles, and canvas crews from town to town. In addition, some equipment still goes by truck, and many of the Ringling performers travel by motor home or truck, preferring to avoid the limited space, noise, and confusion that go with life on a crowded circus train.

Railroading

Technically, the Ringling Brothers and Barnum & Bailey Circus may still be a railroad show, but it's a far cry from the days which followed W. C. Coup's original 1872 move to rail. Because the success of the circus is so intertwined with the rapid expansion of the railroad, the golden days of the railroad circus merit a closer look.

Circuses grew as fast as the trains and the westward development of America would allow. They could now jump hundreds of miles in a single night, instead of five to fifteen miles. In any single season, they could play at a greater distance from their winter quarters than ever before, in virtually any city in the United States serviced by a railroad. They could even bring their audiences to them on special excursion trains, increasing their exposure still more. By 1891, at least seven of the hundred or so circuses in the country were large railroad shows. By 1911, at the peak of the golden age of the railroad circus and only forty years after the first major railroad show, there were thirty-two.

Traveling by train was never an especially cheap proposition for the circus. Transportation of a large circus was an enormous logistical operation: There were hundreds of horses, elephants, and other performing and menagerie animals to

Rounded Warren flats in foreground. Dropped bottom Mt. Vernon flat car at left rear. Photo by W. H. Rough

transport, feed, water, and exercise. They also carried enough canvas to make the bigtop, menagerie, cookhouse, side show, and other support tents, with all of the necessary poles, chains, and miles of ropes; seating for sometimes upwards of 12,000 people; wardrobe; lighting; an adequate food supply for animals and people; wagons for parades and for moving equipment from the rail-yard to the circus lot; and of course all of the workers and performers themselves, who at times may have numbered 1600 people on the Ringling show. The daily task of loading, moving, and unloading a circus train instituted a tradition of clever transportation design that remains typical even in today's truck circuses.

In his first year with Barnum, Coup found that a whole new uniform rail flat car design would be necessary, and he ordered forty new ones from Columbus, Ohio, for the 1872 season. Railroads charged the same rate for all flat cars, long or short, so Coup's cars were twice the usual length of 30 feet, in order to carry more wagons for the money. They were reinforced to stand the great weights of the circus wagons. They were of low uniform height, to keep the center of gravity of the heavy wagons as low as possible, to allow them to clear overhead bridges, and to facilitate load-

ing. Brake wheels on the ends of the cars were removable, so as not to interfere with rolling wagons on and off the car. Because railroads had not yet agreed on a standard gauge, Coup's cars also had a system for changing the width of the wheel axles.

Later, circus flat cars grew to a standard 72 feet long by 9 feet, 9 inches wide, long before the railroad companies had ever conceived of "piggy-back" cars for themselves. After 1922, most of the new steel circus flat cars were made by either Mt. Vernon Co. in Mt. Vernon, Illinois or the Warren Co. in Warren, Pennsylvania. The Warren cars are easily recognizable in profile, because they bow upwards in the middle, unless they are fully loaded, whereas the Mt. Vernon flat cars have a straight top edge and an angular straight bottom edge.

Uniform circus flat cars permitted the train to be unloaded from either end from designated "run" cars. For efficiency, the cars were designed so that a train could be "cut" and unloaded in two or more sections. The 24-hour man phoned the train crew to inform them to load the train with "poles to caboose," or "poles to engine," or "poles to middle." The crew then faced each circus wagon pole or "tongue" in the proper direction on the flat cars for efficient unloading. Ramps called

"The Big One," Cleveland, 1920. Side show tent, with eight center poles of the big top visible behind it. Photo courtesy of Circus World Museum, Baraboo, WI

"runs" would be placed off the end of the designated flat cars. Using horse, elephant, or tractor power, wagons were pulled across steel plate bridges placed between the other cars to the end of the run cars. To prevent the wagon from rolling down the run too fast, a rope attached to the rear was wrapped around a "snubbing" post midway on the side of the run car. Crews eased the wagon down the run, checking its speed by tension on the rope. Guiding the wagon down the run on the front end was the "poler," who had the most dangerous job in unloading a circus train. With one false move he could jackknife the wagon and turn it over onto himself. Not uncommonly, if the "snubbers" lost control and the wagon came down too fast for him to stay clear, the poler could be seriously injured. The whole efficient but dangerous system of loading and unloading circus flat cars can still be seen daily in a fascinating demonstration at the Circus World Museum in Baraboo, Wisconsin. Small "cross cage" wagons, which could be placed side by side across the flat cars, were hefted into place by hand. The term "razorbacks," for the men who load and unload the rail cars, derives from the men who squat under the side cages and position them across the flat cars on the command "Raise your backs!"

After each wagon was unloaded, it was customarily hitched to a team of Percherons. This traditional breed of heavy draft horses, along with Belgians and Clydesdales, were called baggage stock in the circus. They were responsible for pulling the wagons from the railroad siding to the lot. In the old days, the baggage stock was a major portion of the animal population in the circus; in 1916, the Ringling show carried 300 such horses.

The way from the rail yard to the circus lot was marked by arrows chalked on telephone poles, the only kind of arrowing really needed for railroad shows. At night, the way back to the yard would be marked with smudge pots.

A Circus Day

The Ringling show in its heyday used to travel in four separate trains. In the 1923–28 seasons there were a total of 100 cars, not counting the billing cars attached to an earlier passenger train. The efficiency of train travel can best be understood with a look at a typical circus day on a Ringling lot in 1946. The first show train arrived in town at about 5:00 a.m. It was called the "Flying Squadron," after the name for the 1873 crew who arrived a day early to pound in stakes and otherwise prepare the lot. The three stock cars, eighteen flat cars, and five coaches of the Flying Squadron brought in everything necessary to lay out the lot, and its two most important items were the cookhouses and the stake drivers. As a crew of 174 men began to prepare breakfast, the second train, containing the big top, arrived at about 6:30 a.m. By the time the third train with the seating arrived at 7:30, the stakes had been driven for the major tents, and the wagons were already rolled onto the lot. Poles were up by 8:30, and an hour later the great canvases rose from the ground like enormous mushrooms. The fourth and last train, consisting of eighteen coach cars, rolled in shortly afterwards, bringing the performers. For the rest of the morning, workers spotted the cages and trunks, erected the seating, and hung the banners for the side show. Aerialists hung or checked their own rigging. By 11:30 a.m., everything was ready for the show, and the cookhouse flag was raised to signal lunch was ready.

At 12:30, the circus opened for business, with the shouting of "DOORS!" and the candy butchers, bugmen, and side-show talkers and grinders went to work, calling out, "Step right up..." Those gentlemen with the canes and straw hats soliciting your business at the circus, by the way, are "talkers," or "grinders," and are never to be called "barkers"! Following a brief band concert, the first performance of the day began at 2:15 p.m. sharp. There is still today, indeed, a time-honored tradition for the circus, unlike the theatre, to begin promptly as advertised. At 3:00 p.m., during

the show, the side-show workers were fed dinner, so they could be ready for the "come-out." Immediately following the departure of the first audience, everyone else was fed, and the cook tents, known as the "Hotel Ringling," were taken down and loaded on the wagons. They were returned to the Flying Squadron train by 7:00 p.m. As soon as the cages and animals were led out of the menagerie tent for the performance, it too was taken down and packed into the wagons for transport to the train. By 9:30 p.m., the Squadron left town with the cookhouse and menagerie tents, and all the animals except for the elephants who would be needed for labor in dismantling the rest of the circus.

At 10:30 p.m., immediately following the performance and before the public was even out of the tent, the massive job of dismantling the rigging and seating began. The third train was loaded next, with all the seating, rigging, props, and costumes, but it couldn't leave before the second unit, so that the arrival order for the next day could be preserved. The big top was down by midnight, unlaced, baled, loaded on wagons, and bound for the second train, followed by the big poles. The railroad siding power plant, the last item to be loaded on the train, was usually numbered 130, reflecting the 1:30 a.m. time that the managers expected the last train to leave town. The next day, the whole process would start all over again. The overall guiding principle for circus transportation logistics stressed the importance of a loading order which reflected the order that the

Unloading at Circus World Museum. Note poler at center, snubbing post at left, and dropped bottom of Mt. Vernon flat. Photo by Joan Z. Rough

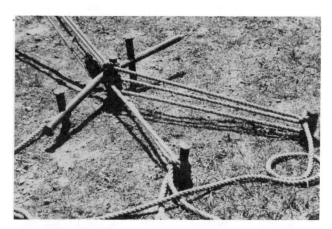

The "Dead Man," for critical strength. Photo by Joan Z. Rough

show required the equipment on the lot: cook-house, menagerie, side show, big top, seats, props, rigging, wardrobe, and lighting.

Roustabout Life

The whole moving process developed into an exacting science. Giving the lie to the old maxim, "It's a real circus in here!" to describe pandemonium and chaos, the circus move was and remains one of the more highly controlled and organized of human activities. Switching from rails to trucks has simplified the moving process only slightly from the old days. The loading and unloading down at the railroad yards and the wagon processions to and from the lot have been eliminated. Even the large tented circuses of today deal with moving far fewer animals and a much smaller population from place to place than did the only moderate-sized railroad shows of yesterday. Shorter average distances between stands have held travel time to a manageable level. Nonetheless, it's not an easy life for those who elect to work for the circus. "Roustabouts," as they are called, may start as members of the canvas or the prop crews, or in any combination of other labor-intensive jobs. They may be paid somewhere around $100 a week, and if they stick out a whole season they'll usually get a bonus that may be enough to buy a car and tide them over during the off-season. They sleep at night in tightly-packed dormitory trucks. Showers can be a rarity on some shows, but are readily available requirements on others. They may be makeshift outdoor camp-shower arrangements, but they are a significant improvement over the old system, when the water truck supplied each man with four buckets of cold water per day, two in the morning and two at night. There is rarely time to leave the circus to explore local towns; and the tradition of not mixing with townspeople, affectionately called "towners," or "lot lice" when they come on the circus lot, remains strong.

On the other hand, there are enough "pluses" to make life as a roustabout worthwhile in the eyes of those who choose it. It offers the freedom of moving about the country in a kind of rootlessness, a spirit of adventure that is reminiscent of pioneer days. Roustabouts still tend to be a tough and self-reliant lot of pioneers. Occasional thefts, fights, substance abuse, and violence on the lot serve as reminders that many circus people don't live ideal lives. But more commonly, roustabouts are good, fun-loving wanderers, risk takers, and adventurers, in flight from boredom. As Doris Earl, co-owner of the Roberts Brothers Circus observes, "Their faces change, from one year to the next, but the men don't." Sometimes called America's French Foreign Legion, circuses offer anonymity: Few questions are asked of prospective roustabouts, so long as they show a Social Security card

"Home on the road." Photo by L. G. Hoh

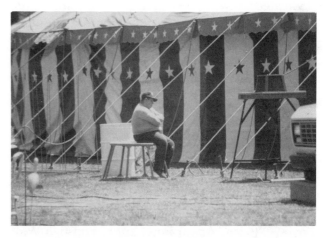

Pre-show leisure time. Photo by Joan Z. Rough

or a green card and a willingness to work. So the circus often serves as a haven for those who would prefer to forget an unhappy life or misdeeds back home.

By contrast, daily life for a performer in the circus can carry significantly greater financial rewards. Headliners like Gunther Gebel-Williams and Dolly Jacobs are among the highest paid performing artists in the world. But weekly salaries of performers with less star appeal at the ticket window can range from $125 to $300. It's not enough to get rich on, but when all family members are working, it's enough to get by. The personal satisfaction brought on by public approval of their demanding performances can feed the ego at least.

On the other hand, many circus performers claim they are sometimes not treated with the respect that is their due as artists. They can be victims of a long-time prejudice which unfairly assigns them to a third-rate "gypsy" status. With restrictive social traditions and the heavy demands of touring, life can be lonely, unless performers are traveling with their families.

Rules and regulations of behavior for circus employees vary considerably. Some show managers are eager to preserve the family image of circus. The Kelly-Miller Circus' David Rawls tolerates no use of drugs or alcohol on circus lots whatsoever, and even discourages the men from smoking in public; he demands a clean appearance at all times, and no swearing. Infractions of the rules can result in immediate dismissal, but he says there are few infractions among a happy and dedicated crew. Other contemporary shows are just as rigid, but some are considerably more lax, and sometimes it's difficult for outsiders to know ahead of time which shows have high standards of behavior. The result of a few unsavory shows is commonly a bad reputation for all circuses.

Grift Artistry

Pay-offs and outright scams are now more the exception than the norm, but the opposite was the case in the early days of American circus. From the 1860's to the 1920's, the circus had an overabundance of shifty grift artists and gamblers. Pogey O'Brien, Adam Forepaugh, and Ben Wallace ran notorious grift shows, and they were among the many who developed clever methods of cheating and short-changing customers. A common practice was for circuses to hire teams of professional pickpockets to work the crowds. Forepaugh even hired a blind woman to "collect alms" in front of his red wagon, 90% of which went into his famous vest pocket and 10% to her. Forepaugh's vest pocket was the notorious repository for all off-the-record fees and pay-offs. Grift privileges were often sold to employees for a weekly fee; according to historian Gordon Yadon, the privilege of stealing laundry from clotheslines while the townspeople were at the circus went for $100 a week.[8] The high ticket window in the red wagon and the high platform of the side show ticket sellers were created specifically to make counting change difficult. Sometimes an invisible slot in the eye-level surface of a ticket stand peeled bills back off the bottom of a pile of change after it had been counted out by the seller and pushed forward towards a naïve customer. Many grift shows were soon forced to avoid towns where they knew tar and feathers and lynch mobs angrily awaited their return from last year's stand. Jaded towners were often ready to believe that circus people were morally corrupt to the last man and woman.

The end result was that the occasional more moral, family-oriented circuses had to protect their wholesome images ever more vigorously. They were called "Sunday School shows" by their less than savory rivals, because they allowed no gambling, swearing, drinking, fraternizing with towners, sloppy or tasteless dress, or contacts between the show girls and anyone else. The Ringlings were particularly adamant about the clean image of their shows, refusing to allow any sort of grift anywhere in their operations. Many oldtimers still feel that the real reason John Ringling was forced to close the American Circus Corporation shows after he bought them in 1929, is that their operators refused to give up their grift operations, and Mr. John would not risk tarnishing the Ringling image.

Seventy years ago, the Ringling Brothers and Barnum & Bailey Circus, the biggest Sunday School show of all, printed a list of "Rules and Suggestions" for its employees. It prohibited among other things sitting cross-legged on any float or

tableaux wagon, smoking or chewing gum or tobacco in public, and gambling and the loaning of money. The ballet girls were required to sign in to their sleeping car by 11:00 p.m., and were not permitted to stop at hotels or talk or visit with any male members of the show company except the management, or with any towners. Even an "accidental" encounter with a man was not considered excusable. Unbeknownst to a general public which was determined to see all circuses as morally corrupt, life on such a show was a family affair. In its heyday, the circus wasn't a bad place to raise kids, in an atmosphere that was often considerably more wholesome than that in many of the cities and towns it visited.

Family Life

Most performers are born into circus families, and do what they must do out of compulsion, or because they know no other life. Circus families are close-knit units; they live together in their own rigs, and the children are often trained into the family act as soon as they can walk. Their schooling may be taken care of by a traveling tutor, as is the case with the Ringling, Pickle Family, and other shows. The state of California requires that a tutor certified to teach in California be available to children traveling with any circus in California. When children travel with it, the Big Apple Circus maintains its own "One Ring Schoolhouse," organized by Michael Christensen, providing a certified teacher for a full academic course load, in addition to weekly classes in circus arts taught by

the performers. During the school year in other shows, children may be left at winter quarters or with relatives. Occasionally they make arrangements to complete their schooling by correspondence with home teachers, or through the popular K–8 home instruction courses offered since 1897 by the Calvert School in Baltimore. Calvert provides a fully accredited structured curriculum by mail; their courses include testing and grading procedures, books, and instructional materials prepared for parents with no teaching experience. Schooling for circus youngsters is not easy to come by. It can be thorough, and full of real-life adventures that surpass the seat of a school desk, but it can also be ignored.

Life for circus children may not always be as relaxed, clean, and wholesome as social agencies might wish. For every child among the circus audience who yearns for a life in the circus, there is probably a circus child looking back, longing for the security, warmth, and space of a permanent home. On some shows, crowded life in a tiny shared train or truck compartment, with dirty windows that don't open, a total lack of privacy, and parental indifference to schooling is not unknown. Living conditions are not always even minimally sanitary. Legally required tutors are not always used, leaving some circus kids woefully weak in reading and math skills and ill-equipped to handle life outside the circus should they ever have to leave. Clearly the circus does not necessarily offer children any idyllic escape from the perils of poverty and drugs. It's a life that can

*Mark Oliver Gebel.
Photo courtesy of Ringling Bros.
and Barnum & Bailey Combined
Shows, Inc.*

*Lorenzo Pisoni. Photo courtesy of Pickle
Family Circus*

*1989 Clyde Beatty – Cole Bros. cook house.
The flag indicates meals are being served.
Photo by W. H. Rough*

make a child grow old fast. But then idyllic child-hoods can be hard to come by in other branches of society these days.

On the other hand, circus kids often demonstrate, along with their impressive performing skills, a little more energy and dedication to hard work, a greater ease in dealing with people, a high degree of tolerance, a worldly self-sufficiency, a better sense of time and space, and a greater facility for travel than some of their non-circus peers. Even if they are "deadheading" non-performers, they learn discipline at an early age. They know not to stick fingers in cages, not to leave the yard, and to watch out for tractors, the back ends of horses, and the front ends of elephants. And finally, performers at an early age learn to control the fears that plague us all, children and adults alike: of failing, and of falling. Among the hundreds of reasonably happy and well-adjusted kids traveling with American circuses is Mark Oliver Gebel, who will take over his famous father's elephant act after the completion of Gunther Gebel–Williams' farewell tour with Ringling. Another is fourteen year old Lorenzo Pisoni, born and raised on the Pickle Family Circus. Lorenzo even did a stint as ringmaster in 1988, and he enthusiastically continues independently as a gifted clown, acrobat, and juggler, despite the retirement of his parents from performing with the show.

For performer and roustabout alike, there is a spirit about the circus which they say can't be found in any other lifestyle. There is the freedom and adventure of travel. There are the personal rewards of transcending limitations. There is at least a steady income, with little opportunity to spend it. There is at least a place to live, and warm, like-minded people to live with. There is at least the opportunity to raise a close-knit family with old-fashioned values. Last, but certainly not least important, there is food on the table; and the food for circus people is legendary.

The Cookhouse

Like the army, the circus also moves on its stomach, and the reputation of the "cookhouse," the dining tent, is often the determining factor for an applicant seeking a circus job. Roustabouts know who has the best cooks, and owners know

that the best way to keep good help is to provide good food. Cookhouse stewards Charles Henry, "Ollie" Webb, Joe Dan Miller, and John Staley are all legendary in the business for the meals they planned. Especially sumptuous were their traditional "Christmas" dinners, always held on the Fourth of July, because circus people were always scattered in the off-season around Christmas time. In the old days, the "Hotel Ringling" fed as many as 1600 people — everyone connected with the circus, three full meals per day. An icebox wagon, a steam boiler, and a kitchen tent with field ranges and steam tables located near the cookhouse were in almost constant use.

Inside, the tables were always strictly organized according to a tight circus caste system. On the "short" side of the tent, so-called because of the short length of their tables, the owners and their families, the ticket sellers, ushers, front door men, and the "candy butchers," who were highest ranked in the circus caste system sat near the front door. Performers also sat on the "short side" of the tent, following the pecking order of riding acts, featured trapezists and wire walkers, animal trainers, acrobats, clowns, and side show "freaks." Last, if they were allowed to eat in the main cook-house tent at all, came the black side show band.

The performers were never allowed to associate with non-performers, and they were separated by a curtain from the "long side" of the cookhouse. There, all the workers and their crew bosses ate at longer twelve foot tables. Black roustabouts had their own separate dining tent. Regardless of racial and caste discrimination, however, everyone connected with the circus was served the same food. A tip to the waiter might have brought some extra milk and butter, but no one went hungry.

On the modern truck shows, it is mostly the roustabouts who are fed in the cookhouse, whereas the owners, managers, and performers tend to eat in their own mobile homes and trailers. Racial discrimination and formal dining traditions have virtually disappeared. But the cookhouse is still the first truck to arrive at a new stand in time to prepare breakfast, and the first to leave late that afternoon for the next stand. And the cookhouse flag still goes up at meal times inviting any hungry circus employee to eat all he or she wants.

Spreading canvas.
Photo by L. G. Hoh

1989 Clyde Beatty – Cole Bros.
Fishersville, VA. Photo by L. G. Hoh

Hammer gang. 1989 Great American
Circus, Charlottesville, VA.
Photo by W. H. Rough

RAISING THE TENT

All major circus big tops are now made of long-lasting polyvinyl, except for the Circus World Museum's and Hanneford's, but fortunately no one talks of raising a "vinyl." Despite the Beatty–Cole Show's retirement of the last canvas three-ring big top in 1988, the word "canvas" is still used. It's relatively rare to hear old-time circus people use the word "tent," which they continue to call a "canvas" or a "top." Stuart Thayer suggests quite logically that the word "top" comes from "topped canvas," so-called to distinguish it from an open-to-the-sky arena with canvas sidewalls.[9] Our use of the word "tent" may be frowned upon by circus purists; nonetheless, for clarity among non-circus audiences, we've slipped it in occasionally.

Circus big tops can easily cover a space larger than a football field. Size is usually expressed first by the diameter of the circular ends, and then by the number and width of the sections placed between the ends. Within the last half-century, in 1946, for example, one of the largest Ringling tents had six center poles joining five 60-foot sections with 200-foot round ends, making it a total of 500 feet long, and providing over 91,400 square feet of circus magic. The old Barnum and Bailey show had even larger tops: In 1886, they used 252-foot rounds with four 59-foot centers, making a tent that was 252 feet wide by 488 feet long (109,350 square feet); and in 1892, their top had 220-foot rounds and five 56-foot centers, making it 500 feet long (99,620 square feet). Historian Joe McKennon reports that an even earlier Barnum & Bailey tent had eight poles and may have been 600 feet long, with a declared capacity of 10,000 spectators. By comparison, the big modern Carson & Barnes push-pole tent has 150-foot rounds, and center sections totalling 246 feet. It is thus 396 feet ("a full city block") long, and provides 54,600 square feet, or about half the space of the 1886 Barnum & Bailey big top. According to their press release, the Italian polyvinyl top is made by Scola Teloni, and it bridges a total of eight center poles. The new Beatty–Cole vinyl tent, made by Anchor Tents in Sarasota, Florida, has 140-foot rounds, and three 48-foot center sections. It is 283 feet long and has four center poles. And the Vargas tent, new in 1988, has 150-foot

rounds and three 50-foot centers. While these contemporary shows are not as big as the biggest, clearly, the charge that the big tented circus is a thing of the past is wholly inappropriate.

One of the first trucks to arrive on a new lot, along with the cookhouse, is the stake driver. The innovation of the mechanical stake driver has all but done away with the "hammer gangs" of yesterday, and has considerably reduced the time and energy required to raise a big top. Stakes can number from a few hundred to thousands, depending on the size of the show. The old wooden bull and jigger stakes which secured the center poles could be as much as four inches thick and six feet long. Today's stakes are usually wooden for dirt lots, and steel for asphalt parking lots. Some circuses carry both varieties for flexibility, and others rely on steel pins for all conditions. The stakes are driven 24 to 30 inches into the ground. The number depends on their function: most are for the "stake line" which secures the edges of the circus top; other stakes are driven for extra tent strength and for high wire and other aerial apparatus.

Elephants have been used for over a hundred years to raise the big top, and they are still the most efficient and impressive power source traveling with the circus. Crowds often gather in the early morning to watch the elephants work, and few owners want to disappoint them. Most shows advertise the tent-raising as a special free event, and it's not unusual to see school buses lined up at the circus lot at 8:00 a.m. Elephant tent-raising has taken the place of the circus parade and the balloon ascent as a way of arousing anticipation and building audiences.

Bale-Ring Method

There are two basic methods for raising the top, and there is still heated debate among circus experts as to which method is the better, safer, faster, or cleaner-looking. Historians don't agree on which was developed first, or whether they evolved at about the same time. The bale-ring top is raised on elevated poles, just as sails were raised on the masts of old sailing ships. The push-pole top is pushed up by the poles as they are dragged into place underneath it. The former thus has a naval origin, and the latter undoubtedly owes its roots to field army traditions.

The bale-ring tent-raising procedure is now used by the Clyde Beatty–Cole Brothers and the Vargas Circuses and others, just as it has been used by most of the larger big top circuses of the last century. The driving process begins before the sun is up, while the crew is positioning the center poles, quarter poles, and the side poles. "Toe pin" stakes are driven to mark the positioning of the center poles and to prevent them from sliding when they are raised. Today's center poles are sometimes made in two or three sections of aluminum that can be sleeved together prior to the set-up. In the early years, they were solid 50- to 70-foot logs of Oregon fir; for strength, the lower, heavier end of the tree served as the top of the pole. A spoked, forged steel "bale ring," anywhere from one to three feet in diameter, is slipped over the base of the center pole. The canvas, as well as all the aerial rigging, will later be laced to the bale ring. A heavy block of wood, approximately one by three feet and rounded on the bottom, is attached to the bottom of the pole with a pin or a sleeve. This "mud block" will allow the pole to roll on its base as it is being raised, distribute its weight over a larger surface, and prevent it from sinking into the mud. All the cables and guidelines which will be used for steadying the poles as they are raised are then lashed to the main guy bull and jigger stakes located beyond the stake line.

A spool truck next makes several passes over the site, unwinding sections of the big top adjacent to the center poles; alternatively, as in the Vargas and many smaller operations, bundles of carefully folded canvas may be dropped at strategic ground locations. For a bale-ring tent, the elephants raise the first center pole, which will be used for leverage in raising the other poles. In 1989, co-owner Johnny Pugh came up with a new method for raising his four center poles on the Clyde Beatty–Cole Brothers Circus. The poles are connected by steel cable; the hydraulic system on the spool truck, identical to that used to haul in the nets on commercial fishing trawlers, is used to winch the four poles up simultaneously.

As soon as the poles are up, the canvas is spread out manually; the sections are speedily laced together by a simple and efficient zipper-like system of rope loops and lashed to the bale ring. When the canvas crew have guyed the big top out to the stake line and inserted all the side poles, it takes on the appearance of an enormous oval soup bowl. In areas where there is any possibility of major wind, storm guys are also used as added safety ties to prevent a potential "blow-down."

A "blow-down" can happen in any freak wind condition, and it is still one of a circus man's greatest fears. Every circus has experienced it at one time or another. It can cause physical injury and considerable damage to the top and circus property. Downpours can create large water pockets heavy enough to rip the canvas and snap the side poles, and high winds can lift quarter poles right off the ground. Dealing with a storm is not much

1989 Clyde Beatty–Cole Bros. stake line. Photo by W. H. Rough

Working elephants. 1989 Carson & Barnes, Menomenee Falls, WI. Photo by W. H. Rough

fun for anyone. Spectators are generally reluctant to leave the deceptive safety of a tent to go out into the weather, and the men know that tugging on wet guy ropes can tear the skin off raw hands. They also know that lightning is an ever-present danger when standing in ankle-deep water, and that stressed tent stakes can pull free from saturated mud at any time. With all these potential dangers, circus managers and all hands pull together. Every possible precaution to prevent a blow-down is taken, including parking the big trucks on the windward side of the tent to act as a wind break, extra storm guys, and regular emergency drills for evacuating and lowering the tent as rapidly as possible in a high wind. As a result, serious injuries from a blow-down are extremely rare.

Once the "guying out" is completed, ropes and chains are attached leading from the bale-ring, over the top of each pole, back through a pulley at its base, and out to a harnessed elephant. On signal, the elephant teams "pull peaks," raising the bale-rings approximately halfway up the poles. Sometimes this is done on one pole at a time, but other circuses pull all peaks at the same time in order to provide less stress on the tent material and the poles. This sight of the giant canvas taking its first breath and heaving itself off the ground has inspired many a poet and young runaway, and it remains a sure crowd-pleaser today. As soon as they can get under the canvas, crews of men and elephants quickly begin to insert the quarter poles into the canvas and pull them to a 35 degree upright position. Cries of "Move up!," "Move Back!," and "Stop!" echo under the tent as the elephant trainers and their beasts "shoot" the quarter poles into place. A quarter pole is a lighter, smaller pole with a long slender prong in one end that stabs through a grommeted hole in the canvas. The supposed invention of Old "Doc" Spalding, quarter poles are necessary for the prevention of water pockets, and to elevate the canvas from sagging onto the patrons' heads if the tent is over 110 feet wide. Still larger tents may use two sets of quarter poles, long ones and shorter ones, to bridge the distance from the center poles to the tent perimeter.

There is considerable variation among methods for "shooting," or raising the quarter poles. Jimmy "the Whale" Whalen, the great boss canvas man for the Ringling show for almost thirty years, preferred to use teams of horses, because he considered them faster and more maneuverable under the low canvas than elephants. Later, the Ringling show, as well as some smaller contemporary circuses elected to use tractors or teams of men to shoot the quarter poles. After they are in place, the bale rings can then be pulled to their full height, often five or more stories high.

Push-Pole Method

The push-pole method of raising a top is simpler, and just as suitable for small circus tents, although many veterans will insist that it can't

Bale ring. Photo by W. H. Rough

Beatty–Cole: "Ready to rise." Note mud block on base of main pole, and bale ring in place. Photo by Joan Z. Rough

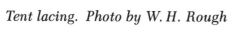

Tent lacing. Photo by W. H. Rough

Spool truck. Photo by W. H. Rough

1989 Clyde Beatty – Cole Bros.
Photo by L. G. Hoh

Ankle-deep. Photo by L. G. Hoh

Pulling peaks.
Photo by Joan Z. Rough

Shooting quarter poles.
1989 Carson & Barnes.
Photo by W. H. Rough

"Heave it. Weave it . . . !"
Photo by Joan Z. Rough

look as tight and finished as a bale-ring tent. On the other hand, the Carson & Barnes Circus has the biggest contemporary tent in the world; yet it's a push-pole design with crisp clean-looking lines. Its owner carries the nickname "Push-Pole Shorty," and indeed D. R. claims his system is faster, simpler, and safer. His big top goes up in under three hours, and comes down in an incredible hour and a half. For the push-pole process, all center and quarter poles are laid out on the ground in assigned locations. The canvas is then spread over the poles; its pieces are laced together and attached to the center poles. Bale-rings, no longer essential for raising the tent, may or may not be used for simplifying the attachment of rigging and allowing a space for heat ventilation at each pole. The pronged side poles at one end are inserted through grommet holes in the canvas, and elephants, horses, or tractors are then used to shoot the base of each quarter and center pole into place. As the canvas slowly begins to rise from one end, small canvas crews work their way down the length of the tent and "hand-guy out," rhythmically tugging on the guy lines, tightening and lashing them in place: "Heave it! Weave it! Shake it! Take it! Break it! Make it! . . . Move along."

Circus Seating

Whichever the method, once the big top is up, other crews go quickly to work attaching the side walls, mounting the rigging for the aerialists, setting up the seating, and spotting all the props and necessary equipment. Seating has been one of the more challenging items for circuses to transport and maintain, and many managers and owners take great pride in the seating systems they have invented. The now-standard jack-and-stringer system, whereby boards are lashed across lightweight wooden jack frames, providing an easily dismantled, portable bleacher-like structure, was another of the inventions of Doc Spalding. But the collapse of even small grandstands which are not properly maintained or are poorly made can lead to major injuries, as was alleged in 1986 with regards to the Toby Tyler Circus. On June 16, in New York State, seventy people were injured when a section of seating collapsed prior to a performance. Subsequent legal actions shut down all operations of the Toby Tyler Circus and all assets were frozen. The operations of all circuses have been adversely affected by increases in insurance rates resulting from this accident. That one event has also resulted in a new wave of anti-circus legislation which has been of as much concern to every conscientious, legitimate, safety-conscious circus owner, as it has been to the less responsible ones.

A great deal of energy has been spent on the design of safe and efficient seating systems for circuses. David Rawls, co-owner of the Kelly–Miller Circus, designed a new modified jack system for his seating. It uses locking steel triangular jacks which are ultra-safe and just as portable. Since the seating requires no lashing, it is much

Jacks and stringers.
Photo by W. H. Rough

faster to erect and dismantle. Often, larger shows, such as the Beatty–Cole, combine a reinforced stringer-and-jack system with folding chairs for its reserve section, with specially designed trailer trucks that cleverly incorporate fold-out bleacher seating. Carson & Barnes uses modular steel seating units, supported by steel jacks. Each unit folds flat and is lifted onto flatbed trucks by elephant-powered winches for transport from site to site. Duke Keller's small open-air Wilder Bros. Circus has two very clever seat wagons designed from converted buses, and a trailer carrying a third section of seating; the units seat 300 people altogether, and each of the three has a canvas canopy that rolls out to shade the seats. The ultimate in circus seating systems, however, was the invention of Art Concello, general manager and former aerialist with the Ringling show in the '40's. His portable "Artony" grandstand revolutionized the circus industry, providing fast, safe, and comfortable seating. Folding upholstered chairs were bolted to accordion-like folding platforms incorporated onto flatbed trailers. Once they were towed into place, a jeep provided the power to unfold them into inclined decks which together formed a great steel bowl.

The Rings

At the center of the bowl, whether steel or wooden, are the 42-foot rings, the real core of the circus experience. The three-ring circus is commonly thought to be a strictly American tradition, and in fact it is one of the characteristics that now distinguish American circuses from their European counterparts. Actually the first use of a three-ring circus was by George Sanger in England in 1860.[10] Barnum didn't get around to it in this country until he joined up with Bailey in 1881, and insisted on giving the American people more for their money. That was nine years after he first claimed to have three rings; but he was counting the hippodrome track as one, solely in order to out-draw Andrew Haight's Great Eastern Circus & Menagerie's two-ring format.

Most American circuses, even some of the small ones, now carry three rings, although there is considerable variation. Some of the newer circuses, like Flora, Pickle, Big Apple, and Soleil, have adopted the European tradition of a single ring. We often forget that the single ring was the norm in American circuses too, before Coup and Barnum made the change to two. Single ring advocates claim it is better to focus attention on one display of artistry at a time, and that more is not necessarily better, even if it's commercially more profitable! On the other hand, the big Carson & Barnes Circus top contains five rings of continuous action, in the grand tradition of Barnum.

Big Top Designs

While the push-pole and the bale-ring systems are the two traditional methods for raising large circus tents, other systems and variations have been and continue to be explored. In 1942, a

Trusses and tent going up. Photo courtesy of Big Apple Circus

The Gold Unit, 1988. Photo courtesy of Ringling Bros. and Barnum & Bailey Combined Shows, Inc.

banner year for the Ringling show, Norman Bel Geddes was the official designer. This theatrical veteran, with many Broadway plays and the interior design of the Pan Am Clipper to his credit, was responsible in that year for Gargantua's special display tent. Furthermore, he dreamed of an ambitious and impressive circus tent of the future, which was described in the official program for that year. It would have been supported by steel scaffolding towers 160 feet high, three times as high as the show's then-current center poles. The canvas would have been supported from these huge towers by steel cabling which was entirely outside the tent structure, leaving the interior free of obstruction. The playing space would have been easily large enough for three rings arranged centrally in a triangular pattern. The tent would have been expensive, and it might have created enormous stress on both the scaffolding and the canvas; it was never built.

The newest and most contemporary circus tents, however, employ structural scaffolding which looks startlingly similar to the Bel Geddes tent. The new French and Italian tents used by the Big Apple Circus, the Circus Flora, the Cirque du Soleil, and the Tarzan Zerbini Circus are designed around four truss-like towers. These towers are joined in pairs by two 40-foot connecting trusses. Initially, the top, lashed to an oval cupola in the center, is located under the towers on a specially designed flatbed truck. As the cupola is raised to a height of 42 feet by cables attached to the towers, the tent unfolds below it. The sides are then guyed out to a conventional stake line. These tents are round and relatively small, containing only the single ring and holding around 1500 people. But in the European tradition, they offer a crisp and colorful appearance, and the more intimate sightlines have minimal interference from poles.

The high-tech tent for the Ringling Brothers and Barnum & Bailey Gold Unit was designed by Ogawa, a Japanese manufacturer, to withstand 90 mph winds and a five inch snow load. It's a square-cornered tent, covering an acre and a half.

Its sixteen cupola'd peaks are created by two rows of eight center poles, and no quarter poles, and it will seat 8,000 people. In 1989, another radically new tent design was being tested for possible use in Ringling's international tours, using aluminum roof trusses and inflatable sidewalls instead of poles. It would seat 8,500 spectators in air-conditioned comfort, a concept that was tried only once before by Johnny North and Art Concello and ended in failure. And still another new top design by Future Tents, Ltd. of Manhattan is under development for the Pickle Family Circus. Traditionally they have played under open skies with a sidewall only, or in auditoriums, but they expect to change all that in the '90's. Clearly, the 1990's could be witness to a revolution in completely new circus tent designs.

One sure indication that the circus business is on the increase is that the tent-makers' business is on the increase. Anchor Industries' custom tent manufacturing operations, one of the nation's largest, moved into a new 41,000 square foot Florida facility at the end of 1989. Only three years earlier, Anchor had bought the Leaf Tent Company, founded by a former Ringling show employee, and the increase in orders required the move to a larger factory. Other major circus tent manufacturers are also doing a brisk business, judging from the number of new vinyl big tops that mushroomed across the country in 1988 and 1989.

Despite the warm, nostalgic feelings that the sight and smell of a circus tent can bring on, it is clear that a tent doth not a circus make. No one would take away the "circus" from the title of the open-air Pickle Family Circus or the arena-bound Ringling Brothers and Barnum & Bailey Circus merely because they do not appear under a big top. And if we could learn all there is to know about life in the back yard, and how a circus advertises and moves, we would still not understand the phenomenon of the circus itself, and what it is that people come to see. The true spirit of the circus is in the people whose skills are exhibited, and it is to them that we now turn our attention.

6.

WHAT A BODY CAN DO

It's time! We're going to the circus. Our first sight is the midway, a gauntlet of colorful temptations that stretches out between us and the main entrance to the tent. In a building, it might only be a concession stand or two, but on a traditional tented circus lot, there is still a glimmer of what the big midways of a half century ago must have looked like. There is much to see and hear, and still plenty of reason for arriving early on the lot: time for exchanging whatever free or reduced-price coupons we have managed to collect for tickets; time for the kids to pull us toward the moon walk, the snake pit, or the elephant rides; time to stock up on a supply of enough cotton candy and cherry snow cones to turn hair and fingers sticky and lips bright red; and time to take in the colored lights and brilliant bannerline paintings of exotic animals and clowns. The bug-men who used to sell chameleons and fish are gone, and the old pirate sword has been replaced by the star-wars variety of light sword as the most popular souvenir, but there are also still balloons, pennants, miniature bullwhips, and a variety of other toys and souvenirs for sale. If we resist them all now, never mind: the candy butchers will continue to hawk their wares during the show, until someone in the family is persuaded to break down and buy. After all, concessions are a major source of income for both the show and the butchers, so Grandma is helping to keep the circus in business when she spoils her grandson.

Circuses no longer carry the big menagerie tents of yesterday, with their hundreds of exotic creatures on display before the show. The side shows have also faded from prominence, although the Kelly–Miller Circus still carries a nice little one with some animals, some snakes, some magic, and some fire-eating. But the midway still con-jures up echoes of the great side shows of the past, which displayed every conceivable variety of human being and strange feat. "LADIES AND GENTLEMEN!" called out the talkers and grinders from their raised platforms, tipping their straw hats and tapping their canes. "STEP RIGHT UP! FOR ONLY ONE THIN DIME, DARE TO EXPERIENCE FOR YOURSELF THE ONE, THE ONLY, THE WORLD'S LARGEST, STRONGEST...IT WALKS, IT TALKS, IT CRAWLS ON ITS BELLY!!!

SIDE SHOWS

Side shows offered a wide range of strange entertainers and "monsters," human and otherwise. The entertainers included among others: magicians, contortionists, ventriloquists, Punch & Judy puppeteers, fortune-tellers and mind-readers, sword swallowers, snake charmers, strong men, tattooed men and women, knife and hatchet-throwers, and minstrels. There were fire-eaters, human blow-torches, and spectacular fire dancers like Queen Dora, a black side show artist. Almost any exhibit suggesting the extremes of human behavior was sought after by the side show entrepreneurs. The Sells–Floto show even tried to hire the notorious "cannibal," Al Packer, to appear as a "freak" on their side show. Packer had allegedly fed on five of his fellow prospectors in order to survive the severe winter of 1874 while trapped in the Colorado wilderness. He was perhaps wrongly convicted of murdering them, and served fifteen years in prison; but he had the sense to reject the Sells–Floto offer and end his days raising rabbits and tending his flower garden.[1]

When the golden days of the side show ended, most performers made the transition to carnivals

1989 Kelly–Miller, Frederick, MD. Photo by W. H. Rough

Side shows at "The Big One," 1934. Photo courtesy of Circus World Museum, Baraboo, WI

Photo by L. G. Hoh

1989 Big Apple, Shelburne, VT.
Photo by W. H. Rough

Snake Pit bill. 1989 Kelly–Miller.
Photo by W. H. Rough

and fairs, as well as to television variety shows like Ed Sullivan's and more recently *That's Incredible* and *Incredible Sunday.*

The word "monster" was initially a medical term derived from the Latin root meaning to warn; the word "monitor" comes from the same root. So "monster" referred to any creature different from the normal, about whom the public must be warned. There were some animal monsters, like giant gorillas and two-headed calves, but for the most part circus "monsters" were all too human on the inside. They ranged from albinos and pinheads to wolf boys and alligator girls, from the world's tallest to the world's smallest, from the hairiest to the baldest, from the fattest to the thinnest. James Bailey, by the way, paid his fat lady fifty cents per pound per week; in a hot midsummer week, she might lose fifty pounds or so, but she was weighed in regularly every Thursday to determine her salary. The grinders often called them "freaks," a word offensive to the performers themselves. The Barnum & Bailey side show performers staged the famous "Uprising of the Freaks" in London in 1898, presumably to protest the use of the word. While there is some conjecture that the whole thing could have been staged as a publicity event, they were successful in getting their banners altered to read "Prodigies." In his book on side show performers, Frederick Drimmer calls them "very special people," because they "carry a special burden and they carry it with dignity and courage."[2]

There are many reasons for the decline of the side show on American circuses. Times change, and the conscience of middle America grew embarrassed by the whole idea of displaying human oddities for commercial gain. Our guilt at having been granted a "normal" body, whatever that is, added to our moral outrage, and we called for an end to the "inhuman" practices of the side show. Not all performers would agree: side shows were in fact one of the few ways in which society permitted them to earn an honest living. As Dick Best pointed out in Drimmer's book, people didn't hire alligator girls for receptionists, nurses, and babysitters.[3] A second factor in the side show's demise was the impressive success of the medical community in preventing or correcting the extreme birth defects like Siamese twins that people were

paying to see. Finally, society itself has made great strides in assimilating the casualties of birth and war into its mainstream. We still have a long way to go, but never before have so many "abnormalities" been accepted as normal variations on the human condition.

"LADEEZ AND GENTLEMEN!"

The main show is about to begin, and it will begin promptly as advertised. "STEP RIGHT UP, LADEEEZ AND GENTLEMEN! FOR ONLY ONE DOLLAR MORE...." There may be one more stop we'll want to make just inside the tent, to buy seats in the "reds," the traditional reserved seats on the front or back side of the tent. The view from there is much better than from the blue seats in the general admission area around the ends, and for some shows, the reds are real chairs, and not bleachers. We reach our seats just in time. As the lights go down, and unread programs are tucked away, a spotlight comes up on the "ringmaster" standing in front of the cage in center ring: "LADIES AND GENTLEMEN, CHILDREN OF ALL AGES! WELCOME TO THE ONE HUNDRED AND TWENTIETH EDITION OF THE...." Every word is crystal clear. Every syllable is stretched to three.

Instinctively, we know he's talking to us, and not to the kids. It's still another paradoxical expression, that: "Children of all ages." So much of the circus is lost on young children. What we are about to see is real, and not magic, but for children everything is still magic. They have no context within which to appreciate just how close-to-impossible many of these performances will be. We ought never to confuse a circus performer with a stage actor or a movie star, whose job is to present us with the illusion of reality and make us believe in it. The circus performer's job is to defy our preconceptions and present us with the real thing itself, and make us believe in that. How often have we seen at the circus a father cradling a wide-eyed young son in his lap, and pointing up at the flying frame: "Look at that. Now watch what she's going to do now. Wooow! Can you believe...?" Of course he believes it; it's the father who is having trouble believing it and is much more impressed. The child addressed by the ringmaster is in the father, and not the son.

We just called that man with the microphone a "ringmaster," but is he really? In all likelihood, he is wearing a bright red jacket, a black silk top hat, white riding breeches, and tall gleaming black boots. It is the traditional formal riding habit of the old English equestrian schools, and this man is the descendant of the riding masters who were proprietors of such schools. According to Joe McKennon, the "ringmaster" is the man in charge of a one-ring circus performance.[4] Stuart Thayer suggests that the title first came into use in the 1820's, to describe a kind of master of ceremonies and straight man for the clown. It was his job also to stand in the center of the ring and hold the leads for the bareback riders; he was always associated with horse acts. When the performances grew to larger two and three-ring productions, the men who arranged and announced the acts, first with bells, and later with whistles, came to be known as "equestrian directors." They did not necessarily

have to be oriented towards horsemanship: The great flyer Alfredo Codona was an excellent equestrian director for the Hagenbeck–Wallace/ Adam Forepaugh/Sells Bros. Combined Show in 1935.

Probably the most famous equestrian director in America was Fred Bradna, who spent over forty years with the Barnum & Bailey and then the combined Ringling Brothers and Barnum & Bailey Circus. He never once made an announcement, but his whistle governed the progress of the entire show. Conversely, his ringmasters, in charge of each ring, could make announcements; but they weren't allowed to blow a whistle. Today, large circuses often use the term "performance director," for an artistic personnel director who doesn't necessarily appear in the ring. Finally, the "announcer," who may sing and be covered with sequins, but who may not have any managerial, equestrian, or ring responsibilities, is the true identity of the man now before us, in the guise of

"Singing ringmaster" Jim Ragona.
Photo courtesy of Ringling Bros. and Barnum & Bailey Combined Shows, Inc.

Clyde Beatty–Cole Bros' Jimmy James.
Photo by W. H. Rough

a riding master and calling himself a ringmaster. On the other hand, just to further confuse the issue, one person often performs several of the roles, as does the very capable ex-clown Jimmy James for the Beatty–Cole show. The end result of all this blurring and mixing of jobs and incorrect usage, is that the word "ringmaster" is gradually coming into use as a general title for the emcee of any circus performance.

We don't mean to imply that the field is entirely limited to men, either. Among the several capable women in the role of "ringmistress" is Miss Charlie Hackett on the Royal Hanneford Circus. Charlie joined the circus as a clown in 1985, but was so convinced that she wanted to be a singing ringmistress that she had her voice surgically lowered to be more effective. She is following in the footsteps of Tommy Hanneford's mother Katherine, who performed as ringmistress in the center ring until she was ninety-three years old, and his grandmother, "Nana."

"AND NOW...
ON WITH THE SHOW!!"

If there are to be lions and tigers at all, the customary opening act for the traditional three-ring circus is the cage act in center ring. The self-supporting bars of the show cage, along with the tunnel cage or cage train bringing in the animals, are usually in place before the performance, because they take a while to set up. All other animal acts, with the exception of the elephants, are traditionally performed before the intermission as well, so they can be promptly fed and loaded following their final performances and on their way to the next stand. The elephants are traditionally the last act of the show, not only because they tend to require extensive clean-up behind them, but because they are often used in the tear-down procedures after the final blow-off.

We'll deal with all the animal acts, including the horses, around whom the modern circus was originally founded, in Chapter 8. But for now, our concern is strictly with those performers who will in the next two hours, stretch our notions of what the human body can do. They are called in circus lingo, "kinkers," presumably because they must constantly be stretching the kinks and sore-

ness out of their muscles. It must be borne in mind that most performers stay with any one show for only a year or two, before moving on to other shows. In this way, each circus maintains its freshness and vitality. Therefore, although contemporary acts discussed in this chapter were recently with the identified circuses as indicated, we use them here as examples. They may no longer be associated with the circus cited.

In his *A History of the Circus in America*, George Chindahl identifies a bewildering 200 or so circus acts. We cannot possibly begin to cover them all in this brief chapter. In *Circus Techniques*, Hovey Burgess simplifies our problem by dividing all the acts into three broad categories: vaulting, which includes leaping and flying; equilibristics, or balancing; and juggling. All three can be combined in a variety of ways, and all three can be done on the ground and in the air.

The aerialists are as good a place as any for us to begin, but before we do, one last brief note applies to all performers, on the ground or in the air, jugglers, vaulters, and balance artists. Every performer learns how to render a "style," as a part of his or her act. A traditional part of every circus performance, a style is the moment when the artist turns to the audience and gestures that it's an appropriate moment to express appreciation for the trick about to be performed or just accomplished. They say to us in the audience, "This trick's hard; watch closely," or "We did it!" Sometimes it happens in an unrehearsed, spontaneous fashion after a particularly difficult trick, and then it's especially hard to resist the resulting exhilaration that sweeps over performers and audience alike. On the face of the performer, a grimace of concentration changes to a grin of joyous satisfaction as he opens himself up to the audience, probably with a boisterous "Hey!" designed to outdo any earlier styles. He fully deserves our enthusiastic applause.

IN THE AIR

There is perhaps no other circus act which so captures the essence of what it is for a human being to exceed his limitations as does the trapeze. "I can do that," murmurs the mesmerized little girl far below, while the band plays the deceptively

Elvin Bale on the single trap.
Photo courtesy of Elvin Bale

comforting strains of a waltz. "He makes it look so easy." But it isn't, of course. The job of some circus performers may be to take a basically simple and easily-executed trick and make it look daring and complicated. But it is the job of the trapeze artist to take an inherently dangerous and difficult trick and make it look easy. Flight dreams are the substance of our unconscious, fulfilling our wish for the unattainable like some kind of science-fiction film. The sight of a human body in mid-air, in total defiance of the restrictive laws of gravity, is a magnificent image. It's an image which often serves as a powerful metaphor, re-inforcing our defiance of all the other laws which hold us down to a mundane existence. No wonder that most of us who ever wanted to run away to join a circus, first wanted to be trapeze artists.

"He flies through the air with the greatest of ease. That daring young man on the flying trapeze." That song, written in 1868 by Gaston Lyle and George Leybourne, was modelled on a young man who revolutionized the art of the trapeze. Prior to the middle of the 19th century, trapeze acts consisted of flyers leaping from one ground-based bar to another. Then young Jules Léotard hung two trapeze bars from ropes over the swimming pool in his father's gymnasium in Toulouse, France, and began to train. Nine years later, on November 12, 1859, at Paris' Cirque Na-poléon, which is now the famous Cirque d'Hiver,

Jules dressed up in the new skintight costume which now bears his name, and performed what he had learned. Both his tights and his flying act were an overnight sensation. Soon, single and double somersaults were being thrown by new flyers all over Europe and America. In 1870 a catcher was added on the second bar, which be-came known as the catch trap.

A triple somersault was considered an impos-sibility until a little Latvian teenager named Lena Jordan accomplished it in 1897. But by the fol-lowing year she had grown too big to repeat it. It took twelve more years for Ernest Clarke to be-gin a thirty year career of throwing triples into the hands of his brother Charles. Antoinette Concello, billed as the "world's greatest woman aerialist," and the Ringling show's future aerial director, was the first woman to perform the triple regularly. It is still only rarely performed, and has earned the legendary title of "the Big Trick." The effort now is to achieve the longest unbroken string of triples, a record held as of this writing by eighteen-year-old Jaime Ibarra. Ibarra established a new record of 118 consecutive triples, at Circus World Museum on September 17, 1989, breaking Martin Alvarez' 1984 record.

In January of 1981, after years of effort, Tito Gaona was probably the first to succeed in throw-ing a quadruple backward somersault, but it was only in a rehearsal, witnessed but not recorded,

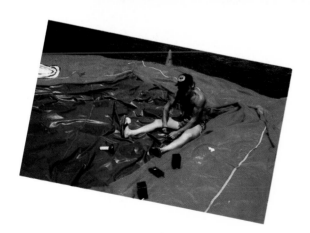

★★★★★★★ TENTS ★★★★★★★

Clockwise from left: Photo by L. G. Hoh. Carson & Barnes, 1989, photo by W. H. Rough. "Heave it . . ." 1989 Great American Circus, photo by W. H. Rough. Franzen repairs, photo by L. G. Hoh. Center: 1989 Great American Circus, photo by W. H. Rough.

✦✦✦✦✦✦✦✦ ANIMALS ✦✦✦✦✦✦✦✦

Clockwise from left: Photo by Joan Z. Rough. Photo by L. G. Hoh. Circus World Museum, photo by Joan Z. Rough. Josip Marcan, photo by Jim Carpenter, courtesy of The Daily Progress, *Charlottesville, VA. David Rosaire's Stagecoach West, 1990 Big Apple, photo by Joan Z. Rough. 1989 Clyde Beatty – Cole Bros., photo by Joan Z. Rough.*

★ ★ ★ ★ ★ ★ ★ ★ ARTISTS ★ ★ ★ ★ ★ ★ ★ ★ ★

*Clockwise from left: Ron, 1989 Roberts Bros., photo by Joan Z. Rough. Father David Tetrault, the Circus Priest, photo by W. H. Rough.
Gunther Gebel – Williams, photo courtesy of Ringling Bros. and Barnum & Bailey Combined Shows, Inc. Photo courtesy of Circus of the Kids.
Circus World Museum Windjammers, photo by W. H. Rough. Longjeans (John Kelly), photo courtesy of John Kelly. Ben Williams and Anna
May, The Woodcock Performing Elephants, 1989 Big Apple Circus, photo by W. H. Rough. 1989 Clyde Beatty – Cole Bros., photo by Joan Z.
Rough. Center: Ten-year-old Enrique Suarez, Jr. in flight, 1990 Big Apple Circus, photo by Joan Z. Rough.*

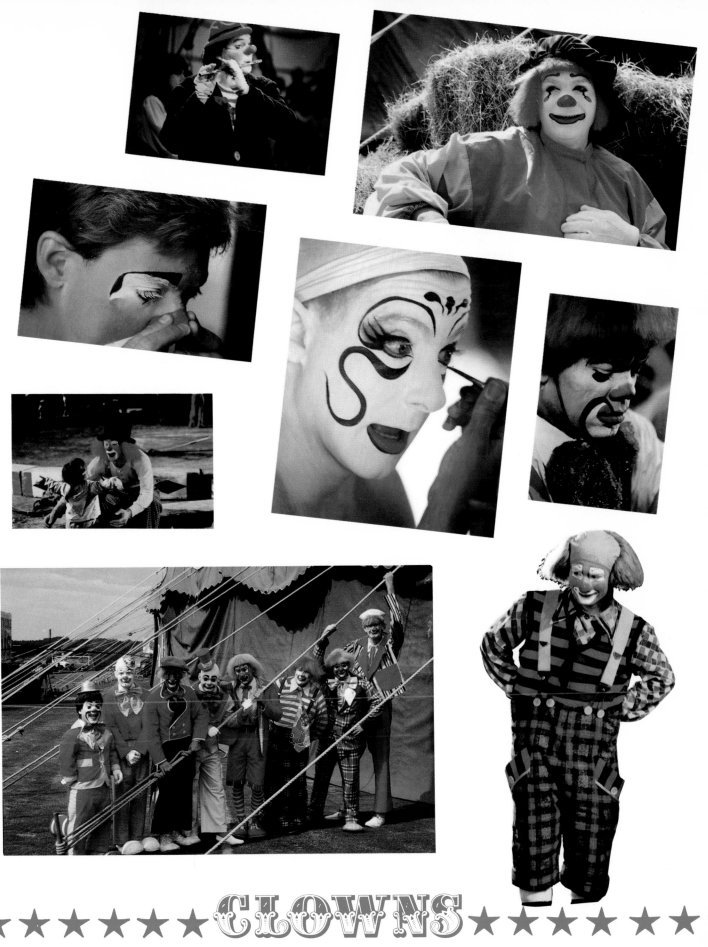

★★★★★★★ CLOWNS ★★★★★★★★

Clockwise from left: Lorenzo Pickle (*Larry Pisoni*), 1989 Circus Flora, *photo by* W.H. Rough. *Tom Caguin, photo by* D.M. Chambers *(Elmo Gibb). David Williams, 1989 Clyde Beatty–Cole Bros., photo by Joan Z. Rough. Whizzer (Don Bridwell), photo by* D.M. Chambers. *Topper* and *friend, 1989 Clyde Beatty–Cole Bros., photo by Joan Z. Rough. Center: Sandy Kozik, photo by Jim Carpenter, courtesy of* The Daily Progress, *Charlottesville, VA.*

★ ★ ★ ★ ★ ★ ★ POSTERS ★ ★ ★ ★ ★ ★

Clockwise from left: 1932. 1904 Spec. 1913 Spec. Hagenbeck–Wallace Train, 1934. Tiger. All photos courtesy of Ringling Brothers and Barnum & Bailey Combined Shows, Inc.

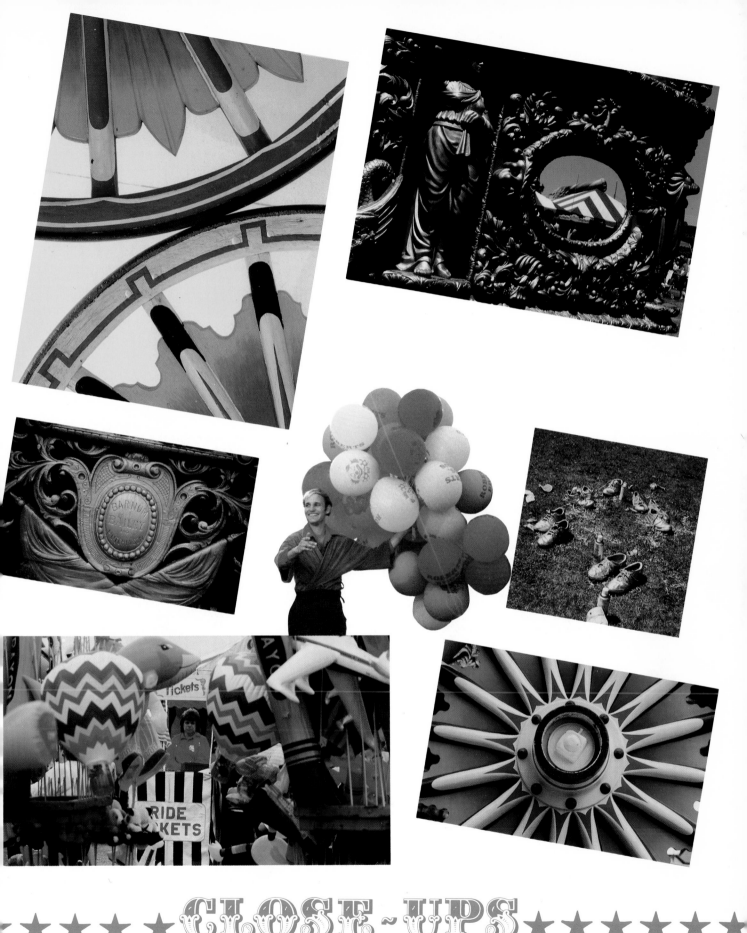

★ ★ ★ ★ ★ CLOSE-UPS ★ ★ ★ ★ ★ ★

Clockwise from left: Circus World Museum, photo by Joan Z. Rough. Photo by W. H. Rough. Photo by L. G. Hoh. Photo by W. H. Rough.
Photo by Joan Z. Rough. Photo by L. G. Hoh. Center: 1989 Roberts Bros., photo by W. H. Rough.

★ ★ ★ ★ ★ ★ ★ ★ WAGONS ★ ★ ★ ★ ★ ★ ★

Clockwise from left: Twin Hemispheres bandwagon and 40-horse hitch, photo by L. G. Hoh. Swan bandwagon, photo by L. G. Hoh. Bell wagon, photo by L. G. Hoh. Cage wagon, photo by L. G. Hoh. Center: Photo by L. G. Hoh.

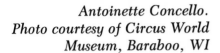

Antoinette Concello.
Photo courtesy of Circus World
Museum, Baraboo, WI

and he was never able to repeat it. Miguel Vasquez completed one in August of that year in a practice, but not until July 10, 1982, in Tucson, Arizona, did he throw a successful "quad" in performance, into the hands of his brother, Juan. Since then, the quad has been performed by relatively few flyers. Ruben Caballero, Jr. has performed them on the Carson & Barnes show. Ricardo Morales was the youngest to throw the quad in 1985, when he was thirteen, with Carson & Barnes. And sixteen-year-old Jose Luna threw two in April 1989. But Vasquez is still the champion, with more than 1,100 completions to his credit since he threw his first. He has a 65% success rate, according to the 1989 Ringling program. The quad is often called "the Biggest Trick," both because flyers dream of accomplishing it and because of its difficulty. The flyer's body is moving at about 70 mph, fast enough so that he may momentarily black out; it is up to his catcher to be there at the right time and make the catch safely.

Despite the publicity surrounding the quad, or the importance of any record-setting acrobatic "trick," the way in which it is executed is just as important as the trick itself. Trapeze artistry is about much more than records and speeds and somersaults. It's about style, precision, grace, timing, and joy. It's about discipline, love, trust, and the fluid ease with which a flyer meets his catcher in that weightless state at the top of his arc. Often even a busted attempt can result in a graceful fall. In fact, for the performer, learning how to fall into the net properly on the back or rear end is the first step in mastering a trap act; falls must happen constantly in the learning process. Other moves are just as challenging as multiple backward somersaults. Pirouettes, whirling the body in an upright position, and forward somersaults can be extremely dangerous, because the flyer can't see his target until the last minute, although these are often unappreciated by an unaware public. Passing leaps involving two flyers in the air at the same time, both returning on the same bar, are spectacular tricks. Dismounts into the safety net often involve diving twists and turns and floating double layouts which can easily result in serious injury if the flyer lands on his feet or head, and some bad cuts and bruises even if he lands on his front. A difficult rebound from the net to the catch trap makes a stunning finale to an act.

The Valentines, the Eagles, the Wards, and the Concellos were among the many talented flying troupes of the early 20th century. Art Concello was born in Spokane, Washington, of Portugese extraction. He and his wife Antoinette, who grew up in Vermont, together with their catcher, Eddie Ward, Jr. made up the Flying Concellos act, featuring two triple artists. They headlined the Ringling show soon after Alfredo Codona's injury and

Miguel Vasquez performing the "Quad." Photo courtesy of Ringling Bros. and Barnum & Bailey Combined Shows, Inc.

Lillian Leitzel. Photo courtesy of Circus World Museum, Baraboo, WI

The Flying Vasquez complete a passing leap. Photo courtesy of Ringling Bros. and Barnum & Bailey Combined Shows, Inc.

Alfredo Codona. Photo courtesy of Circus World Museum, Baraboo, WI

The Codona–Leitzel wedding day.
Photo courtesy of Circus World Museum,
Baraboo, WI

retirement in 1933. As much a businessman as an artist, Concello would eventually own every flying act in the country, rescue John Ringling North from financial disaster, and take over the managerial duties of the "Big One" after North's return in 1947. Today the flying trapeze is almost entirely dominated by outstanding proud Mexican families of artists. Among the many talented flyers are Gaona, Vasquez, Luna, Rodriguez, Rodogel, Neves, Tabares, Ibarra, Ramos, Alejandros, and Caballero—all great names, all Mexican and South American, and all following in the footsteps of the acknowledged greatest, Alfredo Codona himself.

Codona and Lietzel

Codona truly did "fly through the air with the greatest of ease." Every bit as much at home in mid-air as he was with his feet on the ground, he appeared with the Ringling Brothers and Barnum & Bailey Circus for twenty years. On his trapeze, he was almost continuously in motion, a relaxed and fluid blur of triple somersaults and double pirouette returns that displayed his brilliant perfectionism. It was said that the graceful beauty of his movement and the dreams he inspired often moved the spectators below to tears. The story of his obsessive love for the Queen of the Air, Lillian Lietzel, is a tragic circus legend.

Lillian Lietzel was another aerialist star for the Ringling show in the '20's who captured the imagination of her audiences. She opened her act

with a graceful display on the Roman rings. Roman rings suspended from ropes had come into use in gymnasiums for athletic competition in the middle of the 19th century, but they were hung at a certain height off the floor and could not be set in motion. In the circus, Lietzel and others used them in much the same way as a single trapeze, accomplishing a variety of knee or ankle hangs, dislocates, iron crosses, splits, and other acrobatic maneuvers, high over center ring and without a safety net. For the second and more famous half of her act, Lietzel worked on a single length of rope, or corde lisse, onto which a loop was attached with a swivel. Raised high in the air, she inserted her right wrist into the loop and began a series of planges, throwing her whole body over her shoulder for up to 239 revolutions. It was an incredible test of strength and endurance, if not grace. The drums rolled, and the crowd counted out each one. Less than five feet tall and under a hundred pounds, her deceptive vulnerability made thousands of fans and circus workers alike want to take her home and adopt her. Lillian was loved for her grace on the rings and her strength and determination in the plange act, a love only magnified by her reputation for childish temper tantrums and her disdain for the many men who chased her. Both the love and the tantrums resulted in her own private railroad car equipped with a piano, an unheard-of luxury for a performer. And in Lillian's turn, she came to love more than anything else her work and Alfredo Codona.

Dolly Jacobs.
Photo: Martha Swope,
courtesy of Dolly Jacobs

They were married on July 20, 1928, but less than three years later, Lillian fell from the swivel-rope on which she was performing in Denmark and died shortly afterwards. Frank McClosky, the same man who would later become an owner of the Beatty–Cole show, was her rigger at the time. He pointed out how the excessive strain of the planges had caused an invisible crystallization of the metal swivel and resulted in the fall. Codona was devastated. He remarried two years later, but he would never recover from the loss of his beloved Lillian. A year later a fall ruined his own flying career, and on July 31, 1937, he walked into a lawyer's office where he was to discuss a divorce from his second wife. Instead, he pulled out a revolver and shot both her and himself to death.

Today's Aerialists

There is a new "Queen of the Air" working in the contemporary circus who is following in Lietzel's footsteps on the Roman rings. She is Dolly Jacobs, eldest daughter of Ringling master clown Lou Jacobs and revolving ladder show girl Jean Rockwell. Dolly grew up with the circus, and as a Ringling show girl came under the influence of her godmother, Margie Geiger, the wife of a Wallenda troupe member, and the first aerialist to fully use the Roman rings as a swing. Dolly had found her element. She feels that rings give her more freedom because they are independent from each other, and they offer more possibilities than the trapeze.[5] She débuted her own swinging rings act with the Ringling show in 1976. In the next fourteen years she has also worked for the Big Apple and the Royal Hanneford Circuses, preferring the greater intimacy with the audience provided by the single ring: "Before, they were so far away I mostly worked for myself and just pretended. I couldn't see them. Here...I feel the audience and their reaction."[6] A deceptively warm and down-to-earth woman on the ground, who loves the simple things in life, Dolly soars on the rings with startling strength and grace. A fly-away dismount has become the major finale for her act: she somersaults from her rings to the web rope hanging in front of her. It's a stunt she borrowed from Frank Sheppard, although unfortunately he was killed while performing it. Dolly has twice won the Dame du Cirque Award at Monaco's Festival International du Cirque; in 1979, she also won there the City of Monte Carlo Award, and in 1988 the Silver Clown. Both the Gold and Silver Clown Awards, first and second place respectively, are the circus world's equivalent of an Oscar.

The Roman rings are only one of the variations on the trapeze which comprise aerial acts. Spanish webs, long cloth-covered ropes, hung throughout the arena are often used in those "astonishing array of aerial artistry" ballets by the show girls, who thus derived the nickname "bally broads." Their routines are far less demanding than Lietzel's on the web, but dancers often welcome the opportunity to work on aerial choreography because it allows full three dimensional movement. The big aerial ballets like that featured in Vargas' "Let Freedom Ring" spec can be quite challenging, as well as spectacular and beautiful.

The single suspended trapeze is a very different kind of act from the flying acts with which we opened our discussion. There is usually no safety net, although the performer may from time to time use a "mechanic," or safety cable attached from the equipment to a belt around his waist. Single traps are more oriented toward displaying balancing skills than vaulting, although they can do both. Their simplicity can be an ideal setting for beautiful demonstrations of skill: Marie Cristine's with Vargas, Miss Sylvia Zerbini's with Zerbini, Lorraine Flores' with Ringling, and Mark Lotz' with Beatty–Cole among them. Juggling while balanced on or hanging from the trap is a frequent addition. Solo trap acts often display the artist balanced on every conceivable portion of the human body. The head stand was introduced in 1870 by an American named Keyes Washington; modern acrobats use a small round cup screwed to the bar to better fit their head and distribute their weight. A particularly impressive stunt is one in which the performer balances on the bar as it moves in a lateral swing, rather than in the conventional front-to-back movement, thus removing the small added footing provided by centrifugal force. Cristina Kiss, part of the talented Hungarian Kiss trio, features such a routine over the center ring on the Carson & Barnes show. Some performers balance a table and chair with them on the swaying bar, or hang precariously from a heel or instep.

A pair of performers on a single trap adds even more variety and excitement. Here the terminology can also be a little confusing. According to Fred Bradna's Glossary in *The Big Top*, the routine is called a double trap act, as opposed to a trap duo, which involves two trapezes. Swinging from the bar, the upper acrobat suspends his partner below him in a variety of precariously bal-

anced positions, and some limited leaping and catching can be done. Double trap acts offer superb opportunities for artistic choreographers, and the result is often stunning. There are many fine acts in this genre who appear in almost all circuses, ranging from the powerful gymnastic athleticism of the Ringling show's Ayak Brothers, to the popular daring of Chris Kennington and Ron Pace, performing as "Sugar and Spice," with Zerbini. "Satin," featuring Pa-Mela Hernandez and Denise Aubrey, was the first aerial black act to appear with Ringling, in a 115th edition display of paired gymnastics on the bar. In an unusual twist, one of the 1989 Circus Flora's moving aerial duets began and ended on horseback. It was performed by Lisa Giobbi and Sacha Pavlata, to

Sylvia Zerbini. Photo courtesy of Tarzan Zerbini Circus

Mark Lotz, 1989 Clyde Beatty – Cole Bros.
Photo by W. H. Rough

Lynn Jacobs. Photo courtesy of
Culpepper – Merriweather Circus

Cristina Kiss, with 1989 Carson & Barnes.
Photo by W. H. Rough

Sugar and Spice.
Photo courtesy of Tarzan Zerbini Circus

Satin. Photo courtesy of Ringling Bros. and
Barnum & Bailey Combined Shows, Inc.

Lisa Giobbi and Sacha Pavlata.
1989 Circus Flora.
Photo by W. H. Rough

Jessica Hentoff and Kathie Hoyer.
1989 Circus Flora.
Photo by W. H. Rough

gentle operatic strains which coaxed them through a tender mid-air pas-de-deux. A second Flora double trap act was performed by the charming and popular team of Hentoff & Hoyer; these two young women demonstrated a lively series of unusual configurations of arms, heels, and legs. Kathie Hoyer has indicated she will move on to other areas after the 1989 season, so their double act is now history. But Jessica Hentoff, who is the daughter of jazz critic Nat Hentoff, plans to remain both as an aerialist with Flora and as a teacher with its Circus Arts School.

Double trap acts can also grow more intricate with extra props and gadgetry. A performer might employ an "iron jaw," a device inserted into the mouth which allows her to hang and spin from the bar by her teeth alone. A double iron jaw may be used by a usually lighter female under-hanger supported from the mouth of her partner, who is hanging by his knees or ankles from the bar above.

A variation on the double trapeze is the cradle act. A cradle is a stationary, oval or rectangular, tubular steel platform located high over the ring, which may be used by two or more acrobats for many of the same tricks mentioned above. The top performer hangs by his knees over one side of the oval, and hooks his feet under the other side for an extremely secure foothold, while his partner climbs up and down him, flies over him, and maneuvers from his hands, feet, or teeth below him.

Another variation on the trapeze is the "cloud swing," beautiful in its simplicity. It's simply a rope, suspended from both ends, that may have loops attached to it for wrist or ankle holds; the Mexican version has none. Wonderfully flexible but very dangerous, the performer can lie, sit, or stand on it, twist around it, hang from it, spin in it, or tangle himself up with it.

Several performers have developed a stunning climax to their acts that may be done from rings, traps, cradles, or cloud swings. Appearing to let go at the top of their upward swing of whatever devices are supporting them, or of their partners, they sail forward in an apparently suicidal free fall

Aerial cradle act. Photo courtesy of the Pickle Family Circus

Pedro Reis' cloud swing. 1989 Big Apple. Photo by W. H. Rough

dive. A safety cable, a "shock" cord, or the cloud swing rope twisted around an ankle or a wrist, arrests their movement inches before they hit the ground, leaving spectators gasping. Jaqueline Williams did a fly-away from her partner in a cradle act with the 1988 Cirque du Soleil that took her out over the first rows of the audience, somewhat like daredevil Elvin Bale used to do from the single trap. On the Circus Flora, Sacha Pavlata's fly-away from his cloud swing jerks him out over a stunned audience before it deposits him gracefully on his feet at center ring: "I have to work hard to 'sell' an act," he says about his deliberate choice to frighten the audience. Gabriel Flores does a much simpler but equally terrifying one from his cloud swing on the Ringling Brothers and Barnum & Bailey Circus Red Unit, merely wrapping the rope around his ankle before he dives forward. Jens Larsen does his from the Roman rings with the Pickle Family Circus. On the Big Apple, Pedro Reis ends his cloud swing act like

Dolly Jacobs, by leaping to a web rope hung in front of him. The fly-away can often depend on the precise manipulation of complicated equipment and cables. Mark Lotz broke both ankles in the 1989 Beatty–Cole show when he flew away from his single trap with a shock cord that was slightly too long attached to his wrist.

A last aerial act employs minimal rigging, and it can look deceptively easy; it's not. Women with healthy scalps may be suspended merely by their long hair, which is attached by a clasp to a cable or rope. They often perform a juggling routine, in a full swing, or spinning and revolving in an expanding circle which adds to the stress on the hair. When her hair pulled free while doing a spin in 1982, Miguel Vasquez' sister Marguerite Michele fell 25 feet to the ground, fracturing her neck. She would recover and return to the rings, but it was yet another reinforcement of Dolly Jacobs' reminder: "Anything you do up above the ground is dangerous."[7]

Marguerite Michele.
Photo courtesy of Ringling Bros. and
Barnum & Bailey Combined Shows, Inc.

Tino Wallenda Zoppe.
1989 Circus Flora.
Photo by W. H. Rough

Wire Walking

Despite the technical Latin name of "funambulist"—rope-walker—tightropes have rarely been ropes since hemp was replaced with copper wire in 1858. Today they are usually ⅝-inch cables of tightly wound steel strands. For that matter, tightropes haven't necessarily been tight either. But in one form or another, rope-walking is one of the oldest of "circus" entertainments. Wire-walking is a universal tradition spanning thousands of years and many widely diverse cultures. The great wire-walker, like the great trapeze artist, offers stunning images of man surviving, even excelling, in a hostile environment of precision, balance, and fear, far beyond the scope that most of us think we can reach. It is little wonder that those images have been so often used by writers and artists to explore the questions of man's metaphysical place in the universe, the nature of the artist, and the quest for human freedom. In *Also Sprach Zarathustra*, Nietzsche wrote that man is a "rope strung between animal and superman, a rope above an abyss." The wire-walker and the trickster clown who can make him fall represent the two great opposing forces in mankind: the affirmer and the skeptic. [8] In Goethe's *Wilhelm Meisters Lehrjahre*, Wilhelm observes and marvels at the paradox of the tightrope-walkers:

What a precious emotion would it give,
if one could disseminate generous, exalted,

manly feelings with electric force and speed, and rouse assembled thousands into such rapture as these people, by their bodily alertness, have done! If one could communicate to thronging multitudes a fellow-feeling in all that belongs to man by the portraying of happiness and misery, of wisdom and folly, nay of absurdity and silliness; could kindle and thrill their inmost souls, and set their stagnant nature into movement, free, vehement, and pure! [9]

Significantly, both of these great writers are German. If Mexico is the great spawner of trapeze artists, it is Germany that has traditionally supplied the world's great wire-walkers. The Wallenda name is famous because the family came to the United States from Germany, leaving a country full of equally outstanding wire-walkers, and coming to a country where the Ringling publicity crews would turn the great Wallenda into a household word.

But before we get to the Wallenda story, we ought to start with a young blonde-headed Frenchman who first popularized the skill in the 19th century at an international level, Jean François Gravelet. He was called Blondin, and he used to thrill his crowds with walks across Niagara Falls, sometimes with his terrified manager on his back, and sometimes with a chair, table, and lunch, which he would pause to eat in the middle of his trip. Another Frenchman, Philippe Petit, does the same sort of thing today. In 1974 Petit strung his wire between the towers of New York's World Trade Center; in Paris in the fall of 1989, he walked over the Seine to the Eiffel Tower, and he evidently has plans for a stroll across the Grand Canyon in 1990. The public loves endurance walks like these. They are major tests of courage and strength, but they are not necessarily demonstrations of polished circus skills.

More in the spirit of circus was a Miss Cooke, who in 1842 was to be found "sitting on a chair before a table, and pouring a glass of wine from a decanter on it, all on the rope."[10] Camillo Mayer did a variation on Miss Cooke's routine on the Ringling show in 1952, substituting a pot of hot coffee for the wine. There are all kinds of wire acts in the circus today: slack wire, bounding wire, and high and low tight wire.

The principles of slack wire are exactly the opposite from those of tight wire. Here the performer must constantly bring the wire underneath his own center of gravity, instead of concentrating on keeping his center of gravity over the wire. The artist's head and shoulders may remain stationary, while his legs are constantly in movement, pushing the cable wildly from side to side. Slack wire is ideally suited for clowning.

"Bounding" wire is basically an adaptation of tight wire fitted with springs at one or both ends to facilitate somersaults. Alejandro Ibarra's act in the 1989 Circus World Museum show was performed on the bounding wire. The act was modelled on the classical performance of an Oklahoma farm boy born as Hal Smith. As a boy, Smith learned to walk clotheslines in his back yard before he ran away to the circus with his best friend Bunny Dryden when he was fourteen. He was eventually given the more resonant and romantic name of Hubert Castle by ex-clown Pat Valdo, John Ringling's performance director at the time. Ringling featured him as an English import, and Castle soon became a star, the king of the bounding wire. It would flex for about ten inches when his weight hit the wire, and shoot him back off like a bow string. He was known for his somersaults, handstands, and unicycle tricks, all on the wire. His temperament once allowed him to jump down from his wire in the middle of a performance to punch an over-boisterous candy butcher, and then

to remount the wire and coolly complete his act.

Practice tightropes are generally set at four to eight feet off the ground, but the low tightwires used in performance are usually higher. Low tightwire-walkers have traditionally used a parasol for balance. It may not seem like much of a help to those watching from the sides, but air pressure on the large rounded surface provides just enough resistance to help steady the performer. In the golden age of the circus, two of the greatest low tightwire walkers, however, elected not to use a parasol: Bird Millman and Con Colleano.

Bird Millman débuted in a small circus with her parents when she was only six. By the time she was twelve, she was performing her own solo wire act; by 1914 she was a center-ring attraction for the Ringling Brothers and in the same class of excellence as Lillian Lietzel. She was a favorite in

Bird Millman. Photo courtesy of Circus World Museum, Baraboo, WI

*Ayin de Sela. 1989 Pickle Family Circus.
Photo by W. H. Rough*

the early 1920's for the carefree ease and the joy she expressed as she waltzed and ran across her 36-foot wire. It was twice as long as the normal low tightwire and therefore provided more flex. Her story has a much happier ending than Lillian's: She met a Harvard graduate, fell madly in love, quit the circus cold, and lived happily ever after. Contemporary gentle low wire ballet routines, like the magnificent performance by Agathe Olivier and Antoine Rigot on the 1988 Cirque du Soleil, and that of the charming Ayin de Sela with the Pickle Family, are at least in part attributable to the early artistry of Bird Millman.

Con Colleano, one of the finest of low tightwire-walkers, was the first to accomplish the extremely difficult forward somersault on the low wire. When he first performed it in public at the New York Hippodrome in 1923, it took him four tries. No one had believed it could ever be done, because the performer's feet must lead the arc over his head and find the wire before he can actually see where to place them. An Australian by birth, Colleano came to the Ringling show in 1925 with a variety of acrobatic skills and his sister Winnie, a skilled trapeze artist. His routines on the wire included an incredibly rapid blur of bolero dancing and difficult acrobatic twists, spins, and turns. His long career in the circus did not end until his retirement in 1960, during which time, incredibly, he was never seriously injured.

The Evolution of High Wire Acts

The high wire acts have changed substantially in the past twenty years, from tests of endurance to demonstrations of the playful acrobatics and balancing skills that used to be performed on low wires. Contemporary artists perform many of the same somersaults, bicycle and unicycle rides, chair-balancing, juggling, dancing, sword fights, jump-roping, and dangerous spins around the wire. Prominent performers in 1989 included Tino Wallenda Zoppe, Karl Wallenda's grandson, and his family, on the Circus Flora and in their own independent production; the Quiroga Family on Vargas; the Osorio Brothers on the Great American Circus; and the Quiros and the Carillo Brothers on the Ringling shows. All owe much more to the artistry of Con Colleano, Hubert Castle, and others than they do to the high wire endurance tests of Blondin and Petit.

There are still some remnants of the grand old high wire acts in the current routines. Most acts are performed by small teams of equilibrists, rather than as solos. The use of teams adds tricks to the routine like passing, leap-frogging, and stacking a crossing with two or three-man-high pyramids reminiscent of the Wallendas. One of the more impressive and dangerous routines, which was occasionally done in past high wire acts, is a walk up or down the cable which anchors the rigging to the ground, generally set at about a

The famous Wallenda seven-man pyramid. Photo courtesy of Circus World Museum, Baraboo, WI

45 degree incline. The Carillo act and Tino Wallenda Zoppe include such an incline walk. It is done without a balance pole, and may be frontward or backward, a variation for which Zoppe holds a world record. Sometimes but not always, on the horizontal high wire, performers may still use a long somewhat flexible balance pole, designed to lower their center of gravity.

High-wire walkers seldom use safety nets, not only because they feel it would be dangerous to fall onto a net among balance bars and props, but also because they believe a net makes falling psychologically more attractive. They prefer to remain psychologically attuned to not falling, which is a word they don't even have in their vocabulary; it's called "coming down" or "going down." They work to maintain their center of gravity always over the wire itself; if they sense they are about to go down, they never permit themselves to fall to the side; it must be straight down, where they can grab onto and eventually remount the wire — which is their life.

Many performers fatalistically accept the inevitability of coming down sooner or later, and they know the principles of how to land with the least injury. Nonetheless, it's their focused attention on the goal and their power of positive think-

ing which keeps them on the wire. That's what makes walking over the void such a sensational demonstration of the almost supernatural powers of the human mind and body. The wire becomes a threshold between life and death. "On that wire is your life. Down there is your death," said Karl Wallenda. [11]

Wallenda

The Wallenda name remains one of the best recognized in American circus history. Although there is no question that he was a superb showman, businessman, and artist, Karl Wallenda was neither the first nor necessarily the greatest wirewalker to capture the American imagination. Hubert Castle's old friend and partner, the much-loved Bunny Dryden, was killed in a fall from the high wire. Harold Alzana, who came to the Ringling show from England in 1947 was legendary for his walks up the inclined wire and his faked near-falls. Josephine Berosini, the great-granddaughter of Blondin, also did an incline walk in her act in the '40's and '50's. Prominent German high wire artists working for the Ringling show included the Gretonas, the Grotefents (George Grotefent was Karl Wallenda's stepfather and original trainer), and later Camillo Mayer. But it was the Wallenda

The Great Wallendas bicycle pyramid. Photo courtesy of Circus World Museum, Baraboo, WI

family, when they first came to America in 1928, whose performance earned an unprecedented fifteen minute ovation at Madison Square Garden. When they introduced the seven-man three-high pyramid in 1947, after they had left the Ringling show, their fame only increased. It was an incredible sight to see:

> The high wire would arc downward under the tremendous weight of four understanders, two middle men, and a chair-mounter. Once the eight feet halted in perfect unison near mid wire, the girl would slowly rise from her seated position and stand atop the chair. From any angle viewed, the numerous sway guy lines, and seven long restless flexible balance poles all drew the focus in on the triangular human ship of state. With no net below, the tension built up until individual coughs and random gasps became audible from the extremities of the arena. [12]

For fifteen years that stunning act was performed without mishap. Then, on January 30, 1962, before 6,000 people at the Shrine Circus in Detroit, the "ship of state" collapsed. Dieter Schepp, Karl's nephew and a newly arrived escapee from East Berlin, was the first understander. Just beyond the mid-way point, Dieter suddenly shouted "*Ich kann nicht mehr holten!* [I can't hold on anymore!]" He lost his grip on his balance pole and fell forward, and the entire pyramid crumbled behind him. Dieter and Karl's son-in-law, Richard Faughnan, were killed. Karl's adopted son Mario also fell and would be permanently paralyzed. Karl, his older brother Hermann, and Hermann's son Gunther managed to hang on to the wire, and Karl hooked Dieter's sixteen-year-old sister on her way by; she had been in the chair. Despite the devastation, the circus resumed twenty minutes later. Two days later, Karl, Hermann, and Gunther were back up on the wire with Gene Mendez. The following season, the "seven" would be repeated over a dozen times for the Shrine engagement in Ft. Worth, Texas, but after that the act broke up. [13]

Karl continued to perform on his own and infatuate the world with his magnificent obsession: "I feel better up there than I do down here. It's my whole life." [14] To celebrate his fiftieth year on

the wire in 1970, he walked over the Tallulah Falls Gorge in Georgia, standing on his head twice during the crossing. Four years later in 1974, he set a world's distance record with an 1,800 foot walk, sixty feet over King's Island, Ohio. On March 22, 1978, while Karl was making a ten-stories-high crossing between the towers of the Condada Holiday Inn in San Juan, Puerto Rico, a gust of wind dipped his forty pound balance pole, which in turn hooked under his armpit and pulled him off the wire. [15] He was seventy-three years old. Karl Wallenda had devoted his entire life to the wire. "The rest of life is just time to fill in between doing the act," he often said. [16]

The Wallenda name remains a magnetic drawing card even today. Several of Karl's descendants and relatives are still performing in wire acts of their own. In addition to grandson Tino and his family (the "Flying Wallendas"), there are Enrico, another grandson, and Debbie (the "Great Wallendas"), the Carla Wallenda Circus, Steven Gregory Wallenda and his courageous and spirited wife, Angel, who does her high wire walks with an artificial leg ("The Incomparable Wallendas"), and Delilah Wallenda.

Daredevils

Several other circus acts which may be considered here are really ground-based, but since they involve defying gravity, we thought it best to touch on them briefly before we leave our discussion of aerial impressions. We are referring to the daredevil acts, like the globe of death, a 13-foot diameter steel cage inside which up to three motorcycles noisily revolve at high speed, sometimes dodging a chorine. High dives used to be performed, sometimes as a part of the main show and sometimes on the midway. It may sound like a cartoon cliché, but there really was a performer named "Speedy," who dove from an 80-foot platform into a $3\frac{1}{2}$ foot tub of water. Was it a demonstration of courage, foolishness, or insanity? We may also question what "Desperado" thought he was proving when he dove from a 70-foot platform onto a slippery angled slide. More to the point, we may question what audiences were doing encouraging him. Jumps like these, automobile and bicycle races down steep inclines and through loop-the-loops, and all sorts of other

The Bauers on sway poles.
Photo courtesy of Ringling Bros.
and Barnum & Bailey Combined
Shows, Inc.

death-defying stunts have little to do with the genuine artistry and circus skills we have been looking at thus far in this chapter. As we have seen, those are dangerous enough. Daredevils pander to the same thrill-seeking that sends some of us to the speedtracks and tractor-pulls in search of accidental death. So in the minds of many people, both in and outside the circus, they have always been a questionable part of circus entertainment.

In the past, some managers had few compunctions about mounting any "death-defying" act that would draw a crowd. But today, most responsible circus managers refuse to display any act which they deem genuinely life-threatening. They feel the circus has enough genuine skill and art to display without catering to death wishes. Nevertheless, the lines which separate art from the contemplation of death often remain obscure. Some circus artists, as we have seen, are also daredevils, so we must admit that some daredevils may also be artists. Two daredevil acts in particular were many times elevated to the realm of skill and art, often by imbuing them with the paradoxical quality of tongue-in-cheek humor. They achieved tremendous popularity in the heyday of the circus, and they remain a part of many performances today: the sway pole and the human cannonball.

A sway pole, introduced to the circus only in

the 20th century, is a flexible steel pole, built as high as the tent will permit, upon which the performer can climb and balance as the pole sways precariously back and forth. Near the turn of the century, the Winnepecs worked on what they called a "steel ship's mast."[17] More recently, the great Fatini portrayed a red-faced drunken elderly gentleman seeking a light for his cigar. He had to climb a 50-foot "lamp post" to get it; then, seated or standing on the roof of the lamp and occasionally "slipping off," he appeared to hang on for dear life as the swaying pole reached alarming extremes.

Today's masters of the sway pole are the Bauers, descended from seven generations of circus history and now working in close association with the Zerbini shows. They work atop two or more 70-foot aluminum poles which are anchored into tubs and stabilized by 600 gallons of water weighing more than two tons. They do terrifying headstands on top of the poles, which can sway up to 40 degrees, and when two adjacent poles are made to meet in their arcs, the performers can change poles. For the climactic conclusion of the act they may come sliding down the poles headfirst at 60 mph, stopping inches before the ground.

Human cannonballs have been around since the late 19th century. The first spring device was

Elvin Bale and jet-propelled rocket launcher. Photo courtesy of Elvin Bale

patented by an Englishman named George Farini in 1871, and it spawned three of the famous early cannon acts, all of which appeared in England before they debuted in America: "Lulu," who was in reality a man disguised as a woman, was shot 25 feet up into the air to a trapeze by a powerful spring built into the floor at New York's Niblo's Garden in 1873. George Loyal was the first to be shot from a cannon apparatus in America, probably with Yankee Robinson in 1875.[18] And "Zazel," a real woman this time, was first shot from a cannon to land in a net in 1877 and was with the Barnum show in 1880. Eventually she missed the net and broke her back, spending the rest of her life in a steel corset.[19] Ildebrando Zacchini and his circus family revived the cannonball act in 1922, and it was soon copied by the Leinerts in Germany. Using one of the twelve compressed air cannons subsequently built by the family, it would eventually become possible for the "bullet" to travel 100 feet high and 200 feet in distance. Hugo, the second brother, was the first bullet, but five brothers and eight of their children, including Hugo II and Hugo Jr., served as bullets. Zacchini, like Hanneford, is another of the oldest names in the circus business still active today: The Hugo Zacchini cannon act appeared with the 1989 indoor Hamid–Morton Shrine Circus, continuing a

sixty year association between the Zacchini and Hamid families. This is Hugo II, Edmondo's son; he holds two engineering degrees from the University of Florida, and is the only remaining Zacchini working as a "bullet." His brother Eddie produces an indoor show with his family's long-lived Olympic International Circus title.[20]

The "World's Greatest Daredevil," Elvin Bale, has developed such torturous devices as the "Monster Machine" and his version of the "Wheel of Death," a complicated revolving girder with a fixed wheel resembling a hamster cage on one end which he first used in 1976. While the device rotates on its axis, the performer must maintain his balance as he tumbles inside the wheel or walks on the outside, sometimes blindfolded. Bale proposed to ride it with a motorcycle on the Ringling show, until Irvin Feld asked him not to because he couldn't afford to lose him from the show. The Marinelles with Vargas, Joseph Dominique Bauer with Zerbini, and Marco & Philip Peters with the Ringling Blue Unit used variations of the Wheel, with cages at both ends of the arm, for their 1989 shows.

Bale also developed a "human rocket" for the Ringling show in 1978. He then built his first cannon for $40,000 and shot dummies out of it until he could get them to land in the net. When he first tried it himself, he was able to fly about 15 feet. Later flights ranged around 100 feet, and Bale said the launch generated a force of 16 G's in the first second. His cannon uses a dozen or so thick elastic ropes for propulsion, rather than the compressed air of the Zacchini models. Climbing inside it, he powdered his costume and the inside of the barrel to prevent any snags, lay on a kind of saddle with his feet against the wall, and waited for the elastic to be released: "The biggest fear is that the thing doesn't go off. Because [you] have to climb out. When you're in there, you're all tensed up, feet planted, waiting for the shock. But if you're just six inches from the bottom, that's enough to break your back. And if you were halfway out, I'm sure it would cut you in half. It's a very powerful cannon. Put a sandbag in there and I'm sure you could knock down a wall."[21] Bale missed the net when coming out of his cannon in Hong Kong in January 1987. He is now paralyzed from the waist down and can no longer fly, but in the true circus spirit of unwillingness to accept an ordinary life, he remains actively involved by teaching his craft to others. It was Bale who taught his early partner, a Polish teeterboard artist named Christopher Adam Matyska how to be a "bullet." So it was "Captain Christopher" and Commander Weiss who opened the 118th Edition of the Ringling Brothers and Barnum & Bailey Circus Blue Unit. Their shot is a flashy space-age contemporary version of the old Zacchini double act. Elvin Bale also framed the Muñoz cannon act for the 1989 Royal Hanneford Circus, as well as Mark Lotz' high wire motorcycle act with the 1989 Beatty–Cole show.

All of this aerial "daring-do" isn't to everyone's taste of course. Many of us get ourselves to the circus only to glue our eyes to the ground, or bury them on our wives' or husbands' shoulders when any of the aerialists come out. "I won't look!

The Wheel of Death. Silver Clown Winner, Monte Carlo Circus Festival, 1979. Photo courtesy of Elvin Bale

"Dainty Darling Dora," 1989 Kelly–Miller. Photo by W. H. Rough

I can't!!" we protest. We are not all meant to be forced into a metaphorical confrontation with the threshold between life and death, just when we thought we were out for escapist entertainment. On the other hand, that threshold is exactly what many of the rest of us did come for. If solace is needed, we might find it in an an article in *Punch*, which appeared way back in 1862:

> The taste for seeing fellow creatures put their lives and limbs in danger we cannot call 'romantic,' but view rather as disgusting. It is not so much the skill of the performer that attracts audiences, as the peril he is placed in and the chance of seeing his neck broken. If monkeys could be trained to do the tightrope and trapeze business, they would soon eclipse the feats of Blondin and Leotard. Monkeys are by nature better fit for such achievements and having fewer brains than men, have no fear of falling.[22]

ON THE GROUND

To the traditional vaulters, balancers, and jugglers who have made up ground acts in the circus must be added an array of performers who used to be a part of the side shows, but have migrated into the main tent. Among them are the magic acts, which can seem so out of place to circus purists because they are based on illusion rather than the presentation of reality. Nonetheless, magicians and circuses have always had close ties. They traveled together in the old days, and shared the same audiences. Houdini himself appeared in the circus on occasion. Franz Czeisler, the head of the spectacular Circo Tihany tented variety show, is an accomplished magician who features magic in his performances. Big John Strong has virtually mounted a circus of magic, and magic acts are featured in the Great American, Franzen, Roberts Brothers, and Circus World Museum shows, among many others.

Benders

Another group of performers who have successfully moved from the side shows to the main performance in contemporary circuses are the contortionists, more popularly known as the pos-

turers, or benders. Technically, there is a difference: "benders" perform by bending themselves backwards, whereas "posturers" lean forward, keeping their legs straight or folding them behind the neck. The names are often used interchangeably, although it's rare that a contortionist can excel at both backward and forward positioning. In circus parlance contortionists have also been called "Indiarubber men," "elastic incomprehensibles," "klischniggers" or "nondescripts."[23] Their skills are frequently mixed with those of the equilibrists. An example is the 1988 Cirque du Soleil's stunning combination of balance and supple fluidity by "Queen of the Night" Angela Laurier, who learned her skill on her own as a street performer. Other contortionists limit their work to displays of bodily malleability, well demonstrated by Hugo Zamorathe's uncanny ability to tuck himself into a bell jar. That Argentine posturer performed the stunt on the 1989 Royal Hanneford Circus and repeated it on ABC's *Incredible Sunday*. Perhaps the most famous name in the field of contortion belongs to Marinelli, who was an Englishman born as J. H. Walter and also called the "Serpent Man" because of the snakeskin costume he wore. One of the most common bends used by contortionists today was named after him. The "Marinelli Bend" involves bending the body over backwards until the head can look forward between the ankles. A later variation requires the bender to balance and support her body in this position by a mouthpiece only, lifting her legs entirely off the ground. One of the premier contortionists of the turn-of-the-century era was a young black man named Marsh Craig. As a boy he fell in love with the circus and "watered a lot of elephants" to be near the benders. He later became a featured performer with a number of minstrel shows and circuses. It was an act in which blacks were somehow considered more acceptable by white audiences. Other successful black benders included George Crawford, Henry Hunter, and Billy "The Human Frog" Williams.

In 1985, Rudolphe Delmonte was traveling as a bender with the Ringling Brothers and Barnum & Bailey Circus. He claimed that his mother, who had been a showgirl and bender until 1956, had taught him everything he knew. All it takes is practice, he claimed; he is not double-jointed.

Rudolphe Delmonte.
Photo courtesy of Ringling Bros.
and Barnum & Bailey Combined
Shows, Inc.

Since he began to prepare for his career at the age of seven, he practiced every day, with only one month off in his lifetime; that's what it took to remain limber. Rudolphe was twenty-three years old in 1985 and looked forward to a career of less than twenty more years. Muscles grow stiff and less yielding by the time most benders reach the age of forty.

Leapers and Vaulters

Leapers and vaulters were one of the first groups of artists to dominate the circus, partially because they adapted so well to working with horses. Leapers gained momentum with a long running incline or on a springboard of some kind, and usually landed on a pad. In between, they soared and somersaulted sometimes a hundred feet or so over men, or horses, or maybe fifteen lined-up elephants, or anything they could find even more unusual. According to Wisconsin circus historian Gordon Yadon, leapers were one of the primary drawing cards to circuses in the 1860's, before so many of them broke their backs and ruptured their muscles attempting the triple somersault and other near-suicidal tricks.[24] Today's tumbling, perch pole, and teeterboard acts all owe their origins to early spectacular leapers like Frank A. Gardiner, William H. Batcheller, and John Worland.[25]

Tumbling troupes are classical circus acts in which the acrobats use no props. "Acrobat" comes from a Greek word meaning "high walker," or "walker on tiptoe," which suggests the remarkable agility, balance, and strength displayed by these troupes. They perform dramatic leaps, spins, handsprings, flip-flops, cartwheels, twists, turns, and somersaults in a mad free-for-all around the ring, using only each other and the floor for platforms and spring boards. They also feature standing reverse pyramids and totem poles, demonstrating intricate ways in which the weight of the entire troupe can be borne by one man. The man on the bottom, usually the strongest and heaviest, is called the understander; the man on the top is called the topmounter. The traditional troupes were primarily North African; Bedouin acrobats featuring the unique Arab flying sideways somersaults first performed at London's Colosseum in 1836. Among today's many fine traditional troupes are the award-winning Tangier Troupe, who once again appeared with Beatty–Cole in 1989, and the Staneks with Zerbini. Several years ago, the Ringling show's Hassani Troupe included Tahar Douis as the understander. He once held a three-high tower of twelve men totalling 1700 pounds on his shoulders, a world record according to Guinness. Undoubtedly his new career as "Tahar, the Mighty Moroccan Alligator Wrestler" is considerably less of a strain for him.

Over the past decade in American circuses,

Below: The Tangier Troupe. 1989 Clyde Beatty–
Cole Bros. Photo by Joan Z. Rough
Right: The Tangier Troupe totem pole.
Photo by W. H. Rough

extremely sophisticated variations on tumbling and balancing have been performed by the increasingly popular Chinese acrobatic troupes, now generally recognized as the world's best. Their acts tend to defy categorization, and elements of vaulting, balancing, and juggling are often inseparable. The Ringling show, the Big Apple, and the Cirque du Soleil have been particularly successful in showcasing some of the finest of the Chinese acrobatic acts: the Qian Brothers, and troupes from Nanjing, Tianjin, Shanghai, and Shandong among them.

When tumblers and vaulters add one or more of a series of simple props, the act can literally take on a whole new dimension, adding height and increasing the emphasis on balance. Trampolines have always been popular in the circus, both as training devices for flyers and as performance media themselves. Many families of performers will often exhibit both flying acts and "tramp" acts, sometimes using different stage names for each act. The most popular vaulting prop in the circus today is one shared with elementary school playgrounds, the seesaw, but known in the circus only as the teeterboard. It has become a staple

item with several American circuses, and there are dozens of superb acts. The idea is for one acrobat, the flyer, to stand on the lower end; when one or two jumpers leap from a high platform onto the other end, they propel the flyer soaring or somersaulting through the air. Sometimes he lands on a chair on top of a perchpole. Other times he may land on his feet on top of a column of his fellows standing on each other's shoulders. The column can reach a "five-man-high" if supported with a reinforcing perchpole device, but its entire weight is carried by the understander. Often it's the youngest boy or girl in a family teeterboard act who does the most impressive somersaults to the top of the column, simply because he or she weighs the least. The Estrada Company and the Bautista Family perform impressively with the Beatty–Cole show, and the Ringling units boast no fewer than five outstanding teeterboard acts. Two or more teeterboards can add complicated variety to an act and keep several flyers in the air at the same time, as does the delightfully humorous penguin-like waddling troupe with the Cirque du Soleil. Variety is always being sought after. In one impressive variation, Gunther Gebel–Williams

Nanjing Acrobats tumbling lions.
Photo by Martha Swope Associates/
Rebecca Lesher, courtesy of Big Apple Circus

The Mosoianu Troupe.
Photo courtesy of Ringling Bros. and Barnum &
Bailey Combined Shows, Inc.

Marie–Pierre Bernac, David Dimitri, and
Alexandre Pavlata: the Russian Barre.
Photo courtesy of Big Apple Circus

incorporates a teeterboard into his elephant act. It's an elephant that steps onto the raised end of the board, propelling him into an upright position on the back of another elephant.

Another frequently used vaulting device is the Russian swing, first introduced by the Moscow Circus. Two or more people may swing on the framed platform until enough momentum is developed to send one of them flying or somersaulting 30 feet or more to a mat or to the shoulders of a partner. Tady Wozniak and his wife Teresa formed a troupe using the Russian swing in 1975, when they were with the Moscow Circus School. They made their American debut with the Ringling Brothers and Barnum & Bailey Circus in 1977, and in 1983 moved to the Big Apple Circus.

The Russian barre is a vaulting device that has come to us not from the Russians but from the Rumanians. It is a thin, flexible wooden pole, held at shoulder height by two men. The acrobatic artist, traditionally a woman, stands on the barre, and when it is given a slight upward thrust she springs from it into a somersault and returns to the barre. It looks impressively difficult, and it's every bit as much a balancing trick as a vaulting trick. Both the balancer and the men on the ground must work to keep her center of gravity directly over the barre, while she constantly maintains a dancer's grace and poise. One of the more impressive Russian barre acts in this country was with the Big Apple Circus, when David Dimitri and Sacha Pavlata held Marie-Pierre Bernac on the barre. Marie-Pierre appeared to effortlessly and joyfully perform a foot-to-foot backward double somersault, landing back on her feet on the barre with grace.

Ground Balancing

We have already seen that not all balancing acts have to do with great heights. Perhaps the most fundamental demonstration of ground-based equilibristics is hand-balancing, sometimes performed as "living statues." Living statue acts were a popular staple of the circus, especially at the end of the last century. Near nude and near perfect specimens of the male and female figure, covered with white, silver, or gold body paint, would pose motionlessly in a series of tableaux depicting classic works of sculpture like "The Dance

of Life," "Victory," and "The Spirit of Flight." The acts were quite sensuous, and pretty risqué for their day, but since it was all done in the name of fine art there was no attempt at censorship. When a living statues act was stunningly recreated for the Ringling Brothers and Barnum & Bailey Circus 119th edition in 1989, and enhanced with dramatic colored lighting, one startled little girl watching them from the balcony of the Richmond arena was heard to mutter, "They have no pants on, Mommy." She had to be reassured that yes, indeed, body suits were in their proper places, and that the statues were not "anatomically correct."

The more contemporary versions of the living statues are no longer motionless tableaux. In an "adagio" act, two or more partners proceed slowly through a series of bold gymnastic floor moves demonstrating creative choreography and almost superhuman strength. Only one of the partners touches the ground at any one time, while the other

The Living Statues. Photo courtesy of Ringling Bros. and Barnum & Bailey Combined Shows, Inc.

balances on him or her in every conceivable position. The moves are performed, like those of the contortionists, with the goals in mind of displaying graceful suppleness, as well as the harmony and balance of juxtaposed human form and line. The Pivarel act with the Ringling show, the Mayas with the Circus Vargas, and the hand-balancing of Eric Varelas and Amelie Demay with the Cirque du Soleil are stand-outs, but there are many fine similar acts.

Hand-balancing can also be a very impressive solo act, with the artist standing on one hand, or a cane, often on a raised platform. One of the most famous of hand-balancers was an Austrian performer simply named Unus, with the Ringling show in the late 1940's and 1950's. A stylish gentleman, he arrived in the ring dressed to the nines in top hat, white tie and tails, with cane in hand. He approached a table on which rested a lit globe lamp. Using only one index finger for support, he proceeded to stand upside down on the globe. There have been other fine finger balancers as well. Ramon España with the 1989 Roberts Brothers Circus did a very good one-finger stand. Some performers use a brace hidden inside a glove to add support to the first knuckle joint, and some don't, but either way it's an impressively difficult balancing trick.

Once again, the addition of props to ground balancing acts can add interest and variety. A perch pole, anywhere from 20 to 40 feet high, balanced on the shoulder or from the belted pouch of an understander adds a degree of difficulty and risk for the topmounter, who shinnies up to do head and handstands at its top. Rolling globe acts, in which balancing performers walk on top of large balls and maneuver them up and down narrow ramps, are one of the oldest of circus acts. The Royal Hanneford's rolling globe act was televised during the 1989 Milwaukee Circus Parade

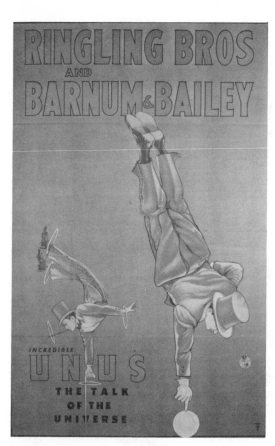

Poster of hand-balancing.
Photo courtesy of Ringling Bros. and Barnum &
Bailey Combined Shows, Inc.

Ramon Espana hand-balancing.
1989 Roberts Bros.
Photo by Joan Z. Rough

festivities. Rola-bola balancing acts, with multiple layers of rolling tubes and balls under a precariously balanced standing board, threatening to shoot out from under a performer in any direction and at any second, are also impressive demonstrations of the art of equilibrism. Ramon España, again with the Roberts Brothers, and the Pickle Family troupe were among those who mounted outstanding rola-bola displays in 1989.

Finally, trick bicycle-riding is another balancing act, which has been developed into a fine art in China. Outstanding among contemporary bicycle acts have been the Chinese Nanjing troupe with the 1989 Big Apple Circus, and the Chinese-inspired bicycle act with the Cirque du Soleil. One of the liveliest of cycling acts in recent years was the appearance of the King Charles Troupe, the first major black act to appear in a modern circus. They debuted with Ringling in 1969, and have entertained millions ever since. Their routines with basketballs on unicycles, a kind of cycling Harlem Globetrotter act, can be counted on to add wit and pep to any circus performance. The troupe's creator, Jerry King, began by teaching his young son Charles how to ride a unicycle in the halls of their Bronx apartment building. Both by example and by active community involvement, the troupe members have served as models of drive, spirit, and originality for thousands of youngsters seeking a way out of the ghetto. "In the Circus, we represent black people in a way nobody else has. When some of the younger kids get homesick, we have to remind them of that and show them we really are a family. Then they don't feel so lonesome," said Leroy Ross, a member of the 1985 troupe with the Ringling show.[26]

Juggling

Juggling acts have a particular appeal for those of us who every day face the prospect of keeping the many facets of our lives all in the air and moving at the same time: the job, the customers, the kids, the spouse, the friends, the budget, the diet, any one or all of which threaten to fall out of control at any minute. The sight of a good juggler is a symbolic and reassuring reminder that it is after all humanly possible to juggle all of the above with a clear head. Through it all, the juggler stays completely relaxed and just keeps on smiling; he makes it all look so easy that it is no wonder his performance has had such a universal magical appeal. No one knows how the art of juggling might have started; perhaps it was as a magic ritual or a religious dance of some kind. We do know that it has been around for at least 4,000 years, in widely separated cultures. Pictures of female jugglers, using the same basic displays and techniques still in use today, have been found on the walls of Egyptian tombs. It is an ancient art in China as well, and the Chinese still produce some of the best jugglers in the world.

The problem for anyone watching a good juggler is that we know it can't be as easy as it looks. It never is. Everything is happening so fast, we have no idea what we're watching. That's part of the fun, but it does help to know that there are two basic styles of juggling: cascading, sometimes called crossing, and showering. For cascades, the objects are alternately caught and thrown by both hands, and they cross in mid-air. For showers, the objects are thrown by one hand and caught by the other, so that they follow each other in one direction and make a circle in the air. In the double shower, a second circular pattern in the opposite direction is created when the object is thrown from the second hand back to the first. And if one spectator is particularly anxious to impress another with his expertise, he might point out that for showering, the throwing hand is kept lower than the hand which is catching and returning, whereas for a cascade, the juggler will keep his hands level. A third pattern may be established with one-handed juggling, when the same hand is throwing and catching the juggled objects. When both hands are doing one-handed juggling, but the objects don't cross, the pattern is called a fountain.

Conventional juggling objects are balls, clubs, flaming firebrands, knives, rings, plates, scarves, and badminton rackets, of all things. But part of the creative ingenuity of a good juggler is to pick unlikely objects for juggling. Dick Franco juggles ping-pong balls from his mouth. The Flying Karamazov Brothers boast they can juggle whatever objects the audience might challenge them with, and have had to make good with combinations of raw fish and bowling balls. The dynamic "Big Juggle" which climaxes a Pickle Family Circus performance uses every member of the company

Rola-bola balancing act. Photo by Joan Z. Rough

Nanjing acrobats. 1989 Big Apple, Shelburne, VT.
Photo by W. H. Rough

Risley act: The Rios Brothers.
1990 Big Apple.
Photo by W. H. Rough

Lorenzo Pickle and the Baldinis. 1989 Circus Flora.
Photo by W. H. Rough

Charlie King and the King Charles Troupe. Photo courtesy of Ringling Bros. and Barnum & Bailey Combined Shows, Inc.

to keep dishes, glasses, and any other loose object on stage in the air in apparent chaos. Judy Finelli, the Artistic Director of the Pickle, no longer works on stage, but she juggled for fourteen years in a comic routine with her husband, Hovey Burgess, and her expert sense of humor and timing can still be felt while watching the Pickle performers.

Sometimes even people are juggled. In what is called a "Risley" act, a foot juggler, or "antipodist," lies on his back in a supportive cradle called a "trinka," and juggles a human body with his feet. There was a very good Risley act on the 1989 Carson & Barnes show; with his trinka mounted on a perch pole, the juggler spun with his feet the curled-up body of his young son. The Rios Brothers performance on the 1990 Big Apple Circus is an outstanding display of acrobatic "Risley" juggling. Richard Risley, for whom the act was named, was an American who toured the world with his own circus, and brought back with him one of the first Oriental tumbling troupes to be seen in Europe and America. Another of the fascinating enigmas that are scattered throughout

circus history, Risley died in a lunatic asylum in 1874.

Vaudeville juggler Homer Stack used to say that the true mark of a great juggler is a good sense of timing, good muscular control, and good concentration. Particularly in humorous juggling, Vaudeville led the way with people like Stack and the great film star W. C. Fields, at one time known as the "world's greatest juggler." Even in the circus the juggler is an over-all entertainer, as we know from the very derivation of his name, from the Latin *joculator*, jester. We might well remember that the French *jongleurs* from the Middle Ages were not merely jugglers, but multi-talented minstrels and troubadours. A sense of style and humor, and a creative inventiveness contributing to variety are paramount.

Enrico Rastelli, born in 1897, is still recognized as one of the greatest jugglers of all time, although he died when he was only thirty-four. His father was a juggler, and because jugglers were paid so little, he forbade his son to take up the profession. The result was that young Enrico practiced in secret until he could juggle seven balls. Since that was two more than his father could do, Enrico was permitted to continue, and by 1922 he was appearing at the Olympia in England. The variety in his act was stunning: "He would sit on a stool with a football on each instep, another on each knee, two balanced one on top of the other on a mouth-stick, two more balanced in the same way on a stick on his forehead, and one spinning on the forefinger of each hand."[27] Contemporary American teenager Anthony Gatto is also recognized as one of the greatest jugglers of all time; he was capable of doing routines similar to Rastelli's when he was only twelve. He was the youngest winner of the Senior National Competition and a gold medal winner at Monte Carlo, and he has already given a command performance for the Queen of England. Other popular jugglers working today are Francis Brunn, Albert Lucas, T. J. Howell, who does a speedy juggling act with traditional balls, rings, clubs, and flaming torches at Circus World Museum, and Daniel "Le Bateleur" Ouimet with the Cirque du Soleil.

Numbers juggling doesn't necessarily convey the true spirit of juggling art, nor is it always more difficult: Apparently a double shower of eight is actually easier than a straightforward shower of seven; on the other hand, an odd number of balls are generally easier to keep track of in criss-crossing showers than even numbers. Jugglers insist above all that it's easier to do all this than to try to explain it. Casual observers must be satisfied with knowing that it is difficult enough to juggle five balls; seven or eight is extremely challenging. Rastelli was reported to have juggled ten balls. Seven clubs seems about a maximum, and maybe ten balls or rings. Although rings are purportedly easier than clubs, no one has ever duplicated for the record the twelve rings reported by Xenophon in 421 B.C., perhaps with some poetic license.

Jugglers frequently perform several variations on the conventional aerial manipulation of objects. There is cigar-box juggling, whereby the artist holds three boxes in the air by clamping them in varying patterns between his hands; and there is the predominantly Chinese art of plate-spinning, whereby a series of dinner plates are kept spinning aloft on pointed sticks. The recent appearance of the Nanjing acrobatic troupe with the Big Apple Circus offered an outstanding example of the art, which is beginning to gain in popularity. There are good plate-spinning acts now on the Circus Vargas, the Roberts Brothers, the Great American, and the Circus Smirkus. The Chinese are also responsible for introducing the mouth-stick and ribbon pattern-waving. New variations and displays combining balance and juggling skills are being developed all the time with contributions from artists representing traditions from all over the world. Even small circuses can contain some stunning juggling performances; they can be mounted very economically, and they are always favorites with the spectators.

7.
MUSIC AND LAUGHTER

Traces of lost images can make us chuckle quietly to ourselves before we even know what we're laughing at: of Lou Jacobs squeezing his long frame into his miniature circus car; of Emmett Kelly forlornly sweeping his spotlight into a dust pan; of a set of teeth chasing a giant toothbrush and tube of tooth paste around the hippodrome track; of the hysterical Firehouse Fun clowns battling a blazing building and all but exterminating those whom they sought to rescue, a routine begun at the Ringling Brothers and Barnum & Bailey Circus in 1924; and of happy children quietly and reassuringly folded into the friendly arms of "Topper" and "Buster," during clown autograph sessions with the 1989 Beatty–Cole show.

Do the images call up the sounds, or is it the other way around? It's perhaps different for each of us at different times. Who can listen to Aram Khachaturian's pounding "Sabre Dance" without also hearing the tiger's snarl or the elephant's trumpet call, closely followed by other memories: shadows of the great beasts performing some rapid bit of deft choreography, or of the juggler's whirling firebrands? And who can watch any of the great slapstick clown routines without also hearing their hooting and yelling, and the wonderful blasts, whistles, slides, and percussion that the great brass circus bands provided to accentuate the action?

By the time we leave a circus performance, perhaps we have been impressed by the spectacle, awed by the aerialists, frightened by the animals, and amazed by the stunts. But the clowns and musicians have tapped directly into our emotions, maybe without our even knowing it. They have made us laugh, and tap our feet, and shout, and sweat. They have just plain made us feel good. Together the bands and clowns control the whole rhythm and flow of the circus performance, providing the real suspense and sense of anticipation that make the circus so memorable. Music and laughter can make the most intolerable of lives tolerable.

So it is to the circus bands and circus clowns that we now turn our attention. This is not the place for any kind of definitive history of either group. They both have their own professional associations, with the attendant newsletters and historians, who have done an admirable job compiling histories of their professions. Our limited survey will let us discover who some of the great masters in both fields are and were, and a little about their backgrounds and methods. Because their effect is often subconscious, and their names are sometimes buried in the back of circus programs, audiences often forget the special significance of their contribution to the overall success of the circus. We group musicians and clowns together here because there is a long tradition of mutual respect between them. The direct connection between them is the singing clown, who played a major part in introducing music into the circus. A more relevant point is that the musicians and clowns share the common goal of having direct impact on our emotional disposition, which ought not to be overlooked.

THE WINDJAMMERS

If circus was considered an immoral activity by many people in 18th century England and America, music was even worse. In England in 1782, Charles Hughes, Philip Astley's arch-rival, was thrown in jail for contempt of Magistracy, for having introduced music to his circus in defiance of the law. No one played music in colonial

"Firehouse Frenzy."
Photo courtesy of Ringling Bros.
and Barnum & Bailey Combined
Shows, Inc.

"Topper," 1989 Clyde Beatty–
Cole Bros. Photo by W. H. Rough

Big Show Band in the early days.
Charles Ringling is second from
the right. Photo courtesy of
Ringling Bros. and Barnum &
Bailey Combined Shows, Inc.

Clyde Beatty–Cole Bros. bandwagon.
Photo by Joan Z. Rough

America: it was an act of the devil. Only when that holiest of instruments, the organ, was introduced into churches did instrumental music begin to be acceptable. Military bands were not common until after the Revolution, when it had become clear that the British regimental bands were more inspirational than the American fifes and drums. Early circus accompaniment was limited to a tambourine, some drums, and perhaps a fiddle, or a fife and a trumpet. More often than not, the clowns were the musicians. But by their heyday, circuses were often judged as much by the strength and quality of their brass bands as by the size of their elephant herds.

Today it's difficult to conceive of a circus without music. Walking into Canada's Cirque du Soleil, our first impressions are established by the overwhelming sound of the music. Its overall impact rests heavily on a stunning modern score by René Dupéré, played by a bank of computer buttons and a live five-piece band conducted by Benoit Jutras. There is nothing traditional about it, either in content or in instrumentation. Nonetheless, the music heightens all the emotions of the audience, ranging from suspense to comic relief. It carefully frames each ring act, just as a film score might set up a scene. The Pickle Family Circus also uses non-traditional music to shape and mold their performances, but in their case a five-piece jazz band under the direction of Jeffrey Gae-

to sets a frenetic pace for the cast with an original high-energy jazz score. On the Big Apple Circus, Director Rik Albani conducts more traditional-sounding, brass-oriented original music created especially for the show by his partner and wife Linda Hudes. For one performance in 1985, their already exciting eight-piece band was joined by the 85-piece Boston Pops Esplanade Orchestra, making them one of the largest circus bands ever assembled. The Circus Flora Band uses a jazzy original score, composed, arranged and conducted by Miriam Cutler, which can also include some operatic elements when called for. In Japan, the Ringling Gold unit discovered that the Japanese wanted to hear up-tempo, recognizable, modern American rock music, and they too have abandoned traditional circus musical fare. In this country, Ringling music is more traditional-sounding, although Music Director Bill Pruyn relies heavily on themes from new Broadway musicals, television, and other non-traditional fare, and musicians are jobbed in at each major stand. On the Tarzan Zerbini Circuses, the circus sound is often provided by several bandmasters, including John Mohan and Clem Toca, with his three-piece musical family. Musical director and busy trumpet player Mark Van Cleave also furnishes bands for Garden Brothers and other shows, by jobbing in local professional musicians.

Among the traditional big three-ring circuses,

there is only one that still maintains a full eight-piece, traditional, all-brass circus band, all of whom stay together for a full season on the road. They are led by young James Haverstrom for the Clyde Beatty–Cole Bros. Circus. Jim traveled with the show for two years before he became the bandmaster in 1988. The musicians select and arrange their material from a wide variety of sources. Only about a quarter of their repertoire is traditional circus fare, and the rest is made up of more contemporary pop and show music. Nonetheless, nowhere else is the traditional sound of the regular live brass circus band so evident, music that can easily fill a tent with old-fashioned excitement and merriment.

Many of the smaller traditional tented shows also still rely on live music, and they are determined to maintain the traditional sound of the circus band. It may be limited to a single organ or synthesizer, which can be supported by drums and one or two brass instruments, but the ingenuity of the musicians can make up for minimal equipment. On the 1989 Roberts Brothers tour, Bud Manley and a small combo were sufficient to call forth the traditional spirit of circus. The four-piece Kelly–Miller band, under the direction of former Beatty–Cole bandleader Clark Wiegle creates a fine circus sound, as does the Bentley Brothers' three-piece band led by Brian Young, and the Great American's group led by Jack Forseen, veterans of the Circus Gatti. Vidbel's Old Tyme Circus and the little one-ring Culpepper–Merriweather Circus both prioritized music in 1989, carrying small live bands. At the Circus World Museum in Baraboo, trumpeter Rick Percy and his little band accompany all performances with a full repertoire of pre-1939 traditional circus music.

Rising costs have driven many circuses to replace their bands with taped music. It's not always easy even to job in talented musicians willing to accept the rigors of circus music unfamiliar to them. And to find talented musicians willing to undergo the challenge of circus life on the road for very little pay is even harder. Music royalty fees from the American Society of Composers, Authors and Publishers (ASCAP) and Broadcast Music Incorporated (BMI) are high, and the bigger the show, the higher the fees. As recently as 1986,

Charlie Stevenson's eight piece brass band was playing a dynamic traditional circus repertoire for the Carson & Barnes show, but royalty fees and the difficulties of finding suitable musicians have proved too much to justify the effort in the minds of the owners. They have replaced their live band with an ingenious sound system designed by Greg Haggard. It enables a single sound director to mix and blend a great variety of studio-recorded music specially composed and arranged by Steven Michael Lack, conducting the Circus Music International Brass Band. The effect is stunningly realistic; tempo is matched to animal and human rhythms, and drum rolls still add appropriate suspense to death-defying acts. The Circus Vargas has taken a similar course with their tape system.

There are of course outcries of protest against even good canned music from all out-of-work musicians. What's more, many experts feel that the real circus spirit can only be evoked when the music is closely following the action, and not the other way around. Horses, for instance do not hear music, and they can't dance in time to a beat. The effect depends heavily on the timing of the conductor in matching his music to the steps of the horse, which are cued by hand or by audible signals from the trainer. Even the best of music recorded in a controlled sound studio is difficult to match to the chaotic rhythms of a live circus performance. Nor can a recording be as readily prepared for accidents, or the slight variations in rhythm in every act from performance to performance. Many fans continue to insist that circuses must carry live bands, capable of playing traditional circus music, although they may be waging a losing battle.

Circus Music

What is "traditional" circus music, anyway? Merle Evans defined it only as music written by circus musicians that is "brighter" than other music. The most often-played circus music is the march, but there are plenty of opportunities for waltzes, rags, serenades, intermezzos, Latin rhythms, smears, and galops. Different styles of music characterize each act. Wild animals may be accompanied by fierce marches with a driving beat like "Bravura," or "Burma Patrol." Waltzes like "Over the Waves" and "Wedding of the

Winds" might lull us through graceful trapeze performances. The pacing for a big slapstick clown act might be set by a galop like "Prestissimo," or "The Homestretch." *Galop*, incidentally, is the French spelling for the horse's gallop, which suggests both the source and the exhausting two-beat pace of the music.

There is no room any more for string instruments in "traditional" circus bands — that is to say in brass bands beginning in the mid-19th century. Since the advent of the three-ring circus, the emphasis has been on drums and brass: the far-reaching clear tones of cornets, trumpets, trombones, French horns, baritones, and tubas. Saxophones and the other reed instruments are debatable, but they have seen frequent use in the circus. Although their music is all original, the "traditional" Circus Flora Band includes a mean Cajun fiddle and a full range of reeds. They harken back to an earlier era when such instruments were the only ones acceptable and available at any public concerts, and when they provided adequate volume under a single-ring tent.

Most "original circus music" was written in the 20th century. Before that, circus musicians were too busy conducting to take time to write their own. In the early 1830's they played narrative songs like "Yankee Doodle," "Billy Barlow," and "Jim Crow."[1] The first full band probably went out around 1830 with the Purdy & Welch Circus. But the first circus brass band didn't appear until Ned Kendall took his new trend-setting Boston musicians out with the New England Caravan in 1832, and they became an all-brass group at Allan Dodsworth's insistence in 1834.[2] Independent brass bands were the rule in circuses by 1837, often riding in the splendid new music carriages made for them. In the 1850's, the cornet began to replace the keyed "Kent" bugle, and Kendall was joined by Tom Canham, Patrick Gilmore, and David W. Reeves, all among the major bandmasters of the country. Gilmore was responsible for setting a trend away from brass and towards a balance with reed instruments, and for introducing the big touring band era. As leader of Providence's American Band, Reeves also became a prominent composer. But for all intents and purposes, there were few circus bands as separate entities until the turn of the century.

Functions

Barnum himself always believed in the power of good music to draw in the public, as is evidenced by his pre-circus-days sponsorship of the Swedish Nightingale, Jenny Lind. The Ringling Brothers were also musicians. Charley Ringling usually played the violin and Alf T. the organ and the cornet. They did one act wherein the two of them played twelve different instruments. Neither brother ever lost his love for music; Merle Evans remembered Charley sitting in with the big top band, often as a baritone soloist for the center-ring concert, right up to 1925, the year before he died.

So despite the fancies of circus purists, there is really no long-term tradition of music written exclusively for the circus. Special music had been written for the circus by bandmasters and composers since the 1870's, but not all circus music was written by circus musicians. Bandmasters have always been free to choose from a wide variety of traditional and non-traditional sources, although in the old days the two were more clearly delineated. It used to be rarer than it is today for a circus band to play pop music during the performance itself. Conversely, it was just as rare to hear circus galops in popular band concerts. In the old days there were special center-ring concerts before the performance, as well as completely separate concerts after the show by the side-show and other bands. For these concerts, standard popular and classical fare was the norm.

However, for the circus acts themselves, a good deal more flexibility is needed. Unexpected animal behavior may require stalling and vamping or a sudden change of pace. It's sometimes easier and more economical to develop music specifically appropriate for the occasion. Short snatches of familiar music may be blended together in an original medley, and occasionally a single piece of music may be written for an entire production number. Such was the case when Igor Stravinsky was asked to write "The Elephant Polka" for the 1942 Ringling show. This famous circus "ballet" was performed by a "corps des elephants" costumed by Norman Bel Geddes and choreographed by no less than George Balanchine, all of which did not prevent it from being roundly despised by the musicians who had to play it.

The trick for good circus music is an alert band equipped to handle improvisation and the up to 200 planned cues a performance might require. Bandmasters must be people of considerable judgment and discipline. They might be required to shift tempos in a split second, or to add extra bars of music to complete an act. Sometimes over 200 different pieces of music had to be prepared for a three-hour show. Scoring a performance happens before the circus ever leaves winter quarters, and it's not an easy task for the band director. He almost always gears his music to the center ring, but on occasion he might be expected to match a medley to the changing pace and style of three acts at once. He also has to be a shrewd psychologist, adept at calming bruised egos: if a Hungarian balancing act wants Hungarian music, and at the same time a Mexican flying act wants Spanish music, the director may have to find a way to convince both that they are getting what they want, as Merle Evans once did. Sound effects, whistles, slides, and snatches of classical music that punctuate every action in the center ring are also provided by the band—the same effects that found their way into cartoons and early film comedies.

Circus music has two other functions that are less apparent to the general public. It serves as a secondary language and signal clock for the full circus family. Since the same music with only minor adjustments is used for every performance, performers know exactly which measure of what song will send them to change costumes. A single familiar bar will bring them to the back door in time for their acts. Roustabouts and other employees will hear when to be ready to tear down the side show tent, when to look for the flag over the cook tent, and when to be ready for the "blow-off," the crowd's departure. In many ways, the whole pacing of a circus day is controlled by the band.

A second in-house function of circus music is to signal any kind of disaster. After a fall from the high wire or trapeze, it was the bandmaster's job to signal for rescue workers and distract the audience by suddenly cutting whatever the band was playing and shifting to fast music anticipating the entrance of the next act. For the Beatty–Cole show, "Twelfth Street Rag" will bring out the clowns en masse for audience distraction after such an accident. Rarely was a John Philip Sousa march heard in a circus tent unless there was a major emergency taking place, and the most recognizable disaster march of all was "The Stars and Stripes Forever." It was the universal signal for circus personnel to come running and evacuate the tent. It was played by bandmaster Merle Evans, for instance, from the moment he spotted the beginnings of the great Ringling fire of 1944, until seconds before the burning quarter poles crashed across his bandstand.

Great Bandsmen

Circus musicians are traditionally called "windjammers" because they "jam wind into cornets, clarinets, trombones, baritones, etc. for six to seven hours a day," according to Merle Evans, the most famous windjammer of all.[3] Contemporary windjammers formed themselves into an official organization of circus music lovers in 1971. Membership in Windjammers Unlimited, Inc. approached 700 in 1989, many of whom are non-playing lovers of circus music. The traditional circus musicians themselves are getting older and scarcer. Still, at their annual convention in 1989, a 140 piece band assembled to record a concert of music written for circus in years past, one of the Windjammers' stated goals. The purpose of the organization is simply to keep traditional circus music and circus concert music alive. They publish a bimonthly magazine called *Circus Fanfare*, and they have established a Windjammer's Hall of Fame. Ward Stauth, the Secretary–Treasurer of the organization, has gathered together an impressive collection of recorded and printed circus music that he hopes will form the basis for a new non-profit American Circus Music Museum in Corydon, Indiana. But as of this writing, the eventual disposition of his collection is not yet clear.

Merle Evans was the band director for the Ringling Brothers and Barnum & Bailey Circus for a half-century beginning in 1919. When he put down his cornet for the last time with the Ringling show on December 4, 1969, this "Toscanini of the Big Top" had played an incredible 18,250 performances without missing a day, even for one severe bout of ptomaine poisoning. His largest all-brass band consisted of thirty-six instruments.

Emmett Kelly with Merle Evans.
Photo courtesy of Circus World Museum, Baraboo, WI

Merle used to be able to blow a clear high-C note on his legendary cornet even while munching popcorn, his favorite food. Humble, gentle, and always smiling, he was remarkably popular among all circus people, and widely respected for his talent. He took almost everything in his stride, and rarely complained about anything, including his salary: He made $60 a week when he first started with Ringling, and $800 when he left. After his retirement from the Ringling show, Merle never went back to visit; he and other traditional windjammers were short on patience with the lack of cornets and the new rock-and-roll music that pervades the modern circus. He never completely retired, however; he remained an active teacher and concert band conductor until his death at ninety-six, on December 31, 1987.

While his least favorite circus music was undoubtedly the "Elephant Polka," some of Merle's favorite circus pieces were the "Battle of Shiloh March," by C. L. Barnhouse; Frederick Alton Jewell's "Quality Plus" and "High and Mighty"; and "Barnum & Bailey's Favorite," by Karl L. King. All three composers were outstanding circus musicians. Barnhouse became the foremost publisher of circus music, and Jewell wrote over 200 compositions while working for Gentry, Sells–Floto, Barnum & Bailey, Hagenbeck–Wallace, and various Shrine circuses. The prolific Karl King was Evans' predecessor at the Ringling show. Before his death in 1971, he had written 282 different band compositions. Other great circus musicians included Charles E. Duble; Walter P. English; A. W. Hughes; Keith Killinger; the "Paul Whiteman of Spangleland," Henry Kyes; the galop king Joseph John Richards; and Everett James. James was the band director and his wife Mabel was a trapezist for the Mighty Haag Circus when their son Harry was born in 1916. That future great jazz trumpeter would grow up as a circus drummer and contortionist. At least one other musical great barely missed becoming perhaps the greatest circus musician of all time: The "March King"

himself, John Philip Sousa, was fully prepared to run away and join the circus in 1867, at the age of thirteen. However, his anxious father prevented it by enlisting him as an apprentice in the U.S. Marine Band.

Black Windjammers

Not all the finest music provided by the circus came from the main big top band. The side show bands, the "jig bands," as they were traditionally called by both blacks and whites, presumably without the ugly racist connotations associated with today's use of the word, were made up of black musicians who exhibited a scope and power equal to their white counterparts. They accompanied many of the side show routines, and were frequently responsible for delivering the after-show concert in the main tent. Undoubtedly the greatest of the side show band directors was P. G. Lowery, a graduate of the New England Conservatory of Music, who directed the side show band for the Ringling show, as well as the bands for several minstrel shows. Both black and white circus musicians frequently traveled with the indoor minstrel shows during the off-season. Lowery's talent on the cornet, his rigid discipline, and his professional modesty earned him respect from

Calliope. Photo by W. H. Rough

many admirers of all races, including Merle Evans, who had insisted on his being hired for the Ringling show. From the time when he was the leader of the Nashville Students Band, Lowery was billed as "the world's greatest solo cornet player." His chief competition for distinction then was another cornet player, W. C. Handy, bandmaster of the Mahara Minstrels. Handy went on to write "St. Louis Blues," among others, and to become known for posterity as the "Father of the Blues." Other well-known black band leaders included Prof. Wolfscale with the Barnum & Bailey Circus, Fount B. Woods with the Cotton Blossom show, Camp Travis with the Russell Brothers shows, "Pop" Simmons with the Virginia Minstrels, Arthur Wright, and Dan Desdunes.

Calliopes, Etc.

"Calliope" Clarence Cottman was another black man who earned acclaim as a circus musician. He was the recognized master of the steam piano, or calliope. No other single musical instrument is so uniquely associated with the circus. Circus people pronounce it *"kall*-ee-yoap," strictly three syllables with the accent on the first, and under no circumstances "kall-*eye*-o-pee," the way everyone else pronounces it. Doc Spalding called the large organ wagon he used on his 1849 circus an "Apollonicon," at the time a relatively common name for a large mechanical organ. The church organ was at last finding its way into Puritan churches, and this was simply a larger and more

elaborate traveling version. A few years later, J. C. Stoddard of Worcester, Massachusetts, took out a patent that harnessed the power of steam for playing the organ. The "calliope," as it was now called, found favor on steam boats, where there was a steady supply of steam, and on elaborately fitted heavy circus wagons, which burned coal to generate their own steam. Calliopes could be heard for miles, and their unique woozy sound was used both to give concerts and to gather audiences. Calliopes were generally the last vehicles in line for circus parades for many reasons, not the least of which was their alleged tendency to explode, although none ever has in a parade.

At the other end of the processions, the giant circus bandwagons led the parade sections, beckoning anyone within earshot to come to the circus. They were elaborate storage wagons for the musical instruments, but they also provided high moving platforms from which band members could perform as "pied pipers."

Circus parades led to other innovations in circus music as well. At the end of the 19th century, the Ringling Brothers Circus carried the only mounted band in the country outside the U.S. Cavalry. There were forty brilliantly arrayed musicians mounted on matched white horses, led by George Granweiler. Other circuses followed suit in displaying unusual eye and ear-catching bands. There was a children's band mounted on ponies, and a ladies' band, and Karl King tried a mounted band with the Sells–Floto Circus.

Singing Clowns

As we have seen, it was not the big brass circus bands, however, who introduced music into the circus. The real credit for that goes to the early musical clowns. The questionable morality of feel-good music somehow became less questionable if what sounded like a moral message was being delivered at the same time, or if it was played with tongue firmly planted in cheek. Musical self-mockery was a popular form of entertainment that found its ultimate niche in the minstrel shows, both black and white. Minstrel stars also worked in circuses: Daniel D. Emmett, for instance, the composer of "Old Dan Tucker," worked for Welch's Olympic Circus.[4] But he was in New York with Bryant's Minstrels in 1859 when he wrote the future battle cry for the southern cause: "Dixie" was composed for the walk-around at the end of the show. The singing clown survives today in the likes of the more conventionally dressed Mark Russell, Tom Lehrer, and Stephen Wade. In fact, he was not unlike today's stand-up comedians and broadside balladeers. But he made his entry into America way back in John Bill Ricketts' circus.

Matthew Sully, a prominent English Harlequin, tumbler, and singer at Sadler's Wells Theatre in London, joined Ricketts' company in the summer of 1795. He became particularly well-known for his hit song, "Four and Twenty Periwigs." Later that fall, they were joined by the man recognized as the first "American-born" circus clown, John Durang. Much of what we know about Ricketts' enterprises we owe to Durang's detailed memoirs. The new clown was an accomplished actor and acrobat, and his variations on the "Tailor's Ride to Brentford" were extremely popular. Joe Pentland was another popular early singing clown and one of the first to get top billing. He worked with Aron Turner's Circus, and then with Sands & Lent. He is one of those often credited with creating still another variation on the tailor's ride, called "The Drunken Sailor." Posing as a drunken sailor, Pentland emerged from the stands offering to ride an ornery horse, and was greeted with various hoots and cheers. After several hilariously unsuccessful attempts, he stripped down to his leotards and rode with consummate skill. A later version of the act was wonderfully

described in *Huckleberry Finn,* and other variations on it survive today in several contemporary equestrian routines. Tony Pastor, often called the "Father of Vaudeville," also began his career in the circus as a singing clown and acrobat before he opened his variety theatre in New York in 1881. Finally, circus pioneer Dan Castello, W. C. Coup's first partner, was not only a courageous owner and frontiersman, but also a renowned singing and riding clown.

However, the first American clown to achieve genuine star status was a jockey, gambler, and strong man who used to catch cannon balls on the back of his neck. He was born as Daniel McClaren, but he is better known by his mother's maiden name of Rice. We first met Dan Rice as a circus owner in Chapter 3. Despite his later notorious drinking episodes, his presidential ambitions, and his ruthless billing wars with Spalding, Rice was best known and loved as America's premier singing clown. Above all, he saw himself as a true jester: "A successful clown must possess more intellect, ability, and originality than a comedian. He must be a crack mimic, an elocutionist, a satirist, and so ready-witted that he — to the ringmaster — is a stupid fool, a buffoon; to the audience — a wise man whose every remark is impregnated with philosophy as well as humor. This is the dual nature of the true clown."[5] Rice's version of the tailor's ride was similar to Pentland's, but instead of the drunken sailor he posed as a country bumpkin named Jenkins. The "Pete Jenkins Ride" thereafter became the most common name for the routine in America. His own "uneducated" vivid satirical variations of Shakespearean English, included this "tragic" opening:

Hamlet, the Dane, of him just 'deign' to hear,
And for the object lend, at least, an ear.
I will a tale unfold, whose lightest word
Will freeze your soul, and turn your blood to
  curd.
. . . .
One night two fellows, standing at their post,
Beheld — my stars! a real, living ghost —
Whose ghost was he, so dismal and unhappy?
It was, my eyes, the ghost of Hamlet's pappy.[6]

Rice's best-known song was the popular "Root Hog or Die"; all America was singing and shouting its many verses:

> I'll tell you of a story that happened long ago,
> When the English came to America, I s'pose
> you all know,
> They couldn't whip the Yankees, I'll tell you
> the reason why,
> Uncle Sam made 'em sing: Root Hog or Die! [7]

It was the circus' musical clowns like Dan Rice who were America's first real troubadours. Thanks to them, songs like "Root Hog or Die," "Turkey in the Straw," "The Man on the Flying Trapeze," and "Down in the Coal Mine" were sung and preserved. "Circus songsters," popular pocket-sized anthologies of traditional and topical secular song lyrics, began to appear with a circus orientation around the middle of the 19th century. They were the precursors of our modern circus souvenir programs. Among them were Sam Lathrop's *Songs, Stump-speeches, Remarkable Sayings, Buncomb Harrangues, and Fools Arguments,* Nat Austin's *Clown Song and Joke Book,* and *Dan Rice's Great Song Book.* The latter also contained Rice's "puns, jokes, tales, grotesque adventures, gibes and flashes of merriment." As the songster concept expanded to include all vocal circus music beyond the purely comic, separate booklets were published and sold containing the music from the separate after-show concerts. [8]

CLOWNS

In America in the second half of the 19th century, the onset of the three-ring circuses spelled the end of the singing solo circus clowns. The subtlety of the solo clown's humor and the sense of personal contact with his audiences could not be conveyed over the vast acreage of the new big tops, when spectators were already distracted by other acts. The talking and singing clowns retired immediately to vaudeville and the touring variety shows, leaving the circus to the riding clowns. Even the pantomime solo clowns, like the great Frank "Slivers" Oakley, who enthralled audiences with his baseball act after the turn of the century, survived only for a while. The new silent clowns could erupt into an arena by the hundreds, all performing their routines at once during the "walk-arounds," or the "come-out" before the perform-

ance begins. When Oakley's act was cut and his salary was reduced from $750 a week to $50 for doing a walk-around only, he walked out of the Ringling show in disgust. He committed suicide in 1915. A whole new style of uniquely American clowning, based on flamboyant costumes, loud noises, oversized props, and aggressively violent routines, was about to begin. Only relatively recently, under the influence of the "new wave" one-ring circuses in America, have solo mime clowns begun to make a comeback, although they are still a relative rarity. The outstanding solo work of Cesar Aedo, the "Travelling Salesman" in the 1990 Big Apple company, is a case in point. In classic mime form, Cesar tugs with all his apparent strength in an effort to move his "samples" case, but it is invisibly fixed in space. Wonderfully funny silent pantomime turns such as this and others by Pickle, Dennis Lacombe, and several other "new wave" clowns, take upwards of ten minutes to present. In the giant late-19th century three-ring circuses they proved no longer feasible.

Grimaldi

American clowns, whether they worked in walk-arounds, in entrées, or as a solo act, were among the thousands around the world owing their inspiration to a man who never set foot in America, or for that matter in the circus. His name was Joseph Grimaldi, from whom all clowns earned the name "Joey," and for whom clowns around the world still celebrate memorial services and enormous gala birthday parties. So profound was his influence on clowning in general that he merits a brief digression from the American circus.

Grimaldi was born in London in 1778, grandson of a performing acrobat, and son of a cruel and quirky pantomime artist. He participated in his father's act dressed as a monkey on a chain, until the old man died when he was ten. Then, while Astley and Hughes were plying their trades in the early days of the circus, young Grimaldi was quickly growing into one of the outstanding Harlequins of his day in the pantomimes. When he introduced his "Clown" to London audiences in 1800, the character quickly gained popularity over Harlequin. By 1806, when he appeared as Clown in an unprecedented ninety performances of the "Harlequin and Mother Goose, or The Golden

Egg," his reputation as the "King of the Clowns" was established for all time. Joey was the first clown to paint his face with geometrical patterns suggesting a grotesque distortion of personality, and his unrestrained acrobatics and antics with swords and other props were challenging tests of physical endurance. His comic songs, like "Hot Codlins," were the hit tunes of the day:

> A little old woman her living got
> By selling hot codlins, hot, hot, hot.
>
> . . . .
>
> To keep herself warm, she thought it no sin
> To fetch for herself a quartern of [GIN!][9]

Enthusiastic audiences were expected to supply the final rhymed word at top volume. While Joey's humor was often vulgar, he was above all warm-hearted and recognizably human. The wide range of his imaginative performances contained models for all clowns to follow. Eventually Grimaldi's broken health required him to retire when he was only forty-five. He was so maimed by all that he had endured on stage that after two return appearances in 1828, he had to sit down during his final performance to bid his audiences farewell. He lived through nine more years as a crippled and bitter recluse, before he died in 1837.

The legend of Grimaldi continued to grow after his death. An impressed Charles Dickens rewrote the clown's memoirs and made them into a bestseller. Other biographers have explored every aspect of his life, from his difficult childhood to the tragic death of his first wife and the loss of his only son to alchoholism. There is a story in circulation that late in his career, Grimaldi went under an assumed name to a doctor for treatment of his profound depression. "There is only one cure for you, my man," said the doctor. "You must go at once to see the clown Grimaldi." "But doctor," replied the weary clown, "I am Grimaldi." Of course a similar story had circulated almost two hundred years earlier about the Italian–French mime clown, Domenique Biancolleli, and another about the American whiteface pantomime George L. Fox, so the historical accuracy of this one is questionable. It does, however, serve to illustrate the strange combination of human joy and pain which is the paradox of the clown's life. Not for naught is the clown often portrayed as a darkly schizophrenic and troubled personality.

The Paradox of Clowning

What is there about clowning that brings out the dark side of human existence along with the bright? Our laughter sometimes seems only a short step removed from horror. With the clowns we learn to laugh as much at human pain and suffering as we do at comic situations. Insults, beatings, falls, and all kinds of tragic disasters can become the substance of comedy; it seems the greater the violence, the more pronounced the laughter. But through the laughter, poverty and deformity are diminished. No matter what the severity of the tragedy, the clown survives, and he does it with dignity. The clown's gag may make us howl with laughter, or create a bout of depression. It may make us smile happily, or create a brief moment of genuine empathy and understanding. Conrad Hyer points out that clowns are both "delight makers" —*koshare* as the Navahos called them — and "disturbers of the peace."[10] Among all the paradoxes of the circus, the clown is the most baffling.

Traditions

There have been thousands of circus clowns, of course, whose names have never been at the tip of America's tongues, and thousands more who never will be. The expanse of the three-ring circus requires armies of clowns at times, all participating in mass routines and gags. Like dancing girls in a chorus line, few of them ever earn anything approaching star status; there is little hope of anything other than minimal pay, and stability and security are unknown. Quitting his traditional college to enroll in Clown College and then travel with the Beatty–Cole Circus under the monniker of "Tomato Soup," as did Greg Long of Charlottesville, Virginia in 1987, didn't exactly thrill his parents. But he is a happy man, nonetheless. Clowns are a dedicated and hard-working troupe of people, who endure many hardships, primitive living conditions, and low salaries in order to perform their art for us. It takes stamina and devotion to be a clown, and many patrons consider them to be the real stars of the circus. Some have lived the clichéed existence of the tragic clown, like Grimaldi, Fox, and Oakley; but still others, like Felix Adler and Lou Jacobs, have been inherently happy people.

Russell-B-Clown.
Photo courtesy of Russell Brown

"Queenie Moon," a.k.a. Joan Mankin, in the "big juggle."
Photo courtesy of Pickle Family Circus

Happy dodges a squirt from his
mischievous car, at Circus World Museum.
Photo by W. H. Rough

Ruth Chaddock. Photo courtesy of Ringling Bros.
and Barnum & Bailey Combined Shows, Inc.

Photo courtesy of Ringling Bros. and
Barnum & Bailey Combined Shows, Inc.

"Buster" helps a visitor to the 1989
Beatty–Cole clown alley.
Photo by W. H. Rough

Most American circus clowns have been male and white. There have been a few great black clowns, like Gordon Bunch and Eph Horn. Horn was America's first black clown, also known as the Black Star. More recently, talented blacks like Russell Brown, featured at the 1989 Milwaukee Parade, have made major inroads into the world of clowning. Despite women's equality in the early history of clowning, and a few notable later exceptions like Evetta, otherwise known as Josey the lady clown, or Josephine Matthews, American clowns were male in accordance with more chauvinistic policies that were established in the 19th century. Several clowns' wives, including Felix Adler's wife Amelia, clowned in the ring, but they usually disguised the fact that they were women. Not until Peggy Williams broke the sex barrier in 1970, and became the first female graduate of Ringling's Clown College, did the traditional all-male bastion of circus clowning open completely. Peggy was a speech pathology major before she decided to become a clown, and she moved on to become an Assistant Performance Director with the Ringling Blue Unit. Another Clown College graduate, Ruth Chaddock, became Ringling's foremost female stilt-walker. A third, Bernice Collins, who also at one time harbored ambitions to be a tiger trainer, became the first black female clown to appear with the Ringling show. In fact, the Ringling show now sports a number of talented female clowns, and universally, clowning is becoming as respectable for women as it is for men, opening up whole new gag and routine opportunities. The Pickle Family Circus' Queenie Moon, performed by Joan Mankin, is one of the funniest feature clowns anywhere in the business. Weighed down by sheer numbers, our use of "he" to refer to all clowns is intended as no slight to the many talented "she's" in the profession of modern clowning. Although there are too many unsung clowns, both male and female, to even begin to name them all, we are advised to remember Barnum's still true maxim that they are one of the two pegs on which to hang a circus.

Clown gags and routines have generally varied very little from one generation to the next, which may be both an advantage and a disadvantage. There is humor in their very predictableness, and fathers and sons can share the same experiences a full generation apart. We know, with some variations, that we can expect the same barbershop routine on the Beatty–Cole show that our grandparents saw fifty years ago. The Ringling Brothers and Barnum & Bailey Circus performed a real service to nostalgia buffs in 1988 when they recreated many of the clown gags from the heyday of the circus. They included the burning house, the "cop" chases, and the inept house painters. All the clown car routines, like the exploding car, the one loaded down with an unbelievable gang of clowns, and the self-driving car, like Happy's at Circus World Museum, are part of our clown vocabulary. When we don't see the old gags performed, some of us leave with a feeling that the circus has been incomplete. Others of us, on the other hand, feel that the old jokes are now too stale and too oft repeated, and that it's time for the infusion of a brand new approach to circus clowning. Therein lies the basis for the never-ending hot debate on the state of clowning in America.

Whitefaces

It all starts in clown alley, a small tent located in the back yard near the performers' entrance to the big top. There is where the various combinations of zinc oxide and oil or grease were mixed to become "clown white" makeup—before it all came in a can; it's where the clowns traditionally dress, and where they traditionally wash in the allotted two buckets of cold water per performance. The nine or so Beatty–Cole clowns are fond of claiming that theirs is the last genuine clown alley under canvas in the country. In the heyday of the three-ring circus, clown alley residents used to number in the hundreds.

Part of the process of learning to clown lies in determining the physical and psychological identity of the clown who lies at the heart of each individual performer. When he puts on his makeup, a good clown usually doesn't think of it as a disguise, but as a conduit through which his inner clown personality can be expressed. Once his clown face has been developed, it becomes his unique personal property, and no one else is ever allowed to duplicate it. Emmett Kelly and his son were well-known for their frequent and bitter disagreements, which were at least in part over the contention that Emmett, Jr. allegedly wanted to

Mike Snider, Clyde Beatty – Cole Bros. Photo by D. M. Chambers "Elmo Gibb"

Felix Adler and porcine friend. Photo courtesy of Circus World Museum, Baraboo, WI

Frosty Little and his canine sidekick Sky. Photo courtesy of Ringling Bros. and Barnum & Bailey Combined Shows, Inc.

expropriate his father's face.

The faces and styles of circus clowning developed historically from specific performers and their routines, and then became generalized. They can be divided into three basic categories. The oldest is the whiteface clown, who had developed by the end of the 17th century into the characters of Gilles and Pierrot, French country fair variations on the Pedrolino character of commedia dell'arte. Over a hundred years later, at about the same time that Grimaldi was entertaining in London, a young Jean-Gaspard Deburau was capturing the imagination of audiences at the Théâtre des Funambules in Paris. Deburau, whose life was the basis for Marcel Carné's French film *Les Enfants du Paradis*, wore white face makeup, a skullcap, and an all-white suit; he was an adept juggler, acrobat, and mime, and he gave Pierrot a new air of sophisticated, dreamy mischief-making bordering on the sinister.

Since then, whiteface circus clowns have fol-

lowed in the footsteps of Deburau: Until recently, they were authoritarian, sophisticated, and exacting. They tended to be pie-throwers and trick-instigators, and rather narrow-minded and bossy pseudo-intellectuals. If their painted features are of a natural size, they are called "neat whiteface," and if they are oversized or otherwise exaggerated, the clowns are in "grotesque" whiteface. Silent screen comedian Harry Langdon worked a traveling medicine show as a neat whiteface clown before he went to Hollywood. Pat Valdo was a prominent whiteface in the 1920's, before he became Ringling's personnel director. Today, Cecil McKinnon, who is "Yo-Yo" on the Circus Flora, is a good example of the 19th century neat whiteface. And finally, Glen "Frosty" Little, the current Master Clown for the Ringling Brothers and Barnum & Bailey Circus, is a well-known neat whiteface clown. His pointed cap is perched over a chalky face, with an only slightly exaggerated red lower lip and nose, and minimal character lines. Neat whitefaces are growing rarer, and modern ones are often characterized more by sadness than by their traditional mischievousness.

Only a few years ago in America, grotesque whitefaces were in abundance. They included the likes of Joe Lewis, one of the first prominent cop clowns; Paul Jung, who was also an inventive producing clown; Bobby Kay; and Paul Jerome, with make-up suggesting widely separated buck-teeth. But the most familiar face of all grotesque whiteface clowns belonged to the great Felix Adler. He carried a tiny umbrella, and his oversized red nose lit up when he was excited. He wore a grossly padded rear-end extension, long yellow shoes, and a tiny hat. Like many of the great circus clowns, including Otto Griebling, Poodles Hanneford, Lou Jacobs, Paul Jung, and Emmett Kelly, Adler set out to be another kind of circus artist before he settled into his clowning role. Born in Iowa in 1895, he ran away to be a tightrope walker in the circus when he was a boy. A few falls converted him into a clown, and for fifty years he was America's "King of the Clowns," a featured star in the Ringling Brothers and Barnum & Bailey Circus. For his most famous routine, Adler worked with a pet piglet, as had Dan Rice. Because piglets tend to grow rapidly into less-than-cute porkers, he estimates that during his career he had to train over five hundred pigs to feed from a bottle, climb a ladder, and slide down a plank. His clowning, like that of so many other circus clowns, was based on simplicity, surprise, and doing something serious that turns out to be funny. Before he died in 1960, Adler had also become one of the first great producing clowns in the country, directing the appearance of the entire troupe of Ringling clowns.

Augustes

A second stock circus clown was probably developed in Germany in 1869, by an American clown named Tom Belling. The story goes that Belling was running away from an angry proprietor in the back yard, and stumbled into the ring. Mortified, he tripped over his own coat tails and incoherently blundered off again, to the sound of roars of laughter and cries of "August!" from the approving crowd—a slang term in Berlin for a stupid bumbling fool. And so the "auguste" clown

was created. It's only one story among many claims for the true origin, but it's as good as any.

Whatever his origins, the auguste clown does abundant pratfalls, gets hit in the face with the pies, and is the butt of all the jokes that are usually instigated by the whiteface. On the other hand, the naïve bumbling of the unsophisticated auguste is responsible for dissolving the whiteface's well-laid if meaningless plans into chaos. The routine or gag they perform together is called an entrée, and for years it formed the basis for most clown entertainment in the circus, on vaudeville, in films, and on television. Gradually, the characters have grown more flexible, and their personalities have merged into a much more prominent auguste, who is a trickster in his own right. The modern auguste is the most recognized circus clown: No longer victimized by the sophisticated whiteface, his routines have grown ever more aggressive, physical, and slapstick in nature. The auguste usually wears the big shoes, the bulbous red nose, the red or orange wig, now shifting in style to purple, lime green, or pink, and the outrageous, color-clashing, oversized costumes. He may leave most of his own facial skin color showing, but he exhibits big features predominantly in the easily visible colors of black and red, and his lower lip and eyes may be thickly outlined in white to exaggerate facial expressions. Much to the consternation of the traditionalists, more and more modern augustes "show skin" abundantly. Ironically, this is actually a return to even earlier traditions, when augustes wore practically no makeup at all. Recently, makeup has grown more minimal again, largely due to the influence of the Moscow school of clowning, in order to reveal more of the true humanity of the clown. "Travelling Salesman" Cesar Aedo, with the Big Apple, wears none at all.

Lou Jacobs, who retired in 1988 at the age of eighty-four, after sixty-four years with the Ringling show, was America's premier auguste. "In clown," he was one of the most recognized men in America, with his distinctive big patches of white around the eyes, and his cone-shaped bald head, fringed with red hair around the ears and topped with a tiny hat. Lou wore a red rubber-ball nose, a variation on the large red noses which had long been a tradition used by clowns satirizing the drunken fool. His face appeared on the 1966

5-cent postage stamp commemorating the American Circus, one of the few living Americans to be so honored by the U.S. Post Office. A capable acrobat and contortionist, he created riotously funny effects by folding his lanky six-foot frame into the "world's tiniest car," that he had designed himself. His amiable Chihuahua dog Knucklehead, "disguised" with rabbit ears, was a master at playing dead and "outwitting" Lou, the "hunter." Lou still teaches at Clown College, where he is joined by another popular auguste, T. J. Tatters, otherwise known as Steve Smith, the director of the College.

The Cirque du Soleil's Benny Le Grand is another featured clown artist with his roots in the auguste, but he represents some significant changes in the development of the contemporary clown. For makeup, Le Grand wears only a large white triangular patch over his upper lip, slightly accented eyebrows, a moderately exaggerated nose, and an out-of-control natural hair line. His character role is far from that of a victim of any whiteface clown. On the contrary, he works alone or banters with the ringmaster, and like a conniving escapee from a mental ward, he seems determined to aggressively avenge all the dirty tricks that have been played on augustes for the past hundred years. Drenching spectators with water, or hauling an unsuspecting onlooker into center ring is not unheard of. The warning inserted into the 1988 Soleil program suggests just how "threatening" a clown the new auguste can be, a word once reserved for the antics of the whiteface:

Not one of our favorite people. We cannot endorse any actions perpetrated by Mr. Le Grand while in the ring or other areas of the Circus. All complaints should be directed to the League of Human Decency, Ottawa, Canada. Since Mr. Le Grand has come into possession of certain documents relative to the affairs of Le Cirque, it is best that we allow him to continue with the show.

Our apologies.

The Management.

The auguste, T. J. Tatters, a.k.a.
Steve Smith, Director of Clown College.
Photo courtesy of Ringling Bros. and
Barnum & Bailey Combined Shows, Inc.

Lou Jacobs.
Photo courtesy of Ringling Bros. and Barnum & Bailey
Combined Shows, Inc.

Also fitting into the category of the auguste are two of America's most famous clowns, but the point must be stressed that neither of them ever appeared in a circus: Ronald McDonald and Bozo. There have been hundreds of "original" Ronalds. Bozo, who celebrates a fiftieth birthday in 1990, began as a story-teller for children on Capitol Records, and made the transition to a TV clown played by Larry Harmon in 1961. In the Chicago market he has become a cultural icon, and a Bozo show has been carried on over eighty TV stations around the country. Two hundred actors have played Bozo, including such notables as Willard Scott, the NBC *Today* show weatherman, and former TV network chief Fred Silverman. Bozo's image, a commercial trademark, is one many people associate with clowns in general, and is based on the auguste face of Albert Fratellini. Unlike most augustes of his era, who wore very little makeup, Fratellini painted his lips black, the areas around his mouth and eyes white, and the rest of his face in shades of flesh tones and carmine.[11]

Characters

A third category of characterization grew out of the "carpet" clown, who independently provided carpeting for the bareback riders, and who in Europe still serves as a solo clown performing short routines between acts. "Character clowns," which seem to have developed from the "carpet," include any clown who has developed a unique, non-categorizable routine, and who usually works alone rather than with a partner or in a large group. The character also derives from the traditional poor auguste for whom nothing can go right, and he is the most realistic of the clowns. Unlike the regular clowns, who appear only in scheduled gags and walk-arounds, the character clown usually has the run of the circus tent, and can work independently whenever and however he chooses, so long as he is not disrupting major action in the rings. The most popular "character" is the hobo or tramp clown, who seems to have developed during the Great Depression and may be the only truly indigenous American clown. The tramp clown owes much of his inspiration to "the Little Tramp" himself, Charlie Chaplin, whose genius was built on centuries of clowning traditions. Chaplin's films are still revered and studied by

clowns all over the world. The tramp clown may be naïve and inherently sad, but he always has the considerable dignity which allows him to triumph over adversity and the basic injustice of the universe. Often he is a well-educated but down-on-his-luck gentleman. His face is usually darkened with black, as though he were unshaven or perhaps covered with a hobo's soot from the old steam engines; his clothes are tattered but usually carefully patched.

Two famous traditional tramp clowns, Otto Griebling and Emmett Kelly, have made a particularly strong impact on their audiences. They are the idols of many young clowns, and have been the models for much of what has followed them and is still to come. Griebling was the lovable round-faced tramp who used to attempt to deliver some odd piece of merchandise to an audience member who he claimed had ordered it. Over and over again during a show he would try to find "Mrs. Jones," the rightful owner of a melting block of ice or an ever-growing potted plant. He couldn't understand it when no one wanted anything to do with it. Otto Griebling also developed the routine of banging his tin pie plates together and pitting audiences on the two sides of the tent against each other in a contest of happy screams and applause. He came to this country from Germany in 1910, and spent his first ten years here as a bareback rider, until he broke both legs in an accident and was persuaded to try clowning. While he was with the Cole Brothers show, he and Freddie Freeman developed a burlesque boxing match that left the audience gasping with every noise-amplified haymaker and fall. They used big flat rubber mitts for gloves, that resounded throughout the tent when they slapped the ring curb for effect. In his later years with the Ringling show, even the removal of his larynx never stopped the much loved Griebling from performing. When he died on April 19, 1972, one of the young clowns in the company tearfully remarked that it was "the first thing I have ever seen Otto do that wasn't funny."[12]

Emmett Kelly was Griebling's close friend and admirer, and the two tramps occasionally worked together. They are often compared, and arguments over who was the better clown can get hot. There is no question, however, that Kelly was the better publicist, and he was able to parlay his

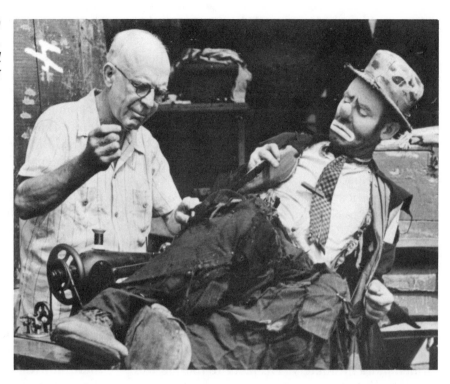

Weary Willie (Emmett Kelly) gets a new patch. Photo courtesy of Circus World Museum, Baraboo, WI

talents into major salary hikes. Working as a young sketch artist, he first created his famous character of "Weary Willie" as a cartoon. Willie was a forlorn little hobo, dressed in dirty rags and a tattered hat, who "always got the short end of the stick, but who never lost hope and just kept on trying."[13] Kelly first entered the circus as a trapeze artist with Howe's Great London Circus in 1921, and began to experiment with his tramp idea as a clown. His boss didn't much like the tattered costume, so it wasn't until much later, at the break-up of his marriage in 1935, while he was with the Cole Brothers and Clyde Beatty Combined Show, that the now-familiar "Weary Willie" character truly began to emerge. Kelly eventually claimed that two men lived in his house: himself, and "Weary Willie," and he wasn't sure which one his wife was most in love with.[14]

Willie's passive face never smiled, never changed at all, no matter what was going on around him. He had a bulbous red nose, a long sad look emerging from natural eyes, and a white, wide down-turned mouth set against a dark "five-o'clock" shadow. His clothes were the same tattered rags worn by the railroad hobos who crowded American boxcars in the thirties. He would peri-

odically enter the arena munching on a head of cabbage, and simply stare unblinkingly at a woman in the audience, occasionally offering her a leaf. Spectators had only to look at him to howl with the laughter of self-recognition. They shared with him his inherent triumph over his appearance as victim and failure. His most famous routine was one adapted from a gag by "Shorty" Flemm. He would enter center ring with a broom and begin to sweep up; when a spotlight spilled a large bright circle of light at his feet, he desperately tried to sweep it away, but to no avail. Eventually, he gave up and walked away, or he succeeded in sweeping it into a tiny pin-spot, which he loaded onto his dust-pan and carried away, only to be confronted with a new spot.

After a period with the Bertram Mills Circus in England, Kelly joined the Ringling Brothers and Barnum & Bailey Circus in 1942, and was its star by 1944, the year of the devastating fire. Caught in the middle of labor difficulties and eager to pursue an independent career, he eventually left the Ringling show, but he continued to play "Weary Willie" in nightclubs and on ball fields for the rest of his life. When he died in 1979, at the age of eighty, his friend Red Skelton remarked,

"The angels must have needed some laughs."[15]

Red Skelton himself ranks as one of the great American tramp clowns, as has once more been confirmed by his induction into the Clown Hall of Fame in 1989. As a boy in 1928, Skelton ran away to join the Hagenbeck–Wallace show. It was in the circus that he began to develop all of his great radio and TV clown personalities: Clem Kadiddle-hopper, Deadeye, Willy Lump Lump, and Freddie the Freeloader.

The American circus has produced many other excellent tramp clowns: Gene Randow, Mark Anthony, Michael Christensen, and Lorenzo Pickle among them. A producing clown who worked for a variety of circuses, Mark Anthony is now semiretired and living in Florida. His "Tony" represented a unique bridge between the tramp clown and the auguste, although he began his career as a whiteface. His gags were big enough to reach the back rows as well as the few to whom he performed more intimately. His favorite routine was his coveted watermelon, which squirted him in the face every time he attempted to sink his teeth into it.

Michael Christensen is a tramp clown whose grounding is outside the traditional American circus. He was a street performer and juggler, and was one of the founders of the Big Apple Circus. Before that he had worked as a whiteface clown to Paul Binder's auguste in a juggling routine at the Nouveau Cirque de Paris, directed by Pierre Étaix and clown artiste Annie Fratellini. He is not performing with the 1990 Big Apple show, but as its clown coordinator, Michael has made clowning a major component of the circus again. He and his colleagues, Fish (John Lepiarz), Oaf (David Casey), and Gordoon (Jeff Gordon) have kept their audiences enthralled with gags that are relatively non-frenetic and refreshingly simple: reviving the magic of soap bubbles; or sending an entire roll of toilet paper flying into the air with a leaf-blower — a Gordoon routine; or performing their impressively complicated but deceptively simple juggling routines and Frisbee games.

*"Mr. Stubs" (Michael Christensen) and the lion.
Photo courtesy of Big Apple Circus*

Another street performer and expert juggler, Larry Pisoni, a.k.a. Lorenzo Pickle, was the inventive creator of the Pickle Family Circus. He is now pursuing an independent career which he hopes will expand the boundaries of the traditional clown into film and stage acting, without ignoring his relatively recent roots in the circus. His 1989 one-man stage show, "Clown Dreams," and a guest appearance with the Circus Flora, as well as his unwillingness to rule out future appearances with the Pickle Family Circus, suggest that the circus is not yet finished with Lorenzo Pickle. Still sporting a red nose, he wears minimal makeup except for a large white mouth, and a red floppy hat, a neat striped pullover, and baggy pants. His routines involve intimate silent conversations with audience members, and a musical facility on his favorite signature prop, a baritone horn. A Pickle routine with balloons is reminiscent of Fanny Brice's vaudeville gag: When Baby Snooks was offered a balloon, "Bigger, Bigger, BIGGER!" she cried, until it burst. Emmett Kelly had a similar but more solitary balloon gag. But Pickle tries to give all kinds of balloons away to a deserving spectator, including one about five feet in diameter, only to have them all burst or sail away. Lorenzo Pickle also represents a bridge: from the traditional American tramp and auguste to the more realistic and modern middle class everyman at the core of the so-called "New Vaudeville" clowns.

It would be a shame to think that future circus clowns will be consigned to replaying over and over the same gags that were a part of our past. Those old gags still have value, and they can still be wonderfully funny, but they are museum pieces. Furthermore, it's not enough that clowns be birthday party entertainers and car salesmen. In the circus it's not enough that they be salesmen and autographers of coloring books, a status to which they have been too often relegated, and from which they are expected to earn a major part of their income. A new breed of clown has developed out of the traditions of the past to indicate that there is more to life than coloring books and museum gags.

"New Vaudeville"

These "Modern" or "New Vaudeville" clowns are called "private clowns" in Europe, a comprehensive term to describe all those who have turned away from the traditional clown "entrée"

"Lorenzo Pickle" (Larry Pisoni) with "Yo-Yo" (Cecil McKinnon). 1989 Circus Flora. Photo by W. H. Rough

between the whiteface and the auguste. Usually, they work alone, and typically they work without makeup. They are often said to be more interested in creating smiles and giggles than in the belly-laughs sought by the entrée clowns. The laughter they seek is created perhaps more from the head than the belly. They believe that the traditional entrée routines have grown sterile and unimaginative. Indeed, it appears they have, when clowns become so bored with their own routines that they fail to inject them with verve, energy, and a personalized connection to their particular audiences. Above all, the new clowns seek that personalized connection to audiences in their own time and space. It is a relationship *with* audience members that they seek — not a performance *at* them.

Some of the new clowns have remained with the circus, like the Cirque du Soleil's Dennis Lacombe. He does the wonderful "Leonard Bernstein" take-off, with his feet anchored to a spring board that allows his frantic baton waving to happen in a near-horizontal position. He is a master of old-fashioned physical pie-in-the-face comedy as well, and he uses a mechanical pie-thrower to suggest his mortal combat with a mechanized society gone berserk.

Barry Lubin was appearing as Grandma in the clown line-up with the Ringling show back in 1977. He was a hit with the Big Apple Circus a few years ago and then spent some time away from the big top exploring other options. A usually quiet but completely unpredictable bespectacled little old lady, Grandma can burst into wild rock rhythms at any minute. Lubin wears a head of gray hair, simple makeup incorporating a red face and nose and white eyes and mouth, and often a simple bright red coat or dress. Grandma's humor thrives on appearing completely out of place and out of context with everything going on around her; yet at the same time she is hip and in touch. In 1989, Lubin was back in the circus fold: He was well-received in his hilarious guest appearance with the Royal Hanneford Circus at the Milwaukee Parade, as "Bat-Grandma," complete with black mask and cape. The entire 1990 Big Apple Circus is oriented around the theme of Grandma's tour through the Old West.

Other new clowns are making their mark in

the theatre, rather than in the circus, although their routines are firmly based on old European and American circus clowning. Avner the Eccentric, a modern tramp clown, and the Flying Karamazov Brothers, a superb group of five unrelated, chattering, musical jugglers, appeared in a frenetic and well-received circus version of Shakespeare's *The Comedy of Errors* at Lincoln Center a few years back. Both Avner and the Karamazovs have also earned rave reviews in their own Broadway shows. Geoff Hoyle is another product of the Pickle Family Circus, where he was the sausage-nosed and fiery-tempered Mr. Sniff. He too is now pursuing an independent stage career with his own one-man show, and he was also the guest director for the 1989 "Café Chaotique" on the Pickle Family show.

Perhaps the most successful of all the new clowns to date is Bill Irwin, another graduate of the Ringling Clown College. Turning down an offer to join the Flying Gaona troupe in Venezuela, he too joined up with the early Pickle Family Circus. While he was with Pickle, he played an odd little whiteface clown named Willy, working alongside Lorenzo Pickle and Mr. Sniff. Since then, he has forsworn all clown makeup and used his own expressive face to suggest realistically much of the same innocence and victimization by the chaos of a mechanized and unfair world that were the province of Charlie Chaplin, Emmett Kelly, and Buster Keaton. The world to which Irwin falls victim is frequently a dehumanized and electronic one. It is always trying to lure him into its grips, to convert him into a TV picture, or to suck him under a curtain. On stage, Irwin is never defeated in these clashes with the modern world; apparent defeats only result in magical resurrections, and the essential humanity of his clown always triumphs over impersonal gadgets, offering invaluable hope to his desperate audiences. Among his other work, his Broadway production entitled *The Regard of Flight* earned him a 1983 National Endowment for the Arts Choreographer's Fellowship. In 1984, he was awarded a Guggenheim Fellowship, and he received the first MacArthur "Genius" Fellowship to go to a performing artist. In 1989, his production of *Largely New York* was another smash hit on Broadway.

A look at today's headlines is sufficient to remind us of how much the world desperately needs its clowns. It is no small relief to know that we are getting them. Despite all the struggles, pressures, psychoses, and phobias associated with life in modern America, or perhaps even because of them, clowning is thriving. Alan Zerobnick, master shoemaker of clown shoes in Sequim, Washington, estimates that there are around 28,000 part-time clowns, including Shrine clowns, jugglers, street vaudeville performers, and about 200 Ronald McDonalds; and perhaps 1,000 professional full-time clowns, as well as "probably millions of 'closet clowns' across the country."[16]

The Clown Hall of Fame and Research Center, Inc. opened a small office and museum in "America's Circus Capital," Delavan, Wisconsin in 1987. There are plans for the construction of a new elaborate multi-purpose facility, including a fully equipped exhibition center with a 400-seat theatre, an educational research center, and accommodations for regularly scheduled clown workshops and seminars. On April 23, 1989, the Hall of Fame inducted its first six clowns: Felix Adler, Otto Griebling, Emmett Kelly, Lou Jacobs, Mark Anthony, and Red Skelton.

The many regional and national clowning organizations in the United States include the World Clown Association, Inc., "dedicated to the art, education, and enjoyment of clowning." The WCA was born in the U.S. in 1982, and held its first convention in Atlanta the following year. Its local units are called "alleys," naturally, and membership numbers in the thousands. It publishes a monthly newspaper called *Clowning Around*. Clowns of America International, the International Shrine Clown Association, and Clowns International also have offices in the United States. Clown schools and the many courses in community colleges all over the country are filled, and Ringling's Clown College has even opened a second campus in Japan. The Japanese faculty are trained in Florida, but their goals are more social than professional: "to show Japanese merchants how to be a little less uptight," and "to give people a new kind of confidence in themselves to better deal with people."[17] Here as well as in Japan, there is a necessary function to clowning related to the mental health of our society, and we might all do well to bear it in mind. Red Skelton, when he was inducted into the Clown Hall of Fame, summed up the positive value of clowning to our world today: "A clown studies his fellow man and can mimic him and still like his fellow man." Or as Conrad Hyer once again puts it, "For those who are not pretenders to thrones that are not theirs or to a divinity they have not attained, or even to some superior form of humanity, the clown enables us to embrace ourselves and one another as the luminous lumps that we are."[18]

8.
ANIMALS AND TRAINERS

"BULLS AND..."

We begin this chapter with the number-one-most-popular attraction in the circus. P.T. Barnum said over a hundred years ago that elephants and clowns were the two pegs on which to hang a circus. A survey of some 1,500 members of the Circus Fans of America completed in 1985, by Pemar Services, suggested that the elephants have not slipped in popularity. What is still the main reason most people go to the circus, the only performing act without a single negative vote in the survey? The elephants![1] Part of the reason is the apparent contradiction between their enormous size and their paradoxically sensitive looks and disposition. They can crush a lion with a single kick or slap with their trunk, and yet we popularly think of them as being afraid of mice — a most decidedly untrue rumor.

What magnificent creatures they are: powerful, and according to many trainers unpredictably dangerous. Both male and female elephants are called bulls, and they are both loved and quietly feared by the men who work most closely with them. They are capable of extraordinary loyalty and genuine affection, both for each other and for their trainers, and their long eyelashes and mournful expressions give them an air of possessing uncannily human emotions and intelligence. Gunther Gebel–Williams, who has worked with elephants, horses, dogs, and a great variety of cats, credits elephants with being by far the most intelligent of circus creatures. At the same time, bull men have learned by experience that it is not smart to completely trust so large, so powerful, and so distinctly not-human a creature. Males are more unpredictable and dangerous than females. Africans are traditionally harder to train, also more unpredictable and dangerous than Asians, who have a longer history of cooperation with man. But that may all be about to change.

Recently, it has been orphaned Africans, whose mothers have been murdered by ivory poachers, who are making ever more frequent appearances in American circuses. It has not been possible to import Asians to the United States for display by zoos or circuses since the mid-70's. Future Asians seen in this country will have to be bred in this country, a process which has heretofore been difficult at best. Now, with increasingly tightening restrictions on elephant exporting in the Asian countries, at the same time that domesticated elephants are being superseded by tractor power, the long history of the Asian elephant in association with man is in imminent danger of collapse. Under the pressure of population and agriculture, the very survival of the Asian elephant is as much at risk as that of the African.

There is no question that the African elephant is in immediate danger of extinction. Over half of the entire population of African elephants has been killed in the last eight years. It is estimated as of this writing that there are a mere 600,000 animals left on the entire continent, and they are being killed at the rate of 80,000 a year. African elephants are the victims of a continuing war of words, in which no one can even agree whether a worldwide ban on trade in ivory would be a help or a hindrance. And they are the victims of the ever-expanding needs of human populations to grow food. Despite all the fervent and genuine wishes of naturalists and animal-rights lovers, this earth can never again sustain the great elephant herds of the past, unless by war, plague, or mismanagement we are successful in killing off substantial percentages of its human population. So while we humans argue about how to protect elephants, and what to do with them once we have

[213]

Photo by Nancy Renner

*Photo courtesy of Ringling Bros. and Barnum &
Bailey Combined Shows, Inc.*

*Baby Barbara carries her own scooper. Photo
courtesy of Culpepper–Merriweather Circus*

them protected, the elephants continue to be slaughtered by the thousands, illegally by poachers for their ivory, legally by "legitimate" ivory traders, and legally by game wardens and farmers protecting their agricultural food supply. In a bitter ironic twist, 1989 may have marked the last year in which baby African elephants can be imported by American circuses and zoos for display purposes. Without a market, many of the orphans will in the future undoubtedly be destroyed along with their mothers. Unless new knowledge and innovative domestic breeding programs are successful in compensating for import restrictions and the lack of respect for animals in their natural state, it is distinctly possible that future generations will not be able to experience what earth's largest living land mammal, either African or Asian, looked like, or how it behaved.

Characteristics

The largest Africans tend to be somewhat taller and leaner than their heavier cousins, the Asians. That distinction doesn't do much good in identifying domesticated animals, which may be younger and smaller than their potential maximum growth

in the wild. Still, it's easy to tell the difference between an Asian and an African elephant: The African has huge floppy ears and a domed head, while the Asian has little ears and two bumps on top of its head. Africans can sport the longer tusks, over twelve feet if they are not broken off in battle or hacked off by poachers.

Among the elephants' more impressive characteristics are their tusks, the middle incisor teeth of the upper jaw; only some Asian females have no tusks. They will grow around two inches a year throughout the elephant's life, new ones replacing broken-off ones. Domestic elephants frequently have theirs trimmed or removed for safety purposes. Elephants are extremely light-footed and able to move in total silence, because they are basically walking on tip-toe, supported by a large pad under the heel that cushions the foot like a running shoe. There are two temporal glands on the elephant's head, from which a gummy substance may ooze when he or she is in an excited state. During "musth," which occurs only in mature males, the substance is thick and foul-smelling. It is apparently associated with sexual dominance during periods of competition for

Beatty–Cole Asians. Note shape of head and small ears. Photo by Joan Z. Rough

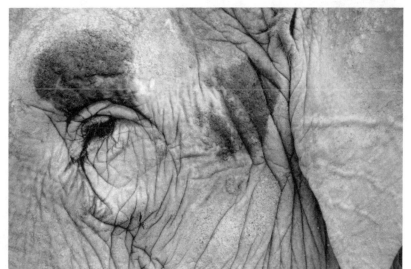

". . .As high as an elephant's eye." Note moisture around temporal gland. Photo by Joan Z. Rough

mating. Trainers agree that elephants can be unpredictably temperamental and dangerously violent during musth.

Elephants are covered with a stiff bristly hair, too tough for razors. Circus elephants are given haircuts ever so delicately, with a blowtorch, and they seem to love it. Their hide is tough and thick, varying from three-quarters of an inch to three inches, but it is extremely sensitive. They can feel mosquitoes landing on them, and a hard slap or blow from the handle of an elephant hook by a trainer is most certainly painful. Most sensitive is the end of his nose, or trunk. The end of an Asian's trunk has a finger for grabbing objects; an African's trunk has two fingers. There is a large hole in the center of an elephant's skull at the base of its trunk, and many people think that the found skulls gave rise to the legend of the Cyclops, Homer's one-eyed giants. The trunk is a multi-purpose instrument for smelling, grabbing, and making a great variety of noises for communication. With it, an elephant can whistle, chirp, squeal, thump on the ground, trumpet, and rumble. Much of the rumbling is at a pitch too low to be heard by human ears, and carries mating calls over great distances to other elephants. The trunk may also be used for holding, blowing, or lifting water to the mouth. It can not be used like a drinking straw, however, since after all, it is primarily a nose.

A circus elephant will drink from 50 to 100 gallons of water a day, much more than little boys who dreamt of running away to the circus to

"You're still thirsty?"
Photo courtesy of Circus World Museum, Baraboo, WI

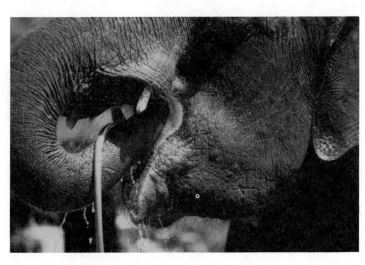

Lisa. 1989 Roberts Bros. Circus.
Photo by Joan Z. Rough

water elephants could ever have managed. A circus elephant will also eat up to 100 pounds of hay and sweet feed every day. Its inefficient digestive system allows it to eat almost anything, half of which is wasted. Fresh grasses are a favorite, but peanuts, tobacco, stale donuts, and paper will do in a pinch. Elephants are sexually mature at around 15 to 20 years; they can live up to 70 years. Pregnancy lasts about 2½ years, and the average female may produce around four 200 pound newborns during her lifetime.

Great Circus Elephants

Elephants have been involved with parades and circus-like activities for over 4,000 years, and they have been a part of the American circus since 1832. Their long tradition of domesticated cooperation with man rivals that of the horse. Their extreme sociability and apparent friendliness, patience, and tolerance, and their great strength and size make them ideal for use in the circus. According to a 1985 census, there were well over 250 elephants in American circuses, and baby Africans are still coming into the country rapidly.[2]

Circus back yards are full of tales of elephant lore. We saw in Chapter 3 how Old Bet and Romeo came to be immortalized on the town squares of Somers and Delavan. According to the *Cincinnati Enquirer* in 1880, another Romeo used to travel with the Uncle John Robinson Circus on the deck of a riverboat. He earned a mischievous but lovable reputation by regularly hauling in the hawser rope, and once almost sinking the ship by banging around a few loose logs. Moved inside for safety, he grew intrigued with the bell wires running from the pilot house to the engine room, and began to ring the bells himself, signalling "all engines stop!" The pilot and engineer had to arrange alternate communications for the rest of the trip.[3] Then there's the one about the elephant who snatched and ate a pack of cigarettes, a lighter, and an envelope containing $1,000 in cash from the shirt of an Oklahoma man. The cigarettes and lighter were done for, but a lot of administered mineral oil produced enough bits and pieces of the bills for the Federal Reserve to replace the cash. . . .Or the one about Tommy Hanneford's elephant, hired by a sleep shop owner for a publicity stunt to test out water beds. She was so distraught

when she couldn't get herself up from the bed that she would have caused an elephant stampede in the basement of the Lansing Civic Center had not Tommy punctured the mattress with his knife.[4]

Not all elephant stories are so lighthearted and benign, however. Most trainers think of their bulls as highly intelligent animals with whom they have formed a partnership, and there is genuine affection between them. But there are also those less responsible would-be trainers who perhaps see themselves as the losers in life's power struggles, victims who set out to avenge themselves by cruel subjugation of these huge beasts. There are plenty of horror stories about elephants who suddenly turned on their trainers, or bystanders, or anyone else whom the elephant deemed its enemy. Not all rampages can be attributed to bad treatment, though, because elephants, like people, are unpredictable individuals, with quirky and little-understood personalities of their own. Many of the stories suggest that the old axiom, "An elephant never forgets," is rooted in fact. Elephants do forget faces, jobs, and tricks, and they can get as frightened and confused as the rest of us. But like the rest of us, they rarely forget strong reactions to punishment and reward, and often they can apparently develop a pathological affection for and loyalty to one man alone. Tichi, one of the Ringling Red Unit's bulls, is fiercely jealous of her trainer, Gunther Gebel–Williams, and won't tolerate the presence of his wife Sigrid. But Black Diamond's jealousy and memory are still talked about by many circus folks. This huge male Asian elephant was brought onto the Al G. Barnes Circus as an occasional stand-in for the notorious Tusko. Black Diamond evidently harbored resentments for some time when he saw his trusted first trainer walk out on him for a woman. Three years later, in 1928, when the trainer and his wife came to visit the circus, he attacked and killed the woman, and threw the trainer across several cars. The old bull was led off to a firing squad for his misguided obsession, and it took 170 bullets to kill him. At the time there were two other elephants of note on the Barnes show that add to our belief in elephantine memory: one-eyed Pearl, and Tusko. Sidney Rink, who had been a superintendent of elephants with Al G. Barnes, once accidentally knocked out Pearl's eye, and she never forgot who had maimed her. According to Slim Lewis, she drove Rink off the show and for the rest of her life sought revenge on all black people.[5]

Along with Henry Clay and Eph Thompson, an independent elephant showman from Europe who later worked with Forepaugh, Sidney Rink was one of the few well-known black elephant trainers in the country. He was one of a family of twenty-nine children, who started as a pony boy with the John Robinson show and became a headliner in charge of three herds of elephants. One day in 1930, the year the Miller 101 Ranch show folded, Rink found himself working for Miller management. His job was to load the elephants for delivery to the receiver in bankruptcy, crossing a picket line of angry unpaid performers and workers. Already seventy-four years old by then, but completely undaunted, he tailed up his elephants, mounted the lead, and had her pick up a logging chain. The line charged for the railroad cars, wildly swinging the chain from left to right, and flew through the picket line. Rink died at eighty-five, on March 14, 1941.

The Mighty Tusko, formerly "Ned," was the biggest elephant on the North American continent since the days of Jumbo. The tusks which earned him his name were about seven feet long. A temperamental Asian male, he was ten feet, two inches tall, and weighed over seven tons. He didn't work or perform on the Al G. Barnes show, but he was a major drawing card all the same, merely from his outlaw reputation. Before Al G. Barnes sold out to the American Circus Corporation, he and Tusko had a very strong mutual affection, and when Barnes left, the elephant became completely unmanageable. No other circus would touch him, and he spent some time as an exhibition road show, accompanied by his keeper and lifelong devotee, young George "Slim" Lewis. Tusko was to finish out his days in the Seattle Zoo, dying of a blod clot on June 10, 1932.

Al G. Barnes, born in 1862 as Alpheus George Barnes Stonehouse, was the gentle owner of one of America's most popular circuses, and widely known for his affinity with animals. It was said that he alone could talk Tusko out of one of his murderous rampages, merely with the sound of his voice. Like Wayne Franzen, that other "Doctor Doolittle" in the modern circus, Barnes grew up on the family farm, where early in his life he acquired his great love for animals and a complete intolerance for cruelty to animals. As a boy he was opposed to joining his father and brother on hunting trips. Once he found an orphaned black bear cub and took it home; within days his dogs and he and the bear were all playfully wrestling together. By the time Al was fourteen, he was breaking horses for his father's stock business, a feat he evidently accomplished mostly by "talking" to them. His father liked to buy cheaper hard-to-manage horses knowing that Al could calm them down. He had a standing $100 bet that Al could break any horse brought to him, and he never lost his bet. During his long life, Al's uncanny ability to talk to wild animals and seemingly be completely understood by them, made him a much-loved legend. Near the end of his life, he could still carry on a friendly howling conversation in the desert

The Al G. Barnes elephants in Hollywood mud, 1935.
Photo courtesy of Circus World Museum, Baraboo, WI

with a skittish coyote. It is little wonder that Tusko saw in him a friend.

Elephants have often been at the center of a circus' life. When "Columbia" was born on the Cooper–Bailey show in 1880, the first elephant to be born in the new world, P.T. Barnum was so impressed he immediately offered to buy the calf for $100,000. Bailey not only refused to sell, but publicized the offer and attracted more customers of his own to see the baby elephant that Barnum would pay so much to have. Finally, Barnum was in turn so impressed with his rival's ballyhooing skills, that he offered to join forces with Bailey to form the Barnum & London Circus. Then there was Toung Taloung, the highly-touted Burmese "Sacred White" elephant acquired by Barnum in 1884, which actually turned out to be a rather boring mottled gray albino. Not to be outdone, Adam Forepaugh scraped down and white-washed one of his elephants, and launched the famous "White Elephant Wars." He nervily claimed that his "Light of Asia" was the only genuine white elephant, and that Barnum's was a complete fraud.

The most highly publicized elephant in history was undoubtedly Jumbo, whose name, shortened from Mumbo-Jumbo, has been added to our permanent vocabulary for denoting enormity. Barnum secretly bought Jumbo from the London Zoölogical Gardens for the paltry sum of $10,000.

The bull had been a resident of Paris and London zoos since he was captured as a baby, and coming into a musth, which was little understood at the time, he was reputed to be growing difficult to manage. He was by then over eleven feet high, a foot taller than the later Tusko, and he weighed about one ton less—6½ tons. [6] So far as anyone knows, Jumbo was the largest elephant ever measured in captivity, although there have been larger Africans in the wild. The example in the rotunda of the Smithsonian's Museum of Natural History is more than a foot taller and probably about a ton heavier. [7] As soon as the sale was made public, the English created a marketing bonanza for Barnum and Bailey by demanding that it be cancelled. Thousands of school children, and even Queen Victoria herself urged that the suddenly beloved Jumbo be kept on British soil. But their pleas fell on deaf ears; for by now, Barnum knew what a plum he had gotten, and he boasted he would even turn down an offer of 100,000 pounds to void the sale.

By the time he arrived in New York, Jumbo had generated such a sentimental hullaballoo on both sides of the Atlantic that he became the single biggest draw in Barnum's career. The world went "Jumbo-crazy," and for his part, the now gentle Jumbo seemed to love all the attention. For 3½ years, he was the much-loved feature attraction on the circus. In his career, he sold millions of

Jumbo. Photo courtesy of Circus World Museum, Baraboo, WI

Woodcock Performing Elephants
Anna May and Ned.
1989 Big Apple, Shelburne, VT.
Photo by W. H. Rough

"Trunk-to-tail." Photo by Lisa J. Rough

Colonel Joe. Photo courtesy of Circus Vargas

Ben Williams and Anna May. Woodcock
Performing Elephants 1990 Big Apple,
Baltimore, MD. Photo by Joan Z. Rough

souvenirs and photos on which he was portrayed, and gave "at least a million children" rides on his back, as well as Queen Victoria, Winston Churchill, and Teddy Roosevelt. When he was killed by a passing freight train on September 15, 1885, in St. Thomas, Ontario, he was mourned by millions all over the world. Jumbo's stuffed hide eventually went on display at Tufts University, where Barnum was a trustee, and it remained there until it was destroyed by fire in 1975. Jumbo is still featured on the school's official logo.

In recent years, only one elephant has been given anything like the star status that was accorded to Jumbo and his early followers. Big Tommy was born in Thailand, and picked up just after his fortieth birthday by the Ringling organization from Tony Diano in 1986. He was renamed "King Tusk," the "Largest Mammal Travelling the Earth Today!" The forty-five-year-old bull stands ten feet high at the shoulder, and weighs about seven tons, shorter but heavier than Jumbo. Lee Keener, who has been his friend and trainer for over twenty years, says that King Tusk is pretty docile and well-behaved, and always does what he's supposed to do. Featured on the Red Unit of the Ringling Brothers and Barnum & Bailey Circus in 1987 and 1988, he was then shipped to Japan to headline the Gold Unit tour. However, if size is what all the fuss is about, Colonel Joe, a castrated male bull now with the Circus Vargas, may soon become the largest mammal traveling with an American Circus. Only fifteen years old, he already weighs an estimated five tons.

Bull Tricks

Performing elephants are taught a number of standard tricks, although every elephant is different, and not all can do every trick. Nevertheless, all individual routines are variations on and combinations of these basic tricks. Hugo Schmidt was one of the best-known boss bull men in the country when he came to the Ringling show from Germany after the war. His son Roman Schmidt has recently enjoyed success in breeding Asian elephants in this country. Hugo told Bill Ballantine that the first hurdle in training is getting past an elephant's kick to get a chain on its leg.[8] Training then starts with keeping the trunk preoccupied

with a stick or "tail-up" trunk-to-tail with another elephant, just to keep it from getting into mischief. Lying down, sitting down, standing on the front or back legs, mounting the pedestal, called a "bull tub," and spinning around are the next lessons. A dangerous trick taught the more trusted bulls is to hold a human being in their mouths while they spin. Their grip must be gentle enough to avoid crushing skulls or leg bones, but firm enough to keep the chorus girls or trainers spinning on a horizontal axis without flying out of the ring. Other difficult variations, like standing on one front foot, or lightly stepping on or half-lying over the body of the trainer, may be taught if the elephant can handle them.

Ben Williams likes to work that trick with Anna May in their fast-paced solo act on the Big Apple Circus, using it to suggest a fearless trust and rapport between man and beast. Ben also puts himself through horizontal spins with his leg in Anna May's mouth. In the 1989 show, Anna May and Ben introduced the newest member of the Big Apple elephant family, an African punk named Ned, perhaps after Tusko's original name. "Punk," a word often used to describe a circus youngster of the human variety as well, is the circus word for a baby elephant. Ned arrived in an oversized baby carriage, pushed around the ring by Anna May in her Sunday best, continuing a long tradition of elephant baby carriages in the circus. Ben Williams is the step-son of William "Buckles" Woodcock, one of the country's foremost bull men, to whom Anna May and Ned belong. Buckles is himself the son of prominent elephant trainers Babe and Bill Woodcock, Sr., who had the center ring bull act with Sells–Floto in 1931. Buckles likes to say that his family was in the circus when the Ringling boys were still wearing their wooden shoes. He acquired his nickname as a tot, when he wanted nothing more than to run away from — not to — the circus, and was buckled into a harness to keep him in sight of his mother. He is most grateful that the harness wasn't fitted with zippers: "Zippers Woodcock wouldn't have the same ring," he says. Ignoring his father's advice to get into the money end of circus, because "an elephant trainer should have a strong back, a weak mind, and a savage disposition, and you don't qualify on any of those accounts," Buckles followed his parents into the business. In 1959 he married Ben's mother, Barbara Williams, the fourth generation of another family of circus animal experts. He is now widely recognized as the reigning authority on elephants in America, and keeps detailed, accurate records on almost every bull that sets foot in the country. Among the other major contemporary bull men are Rex Williams, Barbara's first husband and Ben's father, with the Circus Vargas; and Donnie Carr, who manages one of the largest single herds traveling in the circus with Carson & Barnes.

One climactic trick, which traditionally comes at the end of most multiple elephant acts in the circus, is the long-mount. Fred Logan, the boss bull man for the Clyde Beatty–Cole Brothers Circus, is one of the few who show a walking long-mount: All ten of his bulls walk forward in a straight line on their hind legs, with their front legs braced on the back of the elephant in front. It's an impressive sight. Most other shows use a stationary long-mount, some trainers claiming that it's too hard on the elephants to have them walk during the long-mount. Fred is from Saskatchewan, and came to the United States to work for Terrell Jacobs. He became an assistant to Hugo Schmidt on the Ringling show before he moved off

to be Bill Woodcock Sr.'s assistant on the Kelly–Miller show in 1949. He's been with Beatty–Cole since 1970. Another of Hugo Schmidt's assistants, Axel Gautier, remained with the Ringling show to replace Schmidt, and was in charge of the Blue Unit's herd through 1989. "You cannot make an elephant do anything she doesn't want to do," says Gautier. "My training is based totally on coaxing and rewards."[9] Gautier's elephants, now in their late thirties, were all imported together in 1955 as punks, a brand new herd whose adorable cuteness stole the hearts of the American public. Axel's wife Donna, and his two sons Michael and Kevin, now the seventh generation of circus Gautiers, also participated in the elephant act.

"Buckles" and "Reed."
Photo courtesy of Buckles Woodcock

Fred Logan's Beatty–Cole long mount.
Photo by W. H. Rough

Gunther Gebel-Williams

Over on the Red Unit of the Ringling show, the wünderkind of animal trainers controls the elephant herd — and the tigers, and the liberty horses. It's very easy to get hooked by all the hype surrounding superstar Gunther Gebel-Williams, or to be put off by it. This cheery, blond-headed, muscular man, seemingly full of his own self-importance, is a genuine culture hero, and one of the most charismatic figures the circus has ever produced. But behind all that glitz and hype is a talented, much admired, and widely respected man. Many circus experts are even tempted to call him the greatest animal trainer who ever lived. Standing in center ring, surrounded by three rings of elephants, he can utter a single command in his own unique "elephant dialect," part English, part German, and part grunt, which seems to be interpreted differently by each elephant. As a result, the entire herd executes a variety of tricks all at the same time. Whatever people call him, he genuinely loves his animals, and he is never happier than when he is working with them. Gunther's son Mark Oliver Gebel, formerly "Buffy," helps with the elephant act, and is being groomed to take it over after his father completes his Farewell Tour in 1990. His daughter Tina has a Russian wolfhound act, and his wife Sigrid often presents the liberty horses trained by Gunther. But it is for his caged tiger act that he is now best known — which makes an appropriate transition to the next great category of circus animal acts.

"AND LIONS AND TIGERS AND..."

Born in the then German town of Schweidnitz, now a part of Poland, Gunther Gebel was twelve when he first hooked up with a circus in Cologne, Germany, after the war. At that time, his widowed mother briefly became a seamstress for the Circus Williams. When she left, Gunther stayed on as an apprentice acrobat under the watchful guidance of the Williams family. In the beginning, he wasn't even interested in animal training: "It seemed so much work," he said.[10] But soon his natural instincts and some professional encouragement made him into a proficient horseman and elephant trainer. When Gunther was sixteen,

Harry Williams died in the ring. The boy adopted the name of the man who had been like a father to him, and at Mrs. Williams' request took over the leadership of the circus. By 1968 he and the Circus Williams were widely known for the best animal acts in Europe, and especially for his famous mixed act with elephants and tigers. That year, Irvin Feld came over to make a pitch for him to come to the Ringling show. Out of loyalty to Mrs. Williams, Gunther wouldn't budge until Feld had agreed to pay her $2 million to buy out the whole circus.

Gunther Gebel-Williams made his debut with the Ringling Brothers and Barnum & Bailey Circus in 1969, and has been with them ever since. He put together his renowned large-scale caged tiger act for the first time at Feld's request. Without a single vacation for twenty years, he has spent his entire life with his animals, feeding them, caring for them when they are sick, and rewarding them liberally. Watching him in the ring with his tigers and/or leopards is a study in the mutual respect between man and beast that marks the European "natural" tradition of animal acts. The animals are presented with a minimum of noise and fuss, in a series of tableaux and stunts that display their intelligence and beauty, as well as the power of the trainer's control. There is genuine affection and respect flowing between man and beast, if absolutely no trust. The routine may look casual and relaxed, but it's actually extremely demanding. Gunther must remain agile, and he is acutely aware of every individual personality, and alert to every mood change, tail flick, or flattened ear in the ring with him. The big cats are predictably unpredictable, as he well knows from the 500 stitches that cover his body — scars earned not from cats attacking him, but from trying to keep the peace between rival animals.

Great Trainers of the Past

The American style of caged animal presentation conveys a completely different mood. Now fallen out of favor in the face of more sophisticated "civilized" treatment of animals, the American school of wild animal training began with Isaac Van Amburgh, when he climbed into the National Menagerie's little rectangular cage with a lion, a tiger, and a leopard in 1833. There had been lions

Gunther Gebel-Williams.
Photo courtesy of Ringling Bros. and
Barnum & Bailey Combined Shows, Inc.

Gunther Gebel-Williams' 1969 American début.
Photo courtesy of Ringling Bros. and Barnum &
Bailey Combined Shows, Inc.

Gunther Gebel-Williams with
Bengal tiger.
Photo courtesy of Ringling Bros.
and Barnum & Bailey Combined
Shows, Inc.

Photo courtesy of Ringling Bros. and
Barnum & Bailey Combined Shows, Inc.

A more typical Clyde Beatty: the "American" method.
Photo courtesy of Circus World Museum, Baraboo, WI

Clyde Beatty.
Photo courtesy of Circus World Museum, Baraboo, WI

Patricia White. Photo courtesy of
Carson & Barnes and John McGinn

on display in the new world since the first one arrived in Boston Harbor in 1716, and several men had already dared to enter into the lion's cage. But Van Amburgh was certainly the most famous of early American trainers to enter the lion's den. He emphasized the incredible danger he faced and the magnificent courage it took to face the beast in the cage, especially since his predecessor may have been eaten alive trying the same thing. Dressed like a Roman gladiator, Van Amburgh would force his animals to perform tricks by cruelly beating them into submission with a crow bar; or in a semblance of combat he would jam his blooded arm into the lion's mouth and dare it to bite. Despite his cultivated religious image of lying down with lions and lambs, he was cruel, loud, and brash. However, in the spirit of frontier America, he represented the complete dominance of man over untamed nature that the public evidently needed to be reassured by. From this kind of metaphorical demonstration of the invincibility of man in the primitive, natural world sprang the traditional American style of wild-animal act, characterized by a primitive macho trial-and-error quality. Its popularity caused a rapid growth in imitators. By 1922 there were fifty men and women presenting cat acts on many different circuses. They included such great early 20th century trainers as Peru's rough and ready Terrell Jacobs, who with the help of his wife Dolly worked the largest cat act of all—in a 50-foot cage with an advertised fifty animals—and Jack Bonavita, who lost an arm to a vicious attack by one of his twenty-seven lions.

The legendary Clyde Beatty is our most famous example of the American style. Born somewhere in Ohio, sometime around 1903 (Beatty himself claimed several conflicting versions), he came briefly under the influence of the great Hungarian trainer Louis Roth, did a polar bear act, and acquired his first caged cat act in 1925. He would eventually leave much of the training of his animals to others, while he focused on a theatrical presentation designed to instill fear for his safety among the spectators. Carrying a whip, a chair, and a gun, he advanced on his beasts and encouraged them to "attack." In one favorite routine, Nero, his best large male lion, would knock the chair from his hand and drive him from the arena, from which Beatty would "escape" in the nick of time, slamming the cage door behind him. Pausing to review the situation and wipe his brow, Beatty would then reenter the cage to thunderous applause, and subdue Nero merely by a hypnotic stare into his eyes.

Beatty became a superstar in the circus primarily because of this sense of the theatrical, and a showman's knack for spreading his legend around in books, comic books, movies, and a radio show. He was responsible for spawning in his admirers many dreams of mastery in the cat cage. Among his many cage boys was a young black man named Emanuel Ruffin, whom Beatty called "Junior." Ruffin went on to be one of the few black trainers in the business. He had his own cage act with the Hoxie show under the name of "Prince Bogino," and now works for the Ringling organization in Venice, Florida. After Beatty's retirement from the ring and death from cancer in 1965, the traditional American style of fighting cat act was carried on for a while by men like Pat Anthony and Dave Hoover, but for the most part, the European tradition has become the norm. In his twenty years with the Beatty–Cole show, Hoover even dressed in safari whites and carried a pistol in the grand tradition of Beatty's fighting act, although out of the ring he was a quiet, soft-spoken, cigar-chewing gentleman, and he trained his animals to exhibit their apparently aggressive behavior by rewarding them with food.

Many people also associate the wild animal trapper and dealer Frank "Bring 'Em Back Alive" Buck with the circus, but his connection was minimal; he shared in Edward Anthony a biographer in common with Clyde Beatty, and he worked only briefly for Johnny North in 1938. But two other trend-setting big cat trainers have established high standards for their contemporary counterparts in American circuses: Mabel Stark and Alfred Court. Stark was twenty when she abandoned her nursing career and with a pet tiger went to work for the Al G. Barnes Circus as a bareback rider in 1912. Under Louis Roth's reluctant tutelage, and in defiance of all those who told her "A

Alfred Court.
Photo courtesy of Ringling Bros.
and Barnum & Bailey
Combined Shows, Inc.

woman cannot do these things," she became the famous Tiger Lady and moved to the Ringling show in 1922. Over the years, this plucky little stubborn and courageous woman worked for many different circuses, rarely taking "no" for an answer from either man or cat. She received more than her share of life-threatening maulings, but blamed only her own carelessness and not the natural instincts of her beloved tigers. She was a heroic role model for women all over the country seeking fulfillment in independent careers of their own choosing. Certainly she was an inspiration to Patricia White, the talented trainer currently with the Carson & Barnes Circus. White presents a dangerous and stunning cage act combining male and female Nubian lions, Siberian and Bengal tigers, and a liger. Mabel Stark left the cage for the last time in 1967, after more than a half-century with her tigers. In her autobiography, she expressed a sentiment similar to Karl Wallenda's and one in common with many circus performers: "[Going into the cage is] a matchless thrill, and life without it is not worth living."[11] Four months after her retirement, she was dead.

Alfred Court came to the cage in a different way, following the maxim, "If you want it done right, do it yourself." Already an experienced acrobat and circus manager, the thirty-five-year-old Frenchman had to fire his animal trainer for repeated drunkenness while they were on a Mexican tour in 1917. There was no one to take over the job but himself, and he embraced it with joy. By 1940, with the Ringling show, he was the foremost proponent in the country of the "civilized" European style of animal act. He was famous throughout Europe and America for his mixed acts of Siberian and Bengal tigers, black and spotted panthers and leopards, polar and Tibetan bears, Atlas and Abyssinian lions, cougars, and Great Dane dogs. Although both carried the traditional whip and chair, Court's performance was in marked contrast to the pyrotechnics of Clyde Beatty. His cage acts, whether or not he appeared in them himself, had a much calmer, more stately, and less dangerous appearance; in fact, he and his nephew, Willy Storey, once framed an act in which twelve dangerous leopards worked with six Ringling show girls. An instinctive expert in animal psychology, his training techniques were supposedly marked by the same patient, gentle,

Bombey the liger and Josip Marcan. 1989 Clyde Beatty–
Cole Bros. Photo by W. H. Rough

Josip Marcan.
Photo by Jim Carpenter for The Daily
Progress, *Charlottesville, VA*

Photo by W. H. Rough

Josip Marcan and Bombey.
Photo by Jim Carpenter for The Daily
Progress, *Charlottesville, VA*

soft-spoken extension of friendship to his animals that has come to mark Gunther Gebel–Williams' style. "All training is done by patience and knowledge of the animal's character and mental reactions," said Court. "A flick of the whip for guidance is all that is ever needed, even when an animal is willful or sulky. The trainer's voice must be the final authority in training and in public. The voice must guide the animal."[12] On the other hand, there are those who remember that Court was not always able to abide by his own rules, but was forced to indulge in occasional brutality in self-defense.

Contemporary Trainers

Whether the acts are fighting or natural, American or European, modern trainers insist that the only way to train a wild animal is with a combination of positive and negative reinforcement. The operative word is "train," they emphasize, pointing out that it is never possible to "tame" a wild animal. Positive reinforcement is with food and approval, and negative reinforcement is by disapproval. For all of the American-style trainers, blank-guns and whips were considered no more than noisemakers to add excitement to the act. No one owns up to physical punishment of an animal, with very rare exceptions, primarily because beatings are an ineffective way to teach and an inefficient way to learn. Vicious, torturing animal trainers such as the fictitious Harris Collins portrayed in Jack London's *Michael, Brother of Jerry* are an almost nonexistent rarity in the circus. As any housecat owner knows, an animal will only do what it wants to do; big cats too must be patiently and gently led to an understanding of what it is that the trainer expects them do do in order to earn the reward of a smile, an affectionate pat, or a morsel of meat.

Performing cats may often look lovable, but they are as a rule exceedingly dangerous. Contrary to popular opinion, they are neither drugged, defanged, nor declawed. With more training, they grow increasingly wary and streetwise, and not more manageable. They are not full from a good meal prior to a show, which would only make them sleepy, but hungry and eager to be fed at the end of the performance. Big cats in the circus don't attack because they are hungry or because of any anthropomorphic feelings of hate or revenge.

They attack for reasons of their own because they have a primitive urge to kill. Most trainers much prefer to work with free-spirited, energetic, and intelligent cats, who assert their independence aggressively, even though they are far more dangerous than the "seat warmers," cats bored and lazy by nature, or whose wills have been broken by thoughtless and excessive training. Preferences for species, and claims for the mental superiority of one or the other vary with every individual trainer. The general consensus is that tigers may be more difficult to work with, because unlike lions they are loners; they fend and plot strategies for themselves and do not travel in prides. Their movements are slow and deliberate, but they give less warning of an attack. Participation in a group makes them uneasy by nature. Panthers and leopards, on the other hand, are the most treacherous cats to work with, because they are the fastest attackers.

Lest anyone be lulled into thinking that cage acts are not so very dangerous after all, it would be well to remember that literally every major wild-animal trainer in the circus, including the gentle Alfred Court despite his mythical invincibility, has acquired major scars on his or her body as a reminder of careless moves. Furthermore, since the turn of the century, twenty-one trainers have been killed in the arena. Escapes, while rare, are not nonexistent, and the results can be disastrous for both the animal and anyone who happens to get in his way.

Many circuses do not carry cage acts, for a variety of reasons. There may be animal rights considerations, and insurance coverage for both the animals and the public is growing prohibitively high. The cost of food and of carrying a cage and other necessary equipment for displaying wild animals is also increasingly expensive. Even the Big One has been skeptical of its wild animal acts. Charles Ringling loved the animals, feeling they knew a man better than a man could know his fellow humans: "Unless my animals like me, I am a failure," he said.[13] But he couldn't talk his brothers into having cage acts until 1919, and in 1925 Mr. John once more eliminated them. Only their popularity and tremendous public pressure persuaded him to reinstitute them, despite approval of his ban by both reformers and the press.

Charly Baumann.
Photo courtesy of Ringling Bros. and
Barnum & Bailey Combined Shows, Inc.

Wade Burck.
Photo courtesy of Ringling Bros. and
Barnum & Bailey Combined Shows, Inc.

Today, the popularity of several caged cat acts round the country, including those already mentioned, suggests that they are still appreciated by the public, and that the art or skill of wild-animal training is far from dead. Beyond the thrill of an act, it can teach audiences a great deal about animal psychology and animal behavior, about potential levels of communication and interchange between man and beast, and about man's place in the animal kingdom.

Daniel Suskow shows a popular tiger act with the Tarzan Zerbini Circus. Audiences love Wayne Franzen's obvious affection and extra care for his animals in his little down-home cage act. The Yugoslavian-born former German veterinarian Josip Marcan is currently the cat man on the Clyde Beatty–Cole Brothers Circus. Marcan's gentle European style displays a genuine love and respect for his mixed cats, contrasted with an ironic indifference for his audiences. He is also particularly well-known for his controversial liger breeding program. Overcoming the natural antipathy between lions and tigers, he raised a male lion cub with a female tiger cub and bred them. The resulting ligers have light ocher stripes similar to tigers, and the males also sprout manes, like lions, but they are larger than either of their parents. Bombey, Marcan's male liger, the "gentle giant" currently performing with Beatty–Cole show, now weighs a half a ton, nearly twice the weight of an average adult tiger, and may well be the largest feline in the world. Unlike that other combination of species, the mule, the liger can propagate his own breed. When a male tiger is bred to a female lion, they produce a tili, and when a liger is bred back to a tiger, the result is a "golden tabby," which looks like a faded tiger. Many zoologists question the ethics of such breeding, but the resulting animals seem as happy to be alive as the rest of us, and economic considerations necessitating increased attendance at zoos may make such unusual animals highly desirable attractions.

Since he retired from the cage, Charly Baumann continues to work as the able and gruff Performance Director of the Blue Unit, with the Ringling Brothers and Barnum & Bailey Circus.

But he carries the scars of thirty-five years of working with wild tigers. His father was a popular German movie actor and stuntman before he died in the gas chambers of Bergen–Belsen, and as a boy Charly had often been asked to appear in several films with animals. His first circus work came after the war as an assistant horse-trainer with the Circus Williams in Hamburg, "...when Gunther Gebel was a shoe shine boy,"[14] he says. His courageous rescue of the circus' wild animal trainer from a savage lion attack in 1951 earned him his first spot in the cage.

Two American trainers stepped into Baumann's shoes when he vacated the Ringling Blue Unit cage. In 1989, Larry Allen Dean was presenting fourteen lions, seven male and seven female, in an act framed by English wild animal breeder Jim Clubb. Before Dean, the handsome young North Dakotan Wade Burck had the job of working the Blue Unit's cage act with fifteen tigers, including nine magnificent performing Burmese white tigers from breeder and trainer John Cuneo, the largest such group in the world. Burck's act was a splendid presentation of the beauty and nobility of the wild beast: "The only time I use a stick is to feed a piece of meat. A small buggy whip is sufficient to direct the cats. Prodding only makes them snarl and is usually done to impress the audience with the trainer's bravery. I want the people to be impressed with the cats, not with me."[15] Burck is an articulate spokesman on the issue of endangered wild animals: "I believe with all my heart that the circus makes a substantial contribution in assuring the survival of many endangered species. If this was a perfect world, I'd turn my tigers loose in the wild. But the world is not perfect; they wouldn't survive. There are so many enemies in the jungle. Especially man. In the circus, my tigers get the best of everything— good food, quality medical care and people around them who care...I don't want to buy my sons, Adam and Eric, a picture to show them what a gorilla looked like. Or a whooping crane. Or a tiger."[16] A sensitive caring man and a magnificent performer, Burck planned to spend his life not in the circus but in animal conservation efforts.

"...AND BEARS, AND..."

Caged cats are not the only dangerous wild animal act to make frequent appearances in American circuses. There is an ominous saying in the circus world that bear trainers never retire. The "armless wonder" Jack Hubert lost one arm to a bear and the other to a lion; Chubby Guilfoyle, a student of Beatty's, was maimed by his bears. Trained bears have been around for much longer than the modern circus; after all, England's cruel bear-baiting rings thrived for 700 years. Bears are the most unpredictable and dangerous of all circus animals, because they are "series biters," working their way through a victim by biting continuously and repeatedly, rather than tearing flesh; thus they allow much less of an opportunity for the victim to escape than do the big cats. Furthermore, once a bear decides to latch on to an arm or a leg or whatever, no power on earth can persuade it to loosen its jaws. Finally, bears show no emotion or facial expressions whatsoever, and they will attack out of instinct with no warning or provocation. If they have been given provocation by harsh treatment, they will quietly smolder until the opportunity arises to tear the offender to shreds. Those are but a few of the reasons why bears are almost always kept muzzled in performance, whether in a cage or on a leash. About the only possible upside of a bear attack is that the bite will probably not become as infected as a cat's bite, because bears are normally vegetarian, and their mouths are cleaner.

The most common circus bear is the European or Russian brown bear, but Himalayan black bears and Syrians also appear with some frequency. Emil and Catherine Pallenberg were German bear trainers who were with the Ringling show in the '20's. They worked their bears on leashes, outside the cage, as do most bear acts today, including the Steeples on the Great American Circus, the Weldes with their Russian bears on the Beatty–Cole show, the Bauers on the Tarzan Zerbini Circus, the Lilovs with their Siberians on the Ringling Blue

The Bauer Bears.
Photo courtesy of the Tarzan Zerbini Circus

Ursula Bottcher. Photo courtesy of Ringling Bros. and Barnum & Bailey Combined Shows, Inc.

Unit, and the Berouseks on the Red Unit. An intelligent and curious creature, bears take well to performing tricks. They can roller skate, skip rope, balance on balls and tight ropes, ride bicycles and motorcycles, play the harmonica and concertina, and look much more harmless and cuddly than they really are.

Polar bears are flesh-eaters, unlike their smaller cousins, and their non-retractable three-inch claws and forearms, powerful enough to flip a full-grown seal out of the water, make them the most dangerous of circus bears. They can weigh up to a half a ton and measure up to 9½ feet from nose to tail, with eight to twelve inch wide paws —all of which means that polar bear acts are rare in the circus, and when they are presented, they are usually performed within the steel cage. Clyde Beatty once worked a large polar bear act with the John Robinson Circus at the beginning of his career. Award-winning East German circus star Ursula Bottcher presented her polar bears on the Ringling show in 1976, the first polar bear act in America in thirty years.

"...AND,...OH MY!"

There are many other animals appearing in the circus, of course—the rarer and more unusual, the better. Like Noah, Barnum's original wish was to create a menagerie containing virtually every animal known to man, and in one way or another, it was a prophetic wish. Fox and Parkinson point out that "Virtually all species at some time have been with the circus, sometimes as exhibits of viciousness or rarity, sometimes as examples of man's cleverness and the animal's ability to learn."[17] In circuses of the last three decades there have been horned rattlers, alligators, seals and sea elephants, leaping llamas and guanacos, okapis, orangutans, chimps and other simians of every variety. There are camels, which began to make regular appearances in the circus in the late 1860s, when the U.S. Cavalry imported them for desert duty in the American West. They were a bust in the service, however, and Costello and Coup bought up a bunch of them from Army Surplus for a bargain $80 apiece, for use in their

Photo courtesy of Ringling Bros. and Barnum & Bailey Combined Shows, Inc.

1989 Great American Circus.
Photo by W. H. Rough

1989 Circus World Museum.
Photo by Joan Z. Rough

1989 Circus World Museum.
Photo by Joan Z. Rough

1989 Carson & Barnes.
Photo by W. H. Rough

1870 Egyptian Caravan Circus. They've been a circus fixture ever since. Giraffes have also been circus fixtures, ever since the first two "camelopards," as they were then called, were imported in 1837 for MacComber, Welch & Co. There were a few famous circus hippopotamuses, like "Miss Oklahoma," "Lotus," and "Otto, the Blood-Sweating Hippopotamus," who made their rounds with the circus, sometimes on a leash, and sometimes in heavy cages with built-in bathtubs.

The largest remaining traveling circus menagerie, that of Carson & Barnes, even carried a moose in 1988, and they still carry the big three: a rhinoceros, a giraffe, and a hippo. Many of the more exotic animals are for display purposes only, although some successful acts of performing camels and zebras have been seen. Zebras can be especially stubborn, and they have a vicious kick, developed through years of fending off lions, that makes them less than desirable as performers. Much more manageable is the multitude of conventional performing dog acts that fill up America's large and small circuses. Some are quite good, usually those with a comic angle, and others are little more than canine mock-fashion shows. Bird acts, usually doves and pigeons with pastel-tinted feathers, also seem to be popular. Even the inimitable pig seems to be making a comeback in the circus, in acts reminiscent of "Uncle Henry's Porkchop Review." The intelligence of the pig once made him a circus staple, and as we have seen, a number of clowns used them for partners. One pig trainer used to operate a marvelous scam, by selling his pigs to a local farmer in every town the circus came to, claiming they had grown too large to continue performing. He would collect his money and walk off down the road. Hours later, when the circus was nearing the end of its last performance in town, the band played the customary cue for the pig act. The sharp-eared pigs promptly smashed through their confinement pen and ran off together to rejoin their trainer at the edge of town.

Gorillas

There have been a few animals associated with the circus who were never required to perform. Their mere presence on display was enough to draw circus patrons to the lot. Such a creature was Jumbo, and such was the great gorilla, Gargantua, "the World's Most Terrifying Living Creature." Stories of Gargantua's strength and

*1989 Circus World Museum.
Photo by W. H. Rough*

*1989 Great American Circus.
Photo by Joan Z. Rough*

fierceness were carefully contrived to create long lines of prospective admirers, although he most certainly could and would have torn to pieces any human being foolish enough to enter his cage. He was not the largest or even the most ferocious gorilla outside of Africa, but he was most probably the ugliest. His face had been disfigured in 1931, when he was a baby, by a misguided sailor seeking a meaningless revenge on his captain. The sailor emptied a fire extinguisher full of nitric acid in the face of the valuable little gorilla the captain had brought from Africa, and left him for dead. Terrified and barely alive, he was immediately bought by the kind-hearted Gertrude Lintz, wife of a Brooklyn doctor, who nursed him back to health and named him Buddha, or Buddy for short. Buddy was poisoned by a second psychotic five years later, and again she nursed him back to health. He developed a not too surprising affection for her, together with an extraordinary jealousy and hatred of all males, including the innocent Dr. Lintz, earned from his ordeals with cruelty. The gorilla grew to weigh 550 pounds. While he measured only just over five and a half feet tall, he had a deceptive nine foot arm reach, and he loved to reach through the bars and tear the clothes off curiosity-seekers who came too close to his cage.

At the end of 1937, it became necessary, for the safety of both Buddy and the family, for Mrs. Lintz to sell him to the Ringling show for the secret sum of $10,000. Weeks later, the great circus press agent Roland Butler had transformed him into Gargantua the Great, so named by Johnny North. They were delighted with the malicious, sneering look of hatred acquired from the nitric acid, which would turn Gargantua into the greatest attraction since Jumbo. Almost single-handedly, Gargantua rescued the show from the severe financial bind it found itself in by the end of the Depression years, and in his lifetime he would earn more revenue for the Big One than had Jumbo himself. Gargantua quickly developed a disposition to match his looks and reputation. He almost did in his long-time trainer Dick Koerner, on more than one occasion, as well as North himself, when he walked too close to his first cage one day. He was eventually to be kept in a 9 by 26 foot air-conditioned, glass-enclosed, steel-barred prison on wheels,

which he would never again leave in the remaining twelve years of his life. In 1941, North leased "Gargantua's Bride," Mlle. Toto, from a private source; the highly touted wedding never actually came off. Although their identical cages were parked end-to-end for years, the two gorillas had nothing but indifference to express towards each other. No one ever quite dared to lift the separating doors and allow them access to the same cage for fear of the gentle Toto's safety. On November 25, 1949, Gargantua was found in his cage, dead from impacted teeth and pneumonia he would never have allowed to be treated by any man. The Widow Toto was distraught, but she nonetheless lived happily ever after until she died as an old gorilla in 1968.

Amazing Unicorns

Only one animal since the days of Gargantua has received anything like the old-fashioned ballyhooing of the past: the "Amazing Unicorn," which made its magical appearance in 1985. Nothing was required of this mythical unicorn other than to be ridden around the track displayed on a royal float once or twice in every performance, while being stroked by a lovely maiden. He was healthy, well-fed, and deliriously happy. Nonetheless, armies of animal rights activists prepared to wage war over the cruelty to animals issue, and on the other side armies of Ringling lawyers and publicity agents prepared to meet them head on. "Can we do anything to animals in the name of entertainment?" cried the ASPCA. "Children of all ages believe in Santa Claus, Peter Pan, the Wizard of Oz, and the fabled Unicorn. Don't let the Grinches steal the Fantasy!" screamed back the full-page Ringling ads. No one would ever talk about this creature without tongue planted firmly in cheek, so it's hard to establish just what the facts were. Evidently, it was one of a small herd of angora goats, a word the Ringling folks never owned up to. When they were just born, their original owner had apparently arranged to have their horn buds surgically moved to the center of their foreheads; as the horns grew, they fused together and became one. Kenneth Feld allegedly bought the entire herd of adult goats, in order to prevent any rival unicorns from surfacing in the future, and in order to have available stand-ins as necessary. Those

Photo courtesy of Ringling Bros. and Barnum & Bailey
Combined Shows, Inc.

The Living Unicorn.
Photo courtesy of Ringling Bros. and
Barnum & Bailey Combined Shows, Inc.

Gargantua. Photo courtesy of
Circus World Museum, Baraboo, WI

Gargantua's home awaits restoration at Circus World
Museum. Photo by W. H. Rough

who had believed that unicorns were supposed to look like horses were gently reminded that in the Bible unicorns are generally referred to as goats with cloven hoofs and beards. Throughout the entire debate surrounding the "Is he or isn't he?" controversy, people flocked to the circus to make up their own minds, and P.T. Barnum looked down on his progeny and smiled.

Circus Animals: Yea or Nay?

The whole question of what all these animals are doing in the circus is one which may be justifiably asked. Judy Finelli, whose Pickle Family Circus is one among those who have never included animals in their performances on principle, calls the whole issue of animal rights the "abortion issue of the modern circus world." No issue in today's circus can so pit friend against friend and brother against brother. Nothing can so incense a traditional circus fan as the suggestion that animals are treated cruelly by their trainers, and nothing can so incense an animal rights activist as the suggestion that they are not. The typical argument might go something like this:

"A circus without animals is no circus at all," claim the traditionalists.

"Wild animals belong in the wild," insist the animal lovers. "It is not natural for them to be kept in the confined space of a small cage or a truck compartment, being hauled around the country. It constitutes cruel and unusual punishment."

"What do you mean by 'natural'? Where would you put them? There is less and less 'wild' for them to be in," retort the circus trainers. "These animals are better cared for and better fed than they would be in the wild. They are exercised regularly, more so than they would be in zoos, and with a constant change of environment they are not so bored. They are happy doing what they do."

"Oh come on! No animal jumps through a burning hoop because it wants to. There are vicious beatings, aren't there? Elephants get hit over the head with axe handles and jabbed with your bull hooks, don't they? Lions get punished for instinctive attacks. Broken spirits and cruelty are endemic to the circus way of life."

"There are occasional beatings, and sometimes they may seem excessive to you. Intractable ani-

mals must be taught to obey us. We have to live with them, in close quarters, and our lives often depend on their obedience to us."

"They didn't choose to live with you. What you make them do is undignified. Their tricks are silly and pointless. You are doing this just to show off your power over them. You are playing God!"

"Dignity is your word, not the animal's. What's really pointless is crediting them with human feelings. Animals don't have all the opinions that you do as a human being. What seems undignified to you may be perfectly natural behavior for them. Let them worry about their own dignity. And we do this because we love animals, and because the experience of working with them is humbling and full of its own rewards, NOT because of any macho power trip!"

"Even so, you must admit that you use physical punishment to teach an animal your tricks! Animals are pushed and prodded until they go along with doing whatever you want them to do, just to get you off their backs."

"Even in the wild, animals get both positive and negative reinforcement for their behavior, every day, just like we all do. In the circus, our emphasis is on positive reinforcement and reward. No trainer worth his salt is cruel to his charges. Pain or unnecessary force doesn't help the animal to understand and be content with what is required of him, either in the natural world or in the circus world. Animals only perform well when they like what they're doing."

"But pain happens, doesn't it? Cruelty happens."

"Yes. Every creature on earth feels pain. And all of us feel the results of thoughtless cruelty. We don't like it any more than you do. But the whole circus can't take responsibility for everyone's pain, or for the cruelty of a very few people. It happens everywhere."

"By buying these animals for commercial exploitation, you are depleting the world's supply of animals in the wild, and contributing to the list of endangered species. It is short-sighted and greedy."

"By far the majority of all circus animals are born and raised in captivity. It is the expansion of human populations that is the foremost culprit in depleting supplies of animals in the wild. There is less and less room for them. And as for greed, circus people aren't getting rich quick off of our animals. What ought to concern you is the greed of expanding civilizations, and the greed of ivory hunters and those who supply skins to make coats, and more important, the greed of those who buy the ivory and the skins, and the greed of the consumers who wear the coats and chortle over the ivory at museums and cocktail parties. We're in the business of keeping these animals alive, and preserving them for the future. Aren't you?"

"Yes, but that's not good enough."

"Of course it's not. But in the meantime, we are learning from their behavior, and in our small way we are helping to teach the public that the animals are fellow creatures, as worthy as we are to inhabit this planet."

"How can you believe that? These are magnificent creatures you are keeping in captivity. They are your prisoners. You command them, in spite of an intelligence and a sensitivity of their own which are as valid as a human being's. As a matter of fact, they're even more valid. Your animals aren't systematically detroying the world's environment and bringing us down with them. We are!"

"We agree. And...we are ALL prisoners!"

There is really no logical place to end this argument, and there are no winners; every point has a hundred potential "Yes, but..."s to be appended. Careful listeners will find points on both sides with which they agree, and in fact even the extremists on both sides are in closer agreement than they might care to admit. Circus people were just as horrified and infuriated as the rest of the public at the abandonment by the "Wonder Zoo" of trucks full of animals in a Virginia shopping center during a 1988 heat wave. 1989 circus programs are full of warnings about endangered species, information about how to help with the conservation movement, and exhortations to contribute to the African Wildlife Fund. Circus owners and trainers are constantly considering new training techniques and ways of improving living conditions. For their part, conservationists and animal rights activists are becoming ever more aware of what they have in common with circus animal conservationists. They are beginning to recognize the value of circus breeding programs

in helping to assure the survival of a species, the opportunity for studying animal psychology and animal behavior that the circus provides, and the potential for circus animal trainers to educate the public in all of these areas. Instead of asking for the circus to be boycotted, activists now ask that we "please consider the animals we will see," which is exactly what the circuses want us to do, as well. One recent flyer from the Animal Advocates Network in Richmond, Virginia, informed its readers, "A favorite elephant sport is wallowing in the mud at the edge of a waterhole," and asked "Do you think a circus elephant ever has the pleasure of a mudbath?" Conservationists and circus animal lovers alike might well agree that mudholes and the elephants to wallow in them are tragically becoming an increasing rarity in the world, and that it may not be too long before the circus has a large part of the responsibility for supplying both. No one has supplied us with any answers to the problem of maintaining the richness of life on earth. What all sides must learn to do first is to listen more sensitively to the questions.

"A HORSE! A HORSE!"

Despite all the hubbub over the issues of animals in the circus, there is one animal, a domesticated friend of man for thousands of years, that no one seems to mind appearing in a circus: the horse. Since in both England and America, the modern circus was originally based on exhibitions of equestrian skill, we have now come full circle from our opening chapter: through all the history and logistics of the circus, through the owners and their shows, and through all the different kinds of performers in the circus. It is fitting that at the end we should come back to the old reliable horse, the perennial staple of the circus.

Everything that can be done with a horse has been done with a horse in the circus. They can seemingly perform on their own without leads or riders in the ring; they can pull wagons and tableaux, they can do tricks; and they can carry riders in all manner of styles. Quite often, trainers become adept at mounting a great variety of equestrian acts, like performing as trick riders, as well as serving as trainer and ringmaster for liberty acts. The individual horse, on the other hand, is

a specialist in the one particular kind of performance for which he is best suited by nature and
build.

At Liberty

There is a special kind of magic to the liberty
horse act which opens the 1990 Big Apple Circus.
The ring is dark, lit with leafy shadows suggesting
a forest clearing in the moonlight. Into it comes a
magnificent Arabian stallion, at first alone, and
then joined by his five matching companions.
Completely unencumbered and independent spirits, they mill about briefly, looking for. . .some-
thing, someone? Finally, Katja Schumann walks
quietly into the center of the ring. With no apparent movement or sound from her, the horses
respond and begin to form an ordered circling
line. There is no whip, and there are no bridles or
lead ropes. After a few energetic maneuvers executed in unison and seemingly without command,
the horses suddenly stop, and approach her in the
center of the ring. She appears only to whisper to
them, lovingly. Mysteriously calmed, they form
into a single line and slowly file out of the ring.

Good liberty horse acts depend on a seemingly
telepathic communication between the trainer
and the horses, and when it is done right, it is a
magnicent demonstration of complete cooperation and understanding between man and beast.
Katja Schumann has been doing this and other
equestrian acts for years, and her family has been
one of the top names in European circuses, known
for their horse acts for well over a century. Before
she even came to the Big Apple, Katja was the
winner of the Prix de la Dame du Cirque at the
1974 Monte Carlo International Circus Festival,
and a gold medal at the 1976 Circus World Cham-
pionships in London. The inherent joy in her
spirit was well demonstrated on June 17, 1988.
While counting the paces for her liberty horse act,
Katja was also carefully counting her contractions.
At 10:24 p.m., just after the end of the night's
show, son Max was born into the waiting hands of
her husband, Paul Binder. She was only reluctantly persuaded to skip the next afternoon's performance and delay her return to the ring to the
following night, less than twenty-four hours after
Max's arrival.

There are many fine liberty horse acts that can
be seen in American circuses today. Outstanding
among them is Gunther Gebel–Williams' beauti-
fully trained liberty act, which is sometimes presented by his wife Sigrid. If his tiger act is the
more popularly known, his liberty act is to some
tastes the more artistic illustration of harmonious
respect between man and animal, and an impressive reminder that horses were Gunther's first love
in the circus. Trevor Bale's liberty act with the
Beatty–Cole Circus, now presented by his two
daughters, Gloria and Dawnita, is another example of equine harmony. Also the father of daredevil Elvin Bale, Trevor is another all-round animal man with long roots in European circus traditions. Born on the Circus Schumann, he grew up
in the circus, and quickly learned to perform just
about everything on the circus program from
clown to trapeze. "If you didn't learn, you didn't
eat," he says. Already one of Europe's outstanding
trainers of virtually every species of circus animal
by the end of World War II, he periodically held
down the tiger cage with the Ringling show from
1953 to 1964.

The Work Horse

The traditional link between horses and the
circus does not rest exclusively on performances
and acts. In the early days of the circus horses
were both transportation and labor force. The
heavy Percherons, Belgians, and Clydesdales did
duty as baggage stock, pulling the heavy circus
wagons from town to town, or from rail yard to
lot. They were frequently used in work teams of
six or eight horses for raising tent poles and hauling heavy wagons out of the mud. The most impressive hitch ever developed was the forty-horse
hitch, which was never anything but a brilliant
piece of showmanship used for publicity in the
great circus parades. The Spalding & Rogers
Colossal Dramatic Equestrian Circus had the first
such team in 1853, and Jake Posey drove a team
of forty matched bays for five years beginning in
1898 for Barnum & Bailey's European tour. More
recently, Paul Sparrow handled the reins of a forty-
horse hitch in the 1989 Milwaukee Great Circus
Parade, just as his father Dick had twelve years
earlier.

Old-time baggage stock at the
"Dawn of a New Day."
Photo courtesy of Circus World
Museum, Baraboo, WI

Wonder Horses

Still another category of circus horse is the edu-cated horse, who seems to be able to answer ques-tions from his trainer and perform a variety of tricks. His is a long tradition; the exploits of Morocco in the 16th century were described in Chapter 2. More recently, Wayne Franzen's horse Tonto is still captivating circus audiences, but in the first half of the 20th century, educated horses were the pride of the American cowboy star. Aud-iences seemed to look on Trigger, Champion, Sil-ver, and Topper as intelligent human-like spirits trapped in a horse's body; they were certainly un-derstood to have the ability to perform any "im-possible" trick asked of them by owners Roy Rogers, Gene Autry, the Lone Ranger, and Hop-along Cassidy. Their inspiration, and one of the greatest cowboy teams ever associated with the American circus, was Tom Mix and his Wonder Horse, Tony.

Mix had a checkered career ranging from law-man to pioneer in western movies, but according to his friend Jimmy Cole his weak voice put him at a disadvantage when Hollywood shifted from silents to talkies. He joined the Sells–Floto show in 1929, and had his own private rail car, for him-self and Tony, a Rolls Royce, and $20,000 a week, the highest salary ever paid a circus performer at that time. "I'm not afraid of work," he said, "but

I must have my comfort."[18] Beloved by children and the public for his outward show of courage and wholesomeness, and for Tony, Mix had his share of personal problems, brought on by fame and an overdependence on alcohol. One telltale story of his excessive drinking bouts comes from Joe McKennon in his fictionalized history of the circus in America, *Horse Dung Trail.* It seems that Mix could occasionally have considerable trouble hitting the balloon targets provided for his six-gun trick shooting exhibition. He had to lie down in the ring to steady his aim, but would still miss, hitting the canvas beyond the rising targets. "Look at that dirty s.o.b.!" complained boss canvasman Cap Curtis. "Another hole in my new top. With those goddam scatter shots his cartridges are loaded with, he should never miss!"[19] Nonetheless, Tom Mix's excesses were either forgiven or ignored by an adoring public. In 1934, he elected to start his own circus, and in 1938 it became the first to move entirely across the country on trucks; but it was a disastrous year to make the change. The Tom Mix Circus and seven other shows, including the Big One, plagued by labor strife, weather, and the full impact of the Depression years, had to fold their tents before the end of the season. The show limped through one more season, beset by hoodlums and blowdowns, before it closed for good. On October 12, 1940, Mix, always a lover of fast cars, was on his way to Hollywood when he lost control of his white Cord convertible, went off the road, and was killed instantly. Only sixty years old, but long depressed, he had been pursuing still another film contract. Tony outlived his beloved human partner, and was finally put to sleep in 1944 at the age of thirty-four, the rough equivalent of 120 human years.

Riding Acts

Certainly the biggest group of circus horses performs in the riding acts, which can be roughly divided into two categories: straight demonstrations of formal riding techniques; and acrobatic and trick riding.

The riding schools, from which the circus sprang originally, continued to develop highly artistic styles of formal riding, and many of those styles continue to be the high points of equestrian acts in circuses today. In 1898, Field Marshal Von Holbein of the world famous Spanish Riding School in Vienna, Austria, set the standards for perfection in what is known as the high school, or *haute école*, or *hoche schule* style. In the highest art of horsemanship, dressage, the rider never seems to move around in the saddle, never uses a whip, and never prods with his heels. When the rider has "good seat," there is perfect harmony between horse and rider, who seem to move as a single animal through a variety of trots, gallops, dance steps, and other complicated moves. The rider's display of the high school horse's steps is often referred to as a *manège* act. One of the best high school riders this country has ever seen was a Dutch cavalryman named William Heyer, who starred with the Ringling show in the 1930's. While this more formal side of equestrian art is frequently practiced in more "dignified" settings than the circus, it continues to be an exciting part of modern circus performances.

Acrobatic and trick riding has always been popular in this country, but beginning in the second decade of the 20th century it truly blossomed to become one of the main events in a circus performance. That it did so was due in no small part to two outstanding young women on the Barnum & Bailey show, who accomplished moves on the bare back of a moving horse that no one had thought possible: Ella Bradna and May Wirth. Like Katja Schumann, Ella had been an equestrian star on the Circus Schumann, and her reputation was well-established before she came to the United

Tom Mix and Tony.
Photo courtesy of Circus World Museum, Baraboo, WI

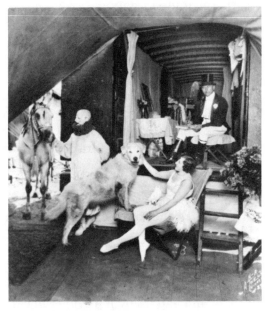

Ella and Fred Bradna and guests.
Photo courtesy of Circus World Museum, Baraboo, WI

States with her husband in 1903. Several years earlier she had been literally thrown into the arms of a young German cavalryman named Frederick Ferber, who was watching her performance from a front row box seat. When the two were married two years later, Fred took her family name. Eventually, the two would share center ring together with the Ringling Brothers and Barnum & Bailey Circus for twenty-nine years, Fred as the distinguished and classically dressed equestrian director, and Ella as the charming balletic equestrienne, who danced "on point" in graceful tableaux on horseback. Her well-known "Act Beautiful," all cloaked in white satin, was an evenly-paced tableau performance incorporating a variety of white horses, dogs, and birds, accompanied by a singing Hungarian midget named Paul Horompo, who played a white-faced Harlequin.

Trick bareback riding of a very different sort was being practiced at the same time by May Wirth, who arrived from her native Australia in 1912. In all likelihood, she was barely seventeen at the time, but the dainty May could perform a difficult forward somersault on the horse from a kneeling position. She was also the first woman to throw a double backward somersault from one horse to another, a feat which she would eventually perform repeatedly while blindfolded. In addition, she could seemingly without effort jump from the ground to the back of a running horse, with her feet planted in awkward baskets, without the use of a "cushion," or small springboard used for most mounts by others. Extremely popular with both show folk and spectators, May Wirth was one of a trio of early 20th century performers, along with Lillian Lietzel and Bird Millman, who are considered the "big three" women of the American circus. She continued to perform with a variety of circuses into the 1930's, when she and her husband Frank, who like Bradna had adopted his wife's last name, opened a booking agency for show people. She died in 1978.

Trick bareback riding is made possible by coating the horse's back and the rider's slippers with resin powder, in order to provide a reliable non-slippery surface. For this reason, the horses are often called resinbacks or rosinbacks. Horses selected for these acts usually have broad backs and even dispositions, like Percherons and Lippiz-

zaners. They often wear soft platform-like pads on which the rider can stand. The pads ease the impact on the horse if the rider's landings and stances are less than gentle. Some say they give the rider a more secure foothold, but others argue they are less stable for landings.

With all bareback acts, the 42-foot diameter of the ring, established two centuries ago by Philip Astley, is usually critical. Every step the horse takes is duly predetermined and noted, and timing is carefully controlled. The bareback horse must learn to move with confidence around the ring at a slow, steady, and reliable pace. Any variation whatsoever in his speed can result in severe injury to the acrobat, who is counting on his launching and landing platforms to be in the right place at the right time. The trick rider also relies on the predetermined level of centrifugal force that his horse's movement generates, to aid and abet his balancing skills, enabling him to lean comfortably into the curve as he is lightly pressed into the horse's back.

A variation on the somersaulting and vaulting bareback acts is *voltige*, a French word for mounted gymnastics. In a voltige act, the rider can vault off the horse's back and run alongside the horse, holding on to a handgrip attached to the harness. Turning cartwheels and somersaults alongside, he might then spring back up to assume a rear-facing position, before he scissors around to the front. According to the late British circus historian Antony Hippisley Coxe, voltige has many variations, including "à la Richard," where the horse is unbridled, "à la cowboy," where a lariat is used. "Tcherkesse," or "Cossack" riding, involves lying across the horse's back with the ankle in a loop attached to the surcingle, the band passed around the horse's midsection.[20] While virtually upside down, the Cossack rider can in this manner retrieve handkerchiefs and other objects from the sawdust floor, while the horse moves at full gallop around the ring. Cossack riding is often a popular high point of the Moscow State Circus on its American tours.

The tradition of pantomimes incorporated into equestrian acts remains strong. We have discussed some of the many variations on Astley's "Tailor's Ride to Brentford," such as the "Pete Jenkins," the "Drunken Sailor," or the "Canadian

Katja Schumann's Pony Express Ride.
1990 Big Apple, Baltimore, MD. Photo by Joan Z. Rough

Timi Loyal and Enrique Suarez, Jr.
of the Loyal – Suarez Riders.
1990 Big Apple, Baltimore, MD.
Photo by Joan Z. Rough

"Poodles" Hanneford performs "Roman Post" style.
Photo courtesy of Circus World Museum, Baraboo, WI

Peasant" acts so popular in early American circuses. Poodles Hanneford, about whom we shall hear more, was to make this kind of equestrian clowning extremely popular in the 1920's. Another popular tale that thrived in the 19th century, both as an equine pantomime and as a narrative poem by Lord Byron, was "Mazeppa." The story told of the exploits of Ivan Mazeppa, a young Polish noble who was discovered in the act of seducing the wife of one of his villainous superiors. He was condemned to be tied naked to the back of a wild horse and turned loose in the wilderness until he died of exposure. Rescued by Cossack soldiers, he was released and became a distinguished prince in the court of Peter the Great. Mazeppa's ride was often incongruously performed by women, and circuses were sometimes successful in gathering large crowds by creating the impression that the ride might be performed authentically in the buff. However, to the relief (or the consternation) of spectators, the rider always wore pink tights and a well-placed sash or two.

Another famous horse pantomime is the "Courier's Ride to St. Petersburg," which presumably portrays a courier carrying urgent war dispatches from Paris for the Czar. The strenuous act was developed in 1827 by Andrew Ducrow, the great equestrian who had taken over Astley's in London. Ducrow entered the ring standing astride two horses, which he eased apart enough to allow more horses to pass forward between his legs. Each new horse carried a flag representing a country the courier had to ride through to reach St. Petersburg. As the horses passed, Ducrow picked up their reins, until he was driving the team of new horses in front of him while standing on the original two. There have been many subsequent variations on the act. Most recently, the impressive Katja Schumann has revived it once more for the 1990 Big Apple Circus, this time called the "Pony Express Rider." The whole style of riding while standing astride two horses is now commonly called "Roman post riding," but at first it was simply called "La Poste," after the French word for Courier. "Roman" apparently did not get associated with the term until after Barnum's great chariot race revivals at the end of the 19th century, in which the act was frequently displayed.

Great riding acts have become a relative rarity

in the American circus. At one time, they occupied the majority of the circus program, but truly talented equestrians who have spent years perfecting their art have gotten somewhat hard to find. As horse ownership declined with the onset of automotive power, audiences lost the ability to appreciate fine horses. Today, when we do find excellent equestrian acts, they are all the more impressive for their rarity. With few exceptions, single riding stars have for the most part been replaced in the modern circus by troupes. There are far too many great equestrian families with long performing traditions to treat in this kind of an introductory format. Names like Clarke, Davenport, Herbert, Herriott, Rieffenach, Zamperla, and many others all deserve a major salute from spectators who appreciate equestrian excellence. Many of the children of original equestrian families are still active in the circus, and the unusual degree of crossover and interaction between them as they share their common interests and talents is an interesting illustration of circus unity. We cannot close this chapter without taking a brief look at four such families, all of whom still thankfully have active performing relatives: the Cristianis, the Hannefords, the Loyals, and the Zoppes.

Riding Families

The Cristiani family, descendants of 100 years of Italian circus history and veterans of Italy's largest circus, were brought to this country in 1934 by the Ringling show, fresh from that ultimate supplier of fine equestrian acts, the Circus Schumann. For a while they entered into a bitter rivalry with the Loyal–Repensky troupe already with Ringling. Seven of the eleven family members eventually did principal riding, including an impressive simultaneous fork jump by five of them onto the back of a single moving horse. Lucio was the most versatile and sensational of the group, with his unmatched full backward twisting somersault from one horse over a second and onto the back of a third. He also demonstrated a liberty act, dressage, and a good clown act. In 1989, Lucio and Gilda Cristiani's two sons, Armando and Tino, mounted a trial performance entitled "A Circus Fantasy," which demonstrated the continuing Cristiani acrobatic skills on the trampoline. Consideration was being given to remounting

The Loyal–Repensky Riders. 1989 Carson & Barnes. Photo by W. H. Rough

*Mark Karoly with the Royal
Hanneford Circus.
Courtesy of Mark Karoly*

once again a full Cristiani Family Circus like the one run by the family in the 1950's.

The 1990 season marks a diamond jubilee anniversary for the Hanneford family: seventy-five years of performing in America. Mrs. Hanneford ("Nana") and her three children, George, Elizabeth, and Edwin ("Poodles"), arrived from Ireland via the Blackpool Tower Circus in England in 1915. George soon established his own separate riding act with his children, and Poodles became the great riding clown who set the whole tone for the popularity of modern equestrian comedy. He remained an active performer for fifty years, right up to two years before his death in 1967. His comic ways of somersaulting off a horse and his challenging "awkward" mounts without a "cushion" were both demanding and outlandishly funny. He also worked with his sister, Elizabeth, his daughter, Gracie, and his wife, Grace White. Meanwhile, his brother George and his nephews, George, Jr. and Tommy, were performing similar comedy in their act, but they also mixed in difficult straight horse-to-horse somersaulting. Following their father's death, George, Jr. went off to develop his own Cossack act; he would eventually start the Hanneford Family Circus, working with such future stars as Timi Loyal and James Zoppe. His brother Tommy's current Royal Hanneford Circus was built from their father's original act, and Tommy called himself "the Riding Fool," modelling his character on his Uncle Poodles' influential style. The show today includes the marvelous Mark Karoly, trained by Tommy to continue in the Hanneford clowning tradition of expert horsemanship. The son of Evy Karoly, another bareback and dressage rider, Mark has a daring routine, including a horse-to-horse somersault with a full twist, which gives a good indication of the demands made on the great riding clowns of the past. In one hilarious routine that always brings roars of laughter, he is energetically propelled by a companion head-first into the southend of a very tolerant and large horse. And what he can do with a coat and hat while standing on horseback at full gallop is impressive indeed.

A third family still active today are the Loyals, a French family, and perhaps the oldest name in the world still active in the circus. So respected is the name in France that a ringmaster there is still called "Monsieur Loyal." The Loyal–Repensky family came to America in 1932 for the Ringling show and subsequently performed in many American circuses. The Repensky name came from Jules Loyal's mother's maiden name, and was used for its impressiveness; there were never any performing Repenskys — only Loyals. Their Ringling act was marked by an unusual seven-man pyramid based on five horses, with four Roman post riders and three top-mounters. The Alfonso Loyal–Repensky troupe of bareback riders, featuring Mme. Luciana Loyal, is currently appearing with the Carson & Barnes Circus. Among Lucy's impressive acrobatic routines with hoops and jump ropes is a very funny modern adaptation of the old Pete Jenkins act. Her uncle, the dynamic Giustino Loyal, formed his own troupe in 1945, and worked with the likes of Ernestine Clarke and Aldo Cristiani, serving in 1960 as the equestrian director for the Cristianis. Currently, the Loyal–Suarez troupe, featuring Giustino's son and Lucy's cousin, Timi Loyal, appears in the 1990 Big Apple Circus. Timi is probably the only man in the world who can do four successive somersaults on horseback within a single circling of the 42-foot ring by his horse. At the opening of the 1990 season in Baltimore in the fall of 1989, he did five, "just for fun." He is joined in the act by his wife Denyse, and the talented Enrique Suarez troupe, a Mexican family with a hundred-year-old tradition of equestrian artistry. Leader Enrique Suarez originally came to the United States to work with Giustino Loyal's troupe; Martha Magdalena Suarez had been a part of the George Hanneford troupe in 1970. The youngest performing member of the family is the irrepressibly spirited ten-year-old Enrique, Jr.

The Zoppe–Zavatta family is a large one, whose talents as bareback riders have enhanced many American circuses since 1936. The Aurelia Troupe, which arrived to perform with the Cole Brothers show in that year, was led by Secondo Zoppe and his half-sister, Aurelia Zavatta. Their cousin Alberto Zoppe arrived in 1948 to play the Ringling show the following season. Alberto's act featured his sister Ruggera and their cousin Cucciolo, who was only 38 inches tall. More recently, in his Circus Italia, Alberto has incorporated lions and other animals into his family's equestrian performances. In 1977 his ten-year-old son Giovanni, later Nino the clown, became the youngest lad to complete a foot-to-foot somersault on a galloping horse. Alberto's daughter, Carla Zoppe–Emerson, is now featured in the Zoppe Riders, framed by the Circus World Museum, and trained by Evy Karoly, Mark's mother. Alberto now produces Zoppe's Circus Europa. Meanwhile, Secondo's and Aurelia's families developed a separate variety of acts over the years, including their "Original Indian Spectacular," the "Bedouin Riders," and "Herman & Petunia." James Zoppe, a grandson of Secondo, debuted with his own troupe in 1978, and has developed a considerable reputation for his grace and style, as he completes difficult horse-to-horse somersaults through large hoops while his horses are leaping over low hurdles at full gallop. He was featured on the Big Apple Circus in 1984 and 1985, and on the Circus Flora in 1988. [21]

It is difficult to watch an outstanding bareback riding performance today without allowing the ghosts of the past to filter into our minds. Some of these riders are performing stunts that Astley, Hughes, and Ricketts never even dreamed of. But the spirit of modern-day riders seems to be a direct link to the spirit of challenge and the drive to excel that marked the riders who were instrumental in creating the modern circus. In the antics of James Zoppe, Mark Karoly, Timi Loyal, and Katja Schumann lie the shadows of eras gone by — horses like Tom Mix's Tony and George Washington's Jack; men like Jacob Bates, who performed his running ground mount in New York in 1722; men like Thomas Pool, Richard Sands, Charles W. Fish, and Andrew Ducrow; and men like the two American riders who vie in the minds of historians for the title of having thrown the first somersault on the bareback of a moving horse: Levi North and John H. Glenroy. In 1912, an aging Jimmie Robinson, the superb horseman known in his day simply as "The Man who Rides," drove his motorcycle 100 miles to see May Wirth perform. Though not yet out of her teens, horse-to-horse somersaults and demanding tricks dumbfounded the old master. Perhaps one day the amazing equestrian acrobatics of Enrique Suarez, Jr., or of some other as yet unknown circus artist will equally impress the outstanding performer of today.

9.
ALL OUT – NOT OVER

"All out and over!" calls out the ringmaster. "Everybody please leave by the front door!" But it's never really over, is it? It will happen again and again, in reality, in our memories, and in our dreams. Some of our most vivid childhood memories are associated with circus, even though we had no way then to understand the depth of its impact on us. Maybe we hadn't gone to the circus for a long time, because we thought we had outgrown it, or we didn't need it. Perhaps, cynically, we thought that we were old enough now to understand the tricks, and the shallowness of the glitz: "So what's the point?" we said. "I've seen the elephants; the leotards are stained; the clowns aren't funny any longer; and the wire isn't so high after all." But then, one day, we took our kids, perhaps because we thought they *deserved* to have our dreams and memories, or because we thought they *needed* to have the experience as a necessary part of their education. Or, maybe, we took *them* because we could finally admit that *we* needed the circus.

We began our look at the American circus by proposing that it had no single national or historical beginning. We have come to believe that as long as there have been human societies, in all the corners of the Earth, there has been some form of circus. And we end this book by proposing that there will always be circus. Simply put, we can't do without it. Even the total collapse of known civilization at the end of the Roman Empire couldn't prevent circus artists from pursuing their vocations, and there is no reason to expect that any modern society can kill off the circus any more readily. Human civilization needs the circus. All that color and noise and glitz which on one level seems to dominate the circus, somehow becomes irrelevant in our dreams, where we constantly wage the battles between our perceptions of truth and illusion. On a higher level, we find elements and images of the circus, which are far more essential to our state of mind, which bring us face to face with what it is to be a human being—a foot on a wire, or the essential humanity of the "freak" who appears so inhuman. In the circus we have found the ultimate balance, strength, and dexterity of humanness, based not on illusion but on risk.

John Steinbeck labelled it "... beauty against our daily ugliness, excitement against our boredom. Every man and woman and child," he said, "comes from the circus refreshed and renewed and ready to survive." The more automated, dehumanized, mechanized and structured our society grows, the more anesthetized, boxed-in, limited, and categorized each of us as individuals will grow; and the more we will need the circus to remind us of what is possible, and of what is essentially human. "A good circus," wrote Oscar Wilde over a hundred years ago in the *English Illustrated Magazine*, "is an oasis of Hellenism in a world that reads too much to be wise, and thinks too much to be beautiful."

Many people have compared the contemporary circus scene to the golden age of the American circus, or even to the circus of their own childhood memories; and they came to the conclusion that the circus is dying. They were wrong. There is plenty of good evidence to suggest that it is now even stronger than ever. Business is booming. New shows are being framed yearly. New ideas are succeeding. And circus themes continue to infiltrate the fabric of American culture: a popular Las Vegas hotel is entirely devoted to circus entertainment and décor, and even the Club Med is offering circus workshops to its clientele. What we

[249]

have seen is not the death of the circus, but merely its ongoing adjustment to the temper of the times. Circus folk are not dying out; like the Roman mimes before them, they are changing and adapting, just as they must, and just as they always have.

Circus people don't think much about the past or about the long-term future. There's no point. Their thoughts are with the here and now. When Johnny Pugh of the Clyde Beatty–Cole Brothers Circus, or Judy Finelli of the Pickle Family Circus, is asked about the future survival of their shows, they shrug their shoulders and say "Sure, we have a future." Only two time references count for circus folks: "Where are we today?" and "Where do we go tomorrow?" Consideration of the possibility of failure is absolutely out of the question. Failure can only be thought of as history; any other attitude toward it would be self-defeating, as well as a jinx. We must remember that it is the nature of circus men and women, even after repeated failures, to get back on the horse, to climb back up the rope, or to drive 200 more miles and do two more shows. Not to do so is not an option. Life must go on! "To be on the wire is life," said Karl Wallenda. "All the rest is waiting."

CIRCUS FUTURES

Will the circus survive? Inevitably! . . . because "The show," like life, "must go on!" Probably more than anything else, the present fad for nostalgia accounts for the recent upsurge in interest in the circus, and such fads can be brief. But the show will go on by whatever means made available to the people who have circus in their blood: "If the public needs the currently trendy nostalgia for the past," they say, "we'll do an old-fashioned show under the big top. If tenting costs grow prohibitively high today, we'll play in the coliseum. If headline performers are sick, or fall and can't go on, we'll mount another act in their place. If no one shows up to see us, we'll go on to the next town. If no one's there either, we'll start a new show." . . . and so on. The determination—the resilience, the pluck—of these people is inspirational, and that's at least in part why the rest of us can't do without them. "The show must go on!"

If the circus will inevitably continue to sur-

vive, in what form it will survive, and under what circumstances it can thrive are separate issues. Are any of the existing shows discussed in these pages, or any others like them, equipped to become the "circus of the future"? Who knows whether any of them will even be around in another ten or twenty years. If they are, will they have changed? Most probably! Will the traditional American three-ring spectacle circus survive? In twenty years, will today's trendy one-ring shows still be unique, or will they be lost in a sea of imitators? Or will they indeed prove in the long run to have made only a brief connection to our communal soul, and have faded from our memory altogether? Will they in turn be supplanted by new and as yet unheard of approaches to circus art? There are no crystal balls here, but the guessing is fun.

One of the largest and most complicated questions looming in the minds of both circus and animal lovers today is whether future circuses will have to do without their animals? Some circus owners see "the writing on the wall," and others claim "You can't have a circus without your animals!" Recently, when the animal-less and relatively high-priced Cirque du Soleil was described to one traditional fan, he responded emphatically, almost angrily, "I'd never go see a show like that!" That's too bad. If he didn't, he'd be cutting off his nose to spite his face, and he'd be missing a good thing. If he went, he would probably miss the presence of the animals, and he might have to spend more for his ticket; but he certainly wouldn't miss the real point of going to any circus: to experience what is not part of our daily lives, what shatters our expectations. For centuries the capabilities of the human animal have fascinated spectators at circus-like performances; we don't believe people would now stop going to the circus merely because other animals might no longer be a part of those performances. The ethical questions of how well the circus is equipped to handle public education, animal breeding and care, and the issues of survival and freedom, will be best dealt with on a case-by-case basis. Some circuses will choose to skirt the whole issue, and others, if allowed, will adjust to meet the very real needs of their animals. Meanwhile, the rhetoric continues, surrounded by the certain knowledge on everyone's part that the wild animals of the world are facing a critical loss of habitat, and their very survival is at stake. Ironically, circus animal enthusiasts complaining of the "bleeding-heart do-gooders," and radical animal rights advocates who cry "cruelty to animals," may well discover that they will have to be on the same side after all.

Will future circuses be in tents or buildings? Will they emphasize the scope and spectacle of the Ringling Brothers and Barnum & Bailey Circus, or the more intimate clowning and acrobatic display of the Pickle Family Circus? Will the rings and stringer seats be replaced by stages and contoured proscenium seating, as in the Circo Tihany? Will circuses grow more traditional, like Carson & Barnes, Beatty–Cole, and the many smaller tented shows? Will they grow more European, like Big Apple and Flora? Will they grow more theatrical and vaudevillian, like the Pickle? Or will they grow more political and satirical, as has Australia's famous Circus Oz, whose acrobatic and clowning routines have dealt with anti-nuclear themes?

The most accurate guess in answer to these questions is probably "All of the above!" Certainly, the circus could not be expected to stay the same as it has been, no matter how much fondness fans may feel for what is past. An awareness of the place of circus in American history, and a knowledge of what the traditional American circus was like are important parts of our education. But we can never really go home again: We can't retrieve what was appropriate to America in her frontier years and make it appropriate for her future. We can't limit the art of the circus by defining it only as what it used to be. It is much too vital to be relegated to a museum, or a mere memory in a photo album. It must have the courage to change and grow to suit the times. Whatever the public and the artists need, the circus will provide. And the adjustment cycles will inexorably continue. At times, the circus may only barely survive, as it struggles to adapt to the rarely understood forces of changing times. There will certainly be many long periods of low circus-profile and minimal activity. It has weathered such times in the past. But at other times, it will thrive.

BREAKING THE BARRIERS

Education is the key to creating an atmosphere in which the circus can thrive. The general public no longer understands just what it is that we are looking at in the circus. We've been spoiled by the high-financed glamour and technological wizardry of the movies. We don't know enough to appreciate just how difficult or how good a circus act is. The performer makes it look so easy, and we've seen a lot more difficult-looking routines performed with the trickery of a camera. In fact, we've been lied to so often by cameras and politicians that we no longer know the difference between excellence and pretense. This has become the age of cynicism, when every promise and every feat is regarded with extreme skepticism.

The result, in part, is that Americans have maintained a historical blinding prejudice which tends to make us look on all circus people as fakes and thieves. Circus people, many of us have assumed, are sleazy nomads, who arrive under cover of darkness, and leave the following night with the hard-earned savings of the middle-class American working man ferreted away in their red wagons. Recently, there was a bank robbery in Greenville, South Carolina, while a circus was playing on the campus of Furman University. On the mistaken assumption that circus people would undoubtedly be involved, officials arrived immediately on the lot to root out the guilty parties. Historically, as we have seen, American circus folk have not been guiltless in earning the mistrust of the "towners," but they have developed in their turn an equally justified mistrust of outsiders, earned from years of slander and false arrests, fights, bureaucratic red-tape, and public antagonism. They have learned to be a closed community, excluding most outsiders and relying only on themselves for sustenance and survival. "Whenever I come into a town in America, I expect to be arrested," one talented circus artist told us. "...But in Europe when I go into a new town, they treat me like a king."

Part of that love–hate relationship between circus folks and outsiders is an inevitable part of the mystique of the circus, and it will never be entirely removed. After all, many circus people have deliberately set themselves outside the norms of society, because they wanted no part of them. And we who are a part of those "norms," whatever they are, need to see the artist as an outsider. Too much familiarity with the mud on hemlines, and worn knees, and other realities of life in the back yard destroys the mystique. Ironically, we must see our artists not only as superior beings, but also as lesser strangers, incapable of blending into our midst. The two visions are part of the paradox of the circus that has surfaced repeatedly in these pages.

Nonetheless, the extreme barriers between circus folk and towners are coming down, and with increased education they will drop further. This book is meant to be a part of the ongoing processes of education and enlightenment. Show owners and performers are slowly growing more eager to participate in the process of public education about the circus. There is recognition that desirable changes in public attitudes must be matched by changes in circus attitudes as well. With the dropping of traditional barriers comes a new understanding of the partnership that must exist between spectators and circus people if the circus is to be anything more than tolerated. Friendly back yard tours and insider stories in the media are opening new channels of communication, and thankfully, the old-fashioned paranoid haughtiness that characterized some circus folks in the past is gradually disappearing.

CIRCUS DAYS

Other changes and experiments are finding healthy expression as well. With an "If you can't beat 'em, join 'em" attitude, the "Big One" and the Circo Tihany are incorporating more and more of the polished glamour of Las Vegas, with their expensive costumes, chorus girls, and glittering lights; and the Cirque du Soleil has incorporated some Hollywood-like high-tech special smoke effects in their performances. Other shows like Car-

son & Barnes and Beatty–Cole are finding new innovative and viable ways to provide circuses more traditional in appearance. At the same time, smaller shows like Flora and Pickle deliberately choose to buck such popular trends and create their own unique form of circus artistry. Owners, managers, and artistic directors are eagerly seeking and trying new approaches to their art, and the result is a healthy variety of circus entertainments from which we may freely pick and choose. Underlying them all, newly identifiable vital missions have been embraced by circus folks in America who are no longer satisfied with mere survival. They are eager to establish their own credibility as professional artists with a serious purpose — not artists of the snobbish sort who appeal only to the fancy investors and the gallery set, but artists of the natural and genuine sort, who appeal to the needs of real, ordinary people. Second, they want to perpetuate the circus as a viable discipline, by establishing new standards of excellence and new opportunities for training.

For their part, better educated audiences are slowly changing too. Knowledge and understanding of what constitutes excellence in circus artistry increases its value to us as a society. As our respect for the circus grows, so does our trust. Circus sponsors now include such benevolent organizations as the SPCA, volunteer fire departments, service clubs, and parent–teacher groups, who find little that is objectionable and much that is admirable about the circus. American audiences are more and more impressed with the live performances of genuinely talented artists, who reach out to us as human beings. We view the performers with increasing respect as people who do what true artists ought to be doing everywhere: Finally, they make us smile; they amaze us; they surprise us; they wake us up; they make us see ourselves.

"May all your days be circus days!"

End Notes

1: LADIES AND GENTLEMEN, STEP RIGHT UP!

1. Flying High Circus, *1989 Program*, 16.
2. Vachel Lindsay. *Every Soul is a Circus* (New York: Macmillan, 1929) 8.

2: TRACES

1. Charles Philip Fox, *A Pictorial History of Performing Horses* (New York: Bramhall, 1959) 36.
2. Homer, *The Iliad* (trans. Richmond Lattimore, Chicago: University of Chicago Press, 1951) 391.
3. Homer, *The Odyssey* (trans. W. H. D. Rouse, New York: Mentor, n.d.) 95.
4. Xenophon L. Messinesi, *A Branch of Wild Olive* (New York: Exposition, 1973) 33.
5. Xenophon, *The Banquet*, trans. O. J. Todd (Cambridge: Harvard University Press, 1922).
6. Constance Carrier, trans., *The Complete Comedies of Terence* (New Brunswick: Rutgers University Press, 1974) 355.
7. George Speaight, *A History of the Circus* (London, Tantivity Press, 1980) 137.
8. H. H. Scullard, *Festivals and Ceremonies of the Roman Republic* (Ithaca, NY: Cornell University Press, 1981) 185.
9. Scullard, 184.
10. John H. Humphrey, *Roman Circuses: Arenas for Chariot Racing* (Berkeley: University of California Press, 1986) 579.
11. Humphrey, 541.
12. Titus Petronius, *The Satyricon and the Fragments* (trans. J. P. Sullivan, Harmondsworth: Penguin, 1974) 66.
13. C. Suetonius Tranquillus, *The Lives of the Twelve Caesars* (trans. Alexander Thomson, M.D., London: George Bell & Sons, 1899) 404.
14. Allardyce Nicoll, *Masks, Mimes & Miracles* (New York: Cooper Square, 1963) 85.
15. William Shakespeare, *Twelfth Night*, III, i.
16. Speaight, 43.
17. Shakespeare, *Richard III*, V, iv, 7.
18. Speaight, 35.
19. Speaight, 34.

3: NEW WORLD ROOTS

1. Mildred and Wolcott Fenner, eds., *The Circus: Lure and Legend* (Englewood Cliffs, NJ: Prentice-Hall, 1977) 15.
2. George Speaight, *A History of the Circus* (London: Tantivity, 1980) 112.
3. C. H. Amidon, "Inside Ricketts Circus with John Durang," *Bandwagon*, XIX.3 (May–Jun, 1975) 16.
4. Amidon, 17.
5. Stuart Thayer, "The Elephant in America before 1840," *Bandwagon*, XXXI.1 (Jan–Feb 1987) 21.
6. *Bandwagon*, XX.4 (Jul-Aug, 1976) 3.
7. Earl Chapin May, *The Circus from Rome to Ringling* (New York: Dover, 1963) 26.
8. May, 36.
9. Stuart Thayer, "Notes on the History of Circus Tents," *Bandwagon*, XXX.3 (Sep–Oct 1986) 28.
10. Marian Murray, *Circus! From Rome to Ringling* (New York: Appleton–Century–Crofts, 1956) 139.
11. May, 112.
12. John Lentz, "In Pursuit of Barnum & Bailey Trivia," *Bandwagon*, XXX.4 (Nov–Dec, 1986) 61.
13. Tom Parkinson and Charles Philip Fox, *The Circus Moves by Rail* (Boulder, CO: Pruett, 1978) 4.
14. John H. Towsen, *Clowns* (New York: Hawthorn, 1976) 139.

15. Mark Twain, *Huckleberry Finn* (New York: Harper, 1906) 196.

16. Ted Schaefer, "When the Big Top Was Big Time in Delavan," *Lake Geneva* I.4 (Aug 1988) 65.

17. Dean Jensen, *The Biggest, the Smallest, the Longest, the Shortest* (Madison: Wisconsin House, 1975) 76.

18. Lentz, 60.

19. Henry T. Sampson, *The Ghost Walks* (Metuchen, NJ: Scarecrow, 1988) 5.

20. Sampson, 543.

21. Jensen, 107.

22. Peru Chamber of Commerce, "Our Circus Heritage."

23. John and Alice Durant, *Pictorial History of the American Circus* (New York: A. S. Barnes, 1957) 133.

24. George L. Chindahl, *A History of the Circus in America* (Caldwell, ID: Caxton, 1959) 108.

25. Chindahl, 150.

26. Durant, 85.

27. Richard Prince, *Old Wagon Show Days* (reprint in *Circus Fanfare* [bimonthly Journal of Windjammers, Ltd., XIX.2, Apr 20, 1989] 18).

28. Earle M. Moss, "A Windjammer's Memories of the Circus, Fifty Years Ago," (reprint from 1972 in *Circus Fanfare* [XVII.2, Apr 20, 1987], 20).

29. May, 184.

30. May, 237.

4: RED WAGONS

1. Clyde Beatty Cole Brothers Circus, *1989 Souvenir Program*.

2. *The Washington Post* (Mar 22, 1989).

3. Joe Kelly, "He's a Popular Fellow," *Circus Reports*, (reprinted from *Utica* [NY] *Dispatch*, Mar 23, 1987).

4. Joe Wallace Cooper, "D. R. Miller. . . A Circus Legend," *White Tops* LIX.2 (Mar–Apr, 1986) 11.

5. Carson & Barnes Circus, *Official 1985 Route Book*.

6. Cooper, 12.

7. *The Washington Post* (Mar 19, 1982).

8. *Emmett Kelly, Clown* (New York: Prentice-Hall, 1954) 175.

9. Rob Mermin, *1989 Circus Smirkus Program*.

10. *People Magazine* (Jan 11, 1988) 58.

11. Alan B. Slifka, "Chairman's Message," *1989 Big Apple Circus Program*.

12. Hana Machotka, *The Magic Ring: A Year with the Big Apple Circus* (New York: Morrow, 1988) 7.

13. *People Magazine* (May 2, 1988) 108.

14. Harriett Swift, "Cirque du Soleil" (*Oakland* [CA] *Tribune*, Aug 6, 1989 [quoted in *Circus Reports*, Aug 21, 1989, 29]).

15. *People Magazine* (May 2, 1988) 108.

16. Cirque du Soleil, *1989 Official Program*.

17. *People Magazine* (Jul 7, 1986) 127.

5: BACK YARDS AND GETTING THERE

1. *Circus Reports*, Aug 21, 1989) 12.

2. John Ringling, "We Divided the Job—but Stuck Together" (*American Magazine* [Sep. 1919], quoted in Charles Philip Fox, *A Ticket to the Circus* [New York: Bramhall, 1959]) 46.

3. Charles Philip Fox and Tom Parkinson. *Billers, Banners and Bombast: The Story of Circus Advertising* (Boulder, CO: Pruett, 1985) 23.

4. Fox and Parkinson, 63.

5. Earl Chapin May, *The Circus from Rome to Ringling* (New York: Dover, 1963) 41.

6. May.

7. Fred D. Pfening III, "The Circus Year in Review," *Bandwagon* XXXIII.1 (Jan–Feb, 1989) 8.

8. Ted Schaefer, "When the Big Top Was Big Time in Delavan," *Lake Geneva*, I.4 (Aug, 1988) 65.

9. Stuart Thayer, "Notes on the History of Circus Tents," *Bandwagon*, XXX.3 (Sep–Oct 1986) 30.

10. George Speaight, *A History of the Circus* (London: Tantivity, 1980) 44.

6: WHAT A BODY CAN DO

1. Lloyd Grove, "How Many Democrats Did Al Packer Eat?" *The Washington Post* (Jun 8, 1989) B2.

2. Frederick Drimmer, *Very Special People* (New York: Bell, 1985) xv.

3. Drimmer, xix.

4. Joe McKennon, *Circus Lingo* (Sarasota, FL: Carnival, 1980) 78.

5. Dominique Jando, "Dolly Jacobs" (Unpublished).

6. Scott Cummings, "An Interview with Dolly Jacobs" (*Theater*, Winter, 1985) 65.

7. Cummings, 64.

8. Marion Faber, *Angels of Daring* (Stuttgart: Hans Dieter–Heinz, 1979) 59.

9. Faber, 106.

10. George Speaight, *A History of the Circus* (London: Tantivity, 1980) 71.

11. Murray Powers, "Karl Wallenda Killed in Fall," *White Tops*, LI.2 (Mar–Apr, 1978) 5.

12. Greg Parkinson, "A Legend is Born," *Bandwagon*, XXII.3 (May–Jun, 1978) 18.

13. Eckley, 133.

14. Powers

15. Powers

16. Parkinson

17. Speaight, 181.

18. Fred D. Pfening, Jr., "Human Cannonballs, Part I" *Bandwagon*, XX.6 (Nov–Dec, 1976) 5.

19. Speaight, 78.

20. Fred D. Pfening, Jr., "The Famous Zacchinis," *Bandwagon*, XXII.6 (Nov–Dec, 1978) 14.

21. Christian Williams, "The Forces Are with Him," *The Washington Post*, (Mar 30, 1983) B13.

22. John Lentz, "Protesting the Perilous Performances," *Bandwagon*, XXI.3 (May–Jun, 1977) 29.

23. Speaight, 63.

24. Ted Schaefer, "When the Big Top Was Big Time in Delavan," *Lake Geneva*, I.4 (Aug, 1988) 64.

25. Durant, 82.

26. Ringling Brothers and Barnum & Bailey Circus, *116th Edition Souvenir Program*.

27. Antony D. Hippisley Coxe, *A Seat at the Circus* (London: Evans Bros, 1952) 183.

7: MUSIC AND LAUGHTER

1. Stuart Thayer, *Annals of the American Circus, 1830–1847*, (Vol. II, Seattle: Peanut Butter Press, 1986) 23.

2. Robert Kitchen, "Nineteenth Century Bands and Music," *Bandwagon*, XXIX.5 (Sep–Oct, 1985) 15.

3. *Circus Fanfare*, XVII.3 (Jun 20, 1987) 28.

4. John H. Towsen, *Clowns* (New York: Hawthorn, 1976) 120.

5. Stuart Thayer, "One Sheet," *Bandwagon* (Sep–Oct, 1975) 23.

6. Towsen, 134.

7. Wilton Eckley, *The American Circus* (Boston: Twayne, 1984) 148.

8. Circus World Museum, *Newsletter*, XX (Jul, 1989).

9. Jean M. Bonin, "The American Circus Songster," *Notes* (Quarterly Journal of the Music Library Assn.) XLV.4 (Jun, 1989) 702.

10. Beryl Hugill, *Bring on the Clowns* (Secaucus, NJ: Chartwell, 1980) 122.

11. Conrad Hyer, *The Comic Vision and the Christian Faith* (New York: Pilgrim, 1988) 57.

12. Towsen, 238.

13. Jack Ryan, "Otto Griebling Dies: The End of an Era Has Come," *White Tops* (May–Jun, 1972) 33.

14. Emmett Kelly, *Clown* (New York: Prentice–Hall, 1954) 49.

15. John Lentz, "Down the Sawdust Trail with Emmett Kelly," *White Tops* (May–Jun, 1972) 19.

16. *White Tops* (Mar–Apr, 1979) 27.

17. Larry Montgomery, "These Toes Won't Drown in Tears of Clown," *Threads Magazine* (Jun–Jul, 1987) 14.

18. Don Marcks, *The Circus Report* (Sep 12, 1988)

19. Hyer, 72.

8: ANIMALS AND TRAINERS

1. Bob Stoddard, "The Survey Said..!" *Circus Report* (May 13, 1985) 21.

2. *The Circus Report* (Feb 24, 1986) 14.

3. *The Circus Report* (Feb 17, 1986) 25.

4. "Strange Bed," *The Circus Report* (Jun 27, 1983) 20.

5. George "Slim" Lewis and Byron Fish, *I Loved Rogues* (Seattle: Superior, 1978) 43.

6. Lewis, 8.

7. Theodore James, Jr. "World Went Mad When Mighty Jumbo Came to America," *Smithsonian*, XIII.2 (May 1982) 135.

8. Bill Ballantine, *Wild Tigers and Tame Fleas* (New York: Rinehart, 1958) 282.

9. Ringling Brothers and Barnum & Bailey Circus, *116th Edition Souvenir Program*.

10. Ringling Brothers and Barnum & Bailey

Circus, *107th Edition Souvenir Program.*

11. D. R. McMullin, "Tiger Lady Mabel Stark," *WomenSports*, III.1 (Jan, 1976) 22.

12. Ringling Brothers and Barnum & Bailey Circus, *1942 Souvenir Program*, 19.

13. Joanne Carol Joys, *The Wild Animal Trainer in America* (Boulder, CO: Pruett, 1983) 61.

14. Christian Williams, "Roar of the Tiger, Thrill of the Crowd," *The Washington Post*, Mar 29, 1983) D11.

15. Betty Bartholomew, "Wade Burck Works to Preserve Future of Wild Animals," *White Tops*, LVII.6 (Nov-Dec, 1984) 29.

16. Ringling Brothers and Barnum & Bailey Circus, *116th Edition Souvenir Program.*

17. Charles Fox and Tom Parkinson, *The Circus in America* (Waukesha, WI: Country Beautiful, 1969) 262.

18. *The New York Times*, (Jan 9, 1931) 26.

19. Joe McKennon, *Horse Dung Trail* (Sarasota, FL: Carnival, 1975) 385.

20. Antony D. Hippisley Coxe, *A Seat at the Circus* (London: Evans Bros, 1952) 43.

21. John Daniel Draper, "Standing Riders and Their Acrobatic Art" Part 2 *Bandwagon*, XXXII.4 (Jul–Aug, 1988) 20–29.

Appendix

LIST OF WORKS CONSULTED

BOOKS

Ballantine, Bill. *Wild Tigers and Tame Fleas.* New York: Rinehart, 1958.

Beatty, Clyde, with Edward Anthony. *Facing the Big Cats: My World of Lions and Tigers.* New York: Doubleday, 1965.

Bishop, George. *The World of Clowns.* Los Angeles: Brooke House, 1976.

Braathen, Sverre O. *Here Comes the Circus! The Rise and Fall of the Circus Band.* Evanston, IL: Instrumentalist Co., 1958.

Bradna, Fred, as told to Hartzell Spence. *The Big Top: My 40 Years with the Greatest Show on Earth.* New York: Simon & Schuster, 1952.

Burgess, Hovey. *Circus Techniques.* New York: Drama Book Specialists, 1976.

Carcopino, Jerome. *Daily Life in Ancient Rome: The People and the City at the Height of the Empire.* New Haven: Yale University Press, 1940.

Carrier, Constance, trans. *The Complete Comedies of Terence*, New Brunswick: Rutgers University Press, 1974.

Carroll, Jon, and Terry Lorant. *The Pickle Family Circus.* San Francisco: Pickle Press, 1986.

Carson & Barnes Circus, *Official 1985 Route Book.*

Chindahl, George L. *A History of the Circus in America.* Caldwell, ID: Caxton, 1959.

The Circus: An International Art. Special Issue of *The UNESCO Courier.* Paris: UNESCO, January, 1988.

Circuses, Carnivals & Fairs in America, in *Journal of Popular Culture*, VI:3 (Winter, 1972).

Cirque du Soleil, *1985 Official Program.*

Clement, Herbert, and Dominique Jando. *The Great Circus Parade.* Photography, Tom Nebbia.

Milwaukee: Gareth Stevens, 1989.

Clyde Beatty Cole Brothers Circus, *1989 Souvenir Program.*

Conover, Richard E. *The Affairs of James A. Bailey: New Revelations on the Career of the World's Most Successful Showman.* Xenia, OH: Richard E. Conover. 1957.

——. *The Circus: Wisconsin's Unique Heritage.* Baraboo, WI: Circus World Museum, 1967.

——. *The Fielding Bandchariots.* Xenia, OH: Richard E. Conover, 1969.

——. *Give 'Em a John Robinson: A Documentary on the Old John Robinson Circus.* Xenia, OH: Richard E. Conover, 1965.

Coup, William Cameron. *Sawdust and Spangles: Stories & Secrets of the Circus.* Washington, DC: Paul A. Ruddell, 1961.

Cox, Harvey. *The Feast of Fools: A Theological Essay on Festivity and Fantasy.* New York: Harper & Row/Colophon, 1969.

Croft–Cooke, Rupert, and Peter Cotes. *Circus: A World History.* New York: Macmillan, 1976.

Derby, Pat, with Peter S. Beagle. *The Lady and Her Tiger.* New York: Ballantine, 1976.

Drimmer, Frederick. *Very Special People.* New York: Bell, 1985.

Durant, John and Alice. *Pictorial History of the American Circus.* New York: Barnes, 1957.

Durov, V. L. *My Circus Animals.* trans. from Russian by John Cournos. Boston: Houghton Mifflin, 1936.

Eckley, Wilton. *The American Circus.* Boston: Twayne, 1984.

Egan, Mary, and Frances Billingsley. *The History of the Elephant Hotel.* Somers, NY: Egan & Billingsley, 1987.

Faber, Marion. *Angels of Daring: Tightrope Walker and Acrobat in Nietzsche, Kafka, Rilke and Thomas Mann.* Stuttgart, Germany: Akademischer Verlag Hans–Dieter Heinz, 1979.

Fenner, Mildred Sandison and Wolcott, eds. *The Circus: Lure and Legend.* Englewood Cliffs, NJ: Prentice–Hall, 1977.

Flying High Circus. *1989 Program.*

Fox, Charles Philip, ed. *American Circus Posters.* New York: Dover, 1978.

——. *A Pictorial History of Performing Horses.* New York: Bramhall House, 1960.

——. *A Ticket to the Circus: A Pictorial History of the Incredible Ringlings.* New York: Bramhall House, 1959.

——. and Tom Parkinson. *Billers, Banners and Bombast: The Story of Circus Advertising.* Boulder, CO: Pruett, 1985.

——. *The Circus in America.* Waukesha, WI: Country Beautiful, 1969.

Freedman, Jill. *Circus Days.* New York: Harmony (Crown), 1975.

Gaona, Tito, with Harry L. Graham. *Born to Fly: The Story of Tito Gaona.* Los Angeles: Wild Rose, 1984.

Hagenbeck, Lorenz. *Animals Are My Life.* Trans. Alec Brown. London: Bodley Head, 1956.

Hammarstrom, David Lewis. *Behind the Big Top.* New York: A. S. Barnes, 1980.

Harlow, Alvin F. *The Ringlings: Wizards of the Circus.* New York: Messner, 1955.

Hediger, Dr. H. *The Psychology and Behaviour of Animals in Zoos and Circuses.* Trans. from German, Geoffrey Sircom. New York: Dover, 1968.

Henderson, J. Y. and Richard Taplinger. *Circus Doctor.* New York: Bonanza, 1951.

Hippisley Coxe, Antony D. *A Seat at the Circus.* London: Evans Bros. 1952.

Homer. *The Iliad.* Trans. Richmond Lattimore. Chicago: University of Chicago Press, 1951.

——. *The Odyssey.* Trans. W. H. D. Rouse. New York: Mentor, n.d.

Hugill, Beryl. *Bring on the Clowns.* Secaucus, NJ: Chartwell, 1980.

Humphrey, John H. *Roman Circuses: Arenas for Chariot Racing.* Berkeley: University of California Press, 1986.

Hyers, Conrad. *The Comic Vision and the Christian Faith.* New York: Pilgrim, 1988.

Jamieson, David, and Sandy Davidson. *The Love of the Circus.* London: Octopus, 1980.

Jay, Ricky. *Learned Pigs & Fireproof Women: Unique, Eccentric and Amazing Entertainers: Stone Eaters, Mind Readers, Poison Resisters, Daredevils, Singing Mice, etc. etc. etc.* New York: Villard, 1987.

Jenkins, Ron. *Acrobats of the Soul: Comedy & Virtuosity in Contemporary American Theatre.* New York: TCG, 1988.

Jensen, Dean. *The Biggest, the Smallest, the Longest, the Shortest.* Madison, WI: Wisconsin House. 1975.

Joys, Joanne Carol. *The Wild Animal Trainer in America.* Boulder, CO: Pruett, 1983.

Kelly, Emmett, with F. Beverly Kelley. *Clown: My Life in Tatters and Smiles.* New York: Prentice–Hall, 1954.

Kirk, Rhina. *Circus Heroes and Heroines.* n.p.: Hammond, 1972.

Lewis, George "Slim" and Byron Fish. *I Loved Rogues: The Life of an Elephant Tramp.* (Republication of *Elephant Tramp,* 1955.) Seattle: Superior, 1978.

Lindsay, Vachel. *Every Soul is a Circus.* New York: Macmillan, 1929.

Llewellyn, Betty Hallff, with A. C. Greene. *I Can't Forget.* Dallas: Walnut Hill, 1984.

MacAllister, Copeland. *People of the Early Circus.* Framingham, MA: Salem House, 1989.

Machotka, Hana. *The Magic Ring: A Year with the Big Apple Circus.* Intro. Paul Binder. New York: Morrow, 1988.

May, Earl Chapin. *The Circus from Rome to Ringling.* (Intro. Leonard V. Farley, reprint 1932 ed.) New York: Dover, 1963.

McKennon, Joe. *Circus Lingo.* Sarasota, FL: Carnival, 1980.

——. *Horse Dung Trail: Saga of the American Circus.* Sarasota, FL: Carnival, 1975.

——. *Horse Dung Trail: Saga of the American Circus INDEX (And a Few Remarks).* Sarasota, FL: Carnival, 1979.

——. *Logistics of the American Circus.* Sarasota, FL: Carnival, 1977.

——. *Logistics of the American Circus (Supplement).* Sarasota, FL: Carnival, 1984.

——. *Rape of an Estate.* n.p. 1986.

McKennon, Marian. *Tent Show.* New York:

Exposition, 1964.

Mermin, Rob. 1989 Circus Smirkus Program.

Messinesi, Xenophon L. *A Branch of Wild Olive: The Olympic Movement and the Ancient and Modern Olympic Games.* New York: Exposition, 1973.

Miller, Art "Doc," *Little Ol' Show.* n.p. 1982.

Mix, Olive Stokes, with Eric Heath. *The Fabulous Tom Mix.* Englewood Cliffs, NJ: Prentice–Hall, 1957.

Moss, Cynthia. *Elephant Memories: Thirteen Years in the Life of an Elephant Family.* New York: Fawcett Columbine, 1988.

Murray, Marian. *Circus! From Rome to Ringling.* New York: Appleton–Century–Crofts, 1956.

Newton, Douglas. *Clowns.* n.p. Franklin Watts, 1957.

Nicoll, Allardyce. *The Development of the Theatre: A Study of Theatrical Art from the Beginnings to the Present Day* (Rev. 3rd Ed). New York: Harcourt Brace Jovanovich, 1948.

——. *Masks, Mimes and Miracles: Studies in the Popular Theatre.* New York: Cooper Square, 1963.

North, Henry Ringling, and Alden Hatch. *The Circus Kings.* New York: Dell, 1960.

O'Brien, Esse Forrester. *Elephant Tales.* Austin: Steck, 1941.

Odell, George C. *Annals of the New York Stage,* Vol. IV. New York: Columbia University Press, 1928.

Parkinson, Tom, and Charles Philip Fox. *The Circus Moves by Rail.* Boulder, CO: Pruett, 1978.

Petronius, Titus (Gaius), Arbiter. *The Satyricon and the Fragments.* trans. J. P. Sullivan. Harmondsworth: Penguin, 1974.

Plowden, Gene. *Gargantua: Circus Star of the Century.* New York: Bonanza, 1972.

——. *Merle Evans: Maestro of the Circus.* Miami: Seemann, 1971.

——. *Those Amazing Ringlings and Their Circus.* Caldwell, ID: Caxton, 1968.

Rennert, Jack. *100 Years of Circus Posters.* New York: Darien House, 1974.

Reynolds, Charles and Regina. *100 Years of Magic Posters.* New York: Darien House, 1975.

Ringling Brothers and Barnum & Bailey Circus. *1942 Souvenir Program.*

——. *107th Edition Souvenir Program.*

——. *116th Edition Souvenir Program.*

——. *118th Edition Souvenir Program.*

——. *119th Edition Souvenir Program.*

Robeson, Dave. *Al G. Barnes, Master Showman.* As told by Al G. Barnes. Caldwell, ID: Caxton, 1935.

Sampson, Henry T. *The Ghost Walks: A Chronological History of Blacks in Show Business, 1865–1910.* Metuchen, NJ: Scarecrow, 1988.

Saxon, Arthur H. *The Life and Art of Andrew Ducrow and the Romantic Age of the English Circus.* Hamden, CT: Archon, 1978.

Scullard, H. H. *Festivals and Ceremonies of the Roman Republic.* Ithaca, NY: Cornell University Press, 1981.

Senelick, Laurence. *A Cavalcade of Clowns.* San Francisco: Bellerophon, 1977.

Sobel, Bernard. *A Pictorial History of Vaudeville.* New York: Citadel, 1961.

Speaight, George. *The Book of Clowns.* New York: Macmillan, 1980.

——. *A History of the Circus.* London: Tantivity Press, 1980.

Stott, R. Toole. *Circus and Allied Arts: A World Bibliography, 1500–1962,* Vols. I–III. Derby, England: Harpur & Sons. Vol. I: 1958; Vol. II: 1960; Vol. III: 1962.

Strutt, Joseph. *Sports and Pastimes of the People of England.* London: Chatto & Windus, 1876.

Swortzell, Lowell. *Here Come the Clowns: A Cavalcade of Comedy from Antiquity to the Present.* New York: Viking. 1978.

Templeton, Francis H. *Circus How-It's-Done Memories, Part I: Big Top Ups and Downs.* Templeton, 1955.

Thayer, Stuart. *Annals of the American Circus, 1793–1829.* Manchester, MI: Rymack, 1976.

——. *Annals of the American Circus, Vol. II: 1830–1847.* Seattle: Peanut Butter, 1986.

Towson, John H. *Clowns.* New York: Hawthorn, 1976.

Twain, Mark. *Huckleberry Finn.* New York: Harper, 1906.

Wilmeth, Don B. *Mud Show: American Tent Circus Life.* Photos by Edwin Martin. Albuquerque: University of New Mexico Press, 1988.

Wykes, Alan. *Circus: An Investigation into What Makes the Sawdust Fly.* London: Jupiter, 1977.

Xenophon. *The Banquet.* Trans. O. J. Todd. Cambridge: Harvard University Press, 1922.

ARTICLES

Amidon, C. H. "Inside Ricketts Circus with John Durang," *Bandwagon*, XIX.3 (May–Jun, 1975).

Ballantine, Bill. "Brutes of the Big Top." *True Magazine*, XLI.276 (May 1960). 62 + .

——. "Circus Kids," *Better Living*, II.7 (July 1952). 20 + .

Bartholomew, Betty. "Wade Burck Works to Preserve Future of Wild Animals," *White Tops*, LVII.6 (Nov–Dec, 1984).

Bonin, Jean M. "The American Circus Songster," *Notes* (Quarterly Journal of the Music Library Assn.) XLV.4 (June 1989).

Circus Fanfare, XVII.3 (June 20, 1987).

The Circus Report, Feb 17 and 24, 1986.

Circus World Museum, *Newsletter*, XX (July 1989).

Cooper, Joe Wallace. "D. R. Miller. . .A Circus Legend," *White Tops*, LIX.2 (Mar–Apr, 1986).

Cummings, Scott. "An Interview with Dolly Jacobs." *Theater*, Winter 1985, 61–65.

Draper, John Daniel, "May Wirth," *White Tops*, LII.2 (Mar–Apr, 1979) 16–18.

——. "Standing Riders and Their Acrobatic Art" (Part 2), *Bandwagon*, XXXII.4 (Jul–Aug, 1988) 20–29.

Gavzer, Bernard. "Are Our Zoos Humane?" *Parade Magazine* (Mar 26, 1989).

Grove, Lloyd. "How Many Democrats Did Al Packer Eat?" *The Washington Post* (Jun 8, 1989).

James, Theodore Jr. "World Went Mad When Mighty Jumbo Came to America," *Smithsonian*, XIII.2 (May, 1982).

Jando, Dominique. "Dolly Jacobs" (Unpublished).

Kelley, Francis Beverly, "The Land of Sawdust and Spangles — A World in Miniature," and (w/ Stewart, Richard H. and Orren R. Loudon) "The Country That Moves by Night." *National Geographic*, LX.4 (Oct 1931). 463 +

Kelly, Joe. "He's Popular Fellow," *Circus Reports*, (reprinted from *Utica* [NY] *Dispatch*, March 23, 1987).

Kirby, E. T. "The Shamanistic Origins of Popular Entertainments" *The Drama Review*, XVIII.1 [T-61] (March 1974). 5–15.

Kitchen, Robert. "Nineteenth Century Bands and Music," *Bandwagon*, XXIX.5 (Sep–Oct, 1985).

Lentz, John. "Down the Sawdust Trail with Emmett Kelly," *White Tops* (May–Jun, 1972).

——. "In Pursuit of Barnum & Bailey Trivia," *Bandwagon*, XXX.4 (Nov–Dec, 1986).

——. "Protesting the Perilous Performances," *Bandwagon*, XXI.3 (May–Jun, 1977).

Little, W. Kenneth. "Pitu's Doubt: Entrée Clown Self-Fashioning in the Circus Tradition." *The Drama Review*, XXX.4 [T112] (Winter 1986). 51–64.

Marcks, Don. *The Circus Report* (Sep 12, 1988).

McMullin, D. R. "Tiger Lady Mabel Stark: She Spent 40 Years Behind Bars." *WomenSports*, III.1, (January 1976). 19 + .

Montgomery, Larry. "These Toes Won't Drown in Tears of Clown," *Threads Magazine*, Jun–Jul, 1987).

Moss, Earle M. "A Windjammer's Memories of the Circus, Fifty Years Ago," (reprint from 1972 in *Circus Fanfare*, XVII.2 [Apr 20, 1987]).

Parkinson, Greg. "A Legend is Born," *Bandwagon*, XXII.3 (May–Jun, 1978).

Pfening, Fred D. Jr. "Human Cannonballs, Part I," *Bandwagon*, XX.6 (Nov–Dec, 1976).

——. "The Famous Zacchinis," *Bandwagon*, XXII.6 (Nov–Dec, 1978).

Pfening, Fred D. III. "The Circus Year in Review," *Bandwagon*, XXXIII.1 (Jan–Feb, 1989).

Powers, Murray. "Karl Wallenda Killed in Fall," *White Tops*, LI.2 (Mar–Apr, 1978).

Prince, Richard. *Old Wagon Show Days*, (reprint in *Circus Fanfare*, XIX.2 [Apr 20 1989]).

Ringling, John. "We Divided the Job — but Stuck Together" (*American Magazine*, Sep 1919, quoted in Charles Philip Fox, *A Ticket to the Circus*, New York: Bramhall, 1959]).

Rogers, Georgia M. "The Greatest Sew on Earth," *Threads Magazine*, (Jun–Jul, 1987) 38–9.

Ryan, Jack. "Otto Griebling Dies: The End of an Era Has Come," *White Tops*, XLV.3 (May–Jun, 1972).

Schaefer, Ted. "When the Big Top Was Big Time in Delavan," *Lake Geneva*, I:4 (Aug 1988). 61–65.

Slifka, Alan B. "Chairman's Message," *1989 Big Apple Circus Program*.

Stoddard, Bob. "The Survey Said. .!" *Circus Report* (May 13, 1985).

"Strange Bed," *Circus Report* (Jun 27, 1983).

Swift, Harriett. "Cirque du Soleil," *Oakland [CA] Tribune*, Aug 6, 1989 (quoted in *Circus Report*, Aug 21, 1989, 29).

Thayer, Stuart. "The Elephant in America before 1840," *Bandwagon*, XXXI.1 (Jan–Feb 1987).

——. "Notes on the History of Circus Tents," *Bandwagon*, XXX.3 (Sep–Oct 1986).

Williams, Christian. "The Forces Are with Him," *The Washington Post*, (Mar 30, 1983).

——. "Roar of the Tiger, Thrill of the Crowd," *The Washington Post*, (Mar 29, 1983) D11.

GLOSSARY OF CIRCUS TERMS

Advance car: Railroad car on the old railroad shows that moved in advance of the show carrying billing and advance crews.

After show: Concert or short play given in the big top after the regular performance, sometimes a Wild West exhibition, sometimes song-and-dance.

Annie Oakley: Free ticket or pass to the circus.

Antipodist: Juggler who lies on his back and juggles with the feet (See **Risley act**).

Auguste: Clown who is the butt of all tricks; he wears no traditional costume, and makeup includes exaggerated facial features and a large red nose; one of the three major clown types.

Back door: Performers' entrance to the tent or arena.

Back yard or **back lot:** Area of the circus lot or arena unseen by the public; the location of dressing tents, animals, trailer parking, etc.

Baggage stock: Large horses used to pull heavy circus wagons, not used in performance.

Bale ring: Large steel ring circling a main tent pole, to which the canvas is lashed.

Ballyhoo: To advertise or talk up a circus performance. Originally, a free show given to attract a crowd in front of the side show; at the 1893 Columbian Exposition, performers were called to the front with the Arabic expression *"Dehalla Hoon,"* then mispronounced as ballyhoo.

Banner: Colorfully painted panel in front of the side show advertising attractions. Also, a cloth sign designed to be tacked to a brick wall by the advance billing crew.

Big Bertha [also **The Big One,** and **The Big Show**]: Titles designating the Ringling Brothers and Barnum & Bailey Circus after they combined in 1919.

Big top: Tent used for the main circus performance.

Billing crew: Advance men charged with putting up circus paper.

Blow a date [or **blow the town**]: To not show up for a performance booked in advance.

Blow-down: Damage suffered when a heavy wind blows down the tents.

Blow-off: Finale of a show, when all performers take their bows and audience leaves.

Blues: General admission seating.

Boss canvasman: Person in charge of putting up and taking down tents.

Boss elephant man: Person in charge of the elephants.

Boss hostler: Person in charge of all baggage horses.

Boss of ring stock: Person in charge of all performing animals.

Break: Point in a flying trapeze act when the flyer drops his legs and begins his trick.

Bugs: Chameleons sold as pets by the "bug men."

Bull: Elephant of either sex, although most circus elephants are female.

Bust out: Entry into the tent or arena of many clowns at once, usually during the pre-show or "come-in."

Calliope: Large musical instrument consisting of steam-driven whistles, frequently used in circus parades. [pronounced *kall*-ee-yoap]

Candy butcher: Concessionaire selling anything before, during, and after the show, outside the tent or in the seats; so-named because the first person to sell concessions on the Old John Robinson show was so successful he quit his regular job as a meat butcher.

Carpet clown: Clown working in the stands or outside the rings who fills in between acts; originally an auguste who supplied the carpet for equestrians in the ring.

Cat: Any tiger, lion, panther, or leopard used in the circus.

Catcher: In a flying act, the partner who hangs from the "catch trap" and catches the "flyer."

Charivari: Boisterous exhibition of acrobatic clowning involving chaotic tumbling; related to old French "Shivaree."

Cherry pie: Doing extra work for extra pay.

Chinese: Doing very heavy extra work, sometimes for no extra pay.

Clown alley: Area reserved for clowns to store props and put on costumes and makeup, usually found just outside the back door.

Come-in: Hour between the opening of doors and the start of the show.

Cookhouse: Tent or complex for supplying meals to circus personnel.

Corporation shows: Circuses operated by the American Circus Corporation of Peru, Indiana.

Daub: Circus paper glued on fences, storefronts, barns or walls where ads are not normally found.

Dead man: Extra strong rigging for the aerial or high wire acts, secured by several stakes driven into the ground with an additional stake lying parallel to the ground.

Donniker [or **Doniker**]: Portable toilet.

Doors: Announcement signalling the opening of the front doors to the public.

Dressage act: Act with trained horse and rider.

Ducat [or **Ducket**]: Ticket to the circus.

Ducat grabber: Person who takes tickets.

Equestrian director: Person in charge of full circus performance.

First of May: Novice going out with a circus for the first time, so-called because seasons traditionally began on May 1.

Finale: Spectacle parade at the end of the circus performance.

Flag [or **Flag's up**]: Flag raised over the cookhouse signalling when a meal is being served.

Flying frame: Frame from which traps and other rigging are hung.

Flying squadron: First section of the old circus trains to arrive in town, bringing everything necessary to lay out the lot and set up the cook tent.

Front door: Main entrance to the big top.

Front end: Everything seen by the public before entering the big top.

Funambulist: Wire-walker or rope-walker.

General manager: Person in charge of all working personnel.

Grease joint: Hot dog and burger stands on the midway or front end.

Grotesque: Whiteface clown with exaggerated facial features and strange style of acting.

Guy out: To tighten guy ropes holding the tent perimeter in place.

Hammer gang: Men who drive stakes.

Hay burner: Any animal that eats hay or grass.

Hey Rube: Traditional call to arms indicating a fight between circus people and towners.

High school horse: Horse taught to do traditional formal steps such as those taught at the Spanish Riding School.

Hippodrome track: Track traditionally separating the seating from the three circus rings.

Home run: Last move of the season returning to winter quarters.

Iron jaw: Aerial act which allows the performer to hang from an apparatus fitting into his mouth.

Jack: "A"-shaped frame which supports stringers for seating planks.

Jackpots: Often wildly exaggerated stories told by former troupers about the circus. To "cut up jackies" is to tell such stories.

Joey: Circus term for a clown, derived from Joseph Grimaldi, famous 19th century English clown.

John Robinson: Quick show, shortened to bare essentials because of storm warnings or to get an early start on the jump to the next town.

Joint: Concession stand on the front end of the show.

Jump: Distance or move between towns.

Kid show: Side show connected to the circus.

Kinker: Any performer, who must work the kinks out of sore muscles.

Liberty horse: Horse performing "at liberty" without reins or rider, executing drills on the subtle command of the trainer in the center of the ring.

Lot lice: Towners who hang around circus lots but spend little or nothing.

Long-mount: Usually the finale of an elephant act, when elephants stand on hind legs, resting front legs on the back of the elephant in front of them. In a "walking long-mount," the line of bulls moves forward or backward in this position.

Manege: To ride a high school horse, showing off its steps.

Mechanic [or **Longe rope**]: Belt worn by the performer, attached to a safety line controlled by another person who can take up slack and prevent disastrous falls.

Mud block: Half-rounded piece of wood or steel placed on bottom of center poles to facilitate raising them into place without their sinking into soft ground.

Mud show: Circus traveling overland on horse-drawn wagons.

Musth [or **Must**]: Periodic condition of male elephants, in which their behavior is dangerously unpredictable, and a sticky substance exudes from glands located between the eyes and mouth.

Nut: Daily expense; "making" or "cracking the nut" refers to successfully meeting circus expenses.

One-day stand: Circus staying in town for only

one day.

Opposition: Competition between circuses.

Paper: Circus advertising, posters.

Perch act: Balancing act in which a performer balances and does tricks on the top of a "perch pole," which is balanced on his partner's head, shoulder, or belted waist pouch.

Performance director: Person in charge of circus artistic performers, who may or may not appear in performance.

Pie car: Dining car on the circus train, or truck or tent supplying food.

Plange [or **Planche**]: Move by an aerialist hanging by one arm from a swivelled loop on a web rope, in which the entire body is thrown over the arm, a trick made famous by Lillian Lietzel.

Poles: The tallest tent poles are called "center poles"; shortest are "side poles"; all those in between, which are used to elevate canvas tops and permit wider tents, and which may vary in length, are called "quarter poles."

Poler: Person guiding heavy circus wagons down ramps from railroad flat cars—one of the more dangerous of circus jobs.

Production number: Lavishly decked act with many floats, props, and performers.

Pulling peaks: Pulling the big top of a bale-ring tent halfway up the center poles.

Punk: Any circus youngster, whether animal or human.

Quad: Quadruple backward somersault by a flyer to the hands of a catcher.

Razorback: Train laborer who loaded circus flat cars; the name is derived from "Raise 'er back—let 'er go!" the command for lifting cross-cage wagons into place.

Reds: Reserved seats in preferred locations available at surcharge.

Red light: Practice of throwing a troublemaker or other undesirable person off the circus train during the night [or to throw someone off the circus lot].

Red Wagon: Main ticket wagon and office, no matter what color it is painted.

Ring curb: Curved curbing, usually wooden and about one foot high, which when combined with other similar pieces forms a standard circus ring of about 42 feet in diameter.

Ringmaster: Originally, the man with the whip in charge of a one-ring equestrian performance; now commonly used to describe the role of circus master of ceremonies and equestrian director.

Ring stock: Circus animals performing in the ring, i.e., horses, camels, llamas, etc.

Risley act: Performance in which a juggler lies on his back and juggles or balances another performer with his feet.

Rosinback [or **Resinback**]: Horse used by trick bareback riders; the name derives from the resin powder rubbed onto the horse's back to provide a sticky footing.

Roustabout: Circus laborer.

Route card: Card listing schedule of dates, towns, miles traveled, for circus stands.

Run: Ramp placed at the end of circus train flat car, used to load and unload wagons.

Sheet: Standard circus advertising paper measuring 28 inches by 42 inches. A "one-sheet" is a standard poster of that size.

Shooting quarter poles: Inserting quarter poles into grommet holes in big top after the peaks have been pulled, and sliding them into position.

Short side: Side of the cookhouse seating the performers and staff.

Sidewall: Canvas wall enclosing perimeter of tent to prevent anyone from sneaking in or seeing a show without paying.

Spanish web: Cloth-covered hanging rope on which aerialists perform in aerial ballets.

Spectacle [or **Spec**]: Parade featuring all performers and animals, usually at the opening of the show; formerly a lavish specially staged production involving hundreds of performers and extravagant sets and props.

Spot: To place wagons, trucks, trailers, or even trunks in designated places in a tent or on the lot.

Stake line: Row of stakes around the tent.

Stand: Town or locale played by the circus.

Straw house: Sold-out performance, when straw was spread in front of seating to accommodate extra patrons.

Stringers: Long pieces of wood supported by "jacks" and used to support seating boards.

Sunday school show: Clean circus with no illegal activity.

Tack spitter: Person who tacked up circus advertising paper or banners, by spitting tacks held in his mouth onto his magnetic hammer.

Talker: Person making "outside openings" and talking in front of an attraction. Also a "grinder," or "opener," and if inside a "lecturer," but never a "barker."

Tanbark: Bark containing tannin, used to tan hides, and afterwards to cover the circus ring floor.

Teeterboard: Seesaw used to propel performers into the air to the back of an animal or the shoulders of other members of the troupe.

Threesheet: Three sheets of advertising paper, thus measuring 42″ by 84″. Also, a self-serving performer who advertises himself more than he deserves.

Top-mounter: Person on top of a totem pole, vaulting act, etc.

Towner: Local person visiting the show but having nothing to do with circus life.

Tramp: One of three major American clown types, a character clown with costume and features of a hobo; also an abbreviation for trampoline, as in a "tramp act."

Trap: Trapeze; a single trap is one trapeze and one performer; a double trap is still one trap but with two performers; a trap duo uses two trapezes.

Triple: Triple backward somersault by a flyer to the hands of a catcher.

Trouper: Person who has spent at least one full season traveling with a circus.

Turnaway: Sold-out performance.

Understander: Person on the bottom of a human pyramid or totem pole.

Wait paper: Circus advertising paper using the words "Wait for. . ."; used in billing wars by a circus wanting to discourage potential patrons from attending an earlier show.

Whiteface: Clown makeup with a white base, usually highlighted with black and red features [or clown character derived from old Pierrot character and other French clowns], one of the three major clown types.

Windjammer: Member of a circus band.

Winter quarters: Where the circus resides off-season, when it is not traveling.

ADDRESSES OF CIRCUS ORGANIZATIONS

The Barnum Museum
Robert Pelton, Curator
961 Main Street
Bridgeport, CT 06604

Circus Fans Association of America
Dale Riker, Sec.-Treas.
P.O. Box 3187
Flint, MI 48502

Circus Historical Society
Johann Dahlinger, Sec.-Treas.
743 Beverly Park Place
Jackson, MI 49203

Circus Model Builders, Inc. International
Sally Weitlauf, Sec.-Treas.
347 Lonsdale Ave.
Dayton, OH 45419

The Circus Report
Don Marcks, Editor
525 Oak Street
El Cerrito, CA 94530

Circus World Museum
Greg Parkinson, Exec. Director
426 Water Street
Baraboo, WI 53913-2597

Clown Hall of Fame & Research Center
Jennie Schilz, Exec. Director
212 E. Walworth Ave.
Delavan, WI 53115

Clowns of America International
P.O. Box 75258
St. Paul, MN 55175

The Hertzberg Collection
Wayne Daniel, Curator
San Antonio Public Library
210 W. Market Street
San Antonio, TX 78205

International Circus Hall of Fame
Fred Weil, Exec. Director
20 North Broadway
Peru, IN 46970

The Joseph T. McCaddon Collection
Mary Ann Jensen, Curator
Firestone Library
Princeton University
Princeton, NJ 08544

McCord Theatre Collection
Betty Llewellyn, Curator
Fondren Library
Southern Methodist University
Dallas, TX 75275

Windjammers, Unlimited
Ward Stauth
2500 Old Forest Road
Corydon, IN 47112

World Clown Association
Pat Frank, Sec.-Treas.
P.O. Box 1893
Huntington Beach, CA 92647

Index

T

"Tailor's Ride to Brentford", 43, 45, 197
Tangier Troupe, 180, 181
    photos, 181
Tarkington, Booth, 18
Tarleton, Richard, 42
Tarzan Zerbini Circus, 102, 103-4, 127, 153, 165,
    177, 180, 191, 231, 232
    photos, 102, 104
Taylor, Zachary, 15, 65
Teeterboard, 181
Ten Nights in a Bar Room, 64
Tent, early Roman origins, 34
Tent raising, 144, 145-150
    bale-ring method, 145-7
    photos, 144, 146, 147, 148, 149, 150
    push-pole method, 147, 150
Tented circus, first American, 58
Tented circuses, 127-8
Tents, 43, 58, 152
    origins of, 58
    photos, 152
Terence, 33
Terrell, Zack, 83, 85
Thayer, Stuart, 22, 56, 58, 145, 158
Theatre Marcellus, 36
Thompson, Eph, 218
Three-ring circus, origins of, 21, 22
    tent interior, photo, 22
Tibbals, Howard, 16, 17
    circus model, photo, 17
Tigers, 226-231
Titus, Lewis B., 57
Toby Tyler, 19
Toby Tyler, or Ten Weeks with a Circus, 126
Toby Tyler Circus, 79, 126, 150
Toca, Clem, 191
Togni, Flavio, 98
Toledo, Ben, 69
Tom McIntosh's "Hot Old Time in Dixie
    Company", 69
Tom Mix Circus, 241
Tom Packs Circus, 18
Tom Thumb, 60
Toulouse-Lautrec, Henri de, 16
"Towners", 27, 28
    photo, 28
Trampolines, 181
Trapeze, 19
Trapeze, 165, 168-9
Travis, Camp, 196
Trucks, 135
Tucker, Hoxie, 69, 95
Turner, Aron, 57, 58, 59, 132
Twain, Mark, 18, 64
Twelfth Night, 42
24-hour man, 133, 136

U

Uncle John Robinson Circus, 217
"Uncle Sam", 65
Uncle Tom's Cabin, 69
    cart, photo, 69
Unicorn, 236, 237, 238
    photo, 237
Unus, 184
"Uprising of the Freaks", 157
U.S. Department of Transportation, 134
Uthoff, Lizzie, 106, 112, 114
    photos, 106, 114

V

Valdo, Pat, 171, 203
Van Amburgh, Isaac, 223, 226
Van Cleave, Mark, 191
Van Doren, Mark, 18
Varelas, Eric, 184
Vargas, Clifford E., 89, 91, 128
Vasquez, Juan, 161
Vasquez, Miguel, 161, 162
    photo, 162
Vaulters and leapers, 180-3
Victoria, 221
Vidbel, Joyce, 91
Vidbel's Old Tyme Circus, 192
Virginia Minstrels, 67, 196

W

Wade, Stephen, 197
Wagons, photos, 52, 53
Wallace, Ben, 69, 72, 140
Wallace, Lew, 35
Wallenda, Angel, 175
Wallenda, Debbie, 175
Wallenda, Delilah, 175
Wallenda, Enrico, 175
Wallenda, Gunther, 175
Wallenda, Hermann, 175
Wallenda, Karl, 172, 173, 175, 250
Wallenda, Mario, 175
Wallenda, Steven Gregory, 175
Wallenda, Tino, 175
Wallenda family, photos, 173, 174
Walter, J.H., see Marinelli
Ward, Eddie, Jr., 161
Washington, George, 54
Washington, Keyes, 165
Wasnak, Diane, photo, 115
Wayne, John, 19
W.C. Coup's Circus, 72
Webb, "Ollie", 143
Welch's Olympic Circus, 197
Weldes, 232
Wells and Wells, 69
Wenatchee Youth Circus, 108
Wenders, Wim, 19
Whalen, Jimmy, 147
Wheel of Death, 177, 178
    photo, 178
White, Grace, 247
White, Patricia, 225, 227
    photo, 225
White, Robert, 67
"White Elephant Wars", 219
Whiteface clowns, 202-4
Wiegle, Clark, 192
Wild West shows, 69, 70
Wilde, Oscar, 249
Wilder Bros. Circus, 151
Wilhelm Meisters Lehrhahre, 170
Williams, Barbara, 222
Williams, Ben, 221
Williams, Bert, 68
Williams, Billy "The Human Frog", 179
Williams, Ephraim, 68, 69
Williams, Harry, 223
Williams, Jaqueline, 26, 169
Williams, John, 42
Williams, Peggy, 202
Williams, Rex, 222
Williams, Tennessee, 16

Wilson, Woodrow, 15
Windjammer's Hall of Fame, 194
Windjammers, 189, 190-6
    black, 195-6
    photo, 190
Windjammers Unlimited, Inc., 194
Wings of Desire, 19
Winnepecs, 176
Wire, "bounding", 171
Wire walkers, 68, 170-3, 175
Wirth, May, 242, 243, 248
Wolfe, Thomas, 18
Wolfscale, Prof., 196
Woodcock, Babe, 221
Woodcock, William "Buckles", 221, 222
    photo, 222
Woodcock, William, Sr., 221, 222
Woods, Fount B., 196
Woods, George, 69
Woods, Pearl, 69
Worland, John, 180
World Clown Association, Inc., 211
Wozniak, Tady, 183
Wozniak, Teresa, 183
Wright Brothers menagerie, 58
Wright, Arthur, 196
W.W. Cole show, 131
Wyler, William, 35

X

Xenophon, 33, 188
Xochitl, photo, 24

Y

Yadon, Gordon, 140, 180
Young, Brian, 192

Z

Zacchini, Eddie, 177
Zacchini, Hugo II, 177
Zacchini, Hugo, Jr., 177
Zacchini, Ildebrando, 177
Zamorathe, Hugo, 179
Zavatta, Aurelia, 247, 248
"Zazel", 177
Zerbini, Elizabeth, 104
Zerbini, John "Tarzan", 102, 103
Zerbini, Sylvia, 104, 165
    photo, 165
Zerobnick, Alan, 211
Ziegfeld, Flo, 74
Ziegfeld Follies, 74
Zoological Institute, 57
Zoppe, Alberto, 247
Zoppe, Cucciolo, 247
Zoppe, Giovanni, 247
Zoppe, James, 247, 248
Zoppe, Ruggera, 247
Zoppe, Secondo, 247, 248
Zoppe, Tino Wallenda, 170, 172, 173
    photo, 170
Zoppe Riders, 248
Zoppe's Circus Europa, 248
Zoppe-Emerson, Carla, 248
Zoppe-Zavatta family, 247-8
Zweifel, John, 50